The Springer Series on Demographic Methods and Population Analysis

Volume 49

Series Editor

Kenneth C. Land, Dept of Sociology, SINET, Duke University, Durham, NC, USA

In recent decades, there has been a rapid development of demographic models and methods and an explosive growth in the range of applications of population analysis. This series seeks to provide a publication outlet both for high-quality textual and expository books on modern techniques of demographic analysis and for works that present exemplary applications of such techniques to various aspects of population analysis.

Topics appropriate for the series include:

- General demographic methods
- Techniques of standardization
- Life table models and methods
- Multistate and multiregional life tables, analyses, and projections
- Demographic aspects of biostatistics and epidemiology
- Stable population theory and its extensions
- Methods of indirect estimation
- Stochastic population models
- Event history analysis, duration analysis, and hazard regression models
- Demographic projection methods and population forecasts
- Techniques of applied demographic analysis, regional and local population estimates and projections
- Methods of estimation and projection for business and health care applications
- Methods and estimates for unique populations such as schools and students

Volumes in the series are of interest to researchers, professionals, and students in demography, sociology, economics, statistics, geography and regional science, public health and health care management, epidemiology, biostatistics, actuarial science, business, and related fields.

Ideas and proposals for additional contributions to the series should be sent either to Kenneth C. Land, Series Editor, Department of Sociology and Center for Demographic Studies, Duke University, Durham, NC 27708-0088, USA E-mail: kland@soc.duke.edu

or to

Evelien Bakker,Publishing Editor, Social Sciences Unit, Springer,Van Godewijckstraat 30,P.O. Box 17,3300 AA Dordrecht, erlands, E-mail: evelien.bakker@springer.com

More information about this series at http://www.springer.com/series/6449

Stefano Mazzuco • Nico Keilman
Editors

Developments in Demographic Forecasting

Springer

Editors
Stefano Mazzuco
Department of Statistical Sciences
University of Padova
Padova, Padova, Italy

Nico Keilman
Department of Economics
University of Oslo
Oslo, Norway

ISSN 1389-6784 ISSN 2215-1990 (electronic)
The Springer Series on Demographic Methods and Population Analysis
ISBN 978-3-030-42471-8 ISBN 978-3-030-42472-5 (eBook)
https://doi.org/10.1007/978-3-030-42472-5

This Springer imprint is published by the registered company Springer Nature Switzerland AG.
The registered company address is: Gewerbestrasse 11, 6330 Cham, Switzerland

Acknowledgements

Nico Keilman gratefully acknowledges financial support from the Department of Economics, University of Oslo, and Stefano Mazzuco acknowledges financial support from miur-prin2017 project 20177BR-JXS, which made it possible to publish this book as an OA publication.

Contents

Chapter 1
Introduction

Nico Keilman and Stefano Mazzuco

1.1 Demographic Forecasting

Future trends in population size, age structure, regional distribution, and other demographic variables are of paramount importance for a wide range of planning situations. Government policy for old-age pensions and long-term care depends on the number of elderly in the future. An assessment of future trends in population variables also is an important prerequisite for exploring environmental issues and the demand of resources in the future. Other things remaining the same, a larger population implies more use of water, electricity, fuel, food etc. in a certain region. Stronger needs for transportation are another effect of growing populations. Local planners have to decide on investments in hospitals and schools. Retailers of certain products (such as baby food) are interested in the size of particular age groups in the future.

Demographic projections and forecasts rely on assumptions of the future developments for components of change for population size, that is, births and fertility, deaths and mortality, and international migration when the interest is in the population for a country as a whole. In case one considers the future state of a certain population sub-group (e.g. persons who live in a specific region or those who are currently divorced), additional components are relevant (regional migration, marriage and marriage dissolution).

N. Keilman
Department of Economics, University of Oslo, Oslo, Norway
e-mail: nico.keilman@econ.uio.no

S. Mazzuco (✉)
Department of Statistical Sciences, University of Padova, Padova, Italy
e-mail: stefano.mazzuco@unipd.it

S. Mazzuco, N. Keilman (eds.), *Developments in Demographic Forecasting*, The Springer Series on Demographic Methods and Population Analysis 49, https://doi.org/10.1007/978-3-030-42472-5_1

Given the importance of insight in future demographic trends, many statistical agencies routinely compute national population forecasts. They do so by means of the so-called cohort-component model, which has become the standard approach in population forecasting (National Research Council – NRC 2000; UNECE 2018). This model requires assumptions on future trends of fertility, mortality, and international migration. We will discuss this approach further in Sect. 1.2.

To make accurate demographic forecasts is both an art and a science, similar to predictions in other fields (Tetlock and Gardner 2016). The scientific part is in the model, and in the fine mathematical and statistical details of the computations. However, to formulate reliable assumptions for the future course of fertility, mortality and migration is an art, largely. Most of the research on demographic forecasting aims at increasing the scientific part, and reducing the impact of selecting the right assumptions – the "art part" in population forecasting. "The quest for knowledge about the future has moved from the supernatural towards the scientific" (Willekens 1990, 9). One way to achieve this aim is to formulate explicit models for fertility, mortality and migration. In that case, one attempts to find a model that describes the historical development of these components of change accurately enough. The model may be an explanatory model with exogenous variables, or a purely statistical (e.g. time series) model. In either case, the model is used to extrapolate the components into the future, and next their future values are used as inputs for the cohort-component model.

The primary aim of this book is to sketch new developments in the scientific part of demographic forecasting. It does not give an extensive review of the field. Such reviews have appeared regularly; see, for example, Hajnal 1955; Keyfitz 1972; Land 1985; Willekens 1990; Keilman and Cruijsen 1992; National Research Council – NRC 2000; Wilson and Rees 2005; Booth 2006; Alho and Spencer 2005; Alho 2015. In contrast, with this book we wanted to show the readers examples of promising new research on demographic forecasting.

In the remainder of this chapter, we discuss selected topics in demographic forecasting, thus sketching the wider context of many of the problems that our authors address. We start with a brief overview of the cohort-component tradition (Sect. 1.2). Next, we describe in Sect. 1.3 how population forecasters account for the inherent uncertainty in their results. Common approaches are to use various deterministic scenarios or, alternatively, a probabilistic model. An important distinction in the statistical modelling of the components of change is that between a Bayesian and a frequentist perspective. We discuss both approaches in Sect. 1.4. Population forecasters often rely on the opinions of experts, when they formulate their assumptions on the future trajectories of demographic components. However, in some cases these trajectories are purely data-driven. This is the topic of Sect. 1.5. Another issue, taken up in Sect. 1.6, is whether one should use data from the country of interest only, or also include trends in other countries. A recent development in demographic forecasting is the evaluation of probabilistic forecasts. Forecasts of this type have been computed since the mid-1980s, and some statistical agencies, too, produce them regularly. After a few decades, one knows the actual development of the variables of interest. Hence, one may want to know how well the forecast, published in terms of a predictive distribution, has performed. This is taken up in Sect. 1.7. Once the forecast has been computed, an important question concerns the best way to communicate its results to the user. Demographers could learn from forecasters in other disciplines, where this question has been analysed. We summarize the most important findings in Sect. 1.8. Section 1.9 gives a brief presentation of the chapters that follow.

1.2 The Cohort-Component Approach[1]

The main idea of the cohort-component model (CCM) is to update a table with known numbers for the population pyramid, taken from a recent census or from a population register, to a new table 1 year later. The update requires assumptions on mortality (the share of persons of a given age who survive 1 year later), fertility (the mean number of children per woman born during the year), and migration (for instance, age- and sex-specific numbers of net-migration). Based on assumptions of this kind for many years in the future, the process can be repeated, resulting in a population forecast for many years in the future. See demographic textbooks such as those by Preston et al. (2001) or Rowland (2003) for technical details, and O'Neill and Balk (2001) for a non-technical introduction.

Edwin Cannan first developed this forecasting approach in 1895. By the 1930s, it had become generally accepted by the statistical agencies of many countries (De Gans 1999). In the 1970s, the model was extended to include a regional breakdown of the population (multiregional model; see, e.g., Rogers 1995), or an extra dimension in general, such as educational level, labour market status, or household status (multistate/multidimensional model). Chapter 10 by Zhang and Bryant and Chap. 11 by Raymer, Bai, and Smith focus on inter-regional migration and follow the tradition of multiregional models.

The CCM is by its nature a pure accounting approach. The new population equals the old one minus deaths and emigrants, plus surviving births and surviving immigrants. This process is repeated for each age group, men and women separately. Assumptions for the three components of change are in terms of age-and sex-specific rates, used as inputs by the CCM. Chapter 4 by Castiglioni, Dalla-Zuanna and Tanturri, and Chap. 9 by Keilman and Kristoffersen discuss certain aspects of this approach.

The mechanical nature of the CCM-approach has been criticized, since it ignores possible feedback mechanisms. Rapid population growth, resulting from high rates for fertility and immigration leads to increasing population density. However, the

[1]Parts of this section and the next one are based upon the paper "Uncertainty in population forecasts for the twenty-first century" by the first author, forthcoming in Annual Review of Resource Economics 2020. Permission to reuse this material is gratefully acknowledged. https://www.annualreviews.org/page/authors/author-instructions/distributing/permissions

CCM does not account for a direct effect of population density on future fertility, mortality, or emigration. More generally, in the long run, one should take into account that the scarcity of resources and degradation of the environment may have an impact on human behaviour and population dynamics (Cohen 2010; De Sherbinin et al. 2007). Also, if the crude birth rate is lower than the crude death rate for a number of decades, population size will fall (assuming that migration has little or no effect), and authorities will likely attempt to promote a pro-natalist policy. Feedbacks of this kind are not included in demographic forecasts that follow the CCM-tradition, at least not explicitly. In some cases, this is reasonable, because demographic variables are much less important than non-demographic variables. For instance, Raftery et al. (2017) combine country-specific probabilistic population forecasts with forecasts of CO_2-emissions and temperature change to 2100. They find that population growth is not a major factor that contributes to global warming, and a feedback mechanism is not necessary. Other studies do include an explicit feedback. For instance, in its population forecast, Statistics Norway assumes that future immigration numbers for various immigrant sub-groups depend, among others, of the stock of migrants already present in the country (Cappelen et al. 2014). See also National Research council – NRC (2000, pp. 31–32) and O'Neill and Balk (2001) for explanations and discussions of the feedback problem, and Sanderson (1998) for the lack of explanatory factors in population forecasts. Burch (2003) gives a more general critical review of the CCM.

1.3 Deterministic Scenarios and Probabilistic Forecasts

Most statistical agencies in the world that compute population forecasts do so using a deterministic approach (NRC 2000). They analyse historical trends in fertility, mortality, and migration, and extrapolate those trends into the future, using expert opinion and statistical techniques. The extrapolations reflect their best guesses. In addition to computing a likely development of population size and structure, many agencies also compute a high and a low variant of future population growth, in order to tell forecast users that future demographic developments are uncertain. For example, the previous official population forecast for Norway, published in 2018, indicates 6.5 million inhabitants in 2060, if current trends continue (see https://www.ssb.no/en/statbank/list/folkfram). However, population growth to 2060 might be weaker or stronger than what current trends suggest, leading to population sizes between 5.8 and 7.8 million persons. The forecasters assumed low and high trajectories for future fertility (leading to 1.6 or 1.9 children per woman on average in 2060), life expectancy of men (between 86.0 and 90.4 years in 2060) and women (between 88.1 and 92.1 years), and international migration (a migration surplus between 10,700 and 41,400 persons annually).

Different projections or scenarios can be produced by systematically combining different assumptions. Collectively, those different scenarios can give some impression of the degree of uncertainty, but not in any quantified way. The probability that an outcome will be within a certain range is unknown (Dunstan and Ball 2016). We do not know if chances are 30, 60, or 90% that Norway in 2060 will have between 5.8 and 7.8 million inhabitants. Yet in many planning situations, it is important for the users to know how much confidence they should have in the predicted numbers. How robust should the pension system be with respect to fast or slow increases in life expectancies? Should we plan for extra capacity in primary schools, in case future births turn out to be much higher than expected? Indeed, as Keyfitz (1981) wrote almost 40 years ago: "Demographers can no more be held responsible for inaccuracy in forecasting population 20 years ahead, than geologists, meteorologists, or economists when they fail to announce earthquakes, cold winters, or depressions 20 years ahead. What we can be held responsible for is warning one another and our public what the error of our estimates is likely to be".

Indeed, the statistical agencies of some countries have started to publish their forecasts in the form of probability distributions, following common practice in, for example, meteorology and economics. A key use of probabilistic demographic forecasts is in modelling the long-term fiscal impact of an ageing population by policy agencies (Tuljapurkar 1992; Lee and Tuljapurkar 2000; Alho et al. 2008; Dunstan and Ball 2016).

Various methods for probabilistic population forecasting have been developed since the 1960s, although Törnquist (1949) was probably the first to integrate probabilistic thinking into population forecasting. In this approach, the fertility and mortality rates, as well as the migration parameters are random variables. This means that the predicted population becomes random. Early contributions were made by Pollard (1966), Sykes (1969), Schweder (1971), Alho and Spencer (1985), and Cohen (1986). The initial aim was to find analytical solutions for the predictive distributions of the variables of interest. Due to correlations between components, between ages and between men and women, as well as autocorrelations in all variables, approximations were necessary (Tuljapurkar 1992). Later work (e.g., Keyfitz 1985; Kuijsten 1988; Lee and Tuljapurkar 1994) used Monte Carlo simulation.

Statistical agencies of some countries have started to publish the results of probabilistic forecasts, following common practice in, for example, meteorology and economics. Statistics Netherlands pioneered the field; see Alders and De Beer (1998). Statistics New Zealand (2011) and Statistics Italy (ISTAT 2018) are the other two known examples. In Chap. 3, Dion, Galbraith, and Sirag suggest that Statistics Canada is likely to follow soon. In addition, we should mention the Population Division of the United Nations, which is responsible for regular updates of population forecasts for all countries of the world. In 2014, the Population Division issued the first official probabilistic population forecasts for all countries, using the methodology developed by Raftery et al. (2012). See also Gerland et al. (2014) and Ševčíková et al. (2016). These probabilistic forecasts do not replace the traditional deterministic UN population forecasts, but supply additional information to the user. After 2014, the UN updated the probabilistic forecasts a few times. The most recent revision is from 2019; see http://esa.un.org/unpd/wpp/Graphs/Probabilistic/POP/TOT/900. The aim of a probabilistic forecast is not to present estimates of future trends that are more accurate than a deterministic forecast, but rather to give the user a more complete picture of prediction uncertainty.

1.4 Bayesian vs Frequentist

What emerges from the pages of this book is consistent with the most recent literature: the Bayesian approach to population forecasting (we would better say to population studies, in general) is rapidly gaining ground. This has already been noticed by Bijak and Bryant (2016) who also highlight that such an increase has certainly been accelerated – if not triggered, by work at the United Nations, when the World Population Prospects in 2014 for the first time were based on a Bayesian hierarchical model (Gerland et al. 2014). The model is "hierarchical" as it considers a single model for all countries, but there are country-specific parameters, leading to a "hierarchy" in the model structure. However, other explanations of the increasing number of Bayesian population forecasts can be given, as Bayesian analysis is on the rise in general, due also to increasingly fast algorithms which make the computational burden of Bayesian inference lighter and lighter. Indeed, in past years, the main obstacle to Bayesian inference was its intractability: apart from specific cases, deriving posterior distributions cannot be done analytically, thus approximation should be used. Nowadays, several algorithms (MCMC, Hamiltonian MonteCarlo, Variational Bayes, to mention some of them) allow fast solutions. Moreover, it should also be noted that forecasting is a natural product of Bayesian inference. As Geweke and Whiteman (2006) note, forecasting means that one uses the information at hand to make statements about the likely course of events, or said differently, to predict future outcomes, conditionally on what we know. Bayesian inference implies conditioning on what we know (data) to predict what is unknown (the so-called posterior distribution), so one might say that Bayesian forecasting is actually Bayesian inference with missing data: missing data is future value of the outcome considered, which posterior distribution is derived based on the prior information, represented by the past values of data. Therefore, it is quite natural that if the number of Bayesian inference applications increases in population studies, also Bayesian forecasting follow the same trend. However, this does not clarify whether the Bayesian approach provides something more (or something different) than the frequentist one. One suggested advantage is that within a Bayesian framework, information from previous studies or from experts' opinions can easily and transparently be incorporated into the forecasting model through a proper informative prior. This is certainly attractive for the field of population forecasting, where experts' opinions have been used in a non-systematic manner, and where it has been already proposed to use such opinions even in the framework of probabilistic population forecasting (Lutz et al. 1996). However, we do not always see the use of priors as elicitation of experts' opinions, neither in Chaps. 2, 5, or 10 proposing a Bayesian approach, nor in the UN methodology (Gerland et al. 2014). Aliverti, Durante, and Scarpa (Chap. 5) use prior distributions to specify the structure of temporal dependence, but experts' opinions are not considered. Graziani (Chap. 2) uses experts' opinion, but she treats them as observed data, while non-informative priors are used. Finally, Chap. 10 uses a "weakly informative" prior for several parameters and a generalized random walk with drift to parameters with a time trend. Even UN methods use priors as a way to include statistical noise and temporal dependence to the forecasting model, and experts' opinions are not included. In facts, if we consider, for example, the UN-model for fertility forecasting (see Alkema et al. 2011), we could say that experts' opinions are rather incorporated in the statistical model while priors are essentially non informative. Thus, while in theory it might look appealing to mix in a formal and transparent way expert's opinions and information coming from observed data, in practice this is rarely done.

Dunson (2001) provides a much more pragmatical answer on why it could be advantageous using a Bayesian approach in some cases: the class of statistical models that can be estimated via Bayesian inference is much broader than would be possible with other approaches. In some cases, this involves retrieving the full conditional distribution of parameters and this might be far from straightforward. For example, Aliverti, Durante, and Scarpa (Chap. 5) use a particular result on skew normal distributions (a posterior distribution from a Gaussian prior combined with a skew normal likelihood gives a unified skew normal distribution, see Canale et al. 2016), while Zhang and Bryant (Chap. 10) combine the Gibbs Sampling algorithm with a Metropolis-Hastings step. In other cases, this is not necessary: for example, the software STAN (see Carpenter et al. 2017) use a Hamiltonian Monte Carlo method for which retrieving the full conditional distribution of parameters is not necessary. Another practical advantage of the Bayesian approach is that once that computation has been implemented and posterior distributions of parameters have been obtained, also the posterior of any function of model parameters can be easily achieved. For instance, Zhang and Bryant (Chap. 10) after the estimation step, provide the predicted posterior distribution of migration rates, which are functions of the estimated parameters.

However, complex models can be estimated using a frequentist approach, too: Basellini and Camarda (Chap. 6), for example, decompose mortality age patterns into three components, with a specific model for each of them, and the parameters of these models are jointly estimated with maximum likelihood. In their case, given the complexity of the model, prediction intervals can neither analytically nor numerically be obtained, so a bootstrap procedure (Efron and Tibshirani 1993) is implemented. Such a procedure involves resampling data for K times, which in some cases can be computationally intensive, but not necessarily more intensive than MCMC algorithms that are needed to obtain posterior distribution (from which credibility intervals can be calculated) of parameters.

Summarizing, we believe that an increasing understanding and application of the Bayesian approach in the field of population forecasting is certainly beneficial to this research area, as it enlarges the forecaster's possibilities by broadening the class of models that can be used. At the same time, frequentist approaches remain a valid opportunity, not necessarily a second choice. Our suggestion is to choose the inference approach to be used after having determined what the most appropriate forecast model is. Once this has been decided, inference method can be determined more easily, on the base of the considerations exposed above.

1.5 Expert Opinions vs Data Driven

In the past, much discussion on population forecasting methods was devoted to experts' opinions based forecasts as opposed to probabilistic ones. Experts' opinions based methods are usually referred to as synonym of deterministic methods, until Lutz and Scherbov (1998) proposed an expert judgment based probabilistic method. Thus the discussion in the literature involves the issue of uncertainty quantification: probabilistic models provide a natural assessment of forecast uncertainty, while experts-based methods specify some scenarios (usually three, labeled "high", "medium" and "low") with no possibility of variation (Booth 2004). However, even in case one uses a probabilistic approach (see Sect. 1.3 for examples), experts-based method are still used but integrated in statistical models that ensure random variability and uncertainty quantification. United Nations population forecasts, for instance, are still strongly based on experts' opinion, and, based on demographic transition theory, the UN World Population Prospects (United Nations 2017) suggest all countries' mortality, fertility, and migration rates will converge, eventually, to the same patterns. Castiglioni, Dalla-Zuanna, and Tanturri demonstrate in Chap. 4 that such a convergence is not confirmed by observed data and that it might be useful to reconsider this assumption. This example shows that, while the opposition between experts' opinions based forecasts and probabilistic forecasts no longer has any reason to exist, forecasters have to decide whether, and to what extent, they can rely on experts' judgments or whether they let the data speak for themselves, by using a data-driven method. In this book, you can find two examples of purely experts' opinion based forecasting method (exposed by Graziani in Chap. 2 and by Dion, Galbraith, and Sirag in Chap. 3) and an example of a strongly data-driven method (exposed by Aliverti, Durante, and Scarpa in Chap. 5). Graziani (Chap. 2) does not consider observed data but embeds experts' judgments into a statistical model, so that prediction intervals can be derived with a proper uncertainty quantification. Of course, we have to bear in mind that experts shape their opinions on observed data, so basing forecasts on their judgment does not mean disregarding evidence coming from data. What is paramount when using experts' opinion is the elicitation process of their judgements. Dion, Galbraith, and Sirag (Chap. 3) show an extremely detailed expert elicitation protocol that allows experts to have an appropriate feedback of their judgments, forcing them to reflect more on the likelihood of their opinion. On the data-driven side, Aliverti, Durante, and Scarpa (Chap. 5) propose an extremely flexible statistical model to make forecast, so that no specific pattern is imposed to the data or to forecasts of the fertility age schedule. Interestingly, Graziani (Chap. 2) reports that the experts-based forecast of the Total Fertility Rate in Italy in 2018 on average is above the actual estimates of the Italian national institute of statistics. The explanation is that "experts did not perceive the persistence of the great recession", and this means that if you want to rely on experts' opinion, you have to bear in mind that such opinions are not necessarily right. On the other hand, Aliverti, Durante and Scarpa (Chap. 5) expect that the mean, variability, and skewness of Italian fertility age schedule will remain approximately constant in the future. The simple explanation of this prediction is that the most recent observed age schedules have remained stable, and this trend has been extrapolated to future years. However, an expert could have objected that also between 1995 and 1999 age schedules have remained stable, but the mean age at childbearing has increased after 1999, while the age pattern became less skewed. These two cases help us to understand that the choice on whether relying more on data or on experts' judgment is a delicate one, as both experts and data can be misleading, and a forecaster needs needs to consider very carefully, for each specific case, which of the two sources is reliable. For example, Bergeron-Boucher, Kjærgaard, Pascariu, Aburto, Alvarez, Basellini, Rizzi, and Vaupel (Chap. 7) show that in the case of Denmark, mortality forecasting is difficult due to broken trends generated by a life expectancy stagnation starting in 1980. Therefore, they compare different extrapolative methods and find a high sensitivity of forecasts to model selection. Actually if we use a cohort perspective, Denmark's life expectancy trend is much smoother than what period life expectancies suggest. This is another example showing that data, even though seemingly "neutral", can also misguide forecasts.

1.6 Coherent Modelling

Another dilemma that a forecaster has to deal with is whether the forecasts of a demographic component of different populations should be considered jointly or separately. Should, for example, male and female mortality be forecast by one common model, or by two distinct models? Recently, coherent forecasting models have gained ground in the field of mortality (not so much in fertility forecasting), since Li and Lee (2005) have proposed a coherent model, assuming that future trends of mortality in similar (or neighbor) countries are mutually dependent. One may use the same argument for mortality of male and female populations of a given country, assuming that they follow similar trends. However, is pooling countries or population sub-groups always beneficial? Raftery et al. (2013) propose information pooling for mortality forecasting, and actually this might be a good idea in case of scarce or bad-quality data for some specific population. However, in other cases, things might go in the opposite direction. Booth (Chap. 8) shows that implementing a coherent model not necessarily improves the forecasts: for example, a sex-coherent model improves forecasts for the mortality of males, but not for females, compared to independent forecasts. Interestingly, she also shows that much of the performance depends on the standard used in coherent modeling and a same-sex low-mortality-standard is optimal. However, the point that we stress here is that pooling information from other countries (or other populations) has not necessarily a positive effect.

Perhaps the concept of exchangeability – well known in Bayesian statistics literature – can help to explain this issue. Exchangeability means that one can re-order and re-label data while the joint density remains the same. In our context, assuming exchangeability with data from multiple countries means that inference (and prediction) can be equivalently done exchanging data even across countries, i.e. data can be pooled together irrespective of the country where the data come from. This is clearly not realistic at a country level (however it is normally done at the regional level, as national forecasts normally pool regional data), even for very similar countries. A "partial pooling" solution might be more acceptable, and this solution is naturally achieved with a hierarchical model: all data are used for inference and forecast but when forecasting for a specific country, data from other countries are differently weighted. In terms of exchangeability, data can be exchanged across countries, but a "penalty" (or a lower weight) is given to other countries' data, the penalty depending on countries' sample sizes and variabilities (see Jackman 2009, Section 7.1.2 on exchangeability in connection with hierarchical models). Thus, whether pooling (completely or partially) countries together or not depends on the extent to which their data are exchangeable. However, in many cases modelling and forecasting without pooling data is not a viable choice. Raymer, Bai, and Smith (Chap. 11) and Zhang and Bryant (Chap. 10), for example, face the challenge of predicting internal migration. Their main issue is that flows from one region to another may have very low sample sizes (see, for instance, Figure 8 in Zhang and Bryant, where it turns out that migration rates from East to North West are estimated only for one age group). Therefore they are obliged to borrow information for these flows, which leads to some kind of data pooling. Raymer, Bai, and Smith use a multiplicative model for that purpose, while Zhang and Bryant implement a hierarchical model. Are data from different region, at least partially, exchangeable? The answer can be given only by experts, not directly by data.

1.7 Evaluating Probabilistic Forecasts

Once a forecast has been published, some 10–20 years later its accuracy can be evaluated, when *ex-post facto* observed data for population size and age structure have become available. Evaluating deterministic forecasts against empirical data has a long history, which goes back at least to the work by Myers (1954). The topic received systematic attention in the 1980s, by Keyfitz (1981), Ahlburg (1982), and Stoto (1983); see NRC (2000) for a review. However, to assess the accuracy of a probabilistic forecast is difficult, because it requires that one compare a forecaster's predicted probabilities with the actual but unknown probabilities of the events under study. For that reason, statisticians have developed "scoring rules": distance measures between the predicted distribution of the variable in question, and the empirical value it actually turns out to have. Gneiting and Raftery (2007) and Gneiting and Katzfuss (2014) review the field. The score that one finds for a certain variable has no intrinsic meaning. Only in a comparative perspective, one can interpret the scores in a useful manner. Indeed, scoring rules are frequently used in comparing two or more competing probabilistic forecasts. A second type of application is to study how fast the quality of the forecast deteriorates with increasing lead-time (forecast horizon).

The results of a probabilistic forecast can be made available in different ways. For demographic forecasting, we distinguish between forecast results in the form of simulation samples or as prediction intervals. Each category has its own scoring rules.

Although the methodology around evaluation of probabilistic forecasts and scoring rules has been known for some time, there are very few applications of scoring rules to population forecasting. Shang et al. (2016) analyse the accuracy of probabilistic cohort-component forecasts for the UK, and compare two forecasting methods. They use a scoring rule for prediction intervals. Shang (2015) and Shang and Hyndman (2017) evaluate interval forecasts for age-specific mortality rates in various countries, and use interval scores to select the best among several methods of forecasting mortality. Alexopoulos et al. (2018) employ interval scores to prediction intervals of age-specific mortality of England & Wales and New Zealand, and evaluate the predictive performance of five different mortality prediction models. All four papers use holdout samples to evaluate the probabilistic demographic forecasts. We are aware of only one example of genuine out-of-sample evaluation of probabilistic demographic forecasts (Keilman 2020).

As an alternative to using scoring functions to prediction intervals, one could check how large the share of actual data is that fall within the intervals. An example is the work by Raftery et al. (2012), who validate their Bayesian method of forecasting populations for 159 countries by estimating the model based on data for the 40-year period 1950–1990. Next, they use the model to generate a predictive distribution of the full age- and sex-structured population for the 20-year period 1990–2010. They compare the resulting 80% and 95% prediction interval distributions with a test data set of actual observations, and check the proportion of the validation sample that falls within their intervals. These proportions are close to the nominal values of 80% and 95%, and the authors conclude that their approach is satisfactory.

Similarly, in Chap. 10, Zhang and Bryant present Bayesian forecasts for internal migration in Iceland. They consider two models: a baseline model that does not include region-time interactions, and a revised model that does. Both models are estimated with data for the period 1999–2008, and 80% prediction intervals ("credible intervals" in the Bayesian perspective) for the migration rates predicted for the years 2009–2018 are checked against a test dataset with empirical rates for these years. The authors inspect the proportion of values of the test dataset that lie within the 80% credible intervals and find that the revised model is much better calibrated than the baseline model, in that actual coverage (71–73% for the revised model) comes quite close to the nominal coverage (80%). Therefore, the authors base their forecasts on the revised model.

Also Raymer, Bai, and Smith (Chap. 11) forecast inter-state migration for Australia for two 5-year periods: 2006–2011 and 2011–2016. The model they use for forecasting was fitted to observed values for 5-year periods from 1981–1986 to 2001–2006. The authors investigate two versions of the model, and note that the proportions of observed data for the two recent periods that lie within 80% or 95% prediction intervals agree quite well with the nominal values of 80% and 95%.

One important drawback of this approach is the fact that the values from the test dataset are not necessarily independent of each other. They may be generated by correlated variables. This means that one has less information in the test data than the sheer number of values suggests. Thus, a comparison between observed proportions and nominal values is not valid, strictly speaking (Alho and Spencer 2005, 248; Gneiting et al. 2007, 253).

1.8 Communicating Forecast Results

As noted in Sect. 1.3, forecasters use deterministic scenarios and probabilistic forecasts to express the inherent uncertainty in statements about the future size and structure of populations. Since many population forecasts and projections are general-purpose calculations that serve the needs of many different users, often there is no frequent systematic contact between users and the producer of the forecast. However, to communicate forecast results in an appropriate way to the users is of paramount importance. Various questions arise in this context. Does the forecast produce predictions of the type of variables (age groups, components of change, regional disaggregation, persons or households, etc.) that satisfy user needs? Is there enough detail in the predicted variables (one-year age groups, short-term versus long-term forecasts)? Are the results available as data files or in print only? Is the forecast updated when new information on current demographic trends becomes available?

Following up on points made by the National Research Council – NRC (2000) on the presentation of demographic forecasts, a Task Force on Population Projections working for the United Nations Economic Commission of Europe (UNECE) recently formulated a large number of recommendations on communicating population forecasts and projections (UNECE 2018). The task force based its work on information from three distinct sources: a survey among users of national and international population forecasts and projections, a survey among national statistical agencies of UNECE member countries, and a consultation round among a small group of experts in the field of population projections. Finally, a literature review using insights from demography, psychology, and science communication complemented the analysis of perspectives from users, statistical agencies, and experts. The task force addressed a number of issues, including ways to provide pertinent and accessible results, the need for transparency, accounting explicitly for uncertainty, and ways to foster relationships with users. Many of the 26 recommendations for good practice seem obvious, although they are not always followed by statistical agencies. Examples are to communicate results in clear and simple language, to disseminate results by single age and calendar year whenever possible, to make electronic dissemination materials accessible, to provide clear descriptions of data, methods and assumptions, or to clearly define key terms used in dissemination products. However, other recommendations are more novel for official forecasts and projections, such as developing an explicit strategy for characterizing and communicating the uncertainty of population forecasts and projections, identifying and characterizing the major sources of uncertainty, providing both sensitivity and uncertainty analyses, and engaging directly with users in a substantive manner, for instance by using new media.

A number of chapters in this book address demographic uncertainty explicitly (e.g. Graziani in Chap. 2, Dion, Galbraith, and Sirag in Chap. 3, Aliverti, Durante, and Scarpa in Chap. 5, Basellini and Camarda in Chap. 6, and Zhang and Bryant in Chap. 10, Scherbov and Sanderson in Chap. 12). Therefore, an important question is whether forecast users want to know about the uncertainty of the forecast. There is little evidence from systematic investigations, but available data suggest that the answer is yes. The survey organized by the UNECE task force mentioned above showed that 69% of the users who answered the relevant question (N = 148) considered quantification of uncertainty of the projections important or very important for their own work. Of 119 users who gave their opinion about the way uncertainty was stated in the projection they use, 42% noticed it was stated, but that it could be stated more clearly, whereas 29% found uncertainty not clearly stated. On the other hand, about one-third of the statistical agencies were of the opinion that the lack of knowledge about uncertainty among users is a challenge in communicating uncertainty. At the same time, one-third of the agencies noted that users are interested in one single scenario.

The interest of population forecast users in forecast uncertainty noted above is similar to the findings by Wilson and Shalley (2019) for Australia. Using data from a small online survey and subsequent focus groups of subnational population forecast users, the authors find that 90% of users who responded were in favour of receiving information on forecast uncertainty. Reasons selected from a list of options for wanting information on uncertainty consist of the need to emphasise the fact that forecasts are not exact (73%), to aid decision-making based on a range of projected population numbers (58%), and to allow consideration of risk or contingency strategies (57%).

In this connection, it is also worth to report the user and producer experiences of Dunstan and Ball (2016) of Statistics New Zealand after they had implemented a probabilistic approach in 2012; see also Dunstan (2019). They stress that the change from a deterministic to a probabilistic forecast was less difficult to make than one might expect. Uncertainty in fertility, mortality and migration can be modelled simply or with more complexity, and progressively applied to different types of forecasts (national forecasts first, followed by derived forecasts: regional, labour market, ethnic groups, level of education, households etc.). A close contact between forecaster producers and main users is essential in the process of preparing the probabilistic forecast. Many users will be interested in deterministic results only and do not need prediction intervals or the full set of sample paths. They can still employ the probabilistic results, for instance the median forecast, possibly supplemented by the upper and lower bounds of the 80% prediction interval. Moreover, probabilistic forecasts, with their quantified measures of uncertainty, can help statistical agencies to define an appropriate horizon for the forecast. Prediction intervals for demographic variables far into the future become progressively wider and flatter, and hence they do not contain much useful information. However, the situation is very different for different demographic variables. Forecasts for subpopulations are often more uncertain than those for aggregate populations. This means that users of probabilistic forecasts can inspect prediction intervals to make their own informed decisions about the usefulness of different forecasts across any projection period.

Closely related is the notion of the "shelf life" of a forecast, recently developed by Wilson and colleagues; e.g. Wilson (2018), Wilson and Shalley (2019), Wilson et al. (2018), Simpson et al. (2019). The concept is borrowed from perishable food labelling to describe the number of years into the future a population forecast is likely to remain of reasonable quality. In practice, 'reasonable quality' could be defined as the period in which the 80% prediction interval (for a probabilistic forecast), or 80% of past errors (for a deterministic forecast for which past errors are available) remain within ±10% error. When the forecast horizon exceeds the shelf life, the forecast is no longer of reasonable quality. In an illustration using Australian data, Wilson et al. (2018) suggest a shelf life of 8 years for forecasts of a population of 10,000 persons, 12½ years for a forecast population of 50,000, and 14 years when population size is 150,000. Using data for a number of past official subnational English forecasts, Simpson et al. (2019) find shelf lives of 6 years for London Boroughs forecasts, and 21 years for Metropolitan Districts. While the choice of 10% for the absolute error is rather arbitrary, the respondents to the Australian user survey found the concept of shelf life very useful (Wilson and Shalley 2019).

Demographers may learn from experiences in other fields when the interest is in communicating the results of a probabilistic forecast. Bijak et al. (2015) remind us of meteorology and climatology, aviation, macroeconomics, as well as cognitive sciences. See also Raftery (2014) and Spiegelhalter et al. (2011). Building upon experiences from weather forecasting, Fundel et al. (2019) highlight several recommendations for communicating probabilistic forecasts. It is important to explain probabilities as relative frequencies to a lay audience, for instance when presenting an 80% prediction interval: "In 80 out of 100 situations with a forecast like this …". At the same time, we should be aware of the limitations of probabilistic forecasts: people may misinterpret them, there may be a mismatch between the information one needs and the prediction interval, and too wide prediction intervals may cast doubt on the competence of the forecaster who produced them (Goodwin 2014). In any case, it is useful to remember the words of Bank of England's Governor Mervyn King. He said, in his Annual Lecture for the British Academy on 1 December 2004: " … in a wide range of collective decisions, it is vital to think in terms of probabilities … (W)e must accept the need to analyse the uncertainty that inevitably surrounds these decisions … (I)n order that public discussion can be framed in terms of risks, the public needs to receive accurate and objective information about the risks. Transparency and honesty about risks should be an essential part of both the decision-making process and the explanation of decisions." (King 2004). For demographic forecasting more specifically, we refer to UN Population Division Director John Wilmoth, who said in 2013: "... I expect that demographers will continue to be surprised by trends that do not follow our prior expectations. It is for this reason that the Population Division has worked hard in recent years to be more explicit and precise about the degree of uncertainty affecting projections of future population trends." (http://www.un.org/en/development/desa/news/population/population-division-director.html as of 6 December 2019).

1.9 A Brief Presentation of Chapters 2–12

In Chap. 2, Graziani proposes a procedure for deriving expert based stochastic population forecasts within the Bayesian approach. The joint distributions of all summary indicators are obtained based on evaluations by experts, elicited according to a conditional procedure that makes it possible to derive information on the centres of the indicators, their variability, their across-time correlations, and the correlations between the indicators. The forecasting method is based on a mixture model within the Supra-Bayesian approach that treats the evaluations by experts as data and the summary indicators as parameters. The derived posterior distributions are used as forecast distributions of the summary indicators of interest.

Chapter 3 by Dion, Galbraith, and Sirag also focuses on modeling experts opinions. Particular care is given to experts' opinions elicitation and their uncertainty quantification: experts are asked to provide estimates of 'most likely' values for a series of demographic indicators, along with corresponding 80% prediction intervals. A flexible distribution (metalog) is used to estimate experts' forecasts uncertainty for all components of population growth.

In Chap. 4, Castiglioni, Dalla-Zuanna and Tanturri evaluate the "convergence" hypothesis that is assumed by UNPD in several population revisions. They find out that in fact, such a convergence does not find empirical support, especially for life expectancy.

Chapter 5 by Aliverti, Durante, and Scarpa provides a data-driven model to forecast age-specific fertility rates (ASFRs). The model is based on a Gaussian process applied to a model of ASFRs. The latter is based on the skew normal distribution, a generalization of the normal distribution that allows for skewed shapes. The Gaussian process allows including model time dependent parameters, used to forecast future values of ASFRs. Forecasting ASFRs might be useful as in many cases forecasts of the TFR are available, but the age schedule is also needed to forecast the number of births.

Basellini and Camarda propose in Chap. 6 to analyse and forecast mortality developments over age and time by introducing a nonparametric decomposition of the mortality age pattern into three independent components corresponding to Childhood, Early-Adulthood and Senescence, respectively. Each component-specific death density is modeled with a relational model that associates a time-invariant standard to a series of observed distributions by means of a transformation of the age axis. This approach allows to capture mortality developments over age and time, and forecasts can be derived from parameters' extrapolation using standard time series models.

Chapter 7 by Bergeron-Boucher, Kjærgaard, Pascariu, Aburto, Alvarez, Rizzi, and Vaupel questions the assumption of linear (or log-linear) development of mortality indicators, such as death rates or life expectancy. This assumption can be problematic in countries where mortality development has been non-linear, such as in Denmark: the country experienced a stagnation of longevity improvement from the 1980s until the mid-1990s. The forecast performance of 11 models for Danish females and males and for period and cohort data are evaluated.

Chapter 8 by Booth focuses on coherent models, where a standard mortality pattern has to be defined. The chapter investigates the impact of different standards used in sex-coherent forecasts and standard-coherent ones. The analysis confirms that low mortality standards usually bring about lower bias, even though some exceptions, especially for males are found.

Chapter 9 by Keilman and Kristoffersen considers the uncertainty in mortality forecasts and analyses the extent to which life expectancy predictions for 2030 and 2050 were revised in subsequent rounds of population forecasts published by statistical agencies in selected countries. In a previous study, the conclusion was that life expectancy forecasts for some European countries for the year 2050 had been revised upwards systematically. Here they show that the period of upward revisions seems to have ended for some European countries.

Zhang and Bryant construct in Chap. 10 a forecasting model for internal migration, with an application to Iceland. The model proposed is a Bayesian hierarchical one. The motivation of using a hierarchical model stems from sparsity of data, which requires information borrowing, especially for flows characterized by low numbers.

Chapter 11 by Raymer, Bai, and Smith also considers internal migration, but the authors propose a log-linear model, which they apply to Australian regions. In particular, they show that multiplicative components can be used to capture the structure of migration flow tables. They combine the model with time series models to produce a hold-out sample of forecasts of interstate migration with measures of uncertainty. Goodness-of-fit statistics and calibration are then used to identify the best fitting models.

Scherbov and Sanderson consider in Chap. 12 a quite different matter: provided that demographic components are evolving over time (especially mortality), ageing could also be defined as an evolving concept. A prospective measure of ageing is considered. This measure could be based on remaining life expectancy or on mortality rates.

References

Ahlburg, D. (1982). How accurate are the U.S. Bureau of the Census projection of total live births? *Journal of Forecasting, 1*, 365–374.

Alders, M., & De Beer, J. (1998). Kansverdeling van de bevolkingsprognose. *Maandstatistiek van de Bevolking, 46*, 8–11.

Alexopoulos, A., Dellaportas, P., & Forster, J. J. (2018). Bayesian forecasting of mortality rates by using latent Gaussian models. *Journal of the Royal Statistical Society: Series A (Statistics in Society), 182*(2), 689–711.

Alho, J. M. (2015). Population forecasting. In J. D. Wright (Ed.), *International encyclopedia of the social and behavioral sciences* (2nd ed., pp. 593–596). Amsterdam: Elsevier.

Alho, J. M., & Spencer, B. (1985). Uncertain population forecasting. *Journal of the American Statistical Association, 85*, 306–314.

Alho, J. M., & Spencer, B. (2005). *Statistical demography and forecasting*. New York: Springer.

Alho, J. M., Hougaard Jensen, S. E., & Lassila, J. (Eds.). (2008). *Uncertain demographics and fiscal sustainability*. Cambridge: Cambridge University Press.

Alkema, L., Raftery, A. E., Gerland, P., Clark, S. J., Pelletier, F., Buettner, T., & Heilig, G. K. (2011). Probabilistic projections of the total fertility rate for all countries. *Demography, 48*, 815–839.

Bijak, J., & Bryant, J. (2016). Bayesian demography 250 years after Bayes. *Population Studies, 70*(1), 1–19. https://doi.org/10.1080/00324728.2015.1122826.

Bijak, J., Alberts, I., Alho, J., Bryant, J., Buettner, T., Falkingham, J., Forster, J. J., Gerland, P., King, T., Onorante, L., Keilman, N., O'Hagan, A., Owens, D., Raftery, A., Ševcíková, H., & Smith, P. W. F. (2015). Letter to the editor: Probabilistic population forecasts for informed decision-making. *Journal of Official Statistics, 31*(4), 537–544.

Booth, H. (2004). On the importance of being uncertain: Forecasting population futures for Australia. *People and Place, 12*, 1–12.

Booth, H. (2006). Demographic forecasting: 1980 to 2005 in review. *International Journal of Forecasting, 22*(3), 547–581.

Burch, T. K. (2003). The cohort-component population projection: A strange attractor for demographers. In J. Fleischhacker, H. A. de Gans, & T. K. Burch (Eds.), *Populations, projections and politics* (pp. 39–57). Amsterdam: Rozenberg Publishers.

Canale, A., Kenne Pagui, C. E., & Scarpa, B. (2016). Bayesian modeling of university first-year students' grades after placement test. *Journal of Applied Statistics, 43*(16), 3015–3029.

Cappelen, Å., Skjerpen, T., & Tønnessen, M. (2014). Forecasting immigration in official population projections using an econometric model. *International Migration Review, 49*(4), 945–980.

Carpenter, B., Gelman, A., Hoffman, M. D., Lee, D., Goodrich, B., Betancourt, M., Brubaker, M., Guo, J., Li, P., & Riddell, A. (2017). Stan: A probabilistic programming language. *Journal of Statistical Software, 76*(1). https://doi.org/10.18637/jss.v076.i01.

Cohen, J. (1986). Population forecasts and confidence intervals for Sweden: A comparison of model-based and empirical approaches. *Demography, 23*(1), 105–126.

Cohen, J. (2010). Population and climate change. *Proceedings of the American Philosophical Society, 154*(2), 158–182.

De Gans, H. (1999). *Population forecasting 1895–1945*. Dordrecht: Kluwer.

De Sherbinin, A., Carr, D., Cassels, S., & Jiang, L. (2007). Population and environment. *Annual Review of Environment and Resources, 32*, 345–373.

Dunson, D. B. (2001). Commentary: Practical advantages of Bayesian analysis of epidemiologic data. *American Journal of Epidemiology, 153*(12), 1222–1226. https://doi.org/10.1093/aje/153.12.1222.

Dunstan, K. (2019). *Stochastic projections: The New Zealand experience*. Paper presented at the Eurostat/UNECE Work Session on Demographic Projections, Belgrade, 25–27 November 2019.

Dunstan, K., & Ball, C. (2016). Demographic projections: User and producer experiences of adopting a stochastic approach. *Journal of Official Statistics, 32*(6), 947–962.
Efron, B., & Tibshirani, R. J. (1993). *An introduction to the bootstrap*. Chapman and Hall/CRC Press.
Fundel, V. J., Fleischhut, N., Herzog, S. M., Göber, M., & Hagedorn, R. (2019). Promoting the use of probabilistic weather forecasts through a dialogue between scientists, developers and end-users. *Quarterly Journal of the Royal Meorological Society, 145*(Supplement 1), 210–231.
Gerland, P., Raftery, A., Ševčíková, H., Li, N., Gu, D., Spoorenberg, T., Alkema, L., Fosdick, B., Chunn, J., Lalic, N., Bay, G., Buettner, T., Heilig, G., & Wilmoth, J. (2014). World population stabilization unlikely this century. *Science, 346*, 234–237.
Geweke, J., & Whiteman, C. (2006). Bayesian forecasting. In *Handbook of economic forecasting* (Vol. 1, pp. 3–80). Boston: Elsevier.
Gneiting, T., & Katzfuss, M. (2014). Probabilistic forecasting. *Annual Review of Statistics and Its Applications, 1*, 125–151.
Gneiting, T., & Raftery, A. (2007). Strictly proper scoring rules, prediction and estimation. *Journal of the American Statistical Association, 102*(477), 359–378.
Gneiting, T., Balabdaoui, F., & Raftery, A. E. (2007). Probabilistic forecasts, calibration and sharpness. *Journal of the Royal Statistical Society, Series B, 69*, 243–268.
Goodwin, P. (2014). Getting real about uncertainty. *Foresight – The International Journal of Applied Forecasting, 33*, 4–7.
Hajnal, J. (1955). The prospects for population forecasts. *Journal of the American Statistical Association, 50*(270), 309–322.
ISTAT. (2018). Il futuro demografico del paese: Previsioni regionali della popolazione residente al 2065 (base 1.1.2017). Report Statistische 3 maggio 2018. Roma: ISTAT.
Jackman, S. (2009). *Bayesian analysis for the social sciences*. Eastbourne: Wiley.
Keilman, N. (2020). Evaluating probabilistic population forecasts. Économie et Statistique/Economics and Statistics (to appear).
Keilman, N., & Cruijsen, H. (Eds.). (1992). *National population forecasting in industrialized countries* (NIDI-CBGS Publications 24). Amsterdam: Swets & Zeitlinger.
Keyfitz, N. (1972). On future population. *Journal of the American Statistical Association, 67*(338), 347–363.
Keyfitz, N. (1981). The limits of population forecasting. *Population and Development Review, 7*(4), 579–593.
Keyfitz, N. (1985). A probability representation of future population. *Zeitschrift für Bevölkerungswissenschaft, 11*(2), 179–191.
King, M. (2004). *What fates impose: Facing up to uncertainty*. Speech given by Mervyn King, Governor of the Bank of England at the Eighth British Academy Annual Lecture, London 1 December 2004. https://www.bankofengland.co.uk/speech/2004/what-fastes-impose-facing-up-to-uncertainty. (As of 6 December 2019).
Kuijsten, A. C. (1988). Demografische Toekomstbeelden van Nederland. Verkenningen no. 49 Planologisch en Demografisch Instituut, Universiteit van Amsterdam.
Land, K. (1985). Methods of national population forecasts: A review. *Journal of the American Statistical Association, 81*(396), 888–901.
Lee, R., & Tuljapurkar, S. (1994). Stochastic population forecasts for the United States: Beyond high, medium and low. *Journal of the American Statistical Association, 89*, 1175–1189.
Lee, R., & Tuljapurkar, S. (2000). Population forecasting for fiscal planning: Issues and innovations. In A. J. Auerbach & R. D. Lee (Eds.), *Demography and fiscal policy* (pp. 7–57). Cambridge: Cambridge University Press.
Li, N., & Lee, R. (2005). Coherent mortality forecasts for a group of populations: An extension of the Lee-Carter method. *Demography, 42*(3), 575–594. https://doi.org/10.1353/dem.2005.0021.
Lutz, W., & Scherbov, S. (1998). An expert-based framework for probabilistic national population projections: The example of Austria. *European Journal of Population, 14*, 1–17.
Lutz, W., Sanderson W. C., & Scherbov, S. (1996). *Probabilistic world population projections based on expert opinion* (IIASA Working Paper). IIASA, Laxenburg: WP-96-017.

Myers, R. J. (1954). Comparison of population projections with actual data. In *Proceedings world population conference 1954* (Vol. III, pp. 101–111). New York: United Nations.
National Research Council – NRC. (2000). Beyond six billion: Forecasting the World's population. Panel on population projections. In J. Bongaarts & R. Bulatao (Eds.), *Committee on population, commission on behavioral and social sciences and education*. Washington, DC: National Academy Press.
O'Neill, B., & Balk, D. (2001). World population futures. *Population Bulletin, 56*(3), 3–40. Washington: Population Reference Bureau.
Pollard, J. H. (1966). On the use of the direct matrix product in analysing certain stochastic population models. *Biometrika, 53*, 397–415.
Preston, S. H., Heuveline, P., & Guillot, M. (2001). *Demography: Measuring and modeling population processes*. Oxford: Blackwell Publishers.
Raftery, A. E. (2014). *Use and communication of probabilistic forecasts*. Mimeo, University of Washington. http://arxiv.org/abs/1408.4812. (As of 6 December 2019).
Raftery, A. E., Li, N., Ševčíková, H., Gerland, P., & Heilig, G. K. (2012). Bayesian probabilistic population projections for all countries. *PNAS, 109*, 13915–13921.
Raftery, A. E., Chunn, J. L., Gerland, P., et al. (2013). Bayesian probabilistic projections of life expectancy for all countries. *Demography, 50*(3), 777–801.
Raftery, A. E., Zimmer, A., Frierson, D. M. W., Startz, R., & Liu, P. (2017). Less than 2° C warming by 2100 unlikely. *Nature Climate Change, 7*, 637–641.
Rogers, A. (1995). *Multiregional Demography*. Chichester: Wiley.
Rowland, D. (2003). *Demographic methods and concepts*. Oxford: Oxford University Press.
Sanderson, W. (1998). Knowledge can improve forecasts: A review of selected socioeconomic population projection models. *Population and Development Review, 24*(Supplement), 88–117.
Schweder, T. (1971). The precision of population projections studied by multiple prediction methods. *Demography, 8*(4), 441–450.
Ševčíková, H., Li, N., Kantorová, V., Gerland, P., & Raftery, A. (2016). Age-specific mortality and fertility rates for probabilistic population projections. In R. Schoen (Ed.), *Dynamic demographic analysis* (pp. 285–310). Cham: Springer.
Shang, H. L. (2015). Statistically tested comparisons of the accuracy of forecasting methods for age-specific and sex-specific mortality and life expectancy. *Population Studies, 69*(3), 317–335.
Shang, H. L., & Hyndman, R. (2017). Grouped functional time series forecasting: An application to age-specific mortality rates. *Journal of Computational and Graphical Statistics, 26*(2), 330–343.
Shang, H. L., Smith, P., Bijak, J., & Wisniowski, A. (2016). A multilevel functional data method for forecasting population, with an application to the United Kingdom. *International Journal of Forecasting, 32*, 629–649.
Simpson, L., Wilson, T., & Shalley, F. (2019). The shelf life of official sub-national population forecasts in England. *Applied Spatial Analysis and Policy*. Published online 21 November 2019. https://doi.org/10.1007/s12061-019-09325-3. (As of 6 December 2019).
Spiegelhalter, D., Pearson, M., & Short, I. (2011). Visualising uncertainty about the future. *Science, 333*, 1393–1400.
Statistics New Zealand. (2011). National Population Projections: 2011(base)–2061. Bulletin published 19 July 2012, ISSN 1178-0584. http://archive.stats.govt.nz/browse_for_stats/population/estimates_and_projections/NationalPopulationProjections_HOTP2011.aspx. (As of 6 December).
Stoto, M. A. (1983). The accuracy of population projections. *Journal of the American Statistical Association, 78*, 13–20.
Sykes, Z. M. (1969). Some stochastic versions of the matrix model for population dynamics. *Journal of the American Statistical Association, 64*, 111–130.
Tetlock, P., & Gardner, D. (2016). *Superforecasting: The art and science of prediction*. New York: Crown.
Törnquist, L. (1949). Om de synspunkter, som bestämt valet av de primära prognos-antaganda. In J. Hyppolä, A. Tunkelo, & L. Törnquist (Eds.), *Beräkningar rörande Finlands Befolkning, dess*

Reproduktion och Framtida Utveckling (Statistiska Meddalanden 38) (pp. 69–75). Helsinki: Statistiska Centralbyrån. (in Finnish, Swedish and French).

Tuljapurkar, S. (1992). Stochastic population forecasts and their uses. *International Journal of Forecasting, 8*(3), 385–391.

United Nations. (2017). Department of Economic and Social Affairs, Population Division. *World population prospects: The 2017 revision, methodology of the United Nations population estimates and projections* (Working Paper No. ESA/P/WP.250). New York: United Nations.

United Nations Economic Commission for Europe – UNECE. (2018). *Recommendations on communicating population projections* (Report no. ECE/CES/STAT/2018/1). Geneva: United Nations.

Willekens, F. J. (1990). Demographic forecasting: State-of-the-art and research needs. In C. Hazeu & G. Frinking (Eds.), *Emerging issues in demographic research* (pp. 9–66). Amsterdam: Elsevier.

Wilson, T. (2018). *Communicating population forecast uncertainty using perishable food terminology*. Darwin: Northern Institute, Charles Darwin University (Research Brief RB03/2018). http://www.cdu.edu.au/sites/default/files/research-brief-2018-03_0.pdf. (As of 6 December 2019).

Wilson, T., & Rees, P. (2005). Recent developments in population projection methodology: A review. *Population, Space and Place, 11*, 337–360.

Wilson, T., & Shalley, F. (2019). Subnational population forecasts: Do users want to know about uncertainty? *Demographic Research, 41*(13), 367–392.

Wilson, T., Brokensha, H., Rowe, F., & Simpson, L. (2018). Insights from the evaluation of past local area population forecasts. *Population Research and Policy Review, 37*(1), 137–155.

Chapter 2
Stochastic Population Forecasting: A Bayesian Approach Based on Evaluation by Experts

Rebecca Graziani

2.1 Introduction

Probabilistic population forecasting has recently received growing attention from researchers and, to a lesser extent, from official agencies, which traditionally derive population projections deterministically. As discussed in Keilman et al. (2002) and Keilman (2018), there are three main approaches to stochastic population forecasting. The first approach relies on the theory of time series, with models suggested both by the frequentist and the Bayesian approaches. The best-known time series approach in a classical framework is due to Lee and Carter (1992), originally proposed to forecast mortality, and later modified to address fertility forecasting, see Lee (1993) and Lee and Tuljapurkar (1994). Many extensions, generalizations and modifications have been proposed: see, among others, Booth et al. (2002), Booth and Tickle (2008), Booth (2006) Cairns et al. (2006, 2011), Hyndman and Ullah (2007), Hyndman and Booth (2008), and Hyndman et al. (2013). Using the Bayesian approach, Alkema et al. (2011) suggest a Bayesian hierarchical time series model for fertility forecasting, Raftery et al. (2013) for mortality forecasting, and Bijak and Wiśniowski (2010) and Bijak and Bryant (2016) for migration forecasting. As a sign that probabilistic approaches are entering

Electronic Supplementary Material The online version of this chapter (https://doi.org/10.1007/978-3-030-42472-5_2) contains supplementary material, which is available to authorized users.

R. Graziani (✉)
Department of Social and Political Sciences, Bocconi University, Milan, Italy

Dondena Centre for Research on Social Dynamics and Public Policy, Milan, Italy

Bocconi Institute for Data Science and Analytics, Milan, Italy
e-mail: rebecca.graziani@unibocconi.it

S. Mazzuco, N. Keilman (eds.), *Developments in Demographic Forecasting*, The Springer Series on Demographic Methods and Population Analysis 49, https://doi.org/10.1007/978-3-030-42472-5_2

the mainstream of demographic forecasting, in 2014 the United Nations for the first time issued official probabilistic population projections for all countries up to 2100, see Alkema et al. (2015).

The second approach derives population forecasts based on the extrapolation of empirical errors. The observed errors from historical forecasts are used in the assessment of the uncertainty, see, among others, Stoto (1983). Following this approach, Alho and Spencer (1990) proposed the Scaled Model of Error, which was used to obtain stochastic population forecasts within the UPE (Uncertainty Population of Europe) project, see Alders et al. (2007).

The third approach, known as random scenarios or expert based approach, derives the forecast distribution of demographic components based on suitably elicited expert evaluations on their future trend, see, among others, Lutz et al. (1998). This is the approach that we follow in the present paper. The advantages and disadvantages of methods that rely on expert evaluations have been widely discussed in the literature. Goldstein (2004) and Lutz and Goldstein (2004), among others, stress how the random-scenario approach might be appealing to official agencies, due to its simplicity, the fact that its framework is based on scenarios, and the direct involvement of experts. The use of expert opinions allows taking into account behavioural theories on the future of the population (as argued by Lutz 2013) and allows incorporating in the forecasting exercise the knowledge of trends (such as policy changes and environmental changes) that might have an impact on the population dynamics. A further important advantage of expert based forecasting is that it does not require data on the past and therefore can be especially useful for developing countries, for which past data are usually poor. The main criticism of the expert based approach is related to the well-known and widely observed tendency of experts to underestimate the uncertainty. Keilman (1990) observed that, particularly when recent trends have been stable, the overconfidence of experts results in overly narrow prediction intervals. Among others, Alho and Spencer (1990) stress the conservativeness of expert opinions with respect to the decline in mortality, while Lee (1993) and Booth (2006) express concerns with respect to the accuracy of fertility forecasts. A further recognized drawback is that a forecast approach based on expert evaluations needs to focus on summary indicators of the demographic changes, and therefore turns out to be inflexible in forecasting age-schedules. Moreover, existing random-scenario methods, being generally based on trajectories that are obtained by the interpolation of a starting known and a final random value, are characterized by a variance and covariance structure which is not particularly flexible. Finally it is commonly emphasized that it is not easy to elicit from experts opinions on the across-time correlations for a single indicator and correlations between indicators.

Our method derives probabilistic population forecasts based on expert opinions in such a way as to take into account relations both between the demographic components and between the expert evaluations. As for the first kind of relation, between demographic components, there is a certain debate about the advisability and/or need to model such dependence. Indeed, if for some pairs of indicators the dependence is not under scrutiny, as for male and female life expectancies at birth, in other cases, as for immigration and fertility, it is more questionable. It is common practice in population forecasting to assume independence between the three components of demographic change, fertility, mortality and migration, for which separate forecasts are provided. Our method lets expert evaluations on the future trends of the demographic components drive the detection of the presence and assessment of the strength of any relations between them. Indeed, in principle the method we suggest can take into account any type of dependence between any pair of indicators. Our method does not exclude independence between the demographic components, an independence that can be the result of expert opinions.

Our method also takes into account any dependencies between expert evaluations. Indeed, we expect that experts who have been trained and work in the same field would share a certain amount of knowledge and information, which could induce associations between their opinions. In an expert based approach, an important and delicate issue to face is how to combine the opinions provided by several experts. A wide literature is available on the problem of the aggregation of expert opinions, see, among others, Genest et al. (1986) for a review. Popular pooling methods suggest combining expert opinions by working out averages. For instance, the linear rule derives the collective assignment through their (possibly weighted) average. Similarly, one can define geometric or logarithmic pooling rules. Such pooling techniques take into account the variability of the expert evaluations, but do not take into account their potential associations, associations that we think cannot be neglected. Here we suggest a method for combining expert opinions that allows modelling both the associations between them and their diversity, taking into account several sources of uncertainty.

We suggest combining the expert evaluations by resorting to the so-called Supra-Bayesian method of pooling, introduced by Morris (1974) and then developed by many authors, see, among others, French (1980, 1981), Winkler (1981), Lindley (1983, 1985), Gelfand et al. (1995), and Roback and Givens (2001). In this approach, expert opinions on unknown quantities are treated as observations and combined based on the theoretical framework provided by the Bayesian approach to statistics. The analyst specifies a likelihood function, to be parametrized in terms of the unknown objects, and a prior distribution for the parameters. The posterior distribution, obtained by applying Bayes's theorem, updates the analyst's prior opinion, on the basis of the evaluations provided by the experts, and can then be used as a forecast distribution for the unknown quantities of interest. This approach takes into account and exploits the variability of the expert evaluations. Hence, the larger the number of experts, the more informative the procedure is.

In the next section, we provide a description of the method that was first suggested in Billari et al. (2014). We discuss in detail the elicitation procedure, the model, and the Markov Chain Monte Carlo algorithm. In Sect. 2.3 we describe the results of applying the model to forecasting of the Italian population from 2010 to 2065. In Sect. 2.4 some concluding remarks are provided.

2.2 The Supra-Bayesian Forecasting Method

As is common practice in the expert based approach, our method focusses on summary indicators of the three components of demographic change: fertility, mortality and migration. Population forecasts by age and sex are then obtained, relying on the commonly used cohort-component model, with age-schedules derived from the corresponding summary indicators, based on suitable models. In the following we describe the method, considering the case of two summary indicators R_1 and R_2 to be jointly forecast from time t_0 to time T. The inputs of the method are the expert opinions, which we presume to have been elicited according to the conditional elicitation procedure suggested in Billari et al. (2012).

The elicitation procedure works as follows. Split the forecast interval $[t_0, T]$ into two subintervals, considering a time point t_1 in it. In the first stage, the expert is asked to provide a forecast for each indicator at time t_1 and at time T, and an upper quantile for one of the two indicators at time t_1, say for instance R_1, as a value such that R_1 takes on a greater value with a predetermined probability. In the implementation of the method, this probability is set equal to 10%. In the second stage, the expert is asked to provide the following conditional forecasts:

- A forecast and an upper quantile at t_1 for the second indicator R_2 presuming that R_1 takes at t_1 a value equal to the elicited upper quantile and the forecast respectively;
- A forecast and an upper quantile at T for R_1 presuming that it takes at t_1 a value equal to the elicited upper quantile and the forecast respectively;
- Three different forecasts at T for R_2 presuming three different combinations of values for R_1 at t_1 and T and R_2 at t_1.

In order to understand how the indicators' mean and variance, along with their correlations, can be derived from the elicited values, consider the case of one single indicator. In the case of the forecast of one single indicator, the expert should provide at the first stage forecasts for times t_1 and T, say m_{t_1} and m_T, and an upper quantile at time t_1, say q_{t_1} as a value such that there is a probability equal to α that the indicator takes on a value greater than q_{t_1}. We assume Gaussian distributions for the indicator at the two time points, with means m_{t_1}, respectively, m_T. Under the Gaussian assumption, the variance $\sigma^2_{t_1}$ of the indicator at time t_1 can be easily derived from m_{t_1} and q_{t_1} as follows:

$$\sigma^2_{t_1} = \left(\frac{q_1 - m_1}{z_{1-\alpha}}\right)^2$$

with $z_{1-\alpha}$ being the quantile of order $1-\alpha$ of a standard Gaussian random variable.

At the second stage, the expert is asked to provide a forecast, say $m_{T|t_1}$, of the indicator at time T presuming that it takes at time t_1 a value equal to the elicited quantile q_{t_1} and an upper quantile of the indicator at time T, say $q_{T|t_1}$, presuming that at time t_1 the indicator is m_{t_1}. Under the assumption of Gaussian distributions at the two time points, the conditional distribution of the indicator at T given that it is equal to q_{t_1} at t_1 is Gaussian, has mean $m_{T|t_1}$ and variance $\sigma^2_{T|t_1}$ that can be derived as before from $m_{T|t_1}$ and $q_{T|t_1}$. The conditional distribution of the indicator is in this way completely specified, so that the correlation between the indicator at the two time points can be derived from standard results on Gaussian distributions.

This method can be easily generalized to the case of two indicators to be jointly forecast at t_1 and T. Therefore, the elicitation procedure allows indirectly eliciting across-time correlations for a single indicator, as the correlation between the rates at the two considered time points t_1 and T, and correlations both at the same time and across time for a pair of indicators, by asking for conditional forecasts.

This elicitation procedure yields vectors of forecasts of the two indicators at the two time points and their covariance matrix, one vector for each expert. In the method we suggest, the forecasts and the covariance matrices are used in a different way. We follow the Supra-Bayesian approach and suggest treating as data the forecasts provided by each expert at the two time points. In a Bayesian approach to inference, the analyst should, then, specify both the likelihood function, describing the random mechanism generating the evaluations and therefore to be parametrized in terms of the demographic summary indicators, and a prior distribution of these parameters, incorporating any information the expert has on them.

The likelihood function shapes the dependences between the expert evaluations. In Lindley (1983, 1985) a multivariate Gaussian distribution is used. Such a choice is motivated primarily by mathematical convenience, since it simplifies all computations related to the derivation of the posterior distributions. Nevertheless, the construction of a likelihood function of this kind is cumbersome, due to the large number of terms to be specified. Indeed, in the case of opinions elicited on several indicators at different time points, the choice of a multivariate Gaussian distribution requires the specification of all marginal means and variances and covariances.

Albert et al. (2012) suggest relying on a hierarchical random effects model, as a more parsimonious approach. At the beginning of the analysis, the experts are grouped by the analyst into a fixed number of homogeneity classes, corresponding to similar backgrounds or similar schools of thought. At the first level of the hierarchy, the opinions provided by the experts belonging to the same group are assumed to have the same distribution, indexed by parameters varying across groups. Then the different groups are assumed to have a common knowledge that is linked through a common distribution assigned to the group parameters and indexed by the parameter that represents the object of the expert evaluations. Finally, at the last level, a prior is assigned to this parameter, representing the overall uncertainty of the elicitation.

We suggest choosing a mixture model for the likelihood. Through this choice, we assume, as in Albert et al. (2012), that there are several different random mechanisms generating the expert evaluations, but we do not know which is the random mechanism generating the evaluations provided by each expert. Again, we presume that the experts can be grouped into a given number of classes, based on their shared knowledge and information, but for each expert we do not know which is the class the expert belongs to. We let the opinions provided by the

Likelihood

$$x_i|\mu_1,\ldots,\mu_J,\Sigma_1,\ldots,\Sigma_J,p_1,\ldots,p_J \text{ ind} \sim \sum_{j=1}^{J} p_j N_4(\mu_j,\Sigma_j) \quad i=1,\ldots,K$$

Priors

$$\mu_j|\Sigma_j \text{ ind} \sim N_4(R, \frac{1}{k_0}\Sigma_j) \quad j=1,\ldots,J$$

$$\Sigma_j \text{ iid} \sim IW(\Sigma_0, n_0) \quad i=1,\ldots,J$$

$$p_1,\ldots,p_J \sim Dir(\alpha_1,\ldots,\alpha_J)$$

$$R \sim N_4(\mu_R,\Sigma_R)$$

Fixed Hyperparameters

$$J,\Sigma_0\ k_0,\ n_0\ \alpha,\mu_R,\ \Sigma_R$$

Fig. 2.1 The mixture model

experts determine their group membership, so as to implicitly derive the dependence structure of the expert evaluations.

On the side of the prior distributions, as in Albert et al. (2012), the group centres are assumed to be independent and to have the same distribution, centred at the vector of summary indicators. In this way, we take into account the heterogeneity of the expert evaluations due to their possessing different pieces of information. Finally, we use the elicited covariance matrices to specify the prior distribution of thc unknown clusters covariance matrix.

The resulting hierarchical model can be schematized as in Fig. 2.1, for the case of K experts where x_i is the vector of forecasts provided by expert i on the two indicators at two time points and $R = (R_{1t_1}, R_{1T}, R_{2t_1}, R_{2T})$ with R_{jt} being the random variable associated with indicator j at time t. The evaluations of the two summary indicators at the two time points are assumed to be conditionally independent and drawn from a mixture of J multivariate Gaussian distributions of dimension 4, each denoted by $N_4(\mu_j, \Sigma_j)$, for $j = 1, \cdots, J$ and with J fixed by the analyst, being the number of groups of experts, with weights $p_1, \ldots, p_J$. We assume in this way that each expert evaluation is distributed according to $N_4(\mu_j, \Sigma_j)$ with probability p_j. As for the prior distributions, the group means μ_j are assumed to be independent conditional on the covariance matrix Σ_j and distributed according to a multivariate Gaussian distribution centred at the vector of summary indicators at the two time points R, and with covariance matrix equal to Σ_j scaled by k_0 so as to end up with a diffuse prior, as discussed below. The covariance matrices Σ_j are assumed to be independent and identically distributed according to an inverse-Wishart distribution with scale matrix Σ_0 and n_0 degrees of freedom. The group probabilities $p_1, \ldots, p_J$ are assumed to have a Dirichlet distribution with parameters $(\alpha_1, \ldots, \alpha_J)$. The vector of summary indicators at the two time points R is assumed to have a multivariate Gaussian distribution. It is worth emphasizing that this choice of prior distributions ensures conditional conjugacy (see, among others, Lavine and West 1992), which is something we draw on in the design of the Markov Chain Monte Carlo algorithm needed for the simulation of the posterior distribution of the vector of summary indicators R, described later.

The analyst needs then to specify the number J of components of the mixture and the parameters of the priors $\Sigma_0, k_0, n_0, \alpha, \mu_R, \Sigma_R$. The number of components can be chosen by fitting models with different J and then comparing them on the basis of indexes such as the Bayesian Information Criterion (BIC) or the Akaike Information Criterion (AIC). Since Σ_0 is the centre of the prior on the groups covariance matrix, we suggest specifying it based on the elicited covariance matrices. In our implementation of the model, we set Σ_0 equal to the arithmetic average of these covariance matrices, scaled so as to increase the variance of the elicited indicators. In this way we take into consideration and can correct the over-confidence of the experts, who tend to underestimate the variability of their forecasts. Since μ_R is the centre of the prior assigned to vector R, it represents a prior guess of the future values of the indicators and can then be specified using all available information. For instance, it can be fixed based on the central scenarios provided by national and international statistical agencies.

As for the remaining hyper-parameters, we suggest specifying them so as to end up with very diffuse priors. In this way, the posterior distribution can be mainly determined by the data, the expert elicited forecasts. Indeed, k_0 and n_0 affect the spread of the prior distributions on the group means and on the group covariances, respectively: the smaller they are, the larger is the spread. We suggest setting them as small as possible in order to increase the variability of the priors. Due to the properties of the Dirichlet distribution, the smaller is the value of α_j, the larger is the variability. Moreover α_j is the probability for an expert to belong to group j. A standard choice to depict no prior information on the group membership is $\alpha_j = \frac{1}{J}$. Σ_R is the covariance matrix of the prior distribution on R. We suggest choosing rather high variances so as to end up with a diffuse prior, and setting the covariances equal to 0, which corresponds to assuming the a priori independence of the indicators.

The joint posterior distribution of the indicators $(R_{1t_1}, R_{1T}, R_{2t_1}, R_{2T})$ can then be used as their forecast distribution at the two considered time points. Since this cannot be expressed in closed form, we suggest a Markov Chain Monte Carlo algorithm to draw samples from it. More precisely, we develop an auxiliary variables Gibbs-sampler, with full-conditionals that are all available in closed form due to the conditional conjugacy ensured by the choice of the prior distributions. For each observation, we introduce at each iteration an auxiliary variable Z_i taking values in $\{1, 2, \ldots, J\}$, which flags its group membership and is updated each iteration. At each iteration of the algorithm, the group means and covariance matrices are updated by drawing them from a multivariate Gaussian distribution and an inverse-Wishart distribution respectively, the vector of latent variables is updated by drawing each component from a discrete distribution on $\{1, 2, \ldots, J\}$, the vector of group probabilities $(p_1, \ldots, p_J)$ is updated by drawing it from a Dirichlet distribution and the vector R of summary indicators is updated by sampling it from a multivariate Gaussian distribution. The draws of the summary indicators from the joint posterior distribution are used as forecasts of the two summary indicators at the two time points, while forecasts for all points of the interval are obtained by resorting to suitable interpolation methods. In the application discussed in the next section, standard elementary quadratic interpolation techniques are used. As a by-product, the draws of the latent variables $Z_1, \ldots, Z_K$ can be used for the estimation of the composition of the groups, that is, the clustering of experts in the J groups.

The Matlab package supraBayesian_popproj, downloadable from the web site of the publication, provides the codes implementing the Gibbs-sampler along with the codes for the derivation of the population forecasts by age and sex based on the simulations from the posterior distribution of the summary indicators.

2.3 An Application: Forecasting the Italian Population

In this section we illustrate an application of our forecasting method. The experts opinion used as inputs of the model were elicited according to the described procedure, through a questionnaire administered in 2012 in collaboration with the Italian Statistical Office (ISTAT). Experts were provided with information on the latest scenarios depicted by Eurostat and by the United Nations on the Italian summary indicators of demographic change. In 2015 the first official probabilistic population forecasts of the Italian population were issued by ISTAT starting from such elicited opinions. The Italian Statistical Office followed the method suggested in Billari et al. (2012) for the derivation of expert-based forecasts of the summary indicators. In the ISTAT forecasting exercise, the indicators were treated as independent and a multivariate Gaussian distribution was taken as the forecast distribution, with mean and covariance matrix obtained by averaging across the experts' elicitations. In 2017, ISTAT provided an update of the population projections of 2015, based on the same elicited opinions; a detailed description of the implemented methodology is provided in ISTAT (2017).

The forecasting period was 2010–2065 and was split into two sub-intervals, employing 2030 as the midpoint. The opinions were elicited on the following summary indicators: Total Fertility Rate, Mean Age at Birth, Male and Female Life Expectancies at Birth, Total Number of Immigrants and of Emigrants. The opinions on Total Fertility Rate and Total Number of Immigrants were jointly elicited, as were the opinions on Male and Female Life Expectancies at birth. Figure 2.2 displays the forecasts of the Total Fertility Rate and of the Total Number of Immigrants at 2030 and 2065 provided by 14 experts, while Fig. 2.3 depicts the corresponding correlations indirectly elicited.

With the Total Fertility Rate, there was low variability across expert evaluations: almost all the experts foresee a moderate increase in the rate from 2030 to 2065. With the Total Number of Immigrants, the evaluations show a higher variability,

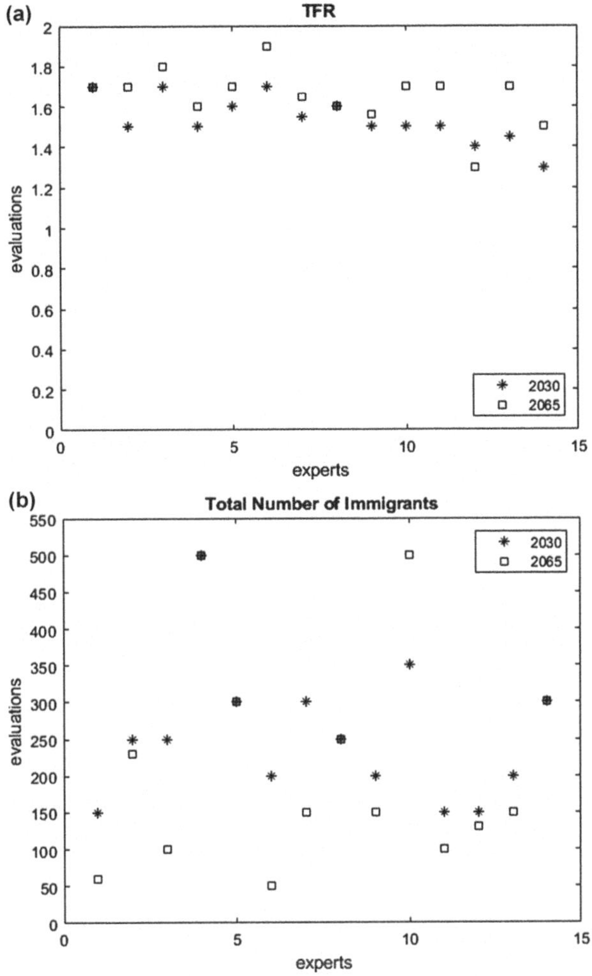

Fig. 2.2 Expert forecasts of Total Fertility Rate and Total Number of Immigrants

especially for 2065; the majority of experts forecast a decrease in the Total Number of Immigrants. As to the correlations, there is a general agreement on a positive high correlation between Total Number of Immigrants at 2030 and Total Number of Immigrants at 2065 and on a positive moderate/high correlation between Total Fertility Rate at 2030 and at 2065. For the majority of experts there is a positive correlation between Total Number of Immigrants at 2030 and Total Fertility Rate at 2030 and no correlation between the two rates at 2065. With regard to the correlation between Total Number of Immigrants and Total Fertility Rate at two different time points, for one-half of the experts there is no correlation and for the other half a moderate/high negative correlation between Total Number of Immigrants at 2030 and Total Fertility Rate at 2065, while all experts agree on there being no correlation between Total Fertility Rate at 2030 and Total Number of Immigrants at 2065.

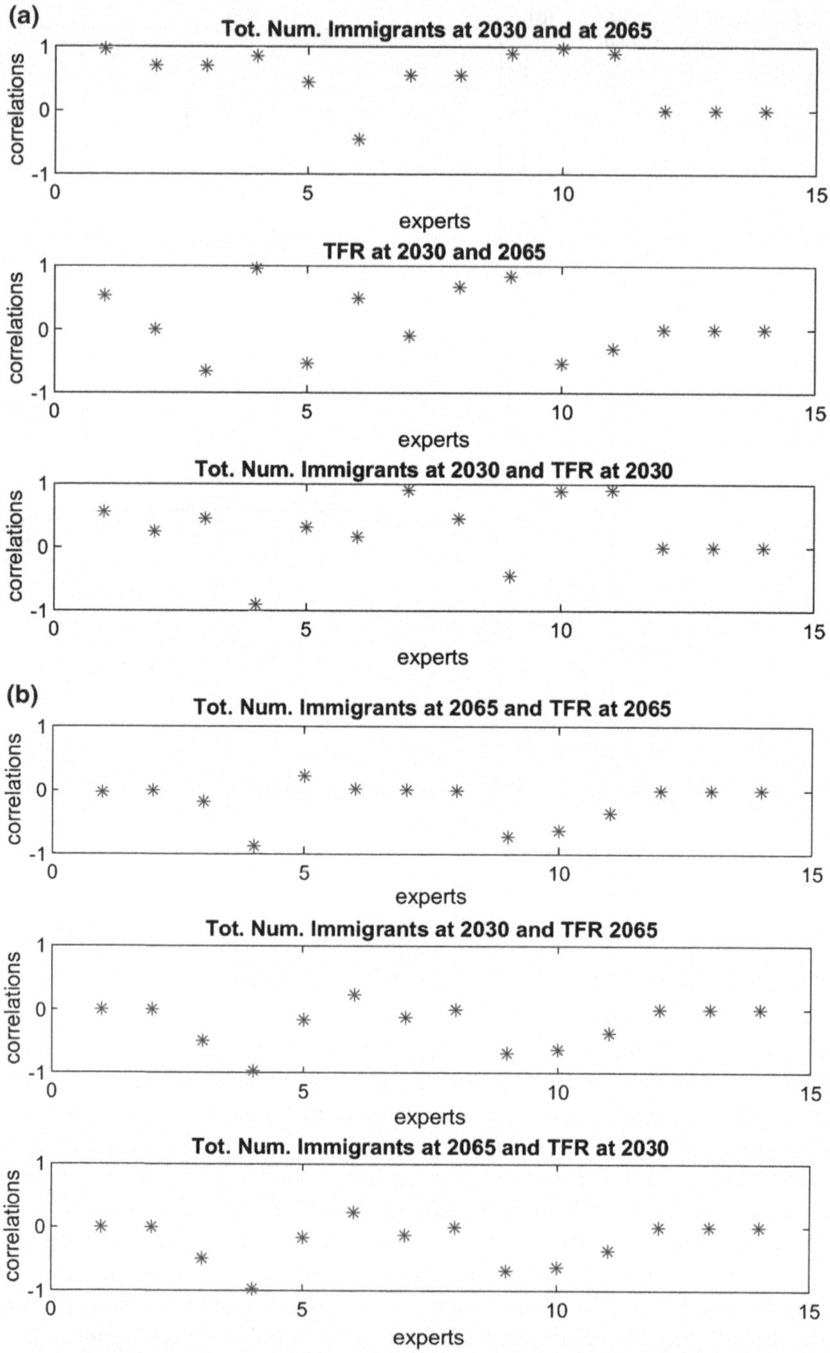

Fig. 2.3 Elicited correlations: Total Fertility Rate (average number of children per woman) and Total Number of Immigrants (in thousands)

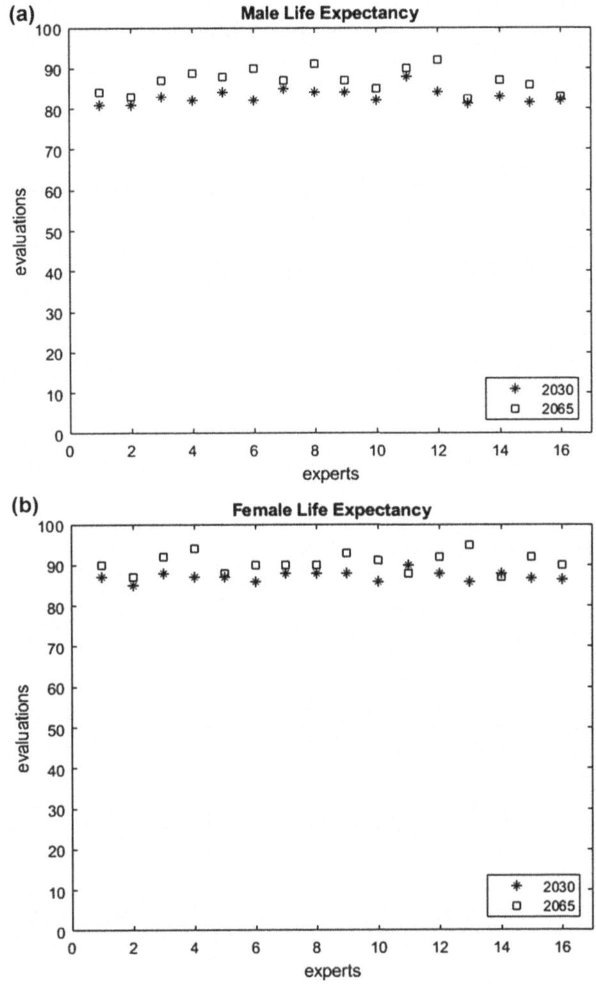

Fig. 2.4 Expert forecasts of Male and Female Life Expectancies (years)

Figure 2.4 presents the forecasts of the Life Expectancies for males and females and Fig. 2.5 presents the corresponding correlations. Note that the forecasts were provided by 16 experts, but only nine provided all inputs needed for the derivation of the correlations. All forecasts show a low variability, both at 2030 and 2065. With regard to the correlations, there is agreement among the experts on the correlation of Male Life Expectancy at the two time points and on the correlation between Male and Female Life Expectancies at 2030, all experts forecasting a positive high correlation. Similarly, almost all experts forecast a positive high correlation between Female Life Expectancy at 2030 and Male Life Expectancy at 2065. Regarding the correlation between Female Life Expectancy at the two time points, we observe for three experts a positive high correlation, for one expert a negative high correlation, and for all other experts, correlations almost equal to zero. In the case of the correlations between Male and Female Life Expectancies at 2065, three experts

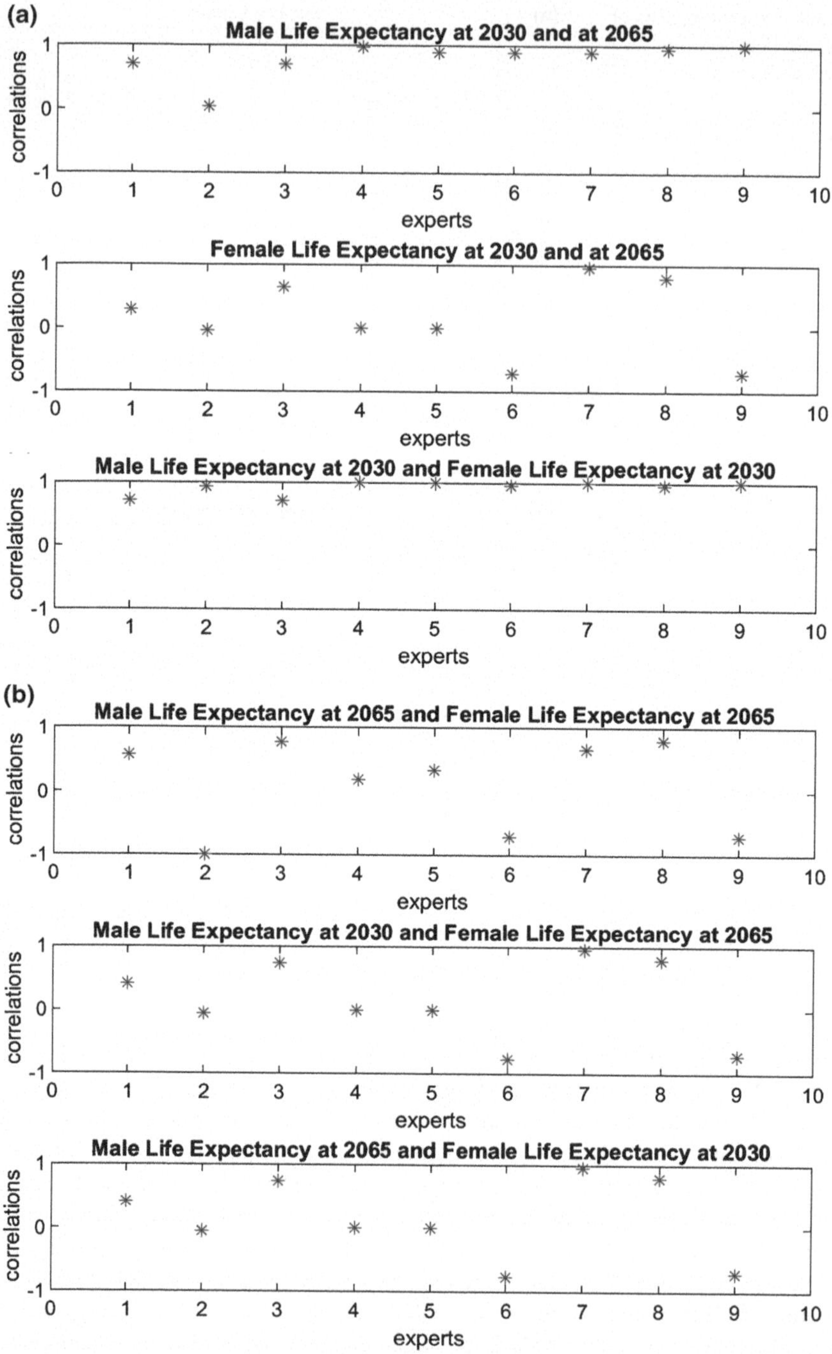

Fig. 2.5 Elicited correlations: Male and Female Life Expectancies

forecast a negative high correlation, one expert a very low positive correlation and the remaining five experts a positive high correlation.

Similar disagreement is expressed about the correlation between Male Life Expectancy at 2030 and Female Life Expectancy at 2065: Two experts forecast a negative high correlation, three experts a zero correlation and four experts a positive high correlation.

Figure 2.6 displays the forecasts and correlations for Total Number of Emigrants provided by 16 experts. There is a high variability in the forecasts, both for 2030 and 2065. In particular, we can notice that six experts provided the same forecasts at 2030 and 2065, this is the reason why in the top panel of Fig. 2.6 only red asterisk is displayed for these experts. Regarding the across-time correlations, almost all experts forecast a positive high correlation. We could work out correlations only for 14 experts, since two of them did not provide the needed conditional forecasts.

Based on the results of the elicitation procedure, the forecasting method explained in the previous section was then used to simulate the joint forecast distribution of Total Fertility Rate and Total Number of Immigrants at 2030 and 2065 and of the joint forecast distribution of Male and Female Life Expectancies at 2030 and 2065. The same method was applied to the separate simulation of the forecast distributions of the Total Number of Emigrants and of the Mean Age at Birth at 2030 and 2065. The prior parameters were specified as described in the previous section. In particular, the means and variances of the priors for the summary indicators were specified based on the ISTAT scenarios available in 2012: μ_R was set equal to the vector of central scenarios and the variances for Σ_R were derived from the high–low ISTAT scenarios available in 2012. The covariances were all fixed to 0. The mixture model was fit for different choices of the number J of components of the mixture, ranging from two to five. The model with two components was selected, since it had the smallest BIC.

The results shown in Tables 2.1, 2.2, 2.3, and 2.4 were obtained through a long run of the MCMC algorithm that provided 20,000 samples from the joint

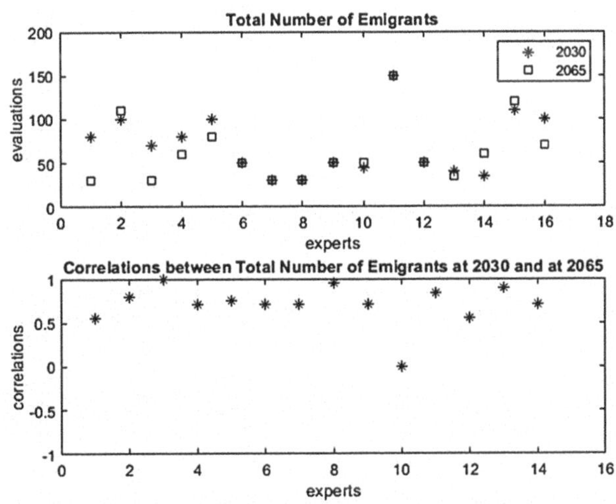

Fig. 2.6 Expert forecasts (in thousands) and correlations, Total Number of Emigrants

Table 2.1 2030 and 2065 Demographic Indicators: Prior, expert evaluations and posterior means and standard deviations, TFR as average number of children per woman, Life Expectancies as number of years, Total Number of Immigrants and of Emigrants in thousands

Demographic Indicator	2010	Prior Mean		Prior SD		Opinions mean		Opinions SD		Posterior Mean		Posterior SD	
		2030	2065	2030	2065	2030	2065	2030	2065	2030	2065	2030	2065
Total Fertility Rate	1.42	1.50	1.50	0.50	0.50	1.55	1.65	0.12	0.14	1.53	1.64	0.10	0.16
Mean Maternal Age	31.40	31.80	32	1	1	31.95	32.52	1.50	2.17	31.80	31.80	0.81	0.93
Male Life Expectancy	79.50	82.80	86.60	3	3	83.01	86.96	1.84	2.94	82.93	86.89	1.76	2.04
Female Life Expectancy	84.60	87.70	91.50	3	3	87.24	90.88	1.21	2.37	87.21	91.02	1.54	2.88
Number of Immigrants	408.66	321	304	100	100	253.57	212.14	94.99	145.68	280.20	262.55	66.28	88.22
Number of Emigrants	83.81	101	128	30	30	70.00	62.81	34.69	35.76	91.48	91.01	23.13	24.23

Table 2.2 Prior and posterior correlations, Total Number of Immigrants and Total Fertility Rate

	Prior correlation	Posterior correlation
Tot. Num. Immigrants in 2030 and 2065	0.4473	0.4381
TFR at 2030 and 2065	0.2084	0.3233
Tot. Num. Immigrants in 2030 and TFR at 2030	0.2448	0.1288
Tot. Num. Immigrants in 2030 and TFR at 2065	−0.2175	−0.0814
Tot. Num. Immigrants in 2065 and TFR at 2030	0.0003	−0.0233
Tot. Num. Immigrants in 2065 and TFR at 2065	−0.476	−0.0712

Table 2.3 Prior and posterior correlations, Male and Female Life Expectancies at birth

	Prior correlation	Posterior correlation
Male Life Expectancies at 2030 and 2065	0.8569	0.6702
Female Life Expectancies at 2030 and 2065	0.1413	0.082
Male Life Expectancies at 2030 and Female Life Expectancies at 2030	0.9636	0.9066
Male Life Expectancies at 2030 and Female Life Expectancies at 2065	0.1017	0.018
Male Life Expectancies at 2065 and Female Life Expectancies at 2030	0.8418	0.6427
Male Life Expectancies at 2065 and Female Life Expectancies at 2065	0.0496	−0.0065

Table 2.4 Total population forecasts and ISTAT estimates (in millions)

Year	Forecast	%85 forecasts interval	ISTAT estimates
2011	60,484	(60,479 60,490)	60,626
2012	60,659	(60,637 60,679)	59,394
2013	60,814	(60,767 60,862)	59,685
2014	60,952	(60,870 61,045)	61,035
2015	61,073	(60,948 61,199)	60,796
2016	61,180	(61,004 61,357)	60,666
2017	61,275	(61,041 61,512)	60,589
2018	61,361	(61,061 61,666)	60,484

posterior distribution of the indicators at the two time points, 2030 and 2065; the first 10,000 were discarded, as burn-in. The convergence of the algorithm was assessed though different techniques, the trace plots of the chains run for Total Fertility Rate and Total Number of Immigrants and discarding the first 10,000 draws are depicted in Fig. 2.7. The analysis can be replicated using the Matlab code "supraBayesian_popproj" available in the online material of this book.

Table 2.1 shows the prior and posterior means and standard deviations for the summary indicators at 2030 and 2065, along with the arithmetic average and standard deviations of the corresponding expert opinions. For all indicators, as expected the posterior standard deviation at 2030 is smaller than the one at 2065, and both posterior standard deviations are smaller than the prior ones, since noninformative priors are used. Our forecasts show a lower variability compared

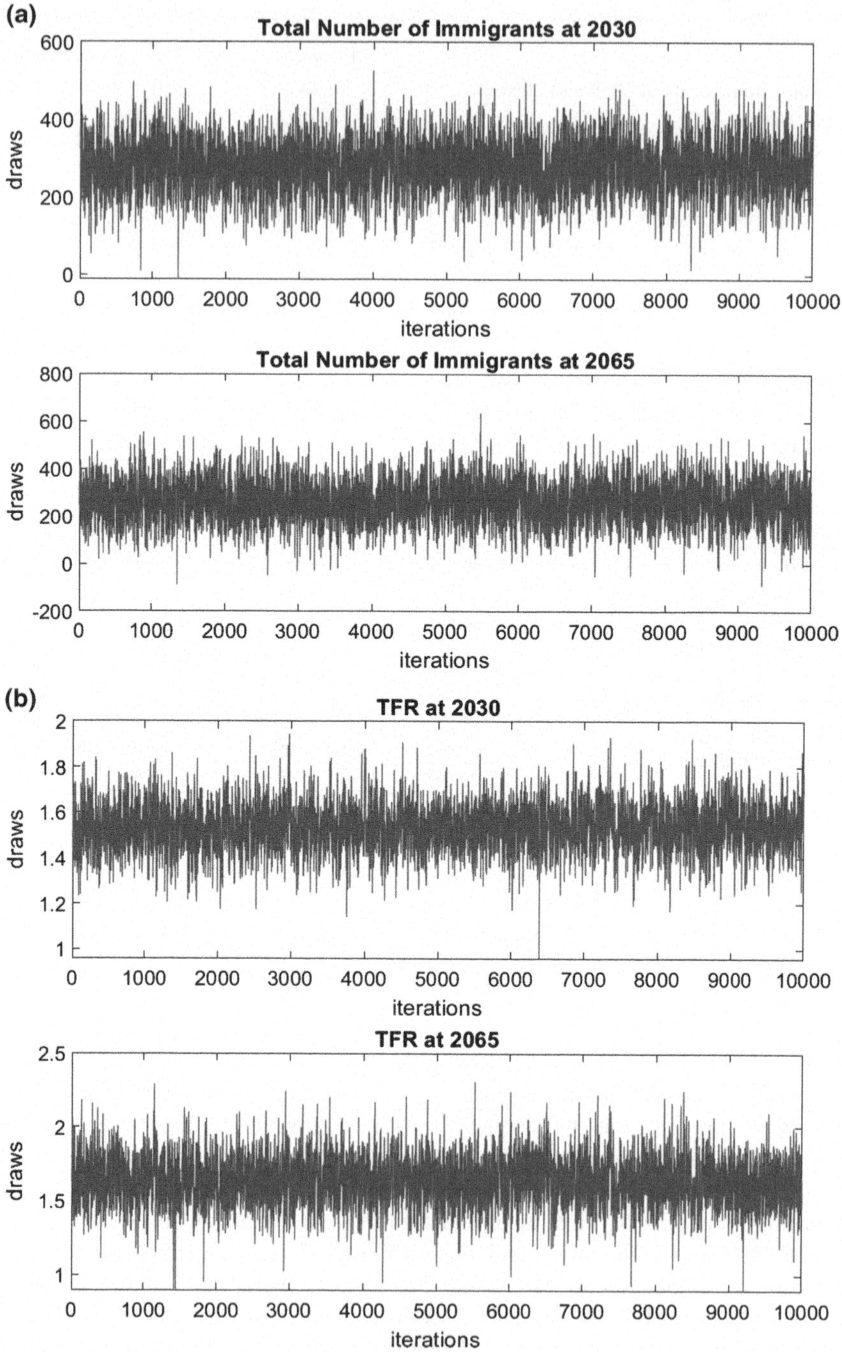

Fig. 2.7 Trace plots, TFR as average number of children per woman, Total number of Immigrants in thousands

against the one induced by ISTAT scenarios. The ISTAT central scenario, used as prior mean, predicts a Total Fertility rate equal to 1.5 both for 2030 and 2065, the arithmetic average of the expert opinions is 1.55 at 2030 and 1.65 at 2065, and our model predicts, as posterior mean, 1.53 at 2030 and 1.64 at 2065. The same kind of pattern can be observed for the Total Number of Immigrants, for which the ISTAT central scenario, used as prior mean, predicts for 2030 321,000 and for 2065 304,000; the arithmetic average of the expert elicitations is around 254,000 for 2030 and 212,000 for 2065; while the model forecasts, as posterior mean of the indicator, are 280,000 for 2030 and 262,000 for 2065. Regarding the Life Expectancies, the ISTAT central scenario, used as prior mean, predicts a Male Life Expectancy equal to 82.80 at 2030 and equal to 86.60 at 2065, a Female Life Expectancy equal to 87.70 at 2030 and equal to 91.50 at 2065, while the arithmetic averages of the expert opinions are 83.01 for 2030 and 86.96 for 2065 for males and 87.24 and 90.88 for females. The mixture model predicts posterior means of Male Life Expectancy equal to 82.93 at 2030 and to 86.89 at 2065, and a Female Life Expectancy equal to 87.21 at 2030 and to 91.02 at 2065. The ISTAT central scenario on Total Number of Emigrants predicts 101,000 emigrants in 2030 and 128,000 in 2065; the arithmetic average of the expert evaluations is 70,000 and 62,810 for 2030 and 2065 respectively; and the model predicts a Total Number of Emigrants equal to 91,480 in 2030 and 91,010 in 2065.

Table 2.2 provides the prior and posterior correlations at the same time (2030 and 2065) and across time for the Total Fertility Rate and the Total Number of Immigrants, and the correlations at the same time and across time between the two summary indicators. It is worth emphasizing that the prior correlations are derived from Σ_0, which was obtained as the scaled arithmetic average of the covariance matrices elicited from each expert, while the posterior correlations are obtained from the 10,000 draws of the two rates at the two time points. The model predicts a moderate positive posterior across-time correlation for the Total Number of Immigrants and a moderate/low positive across-time correlation for Total Fertility Rate. All posterior correlations between the two rates are around zero, apart from the correlation between Total Number of Immigrants at 2030 and Total Fertility Rate at 2030, equal to 0.1288. The forecast of this positive, even though weak, correlation is in concordance with Sobotka (2003), Sobotka et al. (2008), Haug et al. (2002), Coleman (2006), and Goldstein et al. (2009), who argue that fertility rates in many European countries may have been increased by the compositional effect of the rising share of higher-fertility immigrants. The fact that the correlation between the two rates is almost zero at 2065 is due, in our opinion, to the difficulty for the experts to express, even indirectly, opinions on the long term associations.

Table 2.3 presents the prior and posterior correlations at 2030 and 2065 and across-time for the Male and Female Life Expectancy. Based on the elicited opinions, our model predicts a moderate/high correlation between Male Life Expectancy at 2030 and 2065, between Male and Female Life Expectancy at 2030, and between Female Life Expectancy at 2030 and Male Life Expectancy at 2065. All other correlations are predicted to be around zero.

For each of the summary indicators, from the 10,000 values obtained as draws from the corresponding posterior distribution, 10,000 trajectories over the time interval from 2010 to 2065 are obtained by relying on standard quadratic interpolation techniques. The forecast of the Italian Population from 2010 to 2065 was then derived based on the cohort-component model. The inputs of the model are the age- and time-specific fertility rates, age- and time-specific male and female survival rates, and age- and time- specific net migration rates, obtained from the corresponding summary indicators by applying standard smoothing techniques. In particular, the matrices of male and the matrices of female age- and time-specific mortality rates are obtained from the corresponding life expectancies at birth on the basis of the extended model life tables provided by the United Nations. The matrices of age- and time-specific fertility rates are derived from the vectors of total fertility rates and the vectors of mean maternal ages at birth, using a rescaled normal model. For migration, the matrices of male and female age-specific net migration flows are derived from the corresponding vectors of total net flows, applying a rescaled gamma model. This is a simplifying assumption that assumes the absence of pre-school, retirement, and post-retirement peaks in the age profile of migrations, with the only peak being related to labour migration.

Starting from an estimated total population at 2010 of 60,343 million, our model predicts a slight increase at 2030, with the total population forecast to be 61,795 million with an 85% forecast interval ranging from 60,137 million to 63,475 million. After 2030, the total population is predicted to decrease, reaching 57,146 million, with an 85% forecast interval from 50,135 to 64,503 million. As expected, the latter forecasts have a higher variability.

Table 2.4 presents the Italian population forecasts and prediction intervals obtained through our method and the values estimated by ISTAT from 2011 to 2018. Overall, our forecasts are above the ISTAT estimates, with differences in absolute value ranging from 142,000 in 2011 to 1,265,000 in 2018. One explanation of this over-prediction might be found in Table 2.1, where we see that on average, expert opinions at 2030 and especially at 2065 on Total Fertility are well above what is expected by the ISTAT central scenarios, and the same for Male Life Expectancy. It is as well plausible that the experts did not perceive the persistence of the great recession, which was linked to lower fertility (see Goldstein et al. 2013, Comolli and Bernardi 2015, Comolli 2017 and Matysiak et al. 2018) and to lower levels of net migration (see Anelli and Peri 2017), leading to smaller population sizes. The failure of our method to capture the decrease in the total population estimated by ISTAT from 2014 to 2018 might be due as well to the interpolation techniques used for the derivation of the forecast indicators between the starting time 2010 and 2030 and between 2030 and 2065.

2.4 Concluding Remarks

The method we have suggested makes explicit use of expert evaluations to derive probabilistic forecasts of the future trends in the population by age and sex. Our method makes use of expert opinions not only about the expected future behaviour of the demographic components but also about the across-time correlations of single indicators and about the correlations between the indicators. The expert evaluations are then combined in such a way as to take into account their associations. The advantages and limitations of an expert based approach have been discussed in the Introduction. Here, it is worth emphasizing the fact that experts are always involved in the population forecast at different levels of the forecasting procedure and to different degrees. In the time series approach, experts contribute to the choice of the model and the specification of the prior distributions. In the extrapolation from past errors approach, experts provide the central trajectories and contribute to the evaluation of the forecasts. Furthermore, we do not neglect information on past trends when considering expert evaluations as the main source for deriving the population forecasts. Indeed, expert evaluations should be based as well on such information. Our method allows taking into account the overconfidence of experts in their opinions, which might produce an undervaluation of the uncertainty of the forecasts. The entire process is treated within the formal framework provided by the Bayesian paradigm.

Our modelling strategy has some specific limitations. The main limitation is that we have focussed on summary indicators of the demographic changes, which are then converted into age schedules based on parametric models. An extension of the method is in principle feasible, the main difficulty being related to the elicitation of opinions on curves, depicting age patterns. Moreover, our method does not take into account the uncertainty in the initial distributions of the population by age and sex, this being particularly problematic in the case of inconsistencies between the census-based and register-based population records. Experts could be asked to express their opinion on the initial structure by age and sex of the population as well. Lastly, our method exploits expert opinions to derive the forecast distribution of two summary indicators at two time points, while forecasts for the years between the starting one and the midpoint, t_1 and between t_1 and the final time T, are obtained relying on standard interpolation techniques. In principle, our method can be generalized to the case of more than two indicators at more than two time points. The main limitation is on the side of the inputs of the forecasting procedure for the indicators. The indirect elicitation of the correlations requires, as seen in Sect. 2.2, questions on conditional forecasts that in the case of more than two time points and more than two indicators can be extremely cumbersome. More work should then be devoted to the selection of suitable interpolation techniques and experts could be involved in this choice as well, by asking them to express their opinion on the expected trends between the considered time points.

As a general consideration, the performance of the forecasting procedure relies on the number of experts and their commitment. The application of the method discussed in the previous section was based on the results of the first round of the questionnaire, when at most 16 experts contributed. A new round of the questionnaire is currently running, the results of which are not yet available. However, almost 100 experts have contributed, and we expect a better performance of the method here suggested.

Acknowledgements The author would like to thank Francesco Billari, Eugenio Melilli and an anonymous referee for extremely useful comments and suggestions.

References

Albert, I., Donnet, S., Guihenneuc-Jouyaux, C., Low-Choy, S., Mengersen, K., Rousseau, J., et al. (2012). Combining expert opinions in prior elicitation. *Bayesian Analysis, 7*(3), 503–532.

Alders, M., Keilman, N., & Cruijsen, H. (2007). Assumptions for long-term stochastic population forecasts in 18 European countries. *European Journal of Population/Revue Européenne de Démographie, 23*(1), 33–69.

Alho, J. M., & Spencer, B. D. (1990). Error models for official mortality forecasts. *Journal of the American Statistical Association, 85*(411), 609–616.

Alkema, L., Raftery, A. E., Gerland, P., Clark, S. J., Pelletier, F., Buettner, T., & Heilig, G. K. (2011). Probabilistic projections of the total fertility rate for all countries. *Demography, 48*(3), 815–839.

Alkema, L., Gerland, P., Raftery, A., & Wilmoth, J. (2015). The United Nations probabilistic population projections: An introduction to demographic forecasting with uncertainty. *Foresight (Colchester, Vt.), 2015*(37), 19.

Anelli, M., & Peri, G. (2017). Does emigration delay political change? Evidence from Italy during the Great Recession. *Economic Policy, 32*(91), 551–596.

Bijak, J., & Bryant, J. (2016). Bayesian demography 250 years after Bayes. *Population Studies, 70*(1), 1–19.

Bijak, J., & Wiśniowski, A. (2010). Bayesian forecasting of immigration to selected European countries by using expert knowledge. *Journal of the Royal Statistical Society: Series A (Statistics in Society), 173*(4), 775–796.

Billari, F. C., Graziani, R., & Melilli, E. (2012). Stochastic population forecasts based on conditional expert opinions. *Journal of the Royal Statistical Society: Series A (Statistics in Society), 175*(2), 491–511.

Billari, F. C., Graziani, R., & Melilli, E. (2014). Stochastic population forecasting based on combinations of expert evaluations within the Bayesian paradigm. *Demography, 51*(5), 1933–1954.

Booth, H. (2006). Demographic forecasting: 1980 to 2005 in review. *International Journal of Forecasting, 22*(3), 547–581.

Booth, H., & Tickle, L. (2008). Mortality modelling and forecasting: A review of methods. *Annals of Actuarial Science, 3*(1–2), 3–43.

Booth, H., Maindonald, J., & Smith, L. (2002). Applying lee-carter under conditions of variable mortality decline. *Population Studies, 56*(3), 325–336.

Cairns, A. J. G., Blake, D., & Dowd, K. (2006). A two-factor model for stochastic mortality with parameter uncertainty: Theory and calibration. *Journal of Risk and Insurance, 73*(4), 687–718.

Cairns, A. J. G., Blake, D., Dowd, K., Coughlan, G. D., Epstein, D., & Khalaf-Allah, M. (2011). Mortality density forecasts: An analysis of six stochastic mortality models. *Insurance: Mathematics and Economics, 48*(3), 355–367.

Coleman, D. (2006). Immigration and ethnic change in low-fertility countries: A third demographic transition. *Population and Development Review, 32*(3), 401–446.

Comolli, C. L. (2017). The fertility response to the great recession in Europe and the United States: Structural economic conditions and perceived economic uncertainty. *Demographic Research, 36*, 1549–1600.

Comolli, C. L., & Bernardi, F. (2015). The causal effect of the great recession on childlessness of white American women. *IZA Journal of Labor Economics, 4*(1), 21.

French, S. (1980). Updating of belief in the light of someone else's opinion. *Journal of the Royal Statistical Society: Series A (General), 143*(1), 43–48.

French, S. (1981). Consensus of opinion. *European Journal of Operational Research, 7*(4), 332–340.

Gelfand, A. E., Mallick, B. K., & Dey, D. K. (1995). Modeling expert opinion arising as a partial probabilistic specification. *Journal of the American Statistical Association, 90*(430), 598–604.

Genest, C., Zidek, J. V., et al. (1986). Combining probability distributions: A critique and an annotated bibliography. *Statistical Science, 1*(1), 114–135.

Goldstein, J. R. (2004). Simpler probabilistic population forecasts: Making scenarios work. *International Statistical Review, 72*(1), 93–106.

Goldstein, J. R., Sobotka, T., & Jasilioniene, A. (2009). The end of "lowest-low" fertility? *Population and Development Review, 35*(4), 663–699.

Goldstein, J., Kreyenfeld, M., Jasilioniene, A., & Örsal, D. D. K. (2013). Fertility reactions to the "Great Recession" in Europe: Recent evidence from order-specific data. *Demographic Research, 29*, 85–104.

Haug, W., Compton, P., Courbage, Y., et al. (2002). *The demographic characteristics of immigrant populations*, Vol. 38. Strasbourg: Council of Europe Publishing.

Hyndman, R. J., & Booth, H. (2008). Stochastic population forecasts using functional data models for mortality, fertility and migration. *International Journal of Forecasting, 24*(3), 323–342.

Hyndman, R. J., & Ullah, M. S. (2007). Robust forecasting of mortality and fertility rates: A functional data approach. *Computational Statistics and Data Analysis, 51*(10), 4942–4956.

Hyndman, R. J., Booth, H., & Yasmeen, F. (2013). Coherent mortality forecasting: The product-ratio method with functional time series models. *Demography, 50*(1), 261–283.

ISTAT. (2017). Il futuro demografico del paese. Nota metodologica. Technical report.

Keilman, N. (1990). *Uncertainty in national population forecasting: Issues, backgrounds, analyses, recommendations*, Vol. 20. Boca Raton: CRC.

Keilman, N. (2018). Probabilistic demographic forecasts. *Vienna Yearbook of Population Research, 16*, 1–11.

Keilman, N., Pham, D. Q., & Hetland, A. (2002). Why population forecasts should be probabilistic-illustrated by the case of Norway. *Demographic Research, 6*, 409–454.

Lavine, M., & West, M. (1992). A Bayesian method for classification and discrimination. *Canadian Journal of Statistics, 20*(4), 451–461.

Lee, R. D. (1993). Modeling and forecasting the time series of us fertility: Age distribution, range, and ultimate level. *International Journal of Forecasting, 9*(2), 187–202.

Lee, R. D., & Carter, L. R. (1992). Modeling and forecasting us mortality. *Journal of the American Statistical Association, 87*(419), 659–671.

Lee, R. D., & Tuljapurkar, S. (1994). Stochastic population forecasts for the united states: Beyond high, medium, and low. *Journal of the American Statistical Association, 89*(428), 1175–1189.

Lindley, D. (1983). Reconciliation of probability distributions. *Operations Research, 31*(5), 866–880.

Lindley, D. V. (1985). Reconciliation of discrete probability distributions. *Bayesian Statistics,* 2(375–390), 375–390.

Lutz, W. (2013). *The future population of the world: What can we assume today.* London: Routledge.

Lutz, W., & Goldstein, J. R. (2004). Introduction: How to deal with uncertainty in population forecasting? *International Statistical Review, 72*(1), 1–4.

Lutz, W., Sanderson, W. C., & Scherbov, S. (1998). Expert-based probabilistic population projections. *Population and Development Review, 24*, 139–155.

Matysiak, A., Vignoli, D., & Sobotka, T. (2018). The great recession and fertility in Europe: A sub-national analysis. Technical report, Vienna Institute of Demography Working Papers.
Morris, P. A. (1974). Decision analysis expert use. *Management Science, 20*(9), 1233–1241.
Raftery, A. E., Chunn, J. L., Gerland, P., & Ševčíková, H. (2013). Bayesian probabilistic projections of life expectancy for all countries. *Demography, 50*(3), 777–801.
Roback, P. J., & Givens, G.H. (2001). Supra-Bayesian pooling of priors linked by a deterministic simulation model. *Communications in Statistics-Simulation and Computation, 30*(3), 447–476.
Sobotka, T. (2003). Tempo-quantum and period-cohort interplay in fertility changes in Europe: Evidence from the Czech Republic, Italy, the Netherlands and Sweden. *Demographic Research, 8*, 151–214.
Sobotka, T., et al. (2008). Overview chapter 7: The rising importance of migrants for childbearing in Europe. *Demographic Research, 19*(9), 225–248.
Stoto, M. A. (1983). The accuracy of population projections. *Journal of the American Statistical Association, 78*(381), 13–20.
Winkler, R. L. (1981). Combining probability distributions from dependent information sources. *Management Science, 27*(4), 479–488.

Chapter 3
Using Expert Elicitation to Build Long-Term Projection Assumptions

Patrice Dion, Nora Galbraith, and Elham Sirag

3.1 Introduction

The will to better communicate uncertainty about the future and the ongoing development of probabilistic projections in recent years has triggered new interest in formal methods of expert elicitation (NRC 2000). One benefit of expert elicitation is that experts can envision previously-unseen future developments by taking into consideration theories and knowledge from relevant disciplines (Lutz 2009). In contrast, time series methods can aptly forecast developments in the future, but they do so by assuming a continuation in the way that things have evolved in the past (Hyndman and Athanasopoulos 2018). Moreover, expert elicitation can be used to obtain probabilistic information, but with comparatively fewer data requirements (Hanea et al. 2018)–an appealing trait when data are missing or incomplete (Lutz 1994; NRC 2000; Billari et al. 2012, 2014).

Most national statistical offices undertake some kind of consultation with experts when designing their population projection assumptions (UNECE 2018). The scope and format of these consultations vary considerably, ranging from a simple approval procedure from senior management within the organization to the creation of a formal committee of external experts who participate actively in the development of assumptions and methods.

Electronic supplementary material The online version of this chapter (https://doi.org/10.1007/978-3-030-42472-5_3) contains supplementary material, which is available to authorized users.

P. Dion (✉) · N. Galbraith · E. Sirag
Statistics Canada, Ottawa, ON, Canada
e-mail: patrice.dion@canada.ca

S. Mazzuco, N. Keilman (eds.), *Developments in Demographic Forecasting*, The Springer Series on Demographic Methods and Population Analysis 49,
https://doi.org/10.1007/978-3-030-42472-5_3

In 2013, Statistics Canada conducted a pilot exercise in formal expert consultation to inform its population projection assumption-building process (Bohnert 2015). More recently, Statistics Canada refined its consultation process, designing an elicitation protocol which asks experts to provide complete probability distributions representing a plausible range of the future values of fertility, mortality and immigration in the future. In designing this elicitation protocol, we delved further into the science of *expert knowledge elicitation*, implementing best practices in this regard.[1]

The benefits of this new elicitation protocol are numerous, including what we believe to be an improved elicitation experience for the survey respondents, improved accuracy and communication of expert judgments and resulting response aggregation, and more coherent expressions of uncertainty. The latter benefit in particular lends itself well to the direct incorporation of expert judgments into the assumption-building process in both deterministic and probabilistic population projections.

In the remainder of this paper, we describe the innovative expert elicitation protocol used in the development of Statistics Canada's 2018-based population projections (Statistics Canada 2019a, b). Selected results from the protocol are provided, as well as a description of how the results were utilized directly in the building of deterministic projection assumptions. We follow with an application demonstrating how the results from the elicitation protocol could be used in the context of probabilistic projections. We end with some reflections on the utility of this protocol in the further development of probabilistic population projections.

3.2 The *2018 Survey of Experts on Future Demographic Trends*: Expert Elicitation Protocol

3.2.1 Objectives

There are a number of practical criteria that we wanted our elicitation protocol to meet: a small respondent burden (estimated to 1 h of work or less), relative simplicity (requiring no extensive expertise in statistics or specialized software knowledge), and low cost of implementation (including the possibility of using remote elicitation). To meet these requirements, it was determined that the design of a Microsoft Excel spreadsheet-based tool offered numerous benefits: the software is widely used, has the ability to incorporate a graphical user interface, and accepts both textual and numerical inputs.

---

[1]There has been much research completed on the challenges associated with expert elicitation. There have also been numerous studies completed on the best methods to counter or minimize those challenges. Readers can find comprehensive reviews of these topics in Garthwaite et al. (2005), O'Hagan et al. (2006) and Dias et al. (2018).

A key goal of the protocol, and one sometimes in conflict with the previously-mentioned objectives, was to capture the true belief of the respondent to the greatest extent possible. As part of this objective, *accuracy in the expression of uncertainty* became a main focus of the protocol design. We achieved this by eliciting *complete probability distributions* from experts which, in contrast to eliciting a single point estimate, allows for the expression of the uncertainty about the parameter of interest (Morris et al. 2014). We built our protocol around recent methodological innovations by Keelin (2016, 2018) that led to the development of the *metalog* distribution; a flexible probability distribution that can be used to model a wide range of density functions using only a small number of parameters elicited from experts. The most appealing feature of this distribution is that it is flexible enough to *accommodate different types of distributions* (for instance, left-or right skewed, bounded or, importantly, unbounded).[2] We thus avoid making strong assumptions about the characteristics of experts' distributions (e.g., shape, symmetry), and are able to capture nuanced future possibilities.

Another way to improve the likelihood of accurately capturing the views of experts is to offer them *visual feedback* associated with their quantitative judgments (Garthwaite et al. 2005; Kynn 2008; Speirs-Bridge et al. 2010; Morgan 2013; Goldstein and Rothschild 2014). In particular, a graphical interface may be more apt to capture people's intuitions about a probability distribution or when otherwise eliciting parameters that are not easy to think about (Jones and Johnson 2014). Visual feedback also allows the respondent to assess, confirm or revise their judgments if desired, thus improving their calibration and accuracy.

After eliciting the views of numerous experts, it is necessary to combine their views in some manner. Our protocol's emphasis on the elicitation of complete probability distributions was also driven by the desire to *facilitate the aggregation of experts' responses*, something that is much more difficult and requires many more assumptions when only certain values or quantiles are elicited from experts.

These principal objectives, combined with our current knowledge of best practices in elicitation, guided the design of the 2018 expert elicitation protocol, described in the following section.

3.2.2 Design

The *2018 Survey of Experts on Future Demographic Trends* was inspired by and builds upon several existing protocols, such as SHELF (Oakley and O'Hagan 2014; Gosling 2018), EXPLICIT (Grigore et al. 2017), and the self-administered tools

[2]Collecting information pertaining to an unbounded distribution, which is the case for demographic indicators, appears to be particularly challenging without making strong assumptions about the shape of this distribution. Existing protocols tend to fit a limited number of parametric distributions to the elicited values, such as a normal, log-normal or student's t distributions (see for example the sophisticated SHELF elicitation framework in Oakley and O'Hagan 2014 and Gosling 2018).

designed by Speirs-Bridge et al. (2010) and Sperber et al. (2013) adapted to the remote collection of information from a group of experts.

Experts are first presented a short introduction that explains the context and goals of the exercise. They are invited to answer only sections related to components in which they feel they have a certain expertise and are encouraged to contact us in the event that they have any questions or issues in completing the survey. Following the introduction, a first set of questions aims at gathering background information on the respondent, including the number of years of experience they have in the field of demography or population studies, and their self-rated level of experience in the domains of fertility, mortality international migration and demographic projections. This information is collected for two purposes: firstly, to assess whether the group of respondents is suitably diverse (as recommended by Morgan and Henrion (1990), among others); and secondly, the information is used for the purpose of weighting responses during aggregation, described in more detail in Sect. 3.2.4.

The main part of the survey consists of the elicitation of qualitative arguments and quantitative estimates regarding fertility (period total fertility rate), mortality (life expectancy at birth for males and for females) and immigration (number of immigrants per thousand population) for Canada in 2043. The year 2043 was chosen as the target year since it represented the final year in the eventual projection of the provinces and territories. Having a target year 25 years in the future was also deemed to be a good point of balance, forcing experts to think past the short-term evolutions which are likely to follow recent trends, but not so far into the future as to be inconceivable (i.e. we do not ask experts to predict the major demographic behaviours of generations not yet born at the time of the survey). We describe the process using the fertility component as an example (Fig. 3.1).

In **Step 1**, we ask for qualitative arguments that are likely to influence the future path of the period total fertility rate (PTFR) in Canada between now and 2043. Experts are also provided a series of tables and figures showing historical trends for various fertility indicators. Experts are invited to think about a variety of possible future scenarios (increase, decrease, status quo) when formulating their arguments. Besides providing critical information for putting into context their later quantitative estimates, this procedure is recommended as it encourages experts to think about the substantive details of their judgments and consider a whole range of possibilities, thus reducing potential overconfidence (Morgan and Henrion 1990; Kadane and Wolfson 1998; Garthwaite et al. 2005; Kynn 2008).

Step 2 is modelled in large part by the step-based procedures utilized by Speirs-Bridge et al. (2010), Sperber et al. (2013) and Grigore et al. (2017) and comprises four subparts:

(a) Experts are first asked to provide the lower and higher bounds of a range covering nearly all plausible[3] values of the period total fertility rate in Canada

[3]The term "plausible" was arrived at after much careful consideration. As illustrated by Morgan (Morgan 2013), terms such as "probable", "likely", or "possible" may be interpreted very differently by different respondents.

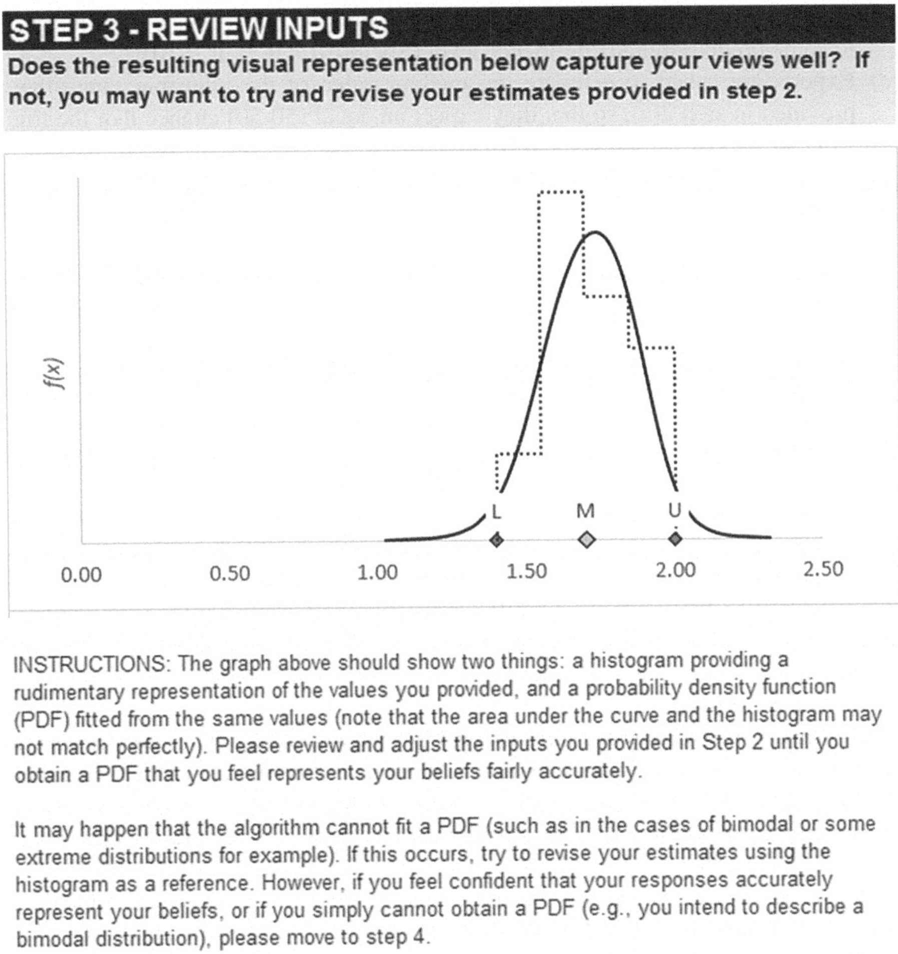

Fig. 3.1 Screenshot from the 2018 survey of experts on future demographic trends: histogram and probability density function generated from an expert's inputs for the PTFR in 2043. (Source: Statistics Canada, Demography Division)

in 2043. Beginning with the contemplation of the extremes of the distribution is an intentional practice used to minimize potential overconfidence (Speirs-Bridge et al. 2010; Sperber et al. 2013; Oakley and O'Hagan 2014; Grigore et al. 2017; Hanea et al. 2018). Indeed, asking experts to first provide a single central estimate such as a mean or a median tends to trigger anchoring to that value in subsequent responses.

(b) Experts are asked to report how confident they are that the true value will fall within the range they just specified in step 2(a). Allowing experts to determine their own level of confidence has been found to reduce overconfidence in comparison with asking them to identify the low and high bounds of an interval to some predetermined confidence level (Speirs-Bridge et al. 2010).[4]

(c) Experts are asked to estimate the median value of the plausible range they provided in step 2(a), so that they expect an equal (50-50) chance that the true value lies above or below the median.

(d) The range of values between the lower bound and the median is split in two segments of equal length and the same is done for values between the median and the upper bound. The respondent is then asked to assign to each segment the probability that the true value falls within each of these segments. Note that each half below and above the median has by definition 50% probability of occurrence, so it is a matter of redistributing that 50% to each segment.[5]

Throughout step 2, several "checks", in the form of pop-up warning signs, were built into the elicitation tool in order to prevent illogical inputs in various forms.

We used Keelin's *metalog* distribution (2016, 2018) to calculate each experts' probability density function based on their responses to the questions above. The metalog distribution – short for "meta-logistic" – belongs to the larger class of Quantile-Parameterized Distributions (QPDs) developed by Keelin and Powley (2011), and refers to any continuous probability distribution that can be fully parameterized in terms of its quantiles. The appeal of using QPDs in modelling uncertainty is that modifications can be made to their quantile functions (through the addition of extra shape parameters, for example), enabling them to represent a broader range of beliefs.

The "meta" in metalog is a term used by Keelin to describe distributions whose original parameters have been substituted in order to incorporate a greater number of shape parameters. In theory, there is no limit to the number of shape parameters the metalog distribution can have, meaning it can be used to model distributional characteristics such as right- or left-skewness, varying levels of kurtosis, and multi-modality. Since the parameters of the metalog are a function of its quantiles, however, the inclusion of additional shape parameters requires the elicitation of a greater number of quantiles. The procedure described in step 2 is designed to elicit five quantiles, enabling the algorithm to fit unbounded metalog distributions with up to a maximum of five shape parameters. In the event that experts' inputs describe a semi-bounded or bounded distribution, log- or logit-transforms are applied to the metalog quantile function, respectively, in order to restrict its range accordingly.

[4]That said, we impose the restriction that the respondent must choose a confidence level of at least 90% or higher; experts are asked to revise their range if they are confident at a level of less than 90%.

[5]This represents the fixed interval method. For this step, the variable interval method, where experts are asked to provide values for predetermined probabilities (as done in step c) was also tested. We found in testing that the fixed interval method performed better than the variable interval method in minimizing the range-principle effect (see Parducci 1963), a problem that has been reported in other elicitation exercises (e.g., Sperber et al. 2013; Gosling 2014). In comparison with the variable interval method, respondents found the task easier and more intuitive with the fixed interval method, and their responses were more plausible.

Moving next to a key and innovative feature of our protocol: in **step 3**, respondents are provided with a visual representation of the parameter estimates they provided in step 2, in the form of a histogram and probability density function (Fig. 3.1). Although we chose to elicit values that are most easily understandable (i.e. median and probabilities instead of parameters of parametric distributions such as mean and variance), it may not be easy for an expert to grasp how a change in median value will precisely influence the corresponding probability distribution. As mentioned earlier, visual feedback allows experts to test if their inputs generate a result corresponding to what they had in mind and reconsider their estimates if desired (Kynn 2008). Implementation of the visual interface was relatively easy thanks to Keelin's free MS Excel distribution program (Keelin 2018).

Despite being highly flexible, there can be instances where our version of the metalog algorithm (having a maximum of 5 shape parameters) is unable to compute a probability density function given the inputs provided. This can occur for example if an expert envisions a largely bimodal probability density function. For this reason, a rudimentary histogram is also presented to the expert which, despite not accurately representing the tails of their envisioned distribution, still reflects their inputs in a crude manner, allowing them to recognize any possible mistakes they may have made or possible biases they may have been subjected to. When a probability density function cannot be computed, experts are informed and instructed to go to the next step if they nevertheless feel comfortable with their inputs.[6]

Once experts have reviewed the graphed densities and are satisfied with their inputs, they are invited to comment on the results in step 4. They are also asked to indicate to what extent the resulting probability density function represents an accurate description of their beliefs (i.e. very accurate, good, poor). Lastly, experts who answered that the visualization of the results did not provide a coherent representation of their beliefs are asked to provide further explanation.

At the end of the survey, experts are asked to confirm whether they would like their names to be acknowledged in future Statistics Canada projections products, while maintaining anonymity in their individual responses. This 'limited anonymity' has been found to be important in limiting any possible motivational biases and permitting respondents to be as unconstrained as possible in their responses (Knol et al. 2010; Morgan 2013). Finally, experts are encouraged to comment on their experience with the elicitation. Allowing the expert to give feedback on the elicitation exercise increases the chances that their knowledge and views are captured accurately (Gosling 2014; Runge et al. 2011; Martin et al. 2011).

[6]The idea is that since an infinite number of distributions could correspond to their inputs, their inputs may be faithful to their assessments of the future, even though a visual representation could not be produced. The histogram remains useful as a way to validate their inputs.

3.2.3 Survey Results

Members of Canada's two demography associations, the Canadian Population Society and l'Association des démographes du Québec, were invited to complete the *2018 Survey of Experts on Future Demographic Trends* questionnaire remotely. In the context of an elicitation on the topic of Canadian demography—a very small field of academic discipline, narrowed further by the fact that we were asking specifically about the future, requiring some level of familiarity with demographic projections—experts are a fairly scarce resource. In total we received 18 responses to the survey. Respondents were found to represent a fairly well-balanced mix of expertise, general years of experience in the field, and current domain of work. The majority of respondents (10 out of 18) reported having high levels of expertise in demographic projections. By and large, respondents reporting low or no expertise in a given component elected to skip the questions relating to that component, as was expected.

3.2.4 Aggregation of Individual Responses

After eliciting the views of numerous experts, it is necessary to combine their views in some manner. The choice of aggregation method was made with the goal of capturing as much information as possible from the experts' individual beliefs, while ensuring that the aggregate result is itself a valid probability distribution from which relevant summary statistics—such as the mean, median, and quantiles—can be derived. For this reason, we adopted a mixture model approach (referred to as a "linear opinion pool" when applied to the context of expert elicitation) in which the aggregate distribution for each component can be thought of as a weighted average of the individual expert distributions. Linear pooling is simple, transparent, and in comparison to other methods, tends to yield distributions with more dispersion, thus offsetting the effect of experts' overconfidence, if present.[7]

Each expert's contribution was weighted on the basis of their self-assessed level of experience about the different components of growth and in population projections. We preferred to weight responses in the context where we solicit a large number of experts in demography with varying levels of expertise in the areas of fertility, mortality, immigration. It also seemed appropriate in the case where a respondent reports a low level of expertise in a given demographic component and somehow expects us to take this information into account.

Despite the fact that experts' responses are parametrized by metalog distributions, the resulting mixture distributions for fertility, mortality, and immigration are not metalog distributions, and do not belong to any defined parametric family.

[7]See Genest and Zidek (1986), Clemen and Winkler (1999) and Dietrich and List (2014) for discussions on various aggregation schemes and their implications.

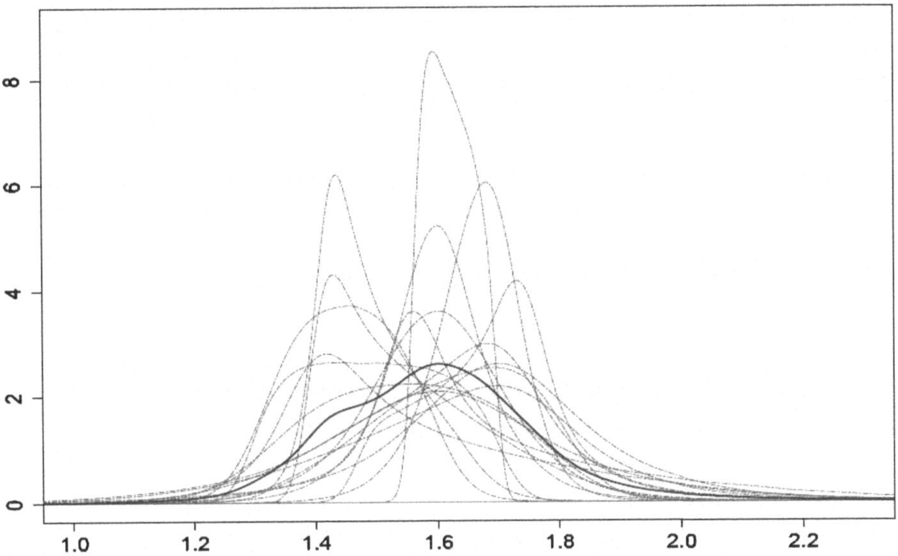

Fig. 3.2 Period total fertility rate, Canada, 2043: Individual expert probability distributions (grey dashed curves) and aggregate mixture distribution (red curve) of the 17 fertility respondents of *the 2018 Survey of Experts on Future Demographic Trends*. (Source: Statistics Canada, Demography Division)

Characteristics such as central moments and quantiles are derived using numerical methods.

Figure 3.2 illustrates the individual probability distributions provided by experts regarding the plausible range of the period total fertility rate in Canada in 2043 and resulting aggregate mixture distribution. Two points should be noted. The first is that there is obviously some divergence among experts, reflecting different opinions about what the future path of fertility in Canada should be. This results in an aggregate density that is asymmetric and, though strictly unimodal, possesses an additional "bump" that reflects a concentration of some experts' distributions around a common range of values (other than the mode).

This is not unexpected: as Lutz et al. (2006) noted, despite factors that are likely to sustain the declining trend in the PTFR, several projection-makers anticipate instead a reversal of trends or some regression toward the mean.[8] These considerations emphasize the importance of the expert survey as a tool to broaden the information base and provide additional perspectives (Bolger 2018). Imagine in contrast what could result from a team of projection-makers in charge of developing assumptions for future fertility and who, after working in the same demographic

[8]A similar schism tends to exist in regard to future mortality between those who believe that we could be approaching a biological limit to life expectancy and those who think that there is room for life expectancy to keep improving further (Oeppen and Vaupel 2002).

projections unit for some time, tend to think along the same lines, either as the result of sharing the same influences or possibly due to some form of *groupthink* effect.[9]

The second point is that it is, for practical reasons, common to adopt a predetermined parametric (most often Gaussian) distribution to model the uncertainty around a parameter in projections. However, we can imagine the loss of information that may have occurred if we had decided to fit only a common two- or three-parameter distribution (such as the normal, logistic, Weibull, etc.) to experts' inputs rather than the more flexible five-parameter metalog.

3.2.5 Incorporation of Expert Judgments into the Deterministic Projection Assumption-Building Process

The aggregate mixture distributions described in the preceding section represent experts' views in 2043, but values are also needed for all interim years of the projection. As Lee (1998) rightly pointed out, expert opinion may be of little help for forecasting intermediate years without information about the autocorrelation structure. This is why we make no inference about what experts had in mind regarding the interim evolution leading to the 2043 distribution; instead, we make our own assumptions about it. To make these assumptions, we privileged time series models, for their capacity to provide probabilistic development over time informed by historical data, calibrated to match experts' densities in 2043. The rationale for this 'hybrid' methodology is that while experts can go beyond past trends and include more information in thinking in the long term, time series models can aptly forecast future trends replicating past autocorrelations—information that experts would have difficulty envisioning. We therefore see this approach as a balanced mix of utilization of time series modelling and expert opinion, benefitting from each method's strengths.

The targets obtained from the survey at the Canada-level are used to derive the regional targets, assuming the same proportional growth in percentage. This method is consistent with the traditional "hybrid bottom-up" approach often used in population projections: assumptions specific to each region are constructed from assumptions initially developed at the national level, but the Canada-level projections exist only by summing the results for the provinces and territories individually. Briefly, medium assumptions for each component are derived as follows:

- Two distinct linear trajectories are produced for the period 2018–2043 for each of the provinces and territories: (1) a short-term trajectory based on the examination

[9]The term was coined by Janis (1972) to refer to the tendency among members of a group to value consensus, harmony and cohesiveness at the cost of making less rational decisions.

of historical trends, and (2) a long-term trajectory based on the results from the *2018 Survey of Experts on Future Demographic Trends*. The 50th percentile (median) of the aggregate expert distribution was used as the long-term national target in 2043.

- These two linear trajectories are combined to obtain a single medium assumption, with the use of a logarithmic interpolation technique that allows for a smooth transition.

The logarithmic interpolation of the two short- and long-term trajectories, yielding a single assumption, makes use of weights selected so that the curve based on the short-term trajectory is given more weight earlier on in the projection years, and the curve based on the long-term trajectory is given more weight in the latter years. The consequence is that in the short-term, assumptions for a given province will reflect mostly recently observed trends, whereas in the long-term, they will be more influenced by beliefs about future trends at the Canada level. Using logarithmic interpolation (as opposed to linear interpolation, for instance), ensures that the short-term trajectory fades relatively quickly in favour of the long-term trajectory. This approach follows best practices in projections to consider the plausibility of outcomes for multiple horizons, in contrast to focusing solely on long-term outcomes (UNECE 2018). Figure 3.3 provides an example of the projected period total fertility rate in the province of Québec according to the medium assumption. The graph displays the short-term trajectory, long-term trajectory and final medium assumption. More details about the methodology can be found in Statistics Canada (2019b).

Low and high assumptions were built based on the medium assumption described above, with targets reflecting experts' uncertainty. The low assumption long-term target (for 2043), was computed by taking the tenth percentile of the aggregate

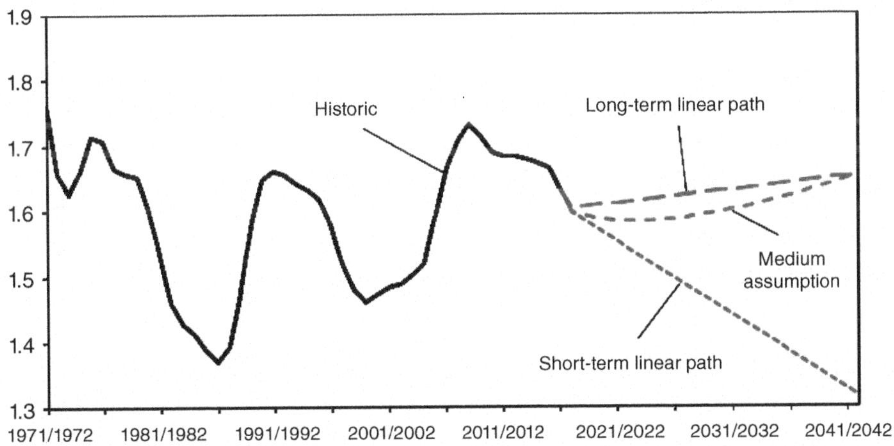

Fig. 3.3 Period total fertility rate, Quebec, historic (1971/1972 to 2016/2017) and projected (2017/2018 to 2042/2043). **Note**: The 2017 data are considered preliminary. (Sources: Statistics Canada, Canadian Vital Statistics, Births Database, 1971 to 2017, Survey 3231 and Demography Division)

probability distribution of experts, and the high long-term target was computed by taking the 90th percentile. Thus, low and high long-term targets represent the bounds of an 80% prediction interval around the medium long-term target. Again, for brevity, we refer readers to Statistics Canada (2019b) for more information about the methodology.

3.3 Application: Using the *2018 Survey of Experts on Future Demographic Trends* to Produce Probabilistic Projections of the PTFR

Producing probabilistic projections of the population requires obtaining probabilistic information on the individual components of population growth. The primary difficulty associated with this is correctly identifying both the individual autocorrelation structures of each of the components, and the structure of the temporal cross-correlation between components. This task becomes exceedingly complex when projections at the subnational level are desired, as regional correlations must also be considered.

In this section, we expand on a method developed by Lutz et al. (2001) in order to provide an example of how results from the *2018 Survey of Experts on Future Demographic Trends* can be combined with traditional time series models – which provide an autocorrelation structure – to produce probabilistic projections. For simplicity, we limit ourselves to the projection of a single demographic indicator (the PTFR) at the national level.

3.3.1 Method

The method utilizes ARIMA models in combination with a priori knowledge about certain properties of the forecast distribution of a given component to derive the full forecast distribution. More specifically, the method assumes that the forecast variance of a component in some year t of the forecast is known, and that the time series parameter(s) can be selected in such a way that the target variance is met in the desired amount of years.[10] Briefly, the model (of, for e.g. the PTFR) can be represented in the following way:

$$y_t = \overline{y}_t + \varepsilon_t$$

$$t = 1, \ldots, T$$

[10] A full description of this method is provided in the supplementary material of Lutz et al. (2001).

Where y_t represents the value of the PTFR in year t of the projection, $\overline{y}_t$ represents the mean value of the PTFR in year t (also assumed to be known in advance), and ε_t represents the deviation from the mean value in year t. The standard deviation of the error in year t, $\sigma(\varepsilon_t) = \sigma(y_t)$, is predetermined according to assumptions about the expected level of future projection uncertainty. In Lutz et al. (2001), a combination of expert opinion and the ex-post analysis of past projection errors is used to obtain standard deviation targets. Given this information, a moving average model of order q (MA(q)) is used to model the ε_t, with the parameters of the model selected in such a way that $\sigma(\varepsilon_t)$ is equal to its pre-specified target.[11] To generate prediction intervals, 2000 simulations are produced.

We modify this method in order to incorporate the aggregate expert probability distribution of the PTFR in 2043 obtained from the survey. Similar to Lutz et al., we use a MA(q) model with $q = 26$ to produce projections of the PTFR from 2018 to 2043, with additional calibration parameters to ensure that in the last year of the projection (in 2043, or when $t = 26$), the forecast distribution obtained from the time series model is identical to the one obtained from the survey.[12] The method is summarized below.

1. The mean of the survey distribution is used as the target mean in 2043; i.e., $\overline{y}_{26} = \overline{y}_{survey}$. Target means for the intermediary years, $t = 1, \ldots, 25$, are obtained using the logarithmic interpolation technique used to derive the medium projection assumption for the PTFR outlined in the previous section. The mean series $\overline{y}_t$ thus reflects both recently observed trends in the PTFR and beliefs about its future long-term level obtained from the survey.
2. The target standard deviation of the error in year $t = 26$ – also the standard deviation of the forecast, $\sigma(y_{26})$ – is set to the standard deviation of the survey distribution.[13] The 27 moving average parameters in the MA(26) model are then set to equal $\sigma(y_{26})/\sqrt{27}$, which guarantees the standard deviation at $t = 26$ is equal to its target value.[14] This also determines the standard deviation in years $t = 1, \ldots, 25$, as they are a function of the moving average parameters.

---

[11] Parameters are not estimated using historical data as is normally the case with time series model. Instead, parameters are derived analytically, conditional on some known properties of the forecast distribution (i.e. the variance).

[12] The choice of q depends on the length of the projection period, as well as what point in the period the desired variance target should be met. An MA(q) model is typically forecastable a maximum of q-periods-ahead.

[13] Setting the standard deviation target to the standard deviation of the expert distribution before calibration guarantees that post-calibration, the structure of the forecast variance remains unchanged. For example, an unmodified MA(26) model with parameters specified as in Lutz et al. (2001) has a forecast variance that increases linearly throughout the projection. By setting the standard deviation of the MA(26) model to the survey standard deviation at $t = 26$, even after calibration parameters have been added to shift the forecast distribution over the course of the projection, the forecast variances in each year remain unchanged (i.e. they increase linearly).

[14] Unlike in a standard MA(q) model, the first term in the moving average series as specified in Lutz et al. (2001) does not have a parameter of 1.

3. Once the mean and standard deviation targets are selected, the full forecast distribution is then obtained using the following 5-step algorithm:
   (a) 100,000 values from the expert survey distribution are drawn at random, and then ranked. The empirical mean, $\overline{y}_{survey}$, and standard deviation, $\sigma(y_{survey})$, are computed.
   (b) 100,000 simulations from a standard MA(26) model are produced for years 2018–2043, with the forecast mean series selected as in 1) and the forecast variance as in 2). Simulations are then ranked in terms of their value in the last year, 2043.
   (c) Each ranked simulation is paired with its corresponding ranked draw from the mixture distribution; i.e. the fifth draw is paired with the fifth simulation.
   (d) The difference between the simulation value in 2043 and its paired draw is computed, and a constant is added to each simulation so that in 2043, the values are the same. The constant is added proportionally over the course of the simulation so that the calibration procedure doesn't cause a "shock" that shifts the simulation drastically.[15]
   (e) The empirical distribution of the time series forecast at year 2043 is now identical to that of the survey distribution, with the mean series $\overline{y}_t$ remaining unchanged. Percentiles can be computed empirically in order to obtain prediction intervals about the median of the forecast distribution.

3.3.2 *Results*

Figure 3.4 displays select percentiles of the forecast distribution of the PTFR from 2018–2043, along with the historical series (1972–2017). The dotted line (50th percentile) is consistent with the Canada-level medium assumption for the PTFR in Population Projections for Canada (2018–2068), Provinces and Territories (2018–2043) (Statistics Canada 2019a).[16]

It should be noted that while the forecast distribution in 2043 is determined by the survey distribution, the forecast distribution in all other years of the projection is determined by the selected parameters ($\overline{y}_t$ and $\sigma(y_t)$) as well as the initial forecast distribution of the ε_t terms. Given that the ε_t series is modelled by an MA(26), a single simulation from this model can be parameterized in the following way:

[15] I.e. a constant is added to the value at every year in the simulation, and not simply to the value in 2043.

[16] A more detailed description of the projections methodology can be found in Population Projections for Canada (2018–2068), Provinces and Territories (2018–2043): Technical Report on Methodology and Assumptions (Statistics Canada 2019b).

Fig. 3.4 Canada historical period total fertility rate (1972–2017) and select percentiles of the forecast distribution (2018–2043). **Note**: The dotted black line corresponds closely to the Canada-level medium projection assumption for the PTFR in *Population Projections for Canada (2018 to 2068), Provinces and Territories (2018 to 2043)*. (**Source**: Statistics Canada, Canadian Vital Statistics, Births Database, 1977 to 2017, Survey 3231 and Demography Division)

$$\varepsilon_t = \sum_{i=0}^{27} \alpha_i u_{t-i}$$

$$u_{t-i} \sim iid\ N(0, 1)$$

where α_i are the moving average parameters. Thus, prior to calibration, $y_t \sim N\left(\overline{y}_t, \sigma\left(\varepsilon_t\right)\right)$. By adding a constant to each simulation to shift the forecast distribution in 2043, the forecast distribution in all other years gradually shifts from being Normal (or approximately Normal) in earlier years of the projection toward a distribution more similar to the metalog mixture in later years of the projection.

Figure 3.5 shows the evolution of the forecast density over the course of the projection. The lighter, orange lines display the distribution in earlier years (symmetrical and approximately Normal) and the darker red lines display the distribution in later years (asymmetrical and closer in shape to the survey mixture metalog distribution). The darkest line, representing the distribution in 2043, is that of the expert distribution. The unusual shape of this distribution suggests that

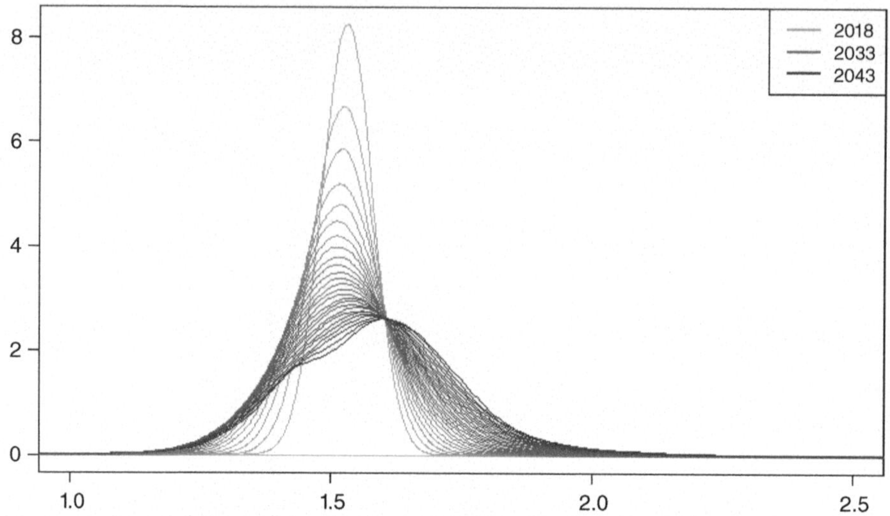

Fig. 3.5 Forecasted density of the period total fertility rate, 2018–2043. (Source: Statistics Canada, Demography Division)

traditional time series models that impose a Normal forecast distribution across all years would fail to accurately represent the aggregate information conveyed by experts.

3.3.3 Future Developments

This method of producing probabilistic projections can be thought of as a simulation-based approach that makes minimal assumptions about the autocorrelation structure of the process. Given the only information known about the full forecast distribution prior to producing projections is: (1) the mean at every year in the projection; and (2) the distribution in the last year of the projection, deriving conditional distributions at all other years requires making no small number of assumptions about the underlying data generating process. ARIMA models, or variations of them, have long been utilized in the projection of fertility (see for example Lee and Tuljapurkar 1994; Keilman and Pham 2004; Alders and de Beer 2004; Dunstan 2011) as well as other demographic indicators. Using simulations from an MA model as a starting point provides both a plausible correlation structure and an initial distributional assumption (Normal).

The way these simulations are modified so that the distribution in the last year of the projection reflects the survey distribution rather than the Normal distribution produced by a standard MA model, however, modifies these assumptions indirectly. The addition of a constant to shift the individual simulations modifies the conditional densities gradually over time, while maintaining the same mean and variance.[17] This process is equivalent to simulating values from the chosen model without explicitly formulating it; the final model is not an MA, but its true form is not derivable – nor does it need to be – from the modified simulations.

In practice, any type of ARIMA model can be used to generate probabilistic projections using this approach. Lutz et al. (2001) tested both AR and MA models to generate probabilistic forecasts and found that the two types of models provided similar results when comparatively parametrized. Their choice for the MA model is not based on how well it fit historical data, but rather on how it could be adapted to integrate different views about the future simply by altering the $\sigma(\varepsilon_t)$ terms. Our modified approach is largely insensitive to the choice of initial model due to the modification process.[18] Assuming a Normal distribution at the start of the projection and the expert distribution at the end restricts the number of ways the process can evolve over time. Our choice of an MA(26) model is based on the view that uncertainty (i.e. the forecast variance) should keep increasing over the course of the 26-year projection horizon (a after which point the variance stabilizes). Overall, in evaluation of the proposed methodology, it is important to remember that we are not so much interested in how one simulation can plausibly mimic the future year-to-year fluctuations of fertility in Canada, but rather in how all simulations together can provide a plausible picture of how uncertainty associated to future fertility propagates over time.

The most difficult aspect of such an approach remains combining it for a number of different indicators (e.g. life expectancy and migration) and across different regions. It is likely that a number of simplifying assumptions will need to be made in order to estimate correlations between both components and regions – in the literature, for example, it is sometimes assumed that components are independent, or that correlations are insignificant enough to be ignored (Billari et al. 2012; Alho 2008; Keilman 1997; Keilman and Pham 2004; Lee and Tuljapurkar 1994). Estimates of correlation may also be elicited formally through expert opinion (e.g., Billari et al. 2012), though this comes at the cost of significantly increasing the burden on respondents. Lutz et al. (2001) used correlation coefficients estimated from various sources – across either regions or indicators – and applied Cholesky decomposition of the variance-covariance matrix to generate correlated random deviations at every point in the projection horizon. Although we have not tested this potential extension, we note that the same methodology can be used to generate correlated simulations resulting from the MA(26) model before calibration to survey results.

[17] An attractive feature of obtaining a normal distribution at the start of the projections is that it is the distribution that makes the least assumptions (i.e. admits the most ignorance) beyond what is stated, here, a known mean and standard deviation (the standard deviation resulting from the chosen MA process). In this context, the normal distribution is the one with the largest entropy. The distribution changes over time as we approach the year 2043, for which we assume having full knowledge.

[18] The approach has only been tested with AR, MA, and random walk (RW) models. Whether this is true for other specifications has not yet been determined.

3.4 Conclusion

We used expert elicitation as a way to better inform the assumption-building process of deterministic scenario-based projections. The resulting scenarios have interesting properties: they share the same definition from one component of growth to another, and they are anchored in real probabilistic information coming from the experts and past data. One of the key advantages of this new approach to projection assumption-building is its conceptual consistency across components: the long-term projection assumptions share the same probabilistic meaning: the "high" assumption represents the 90th percentile of the aggregate probability distribution of plausible future values for that given component according to the experts who responded to the survey; the "medium" assumption represents the 50th percentile, and the "low" assumption the 10th percentile. This leads to greater coherence in the resulting projection scenarios (which combine assumptions about the various components).

Looking forward, the elicitation protocol described in this article can be used to produce a large number of stochastic trajectories that could be combined for the production of probabilistic projections, either as described in the previous section or by utilizing alternative methods.

Acknowledgements Nico Keilman gratefully acknowledges financial support from the Department of Economics, University of Oslo, and Stefano Mazzuco acknowledge financial support from miur-prin2017 project 20177BR-JXS, which made it possible to publish this book as an OA publication.

References

Alders, M., & de Beer, J. (2004). Assumptions on fertility in stochastic population forecasts. *International Statistical Review, 72*(1), 65–79.

Alho, J. (2008). Aggregation across countries in stochastic population forecasts. *International Journal of Forecasting, 24*, 343–353.

Billari, F. C., Graziani, R., & Melilli, E. (2012). Stochastic population forecasts based on conditional expert opinions. *Journal of the Royal Statistical Society: Series A, 175*(2), 491–511.

Billari, F. C., Graziani, R., & Melilli, E. (2014). Stochastic population forecasting based on combinations of expert evaluation within the Bayesian paradigm. *Demography, 51*, 1933–1954.

Bohnert, N. (2015). Chapter 2: Opinion survey on future demographic trends. In N. Bohnert, J. Chagnon, S. Coulombe, P. Dion, & L. Martel (Eds.), *Population projections for Canada (2013 to 2063), provinces and territories (2013 to 2038): technical report on methodology and assumptions* (Statistics Canada catalogue number 91-620-X). Ottawa: Statistics Canada.

Bolger, F. (2018). The selection of experts for (probabilistic) expert knowledge elicitation. In L. Dias, A. Morton, & J. Quigley (Eds.), *Elicitation: The science and art of structuring judgment* (pp. 393–443). New York: Springer.

Clemen, R. T., & Winkler, R. L. (1999). Combining probability distributions from experts in risk analysis. *Risk Analysis, 19*(2), 187–203.

Dias, L., Morton, A., & Quigley, J. (Eds.). (2018). *Elicitation: The science and art of structuring judgment*. New York: Springer.

Dietrich, F., & List, C. (2014). *Probabilistic opinion pooling* (MPRA Paper No. 54806).
Dunstan, K. (2011). *Experimental stochastic population projections for New Zealand: 2009 (base) – 2111* (Statistics New Zealand working paper 11-01).
Garthwaite, P. H., Kadane, J. B., & O'Hagan, A. (2005). *Statistical methods for eliciting probability distributions* (Technical paper 1-2005). Carnegie Mellon University Research Showcase
Genest, C., & Zidek, J. V. (1986). Combining probability distributions: A critique and annotated bibliography. *Statistical Science, 1*(1), 114–135.
Goldstein, D. G., & Rothschild, D. (2014). Lay understanding of probability distributions. *Judgment and Decision making, 9*(1), 1–14.
Gosling, J. P. (2014). *Methods for eliciting expert opinion to inform health technology assessment.* Vignette on SEJ methods for MRC, UK, 2014.
Gosling, J. P. (2018). *SHELF: The Sheffield elicitation framework.* In L. Dias, A. Morton, & J. Quigley (Eds.), *Elicitation: The science and art of structuring judgement* (pp. 61–93). New York: Springer.
Grigore, B., Peters, J., Hyde, C., & Stein, K. (2017). EXPLICIT: A feasibility study of remote expert elicitation in health technology assessment. *BMC Medical Informatics and Decision Making, 17*, 131.
Hanea, A. M., Burgman, M., & Hemming, V. (2018). Chapter 5: IDEA for uncertainty quantification. In L. Dias, A. Morton, & J. Quigley (Eds.), *Elicitation: The science and art of structuring judgment.* New York: Springer.
Hyndman R. J., & Athanasopoulos, G. (2018). *Forecasting: Principles and practice.* Monash University, Australia. Online version at https://otexts.org/fpp2/.
Janis, I. L. (1972). *Victims of groupthink.* Boston: Houghton Mifflin.
Jones, G., & Johnson, W. O. (2014). Prior elicitation: Interactive spreadsheet graphics with sliders can be fun, and informative. *The American Statistician, 68*(1), 42–51.
Kadane, J. B., & Wolfson, L. J. (1998). Experiences in elicitation. *Journal of the Royal Statistical Society. Series D, 47*(1), 3–19.
Keelin, T. W. (2016). The Metalog distributions. *Decision Analysis, 13*(4), 243–277.
Keelin, T. W. (2018). *The metalog distributions – Excel workbook.* Accessible at: http://www.metalogdistributions.com/excelworkbooks.html.
Keelin, T. W., & Powley, B. W. (2011). Quantile-parameterized distributions. *Decision Analysis, 8*(3), 165–250.
Keilman, N. (1997). Ex-post errors in official population forecasts in industrialized countries. *Journal of Official Statistics, 13*, 245–277.
Keilman, N., & Pham, D. Q. (2004). Time series based errors and empirical errors in fertility forecasts in the Nordic countries. *International Statistical Review, 72*, 5–18.
Knol, A. B., Slottje, P., van der Sluijs, J. P., & Lebret, E. (2010). The use of expert elicitation in environmental health impact assessment: A seven step procedure. *Environmental Health, 9*, 19.
Kynn, M. (2008). The 'heuristics and biases' bias in expert elicitation. *Journal of the Royal Statistical Society, Series A (Statistics in Society), 171*(1), 239–264.
Lee, R. (1998). Probabilistic approaches to population forecasting. *Population and Development Review, 24*, 156–190.
Lee, R. D., & Tuljapurkar, S. (1994). Stochastic population forecasts for the United States: Beyond high, medium, and low. *Journal of the American Statistical Association, 89*, 1175–1189.
Lutz, W. (Ed.). (1994). *The future population of the world: What can we assume today?* London: Earthscan.
Lutz, W. (2009). *Toward a systematic, argument-based approach to defining assumptions for population projections* (Interim report IR-09-037). Laxenburg: International Institute for Applied Systems Analysis.
Lutz, W., Sanderson, W. C., & Scherbov, S. (2001). The end of world population growth. *Nature, 412*, 543–545.
Lutz, W., Skirbekk, V., & Testa, M. R. (2006). The low-fertility trap hypothesis: Forces that may Lead to further postponement and fewer births in Europe. *Vienna Yearbook of Population Research, 4*, 167–192.

Martin, T. G., Burgman, M. A., et al. (2011). Eliciting expert knowledge in conservation science. *Conservation Biology*, 29–38.

Morgan, M. G. (2013). Use (and abuse) of expert elicitation in support of decision making for public policy. *PNAS Perspective, 111*(20), 7176–7184.

Morgan, M. G., & Henrion, M. (1990). *Uncertainty: A guide to dealing with uncertainty in quantitative risk and policy analysis*. Cambridge: Cambridge University Press.

Morris, D. E., Oakley, J. E., & Crowe, J. A. (2014). A web-based tool for eliciting probability distributions from experts. *Environmental Modelling and Software, 52*, 1–4.

NRC. [National Research Council]. (2000). *Beyond six billion. Forecasting the world's population*. Washington, DC: National Academies Press.

Oakley, T., & O'Hagan, A. (2014). *SHELF: The Sheffield elicitation framework (version 3.0)*. http://www.tonyohagan.co.uk/shelf/SHELF3.html. Accessed 15 June 2018.

Oeppen, J., & Vaupel, J. W. (2002). Broken limits to life expectancy. *Science, 296*(5570), 1029–1031.

O'Hagan, A., Buck, C. E., Daneshkhah, A., Eiser, J. R., Garthwaite, P. H., Jenkinson, D. J., et al. (2006). *Uncertain judgements: Eliciting experts' probabilities*. Chichester: Wiley.

Parducci, A. (1963). Range-frequency compromise in judgment. *Psychological Monographs: General and Applied, 77*(2), 1–50.

Runge, M. C., Converse, S. J., & Lyons, J. E. (2011). Which uncertainty? Using expert elicitation and expected value information to design an adaptive program. *Biological Conservation, 144*, 1214–1233.

Speirs-Bridge, A., Fidler, F., McBride, M., Flander, L., Cumming, G., & Burgman, M. (2010). Reducing overconfidence in the interval judgments of experts. *Risk Analysis, 30*(3), 512–523.

Sperber, D., Mortimer, D., Lorgelly, P., & Berlowitz, D. (2013). An expert on every street corner? Methods for eliciting distributions in geographically dispersed opinion pools. *Value in Health, 16*, 434–437.

Statistics Canada. (2019a). *Population projections for Canada (2018 to 2068), provinces and territories (2018 to 2043)* (Statistics Canada catalogue number 91-520-X). Ottawa: Statistics Canada.

Statistics Canada. (2019b). *Population projections for Canada (2018 to 2068), provinces and territories (2018 to 2043): Technical report on methodology and assumptions* (Statistics Canada catalogue number 91-620-X). Ottawa: Statistics Canada.

UNECE. (2018). *Recommendations on communicating population projections* (ECE/CES/STAT/2018/1). Available at: http://www.unece.org/statistics/networks-of-experts/task-force-on-population-projections.html.

Chapter 4
Post-transitional Demography and Convergence: What Can We Learn from Half a Century of World Population Prospects?

Maria Castiglioni, Gianpiero Dalla-Zuanna, and Maria Letizia Tanturri

4.1 Introduction

The search for a common path of development has always been present in demographic research, which in general is short on theory and rich in empirical observations and quantification (Thornton 2001). This is perhaps not surprising since demography is the field that has "produced one of the best documented generalizations in the social sciences: the Demographic Transition" (Kirk 1996: 361). This data-driven theory predicts a shared trajectory for all societies, whereby they experienced (or are now experiencing) a shift from an inefficient pre-modern regime of high mortality and high fertility to a post-modern equilibrium characterized by both low fertility and low mortality (Reher 2004, 2011; Livi Bacci 2012). The timing of this process differs across countries, such that its forerunners and latecomers can be identified, knowing that all nations will sooner or later undergo such a change (Reher 2004). Thanks to an impressive series of statistical regularities, for those countries that have begun the transition it is relatively simple to hypothesize a strong convergence in terms of future mortality and fertility trends. These basic elements of population forecasting thus see the eventual convergence of fertility and mortality rates for poor countries as an inevitable destiny, as has already occurred in rich countries.

What it is less clear, however, is what happens after the end of the Demographic Transition, when fertility is close to or under replacement level, infectious diseases are under control, and life expectancy at birth is above 65–70 years. As Reher (2019: 2) observes "after the great fall, fertility gave no indication of rebounding to even remotely similar levels to those holding during the peak of the baby boom" (see

M. Castiglioni (✉) · G. Dalla-Zuanna · M. L. Tanturri
Department of Statistical Sciences, University of Padova, Padova, Italy
e-mail: casti@stat.unipd

S. Mazzuco, N. Keilman (eds.), *Developments in Demographic Forecasting*, The Springer Series on Demographic Methods and Population Analysis 49,
https://doi.org/10.1007/978-3-030-42472-5_4

also, Rindfuss et al. 2016; Billari 2018). Many scholars support the idea that the emerging disparities in the low fertility context are destined to persist (Rindfuss et al. 2016; Billari 2018; Rindfuss and Choe 2015, 2016). It seems, in fact, that developed countries may be on different paths with respect to fertility, aging, and migration, with potentially important consequences for future social and economic stability (Reher 2019; Anderson and Kohler 2015). Given such divergences, the task of population forecasting has become increasingly challenging, due also to the absence of strong theoretical models driving the hypotheses.

In what follows, we examine recent trends, assessing the supposition of a "*weak convergence*" in the aftermath of the Demographic Transition. That is, the notion that countries will converge towards similar fertility and mortality values and contained migration, with birth rates oscillating around replacement level, and as a result, the population growth rate of all countries will approach zero.

While this is far from a simple issue, we argue that it is extremely relevant for population forecasting, given that alternative hypotheses on fertility, mortality, and migration can result in very different population growth rates. Indeed, it is well known that seemingly small differences can have considerable consequences for both population dynamics and structures. For instance, consider a zero-migration stable population with a Total Fertility Rate (TFR) equal to 2.045 children per woman, a mean age at birth of 30 years and a sex ratio at birth of 104/100. A natural growth rate equal to zero can be achieved when mortality is low enough. A TFR of half a child less than replacement level (~1.5) implies that population will decrease at a rate of 1% a year. The decrease would be much stronger (2.4% per year) if the TFR was just 1 child per woman (Kohler et al. 2002).[1]

Weak convergence is clearly the prevailing hypothesis in many of the UN World Population Prospects Revisions. Our aim here is to discuss this supposed convergence through an examination of the near past, comparing actual data with the forecasted fertility, mortality, and migration trends computed in the UN World Population Prospects over the last half century.

While the idea of comparing forecasted trends with real data is certainly not new (e.g. Preston 1974; Calot and Chesnais 1978; Keyfitz 1981; Stoto 1983; Pflaumer 1988; Keilman 1997, 1998, 2000, 2001; National Research Council 2000; Keilman and Pham 2004), our approach is unique in that we empirically test whether or not the convergence projected by the UN population forecasts is substantiated in the aftermath of Demographic Transitions. To this end, we examine the 38 countries that had already reached a TFR below 2.5 children per woman in the decade 1975–85 in order to assess whether or not the generalized expected weak convergence is empirically confirmed up until 2015.

[1] A growth rate close to zero, in the absence of migration, can be achieved even if TFR < 2 and survival continues to improve (obviously with an aging population). As we will see in Sect. 4.2.4, this is precisely the population dynamic forecasted by the UN Population Prospects for the coming decades in countries where the TFR is currently less than 2.5.

The chapter is structured as follows. In Sect. 4.2 we review the literature relative to the notion of convergence and its alternative definitions. We then discuss the hypothesis that has driven different World Population Prospects Revisions, paying particular attention to the 2017 Revision for countries that at present have fertility levels lower than 2.5 children per woman. In Sect. 4.3, we describe the data and methods employed to conduct our comparisons. In Sect. 4.4, we compare demographic forecasts with actual patterns and present our results on fertility, mortality, and migration trends for the countries under analysis. In the final section, we discuss our results, which cast doubt on the idea of weak convergence.

4.2 Background

4.2.1 Convergence vs. Divergence in Population Projections

Demographic forecasts typically rely heavily on current vital statistics and extrapolate their trends into the future. They are rarely driven by behavioral sciences or strong theories that might help to deal with uncertainty. The most relevant exception consists of Demographic Transition regularities, which have aided forecasters in placing each country at a certain point along this well-known trajectory and in projecting future developments in light of that which has occurred in similar countries. That said, also along the Demographic Transition, relevant country/regional specificities can bias projections: the differences in the demographic transition features between more and less developed countries provide a particularly pertinent example to this regard (Livi Bacci 2012).

Establishing accurate hypotheses for population forecasts at the end of the Demographic Transition is even more complex due to a lack (or proved insufficiency) of strong theories that might help to predict demographic behaviors (e.g., the Second Demographic Transition Theory, or The New Household Economics Theory). Moreover, it is commonly accepted that uncertainty relative to population behavior is not only due to a dearth of scholarly knowledge, but is, in fact, inherent: individuals often make unpredictable choices in terms of family formation and childbearing, health-related behavior, and migration (Henry 1987; Keilman 2019). This seems particularly true as social constraints relax and the individualization of choices becomes the norm.

An extensive literature (Preston 1974; Calot and Chesnais 1978; Keyfitz 1981; Stoto 1983; Pflaumer 1988; Keilman 1997, 1998, 2000, 2001; National Research Council 2000; Keilman and Pham 2004) has endeavored to assess the accuracy of historical population forecasts by comparing them to observed statistics. Most studies focus on the accuracy of the size of the population and its growth. A complete and updated survey of previous work and its main inaccuracies in population forecasting is available in Keilman (2019). It is generally accepted that projection accuracy is better for shorter than longer durations, and for bigger as opposed to smaller populations. Previous research also shows that forecasts for the old and young tend to be less precise than those for intermediate age groups, as errors in mortality, fertility, and migration dynamics can significantly affect the size of these groups (Keilman 2019). In addition, it is well known that there is considerable variance in accuracy between regions; large bias can occur where (especially official) data are not reliable or available. Generally, scholars have shown that poor data quality worsens forecast performance. This relationship seems stronger for mortality than for fertility, and for short-term compared to long-term forecasts (Keilman 2019). Weak data on migration can also have a relevant impact on projection precision, particularly in countries where in-flows or out-flows are quantitatively relevant and protracted in time.

While much effort has been dedicated to evaluating the accuracy of demographic population forecasts in terms of population size, structure, and growth, to our knowledge only a handful of studies aim to test the hypothesis of long-run convergence in the aftermath of Demographic Transitions (Wilson 2011, 2013; Dorius 2008; Neumayer 2004). Our paper endeavors to fill this research gap.

Several instances of divergence in mortality trends have been illustrated in the demographic literature (Bloom and Canning 2007; Goesling and Firebaugh 2004; McMichael et al. 2004; Moser et al. 2005; Neumayer 2004). The spread of the HIV-AIDS epidemic in the 1990s, for example, brought the forecasted global mortality convergence observed in the 1980s to a halt (Neumayer 2004, Goesling and Firebaugh 2004; McMichael et al. 2004). Bloom and Canning (2007) show, with regard to the rise in life expectancy observed from 1963 to 2003, that a number of countries appear to have made the jump from the high-mortality cluster to the low-mortality cluster without a clear accompanying convergence. Their results suggest continuous advances among many countries within clusters, with rising life expectancy in some nations resulting in a shift from one cluster to the other. A related study, covering 195 nations during the period 1955–2005, reveals that while life expectancy averages converged across time, infant mortality rates instead continuously diverge; economic development improves life expectancy more than it reduces infant mortality, whereas the situation is reversed among wealthier nations (Clark 2011).

Though not always made explicit, a global fertility convergence is generally expected, with most countries following the path towards replacement fertility as projected by the Demographic Transition theory. Wilson (2001) provides an interesting empirical assessment of the extent to which the fertility revolution has become a worldwide phenomenon in the latter half of the twentieth century, within a "global demographic convergence" framework (both in terms of high life expectancy and low fertility). Yet the simple fact that now much of the world's population lives in countries or areas with below-replacement fertility does not necessarily mean that fertility rates are all destined to converge to the same level (Dorius 2008; Rindfuss and Choe 2015). Dorius (2008: 521), for example, argues that the observed intercountry variation in fertility decline from 1955 to 2005 "points to divergence, rather than convergence" and provides a robust convergence–

divergence test of the magnitude and direction of change in fertility inequality, in contrast to that found several years earlier by Wilson (2001).

Recent studies of expert–based forecasts show that there is now less consensus among scholars on the future of fertility, particularly in countries having reached a TFR well below replacement level (Reher 2019; Basten et al. 2014; Rindfuss and Choe 2015, 2016; Rindfuss et al. 2016). More and more studies have begun to question the mainstream position of a long-term convergence to a same fertility level, both from a theoretical and an empirical perspective. Dorius (2008), cited above, highlights growth in fertility differences at the global level (including less and more developed countries). Meanwhile, Crenshaw et al. (2000) find divergence among less developed countries from 1965 to 1990. Casterline (2001) shows that the fertility transition has been highly unequal at the global level, with birth rates rising and falling over the second half of the twentieth century.

A focus on low fertility countries reveals a sort of bifurcation between countries where fertility has stabilized at relatively high levels (i.e., slightly lower than replacement level) and those where fertility has continued to decline to low or very low levels (less than 1.5) (Rindfuss and Choe 2015; Rindfuss et al. 2016). Sobotka (2017: S20) observes that period fertility rates usually continue to decrease – often to very low levels – even after replacement fertility has been reached, and that there is, in fact, "no obvious theoretical or empirical threshold around which period fertility tends to stabilize." The claimed reversals in reproductive behavior seem more an outcome of a "tempo effect" than a real change in behavior (Sobotka et al. 2017). Such views are in line with the work of Lutz et al. (2006) who envisage an inflection point when fertility is persistently lower than 1.5 children per woman, given that some forces (e.g., stable change in fertility ideals) may act as a "low fertility trap," impeding recovery. A similar result is also predicted by Reher (1998, 2019) who observes the emergence of distinct fertility regimes in post transition societies, along a divide between strong/weak family ties. Billari (2018) as well forecasts the persistence of fertility differentials among a selection of low fertility countries unless a number of conditions – that will not necessarily occur across the lowest-low fertility context – are met: a stronger position of young generations, a higher level of economic development and subjective well-being, and gender equity.

4.2.2 *Defining "Strong" (Beta) and "Weak" (Sigma) Convergence*

Economic forecasts have similarly been informed by the idea of convergence, particularly relative to levels of per capita income and product. Analysts have used a variety of statistical methods to test for such convergence within and between countries across a broad range of indicators and domains. One can distinguish between two types of convergence in growth empirics: beta-convergence and sigma-convergence.

According to Barro and Sala-i-Martin (1992), when partial correlation between growth in income over time and its initial level is negative, there is "beta-convergence," whereby the latter refers to a process in which poor regions grow faster than rich ones, and therefore catch up with the latter. The idea, as explained by Barro et al. (1991: 110), is that "the diminishing returns to capital set in slowly as an economy develops" and these automatic forces ensure convergence over time. In other words, "the condition where former laggards, fueled by higher growth rates, catch up with former leaders is referred to as beta-convergence because it is typically modeled using ordinary least squares regression where the annualized growth rate over the study period is regressed on the observed rate at base measurement" (Dorius 2008: 522; Barro et al. 1991; Barro and Sala-i-Martin 1992). Undoubtedly, demographic transition trends in life expectancy (e_0), infant mortality, and fertility provide excellent examples of beta-convergence (i.e., "strong convergence"). Here, considering various demographic measures, beta-convergence occurs when forerunners increase (e_0) or decrease (TFR) slower than laggards; sigma-convergence occurs when cross-country variation in e_0 or TFR decreases.

Behind this global trend, or reduction of cross-country variation over the long run (i.e., the strong convergence process), it is, however, also possible to observe sigma-convergence when the dispersion of a measure (income per capita, in the previous example) around the average values falls over time (Dorius 2008). The standard deviation describes the overall spread of the fertility distribution (Sala-i-Martin 1996; Neumayer 2004). As Dorius (2008: 522) observes, "If the repeated cross-sectional standard deviation increases, we conclude that countries are diverging on Y and if the variance declines, we conclude that countries are converging."

This standard deviation has been used to test for sigma-convergence in incomes (Sala-i-Martin 1996), infant and child survival rates, and life expectancy (Neumayer 2004; Dorius 2008), among other factors. The utility of the standard deviation in longitudinal designs is its ability to assess inequality under the condition of a relatively constant mean. Yet, as is well known, the TFR and life expectancy for the world have been anything but constant over recent decades. To this regard, Dorius (2008: 523) remarks that "When the mean of Y is trending down, the standard deviation might also be decreasing, but only if the standard deviation is decreasing faster *relative* to the mean is the fertility distribution becoming more equal".[2]

The differences between the two measures should certainly be kept in mind when looking for sigma-convergence, in a world that is beta-converging.

[2]Sigma-convergence occurs when – in considering a group of countries – the mean of an indicator decreases less rapidly than its standard deviation. A good indicator of the sigma-convergence process is consequently the coefficient of variation (the ratio between the standard deviation and the arithmetic mean). In this chapter, we prefer to show parallel trends over time of both mean and standard deviation, as this allows to evaluate both components of the sigma-convergence.

4.2.3 Hypothesis of the UNPD World Population Prospects: A Review

Between 1950 and 2017, the United Nations (UN) published a large set of population projections for the world, its major regions, and almost all countries. While the literature usually considers estimates for pre-transition countries to be problematic (Keilman 2001), it has now become of paramount importance to understand the reasoning behind UN Population Division (UNPD) experts' predictions of mortality, fertility, and migration for those countries that have already completed their Demographic Transition. Indeed, this is an increasingly relevant group. Keilman (2019) reports that data quality for Europe and North America is good, but forecasters' long-run projection of the age structure was inaccurate because they did not expect either the fall of fertility rates in the seventies, or the further increase in life expectancy. As a result, they overestimated the young component and underestimated the old one.

Rather than assess the degree of accuracy in estimating population size and structure (as done by Keilman 1998, 2001), in this chapter we focus on the hypothesis employed by the UNPD to carry out the four Revisions of the World Population Prospects in 1980, 1990, 2000, and 2017. Before turning to a comparison between their hypothesized trends and those actually observed, we briefly describe their assumptions and methods adopted. The World Population Prospects Revisions examined here have different projection horizons: 45 years for the 1980 Revision, 35 for the 1990 Revision, 50 for the 2000 Revision, and 85 for the 2017 Revision.

Until 2008, the UNPD adopted a deterministic scenario-based cohort component method to forecast world population. The approach has been criticized from a statistical point of view as uncertainty is not quantified and no probability is attached to the respective scenarios (usually high, medium, and low variants) (Alho and Spencer 1985; Lee 1998). Moreover, the scenario approach does not include all the different possible combinations of hypothesized mortality and fertility or migration. Indeed, a variant combination that is extreme for one variable is not necessary extreme for another. Moreover, a deterministic approach does not allow for the possibility of distinguishing between a random fluctuation and a structural one; for instance fertility may be high in 1 year due to a specific situation, but not in another (Keilman 2019; Bengtsson et al. 2019). In response to these limitations, the UNPD has adopted a stochastic Bayesian approach since the revision of 2012 (Raftery et al. 2012; UN 2014).

As the UNPD's approach has changed over time, so too have their expectations of fertility, mortality, and migration. With regard to the level of fertility, both the 1970 and 1980 Revisions forecast a decline as countries progress in economic and social development. The target being a TFR of 2.1, whereby countries with close but higher rates than this value will eventually reach replacement level and fertility stabilizes; conversely fertility is expected to rise and return to replacement level in those countries where it had fallen below this level. In 1990, the UNPD observed large variability in paths towards low fertility among developed countries, most of which remained below replacement level. Aware that in these countries trends in future fertility would be mostly affected by shifts in values and lifestyles, the UNPD incorporated hypotheses offered by national statistical offices (with some adjustments) so as to take into account country-specific value orientation and ideational changes. These were used to make medium, low, and high fertility assumptions. According to the three variants, TFR-targets in 2020–2025 were set at 1.9 children per woman in the medium variant, 2.25 c/w in the high variant, and 1.6 c/w in the low variant. This approach was then abandoned in the subsequent World Population Prospects for the low fertility group, with TFR below replacement level in 2000. Countries were grouped by fertility levels around this year. Birth rates are forecasted to catch up in the 5-year period 2045–2050, close to the level of the 1960 cohort (if available), or to 1.7 for those registering a TFR of less than 1.5 in 2000, or to 1.9 for those with a TFR equal to or higher than 1.5 in 2000. In all these approaches, sigma-convergence is assumed, and towards just one target value in the 1970, 1980, and 1990 Revisions, and two values, determined by previous fertility trends, in the following Revisions.

Since the 2012 Revision, the UNPD has adopted a probabilistic approach. In 2017, the general prediction was a convergence towards low fertility, although no specific numerical targets in the post-transition phase are presented. For low fertility countries that have completed the demographic transition, the UNPD estimates fertility change through a time series model, with the assumption that fertility fluctuates around country-specific levels based on a Bayesian hierarchical model (Raftery et al. 2014). The model is based on the specific history of the country and informed by empirical evidence from all low-fertility countries that have experienced fertility increases from a sub-replacement level, with the constraint that fertility cannot be higher than 2.1 births per woman. As the models are constructed relative to the particular experience of each nation, if the latter has experienced extended periods of low fertility without recovery, fertility is projected to remain at low levels. This probabilistic approach, informed on the country's demographic experience and on that of all low fertility nations, does not necessarily lead to convergence.

The assumptions for estimates of mortality change less over time. The computation of age-sex survival probabilities are based on Coale and Demeny regional model life tables, or the national life table if reliable. In the 1970 and 1980 Revisions, quinquennial gains are expected, declining with the lengthening of e_0. In 1970, the maximum e_0 is 68.2 for the sexes combined (3.5 years difference between men and women). In the 1980 Revision, geographical differences are also considered, and for countries with the highest life expectancies, the maximum forecasted e_0 is 73.5 for men and 80 for women. The method adopted for the 1990 and 2000 Revisions is analogous but takes into account regional differences occurring in previous years. In developed countries, the expected gains will diminish, life expectancy will reach very high levels, and differences among countries will continue to narrow. According to the 2000 Revision, in Australia and New Zealand, North America, and in Northern, Western, and Southern Europe in 2045–2050, e_0 will vary between 81.9 and 83.5 years, the only exception being Eastern

Europe, with economies in transition, where e_0 remains below 80. For low mortality countries, a sigma-convergence assumption is undeniable, with the exception of Eastern European countries in the 2000 Revision.

In 2017, the general hypothesis is again one of a continuous and generalized increase in life expectancy. Through a Bayesian hierarchical model, gains in life expectancy are estimated based on country specific experiences in 1950–2015, together with average global trends. For low mortality countries, the double-logistic function incorporated into the model forecasts decreasing gains, which converge towards asymptotic values of increase in post-transition years, and a narrowing sex gap until female life expectancy is set equal to 86 years, then modeled as constant. A convergence in gains is consequently assumed, although future life expectancies will maintain asymptotically constant distances, without a clear sigma-convergence among the different countries.

UNPD experts have tended to be very cautious with regard to migration, usually projecting for several 5-year periods the current statistics in absolute value, and only for a select number of countries. For the first time in 2017 an effort was made to account for the complexity of the phenomenon. The Revision of this year remarks, "Where migration flows have historically been small and have had little net impact on the demography of a country, adopting the assumption that migration will remain constant throughout most of the projection period is usually acceptable. In situations where migration flows are a dominant factor in demographic change, more attention is needed." (UN 2017: 29). Thus some distinctions are made according to either the motivation for migration or the specificity of certain situations. The Revision considers both international migration flows and refugee movements. With regard to the former, it is assumed that recent levels (in absolute values), if stable, would continue until 2045–2050. In terms of refugees, it is assumed that the latter will return to their country of origin within one or two projection periods, i.e., within 5–10 years (UN 2017). After 2050, UNPD experts expect that net migration will gradually decline and reach 50% of the projected level of 2045–2050 by 2095–2100. However, they also admit that "the assumption is unlikely to be realized but represents a compromise between the difficulty of predicting the levels of immigration or emigration for each country of the world over such a far horizon, and the recognition that net migration is unlikely to reach zero in individual countries." (UN 2017: 30).

In terms of net migration, UN experts forecast large variability until 2045–2050, and then a sigma-convergence during the second half of the century. Yet they are aware that – given the present conditions – full convergence is not seriously predictable. In the new 2019 Revision (published just as we finish the writing of this chapter), the idea of convergence toward a 0-migration world is also abandoned.[3]

[3]The UN Population Division published its 2019 revision during the writing of this chapter. Since the methodology used in the new forecasts perfectly follows that of 2017, and the experiences of just a few countries have been updated, our results are not significantly affected. A comparison with the more and the less developed countries, respectively, shows that the differences in the birth and mortality forecasts are very limited. The most notable change concerns the hypothesis on

This shift reflects another "cultural change" within the UNPD (and demography as well), where migrations are not considered "accidents" or "disturbance factors," but rather structural components of complex demographic dynamics.

4.2.4 The Weak Convergence Hypothesis in the UN World Population Prospects, 2017 Revision

Beyond the methodological improvements described above, when the UNPD forecasts the population dynamics of post-transitional countries, it assumes – more or less explicitly – a hypothesis of weak convergence, as we show here.[4]

To this regard, consider the 112 countries around the world where, according to the 2017 Revision, the total fertility rate was below 2.5 in 2010–2015. The World Population Prospects (2017) suggest that during the twenty-first century, these countries will converge to a sort of quasi-stable population with declining mortality, constant TFR of 1.8, net migration rate around +0.2‰, and natural growth rate around −3‰.[5] In addition, fertility and migration – in just a few decades – are projected to be similar in all of these 112 countries, while mortality – continuing its declining trend – should also see decreasing variability (Table 4.1 and Fig. 4.1).

4.3 Data and Methods

Data for this study rely on estimates and forecasts from the World Population Prospects Revisions produced by the UN Population Division in 1980, 1990,

---

migration: in the 2019 Revision, after 2050 migrations are kept constant at the value of 2045–2050 and are not halved, as projected in the 2017 Revision. Consequently, results on migration are the same in the 2017 and 2019 Revisions up until 2045–2050.

[4]If the UNPD demographic forecasts for all countries are considered, including those that had not completed the demographic transition by 2017, beta-convergence proceeds at full speed, because it is assumed that – within a few decades – TFR will be less than 2.5 and e_0 more than 70 in almost all countries of the world. Thus, the UNPD supposes beta-convergence in considering all the countries of the world, while the sigma-convergence manifests among the countries that have completed the demographic transition.

[5]The concept of a quasi-stable population was introduced by Bourgeois-Pichat (1994) to model the populations that during the second half of the twentieth century maintained high levels of fertility while experiencing rapid change in their age structures due to declines in infant and youth mortality; whereas the effect of migration on population age-structure and trends are considered negligible. Now – according to the UN Population Prospects – quasi-stability would be determined by a constant fertility rate around 1.8, and by a continuous decrease in over-50 mortality, with a consequent progressive population aging.

Table 4.1 UN 2017 Revision of World Population Prospects for the 112 countries with TFR ≤ 2.5 in 2010–2015. Number of countries with different values for four demographic indicators

	2010–2015	2030–2035	2050–2055	2070–2075	2090–2095
Total fertility rate	*Number of countries*				
1.01–1.25	5	0	0	0	0
1.26–1.50	22	9	1	1	1
1.51–1.75	22	47	58	45	13
1.76–2.00	26	49	53	66	98
2.01–2.25	20	7	0	0	0
2.26–2.50	17	0	0	0	0
Life expectancy at birth	*Number of countries*				
65.1–70.0	5	1	0	0	0
70.1–75.0	35	13	3	1	0
75.1–80.0	41	45	19	9	2
80.1–85.0	31	50	49	37	19
85.1–90.0	0	3	41	55	52
90.1–95.0	0	0	0	10	39
Net migration rate (per thousand)	*Number of countries*				
≤ − 3.0	24	6	5	4	3
−2.9 – −1.0	18	15	14	14	13
−0.9 – 1.0	30	57	58	65	72
1.1–3.0	12	21	24	25	24
> 3.0	28	13	11	4	0
Natural growth rate (per thousand)	*Number of countries*				
≤ − 7.5	0	1	3	6	6
−7.4 – −2.5	7	22	45	56	69
−2.4 – 2.5	30	37	53	50	37
2.6–7.5	29	43	11	0	0
7.6–12.5	28	9	0	0	0
> 12.5	18	0	0	0	0
TOTAL	112	112	112	112	112

Source: Authors' calculation on data from the UN Population Division. World Population Prospects, 2017 Revision

2000, and 2017. During the period 1975–1985, 38 countries had already reached a TFR < 2.5.[6] This group comprised virtually all the European nations including

[6]The 38 countries are: North-Central Europe excluding German speaking countries (Belgium, Denmark, Finland, France, Iceland, Netherlands, Norway, Sweden); English speaking countries (UK, Canada, USA, Australia, New Zealand); German speaking countries (Austria, Germany, Luxembourg, Switzerland); the former Socialist countries excluding the Balkans (Bulgaria, Czechoslovakia, Hungary, Poland, Romania, USSR); Southern Europe including the Balkans (Cyprus, Greece, Italy, Malta, Portugal, Spain, Yugoslavia); East Asia (Hong Kong, Japan, Singapore, South Korea); and the Caribbean (Barbados, Cuba, Martinique, Puerto Rico).

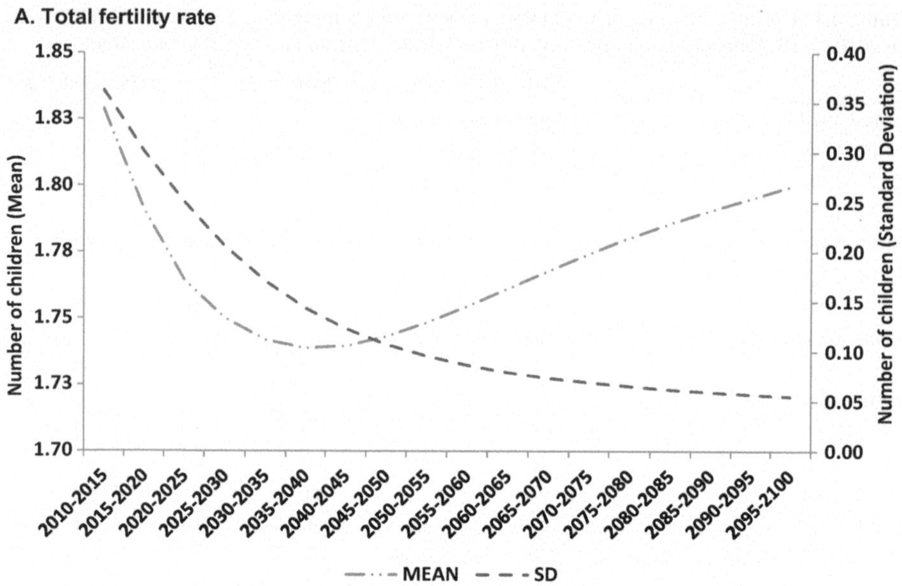

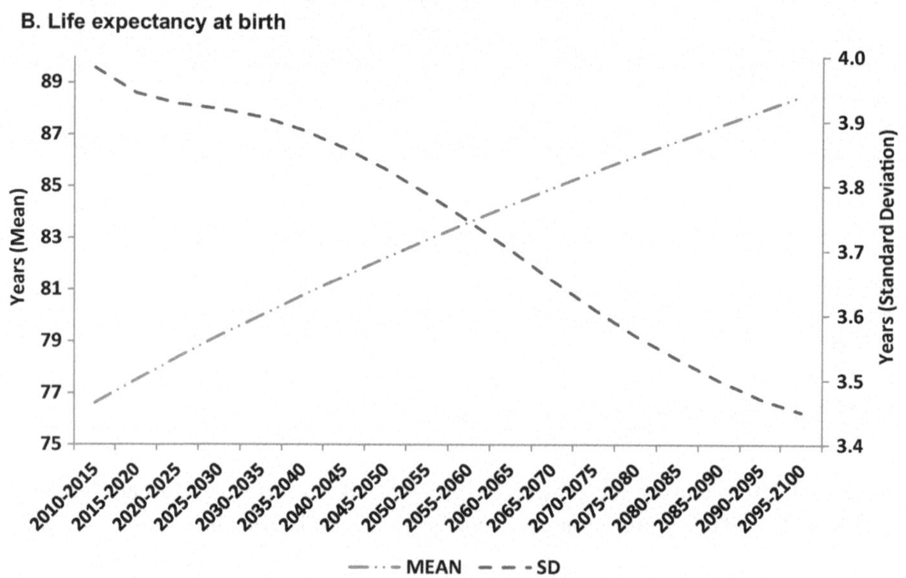

Fig. 4.1 Simple mean and standard deviation of four demographic indicators. UN Population Prospects for the 112 countries where TFR $\leq$ 2.5 in 2010–2015. (**a**) Total fertility rate, (**b**) Life expectancy at birth, (**c**) Net migration rate (per thousand), (**d**) Natural growth rate (per thousand). (Source: Authors' calculation on data from the UN Population Division. World Population Prospects, 2017 Revision)

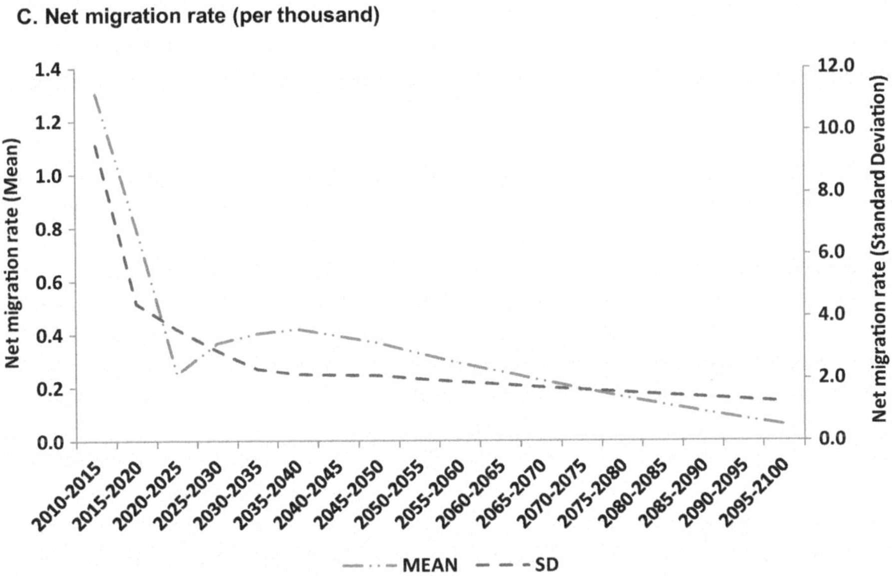

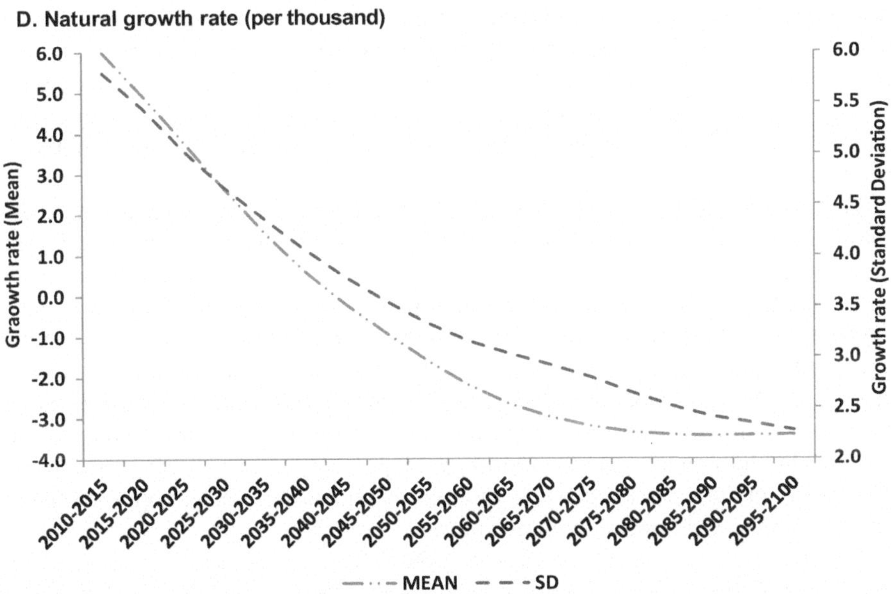

Fig. 4.1 (continued)

Cyprus, with the exception of Albania and Ireland, where the TFR was higher than 2.5 during this time. We do not consider here very small countries and autonomous islands. In order to allow for comparisons before and after the fall of the Iron Curtain, we consider Germany in its post-1989 borders, Yugoslavia, Czechoslovakia, and USSR in their pre-1989 borders. The 38 countries also include six North American states (Canada, USA, Barbados, Cuba, Martinique, and Puerto Rico), four Asian states (South Korea, Japan, Singapore, and Hong Kong), as well as Australia and New Zealand, whereas no African nations had such low fertility in the decade of 1975–1985.

We examine three fundamental demographic forecast indicators: the total fertility rate (TFR), the life expectancy at birth (e_0), and the net migration rate (NMR), defined as the number of immigrants minus the number of emigrants over a period, divided by the person-years lived by the population of the receiving country over that period. We consider TFR, e_0, and NMR for the above 38 countries, comparing the actual levels reported in the 2017 Revision for the period 1980–2015 with the World Population Prospects elaborated in 1980, 1990, and 2000. We also compare the forecasted population growth rate r (a measure of population change that is strictly determined by the estimates of fertility, mortality, and migration), with the actual statistics. Rather than document the "miscalculations" of our colleagues – indeed, it would have been impossible to predict certain historical turning points such as the fall of the Berlin Wall or the collapse of the Lehman Brothers, and their demographic consequences – we aim to understand the extent to which the convergence paradigm has guided forecasters. Thus far we have seen that this hypothesis continues to prevail among those who attempt the challenge of projecting future population trends.

For each World Population Prospects Revision and indicator, we calculate the simple mean and the standard deviation (SD) of the 38 countries, for every 5-year interval between 1980–1985 and 2010–2015. An alternative procedure would have been to calculate the median and the interquartile difference, measures that have the advantage of not being affected by extreme values. While the ratio between the interquartile range and the median would be more robust, previous work (Billari 2018, p. 20, Fig. 2.3) has shown that results given by the two indexes are consistent. Median and interquartile differences are available on request. Moreover, we do not weight the country means according to population size, because we focus specifically on differences between countries as separate entities, as opposed to the proportion of world population they represent.

Finally, we use an analysis of variance (ANOVA) method to assess the proportion of total variability for the four indicators (e_0, TFR, NMR, r) explained by belonging to a given geographical cluster. Countries are grouped into seven clusters, based broadly on the United Nations Regional Groups, and a consideration of fertility trends (see also note 6). The idea being that if a process of convergence was at work during the period 1980–2017, then the differences between these country groups should be less and less relevant. More specifically, the proportion of variance between the groups' averages for the identified demographic indicators should progressively lessen.

4.4 Results: The Lack of Weak Convergence

4.4.1 Fertility

The UN Prospects Revisions of 1980 and 1990 suggest that countries having completed the fertility transition will quickly converge towards similar TFRs around 1.8–1.9. Figure 4.2 shows that over the last 30 years, for post-transitional countries, this convergence has not occurred. The SD between the TFRs of the 38 countries that had already reached a TFR of less than 2.5 during the period 1975–1985, declines slowly between 1975–1980 and 2010–2015, while the coefficient of variation

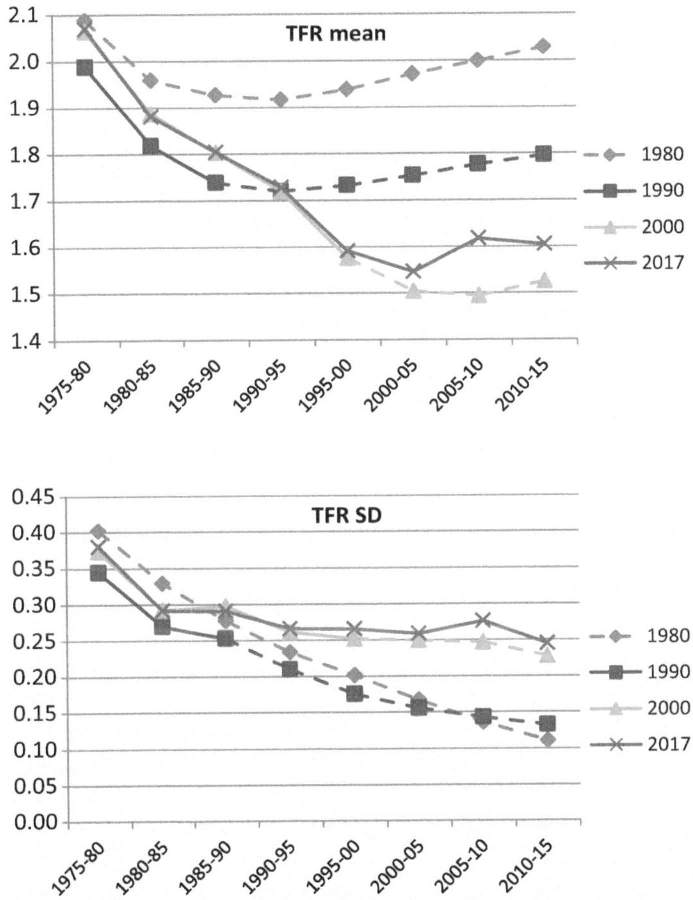

Fig. 4.2 Trends and variation in TFR among the 38 countries where TFR < 2.5 before 1985. UN Population Division: 1980, 1990, and 2000 Population Prospects, and 2017 estimation. (Source: Authors' calculation on data from the UN Population Division. World Population Prospects)

(SD/mean) drops only in the first 5-year period, and then remains almost constant between 1980 and 2015.

The level of the variability in fertility thus basically remains steady between 1980 and 2015, while according to the UN forecasts of 1980 and 1990 it should have lessened. This situation changes when comparing actual trends with the 2000 forecasts. In this case, the Population Division has accurately predicted the average fertility trends and – mainly – the variability and lack of convergence among the 38 countries. However, in light of the correctness of this forecast, it is difficult to understand why, for the following years and decades, a convergence in fertility among post-transitional countries (Fig. 4.1a and Table 4.1) should be seen as inevitable.

4.4.2 Mortality

The 1980 World Population Prospects was unsuccessful in predicting either the spectacular increase in life expectancy (8 years of life gained in just 35 years) or the persistence of profound differences between countries (Fig. 4.3). Even if the 1990 World Population Prospects predicted a convergence that would not occur, it was more cautious in suggesting further increases in average length of life. Meanwhile, the 2000 World Population Prospects – confirming the pace of e_0 increase expected in the 1990 World Population Prospects for the early years of the new century – significantly underestimated (by 2 years) the actual increase in survival, but correctly predicted the lack of convergence between countries. Again, given these results, the progressive convergence of e_0 values expected in the coming decades in the UNPD forecasts of 2017 and 2019 (Fig. 4.1b and Table 4.1) should perhaps be reconsidered.

4.4.3 Migration

Migration rates are by far the most difficult population parameters to forecast as they are more strictly related to largely unpredictable external shocks, such as economic downturns. As already seen for TFR, neither the 1980 nor 1990 World Population Prospects predicted the extent or variability of the NMR (Net Migration Rate) in the first 15 years of the new century (Fig. 4.4). In fact, not even the 2000 forecasts were able to envisage what has actually happened. While the immigration boom of the first decade of the new century and the further increase in the cross-country differences was recorded by the data collected in 2017, such shifts were entirely unforeseen in the projections made 17 years earlier.

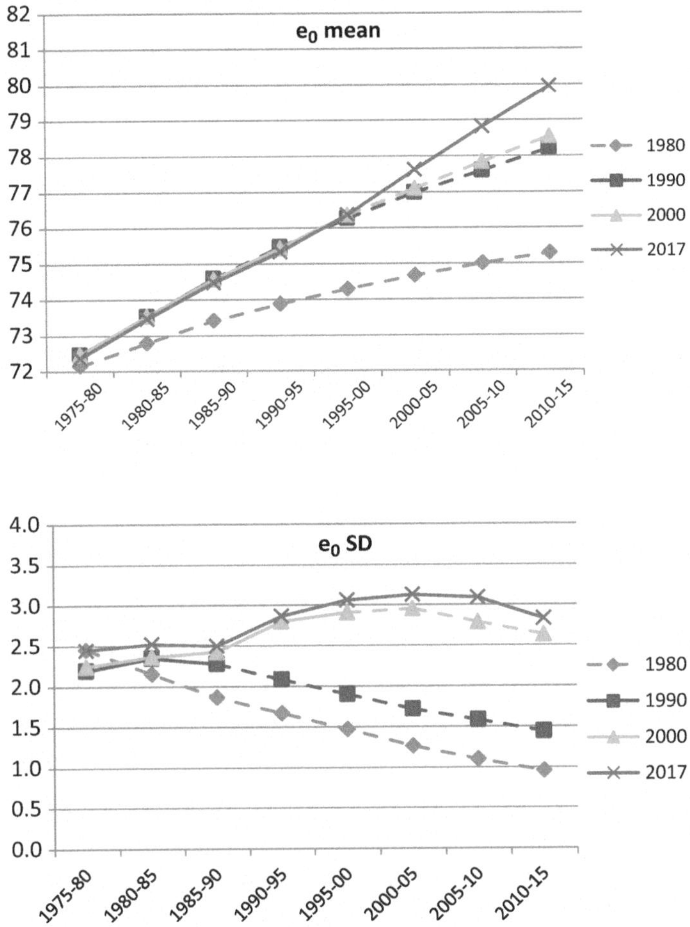

Fig. 4.3 Trends and variation of e_0 among the 38 countries where TFR < 2.5 before 1985. UN Population Division: 1980, 1990, and 2000 Population Prospects, and estimation of 2017. (Source: Authors' calculation on data from the UN Population Division. World Population Prospects)

4.4.4 Growth Rate

The combination of prediction errors of fertility, mortality, and migration significantly impacts forecasts of the population growth rate r (Fig. 4.5). The World Population Prospects of 1980, 1990, and 2000 concur in suggesting, for the first years of the twenty-first century, rapidly declining population growth rates. Yet, in 2000–2015, the growth of the entire population of the 38 post-transitional countries under analysis never dropped below 4‰. This is due in part to the rise in survival rates – with consequent greater growth in the number of elderly – but above all to the increase in the net migration rate, resulting in more young adults and, to some

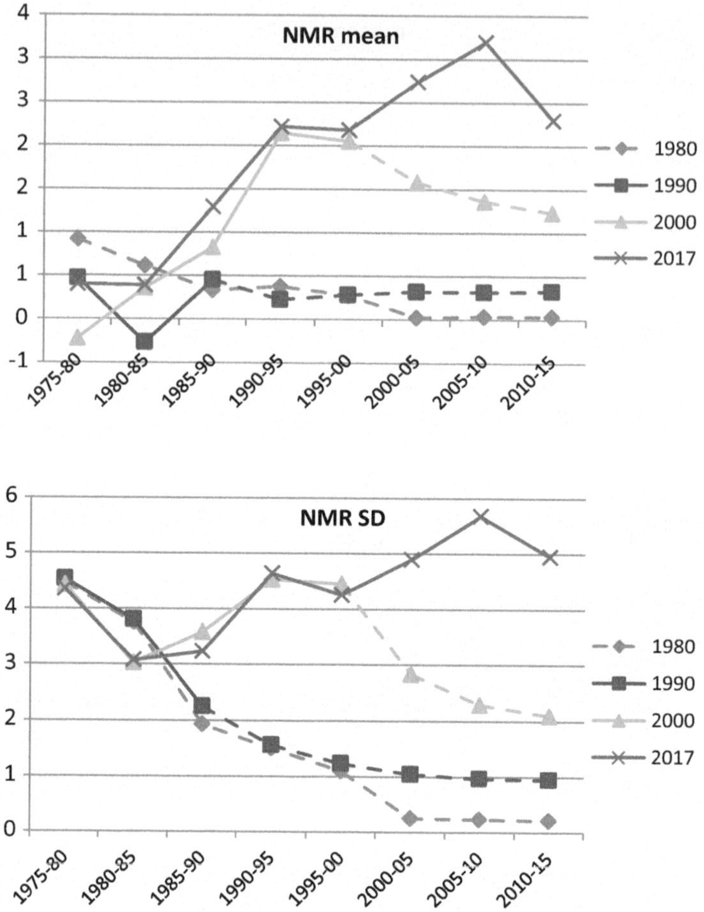

Fig. 4.4 Trends and variation of NMR (per thousand) among the 38 countries where TFR < 2.5 before 1985. UN Population Division: 1980, 1990, and 2000 Population Prospects, and estimation of 2017. (Source: Authors' calculation on data from the UN Population Division. World Population Prospects)

extent, children. The forecasts of r variability also proved to be incorrect. Contrary to that suggested by the World Population Prospects of 1980, 1990, and 2000, during the first 15 years of the new century the variability of r among the 38 countries saw higher levels than those observed during 1975–1990.

This divergence is largely due to the extremely different demography of the ex-communist bloc (i.e., negative migration rates, low fertility, and stagnation or even decrease in life expectancy) compared to that of Northern Europe and the Overseas English-speaking countries (i.e., positive migration rates, less depressed fertility, and continuous rise in life expectancy). For example, in the quarter century of 1990–

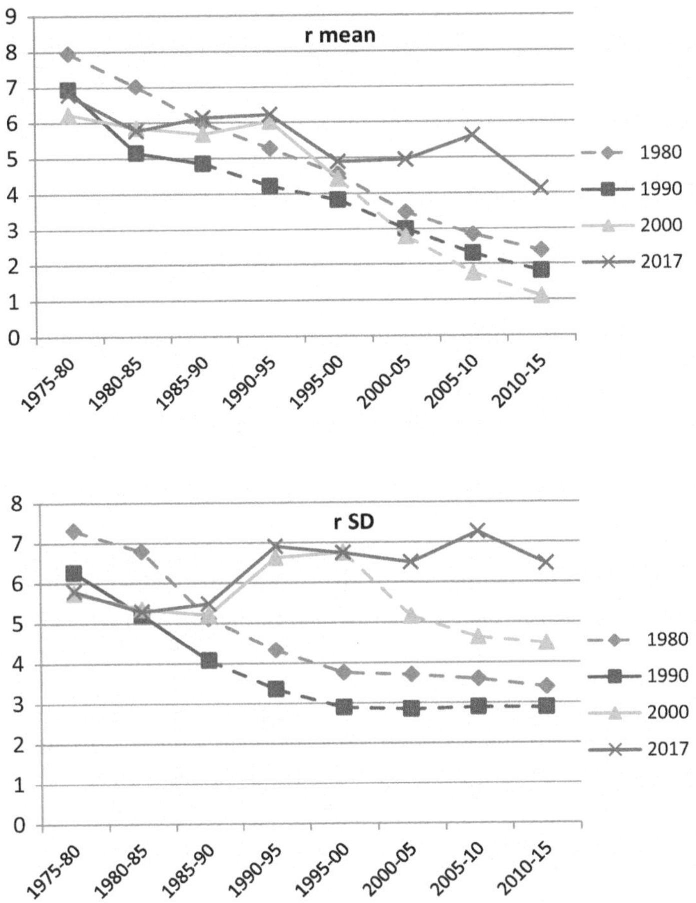

Fig. 4.5 Trends and variation of growth rate r (per thousand) among the 38 countries where TFR < 2.5 before 1985. UN Population Division: 1980, 1990, and 2000 Population Prospects, and estimation of 2017. (Source: Authors' calculation on data from the UN Population Division. World Population Prospects)

2015 the population growth rate was 5.3‰ in the USA compared to −0.2‰ in the former USSR.

4.4.5 *The ANOVA Analysis*

Table 4.2 reports the analysis of variance (ANOVA) results carried out on the estimated and forecasted values for the four indicators (e_0, TFR, NMR, r). As explained in Sect. 4.3, if there would have been convergence, then the share of variance across the seven country groups, as a percentage of the total variance, should have been decreasing. In the 2017 row for each indicator, the ANOVA is based on actual data, taken from the estimates for 1975–2015 published in the 2017 Revision. The table largely confirms the divergence in demographic trends. For mortality specifically, the proportion of variance between the seven groups on the whole variance substantially increases from 40% to 70% in the period from 1975–1980 to 2010–2015. For fertility, the trend is U-shaped, as the proportion of variance between groups decreases up until 1995 and then later increases up to around 80%. For migration, the proportion of variance between groups is less systematic, rising and falling from 1975 to 2000 and then subsequently increasing up to 53% in 2010–2015. These results show that the differences between the groups for the three indicators do not, in fact, narrow over time. Quite the opposite is true, against the hypothesis of convergence.

The other rows in Table 4.2 present the ANOVA outcomes based on the estimates and forecasts for the three indicators in 1980, 1990, and 2000.[7] The forecast results (in italics) share the characteristic of holding the variability explained by the groups nearly invariant on the value of the last 5 years observed (Table 4.2). Therefore, even if the 1980 and 1990 Revisions assumed drastic reduction in the variability of the three indicators among the 38 countries, the geographical differences should have remained constant, in relative terms. The same happens with the 2000 Revision with regard to the NMR. However, things are different in the 2000 edition in terms of TFR and e_0 forecasts for the 2000–2015 period: as seen previously in Figs. 4.2 and 4.3, the projection of variability among the 38 countries remains high, substantially similar to that which actually occurred. However, while for e_0, variability between the seven groups is correctly predicted as high and is in line with actual e_0, for TFR, the polarization of the single countries around the averages of the groups to which they belong was not foreseen.

The main lesson of this analysis is that – after the end of the Demographic Transition – not only does the variability between these countries not decrease, neither does the variability between groups of countries. Again, the notion of weak convergence is not reflected in the actual data: fertility, mortality, and migration rates do not move towards similar and undistinguishable values among the countries that have already completed the Demographic Transition.

[7]Percentages of variance for TFR, NMR and r in 1995–2000, in the rows of prospects 2000 and 2017, are surprisingly different. An explanation is different estimates of empirical indicators mainly in Cyprus, Hong Kong, Barbados, Cuba, and Martinique, based on partial availability of updated recent data.

Table 4.2 Percentage of variance among 7 groups of countries on the total variance among the 38 countries where TFR < 2.5 before 1985 (ANOVA). Variance of life expectancy, TFR, net migration rate, and population growth rate. Groups of countries by geographical area and similar fertility trend. 1980-based, 1990-based, and 2000-based Word Population Prospects, and estimation of 2017

	Proportion of variance among 7 groups on total variance							
UN population prospects	Estimated (normal) or forecasted *(italics)* 5-year periods							
	1975–1980	1980–1985	1985–1990	1990–1995	1995–2000	2000–2005	2005–2010	2010–2015
	Life expectancy							
1980	27%	*28%*	*28%*	*29%*	*29%*	*29%*	*28%*	*30%*
1990	39%	51%	57%	*58%*	*59%*	*59%*	*56%*	*57%*
2000	40%	51%	60%	69%	70%	*71%*	*71%*	*70%*
2017	40%	51%	62%	71%	71%	67%	69%	70%
	TFR							
1980	55%	*56%*	*68%*	*66%*	*62%*	*62%*	*58%*	*50%*
1990	61%	46%	44%	*46%*	*50%*	*51%*	*50%*	*48%*
2000	60%	47%	43%	23%	39%	*45%*	*47%*	*47%*
2017	58%	47%	44%	26%	46%	76%	82%	78%
	Net migration rate							
1980	11%	*8%*	*26%*	*38%*	*46%*	*15%*	*23%*	*17%*
1990	34%	34%	46%	*56%*	*52%*	*52%*	*52%*	*49%*
2000	23%	43%	47%	47%	39%	*40%*	*43%*	*42%*
2017	28%	46%	51%	43%	32%	37%	4%	53%
	Population growth rate							
1980	43%	*42%*	*57%*	*62%*	*64%*	*69%*	*66%*	*63%*
1990	50%	34%	39%	*44%*	*47%*	*46%*	*43%*	*41%*
2000	45%	46%	37%	48%	52%	*53%*	*51%*	*47%*
2017	48%	49%	36%	40%	45%	42%	40%	51%

Note: Values in normal type: estimates. In highlighted italics: forecasts
Source: Authors' calculation on data from the UN Population Division. World Population Prospects
See note 6 for more information on country groups

4.5 Concluding Remarks

The strong paradigm of the Demographic Transition has provided an exceptionally useful tool for describing a common path of demographic change among countries, and their remarkable convergence over time from a regime of high mortality and fertility to a new regime of low fertility and mortality. This well-known pattern drove forecasters to project mortality and fertility in a shared direction of transformation as modernization and economic development spread around the world.

In this chapter, however, we show that the idea of a general convergence also seems to inform the hypotheses and/or the outcome of population projections elaborated by UNPD experts for countries that have already completed their demographic transition, into what we call a "weak convergence." We demonstrate that this idea is not supported by empirical evidence: there are no unequivocal signs of a general convergence in fertility, mortality, and net migration towards common values for the 38 countries that had a TFR < 2.5 before 1985.

While this lack of convergence was correctly predicted in the 2000 Revision of World Population Prospects for mortality and fertility (but not for migration) in the period 2000–2015, the idea of convergence nonetheless seems to inform the hypotheses of UNPD forecasters in subsequent Revisions. In addition, we find that the differences between groups of countries that we identified as homogeneous actually increase between 2000 and 2015, showing a marked characterization of demographic behavior by geographical area.

In light of these results, it is difficult to understand why in the following period of 2015–2050 we should expect the 112 countries with a TFR below 2.5 children per woman in 2015 to converge towards similar values, as suggested by the 2017 Revision of World Population Prospects (Table 4.1 and Fig. 4.1). Further research is necessary to identify new regularities that can aid forecasters who have been "abandoned" by the demographic transition paradigm. The challenge is far from small as these 112 countries are even more differentiated in terms of regional characteristics, institutional settings, level of economic development, and value adherence than the initial 38.

Acknowledgement We acknowledge the contribution of the Project PRIN 2017 (n. 2017W5B55Y_003), titled "The Great Demographic Recession" (GDR).

References

Alho, J. M., & Spencer, B. D. (1985). Uncertain population forecasting. *Journal of the American Statistical Association, 80*(390), 306–314.

Anderson, T., & Kohler, H.-P. (2015). Low fertility, socioeconomic development and gender equity. *Population and Development Review, 41*(3), 381–407.

Barro, R. J., & Sala-i-Martin, X. (1992). Convergence. *The Journal of Political Economy, 100*, 223–251.

Barro, R. J., Sala-I-Martin, X., Blanchard, O. J., & Hall, R. E. (1991). Convergence across states and regions. *Brookings Papers on Economic Activity, 1991*, 107–182.

Basten, S., Sobotka, T., & Zeman, K. (2014). Future fertility in low fertility countries. In W. Lutz, W. P. Butz, & K. C. Samir (Eds.), *World population and human capital in the twenty-first century*. Oxford: Oxford University Press.

Bengtsson, T., Keilman, N., Alho, J. M., Christensen, K., Palmer, E., & Vaupel, J. W. (2019). Introduction. In T. Bengtsson & N. Keilman (Eds.), *Old and new perspectives on mortality forecasting* (Demographic research monographs (A Series of the Max Planck Institute for Demographic Research)). Cham: Springer.

Billari, F. C. (2018). Chapter 2: A "great divergence" in fertility? In D. L. Poston Jr. (Ed.), *Low fertility and regimes and demographic and societal change*. Cham: Springer International Publishing.

Bloom, D. E., & Canning, D. (2007). Mortality traps and the dynamics of health transitions. *Proceedings of the National Academy of Sciences, 104*, 16044–16049.

Bourgeois-Pichat, J. (1994). *La Dynamique des populations. Populations stables semi-stables et quasi stables* (Travaux et Documents). Paris: INED.

Calot, G., & Chesnais, J. C. (1978). La prevision démographique. In A.-C. Dans (Ed.), *Decouflé Traité élémentaire de prevision et de prospective*. Paris: PUF.

Casterline, J. B. (2001). The pace of fertility transition: National patterns in the second half of the twentieth century. *Population and Development Review, 27*(Supplement), 17–52.

Clark, R. (2011). World health inequality: Convergence, divergence and development. *Social Science and Medicine, 72*, 617–624.

Crenshaw, E. M., Christenson, M., & Oakey, D. R. (2000). Demographic transition in ecological focus. *American Sociological Review, 65*, 371–391.

Dorius, S. F. (2008). Global demographic convergence? A reconsideration of changing intercountry inequality in fertility. *Population and Development Review, 34*(3), 519–537.

Goesling, B., & Firebaugh, G. (2004). The trend in international health inequality. *Population and Development Review, 30*, 131–146.

Henry, L. (1987). Perspectives et prévision. In *Les projections démographiques. Actes du VIIIe Colloque National de Démographie (Tome 1)* (Traveaux et Documents Cahier no. 116). Paris: Presses Universitaires de France.

Keilman, N. (1997). Ex-post errors in official population forecasts in industrialized countries. *Journal of Official Statistics, 13*, 245–277.

Keilman, N. (1998). How accurate are the United Nations world population projections? *Population and Development Review, 24*(Supplement), 15–41.

Keilman, N. (2000). Précision et incertitudes des prévisions nationales de population. In C. Wattelar & J. Duchêne (Eds.), *Le défi de l'incertitude: Nouvelles approches en perspectives et prospective démographiques. Actes de la Chaire Quetelet 1995* (pp. 33–67). Louvain-la-Neuve: Academia-Bruylant/L'Harmattan.

Keilman, N. (2001). Data quality and accuracy of United Nations population projections, 1950-95. *Population Studies, 55*(2), 149–164.

Keilman, N. (2019). Erroneous population forecast. In T. Bengtsson & N. Keilman (Eds.), *Old and new perspectives on mortality forecasting, demographic research monographs* (A series of the Max Planck Institute for Demographic Research). Cham: Springer.

Keilman, N., & Pham, D. Q. (2004). *Empirical errors and predicted errors in fertility, mortality and migration forecasts in the European economic area* (Discussion Paper 386). Oslo: Statistics Norway.

Keyfitz, N. (1981). The limits of population forecasting. *Population and Development Review, 7*, 579–593.

Kirk, D. (1996). Demographic transition theory. *Population Studies, 50*(3), 361–387.

Kohler, H.-P., Billari, F., & Ortega, J. A. (2002). The emergence of lowest-Loe fertility in Europe during the 1990s. *Population and Development Review, 28*(4), 641–680.

Lee, R. D. (1998). Probabilistic approaches to population forecasting. *Population and Development Review, 24*, 156–190.

Livi Bacci, M. (2012). *A concise history of world population*. Chichester: Wiley-Blackwell.
Lutz, W., Skirbekk, V., & Testa, M. R. (2006). The low-fertility trap hypothesis: Forces that may lead to further postponement and fewer births in Europe. *Vienna Yearbook of Population Research, 4*, 167–192.
McMichael, A., McKee, M., Shkolnikov, V. M., & Valkonen, T. (2004). Mortality trends and setbacks: Global convergence or divergence? *The Lancet, 363*, 1155–1159.
Moser, K., Shkolnikov, V. M., & Leon, D. A. (2005). World mortality 1950-2000: Divergence replaces convergence from the late 1980s. *Bulletin of the World Health Organization, 83*(3), 202–209.
National Research Council 2000. (2000). Beyond six billion: Forecasting the world's population. Panel on population projections. In J. Bongaarts & R. Bulatao (Eds.), *Committee on population, commission on behavioral and social sciences and education*. Washington, DC: National Academy Press. Available at http://books.nap.edu/books/0309069904/html/index.html.
Neumayer, E. (2004). HIV/AIDS and cross-national convergence in life expectancy. *Population and Development Review, 30*, 727–742.
Pflaumer, P. (1988). The accuracy of U.N. population projections. In *Proceedings annual meeting American statistical association, New Orleans, August 1988*. Social Statistics Section, 299–304.
Preston, S. (1974). An evaluation of postwar mortality projections in Australia, Canada, Japan, New Zealand, and the United States. *WHO Statistical Report, 27*, 719–745.
Raftery, A. E., Li, N., Ševčíková, H., Gerland, P., & Heilig, G. K. (2012). Bayesian probabilistic population projections for all countries. *Proceedings of the National Academy of Sciences, 109*(35), 13915–13921.
Raftery, A. E., Alkema, L., & Gerland, P. (2014). Bayesian population projections for the united Nations. *Statistical Science, 29*, 58–68.
Reher, D. S. (1998). Family ties in Western Europe: Persistent contrasts. *Population and Development Review, 24*(2), 203–234.
Reher, D. S. (2004). The demographic transition revisited as a global process. *Population, Space and Place, 10*, 19–41.
Reher, D. S. (2011). Economic and social implications of the demographic transition. In R. D. Lee & D. S. Reher (Eds.), *Demographic transition and its consequences* (Supplement to Vol. 37 of Population and Development Review). New York: Population Council.
Reher, D. R. (2019). The Aftermath of the demographic transition in the developed world: Interpreting enduring disparities in reproductive behavior. *Population and Development Review*. On-line, 26 June 2019. https://doi.org/10.1111/padr.12266.
Reher, D. S. (2019). The Aftermath of the demographic transition in the developed world: Interpreting enduring disparities in reproductive behaviour. *Population and Development Review*. On-line, 26 June 2019. https://doi.org/10.1111/padr.12266.
Rindfuss, R. R., & Choe, M. K. (Eds.). (2015). *Low and lower fertility: Variations across developed countries*. Cham: Springer.
Rindfuss, R. R., & Choe, M. K. (Eds.). (2016). *Low fertility, institutions and their policies: Variations across industrialized countries*. Cham: Springer.
Rindfuss, R. R., Choe, M. K., & Brauner-Otto, S. R. (2016). The emergence of two distinct fertility regimes in economically advanced countries. *Population Research and Policy Review, 35*(3), 287–304.
Sala-i-Martin, X. (1996). The classical approach to convergence analysis. *The Economic Journal, 106*, 1019–1036.
Sobotka, T. (2017). Post-transitional fertility: The role of childbearing postponement in Fuelling the shift to low and unstable fertility levels. *Journal of Biosocial Science, 49*(S1), S20–S45. https://doi.org/10.1017/S0021932017000323.
Sobotka, T., Matysiak, A., & Brzozowska, Z. (2017). Gender revolution, family reversal and fertility, paper presented at IUSSP Population Conference, Cape Town, November 2017.
Stoto, M. (1983). The accuracy of population projections. *Journal of the American Statistical Association, 78*, 13–20.

Thornton, A. (2001). The developmental paradigm, Reading history sideways, and family change. *Demography, 38*(4), 449–467.

United Nations, Department of Economic and Social Affairs, Population Division (2014). *World Population Prospects: The 2012 Revision*, Methodology of the United Nations Population Estimates and Projections. ESA/P/WP.235. New York: United Nations.

United Nations, Department of Economic and Social Affairs, Population Division (2017). *World Population Prospects: The 2017 Revision, Methodology of the United Nations Population Estimates and Projections*, Working Paper No. ESA/P/WP.250. New York: United Nations.

Wilson, C. (2001). On the scale of global demographic convergence 1950–2000. *Population and Development Review, 27*(1), 155–171.

Wilson, C. (2011). Understanding global demographic convergence since 1950. *Population and Development Review, 37*(2), 375–388. https://doi.org/10.1111/j.17284457.2011.00415.x.

Wilson, C. (2013). Thinking about post-transitional demographic regimes: A reflection. *Demographic Research, 28*, 1373–1388.

Chapter 5
Projecting Proportionate Age–Specific Fertility Rates via Bayesian Skewed Processes

Emanuele Aliverti, Daniele Durante, and Bruno Scarpa

5.1 Introduction

There is an extensive interest on models for fertility rates in statistics and demography (Hoem et al. 1981; Scarpa 2014). Several approaches have demonstrated a satisfactory fit for age–specific fertility rates via standard routine formulations such as the Hadwiger model (Hadwiger 1940), the Gompertz model (Murphy and Nagnur 1972) and the Gamma model (Hoem et al. 1981). These analyses have led to important insights on relevant population patterns and on how education, fertility control and marriage practices have played a key role in determining the shapes of fertility curves (Rindfuss et al. 1996; Billari and Kohler 2004). However, recent studies on developed countries have observed that age–specific fertility rates require more flexible models which are able to capture both symmetric and asymmetric patterns (Mazzuco and Scarpa 2015; Peristera and Kostaki 2007; Chandola et al. 1999).

Electronic Supplementary Material The online version of this chapter (https://doi.org/10.1007/978-3-030-42472-5_5) contains supplementary material, which is available to authorized users.

E. Aliverti (✉)
Department of Statistical Sciences, University of Padova, Padova, Italy
e-mail: aliverti@stat.unipd.it

D. Durante
Department of Decision Sciences and Bocconi Institute for Data Science and Analytics, Bocconi University, Milan, Italy
e-mail: daniele.durante@unibocconi.it

B. Scarpa
Department of Statistical Sciences and Department of Mathematics "Tullio Levi-Civita", University of Padova, Padova, Italy
e-mail: scarpa@stat.unipd.it

S. Mazzuco, N. Keilman (eds.), *Developments in Demographic Forecasting*, The Springer Series on Demographic Methods and Population Analysis 49,
https://doi.org/10.1007/978-3-030-42472-5_5

The above findings have stimulated new research questions and the development of more flexible statistical models which are able to adequately describe these non–standard shapes and characterize their dynamic evolution. Recent approaches include models relying on mixtures of symmetric distributions (Peristera and Kostaki 2007; Bermúdez et al. 2012), smoothing splines (Schmertmann 2003) and skewed distributions (Mazzuco and Scarpa 2015), with some parametric assumptions sometimes relaxed via nonparametric alternatives (Kostaki et al. 2009; Canale and Scarpa 2015). Clearly, the improved fit of these models comes at a price in terms of interpretability. For example, smoothing splines generally provide an excellent fit, but interpretation of the parameters is difficult (Hoem et al. 1981; Peristera and Kostaki 2007). Besides this, few attention has been devoted to forecasts. In fact, until 2011, most demographic projections were based on deterministic predictions of fertility rates produced by the World Population Prospect report of the United Nations (Lutz and Samir 2010). In these forecasts, potential variability is only included via low and high fertility scenarios obtained by manipulating the Total Fertility Rates' (TFR) projections (Alkema et al. 2011; Raftery et al. 2013). However, such an approach does not properly quantify predictive uncertainty, and the extent to which these low or high level scenarios are realistic is still an open question (Alkema et al. 2011).

More recently, United Nations and other agencies have started moving to probabilistic approaches for population forecasting. However, in most of the cases, only summary indicators such as TFR and life expectancy at birth (e_0) are stochastically projected. This means that, in a cohort–component perspective, these indicators have to be converted into age–specific—fertility or mortality—rates, in order to project the population counts. A naive solution would be to assume a standard age schedule that is applied for every year, but this strategy has two major drawbacks. First, it has been shown that mean, variance and even skewness of the age schedule of fertility are not fixed, but time–varying (Mazzuco and Scarpa 2015; Keilman and Pham 2000). Second, in this way a component of uncertainty is missing, whereas we would like to incorporate in our forecasts the uncertainty due to varying age schedules (Ediev 2013).

Motivated by the above considerations, recent approaches for probabilistic forecasting have focused on Bayesian hierarchical models (Alkema et al. 2011; Raftery et al. 2013, 2014; Ševčíková et al. 2016). These methods aim at projecting TFR and life expectancies at birth, while deriving related quantities—such as the age–specific fertility rates—via Markov chain Monte Carlo (MCMC) (Alkema et al. 2011; Ševčíková et al. 2016). Indeed, Bayesian models facilitate probabilistic forecasts via posterior predictive distributions, and incorporate uncertainty in estimation and prediction. For high and medium fertility countries, the proposal to project age schedules of fertility consists in a linear interpolation among a starting fertility age pattern and a target model chosen among different possible age schedules of fertility (Ševčíková et al. 2016). For low fertility countries, it is assumed that a target model will be reached by 2025–2030. Such assumptions are coherent with the United Nations population forecasts, in which both fertility and mortality levels of all countries are assumed to eventually converge to a global value. However, in single population forecasting settings, it is preferable to use a more data–driven approach, without considering target schedules.

In this contribution we propose a Bayesian dynamic model for *proportionate* age–specific fertility rates (PASFRS)—i.e. the age–specific fertility rates divided by the TFR to obtain values summing up to one. Our goal is to provide a parsimonious, yet flexible, representation of PASFRS based on densities of skew–normal variables with moments evolving in time via flexible Gaussian process priors. Such a specification allows to model proportionate age–specific fertility rates across different years via a skewed process, and to characterize their temporal evolution flexibly, while quantifying the uncertainty in estimation and prediction. We refer to our Bayesian skewed processes as BSP. Unlike available Bayesian solutions, BSP provides a direct model for PASFRS, thus allowing to define the entire distribution of these quantities across all the ages, while characterizing its dynamic evolution over time.

5.2 Bayesian Skewed Process

A fertility curve defines the fertility rates at each age or age group y—i.e. the annual number of births to women of a specified age or age group y per woman in that age group. Following Hoem et al. (1981), such a function may be written as

$$g(y; R, \theta_2, \ldots, \theta_r) = R \cdot f(y; \theta_2, \ldots, \theta_r), \tag{5.1}$$

where R is the TFR, i.e. the expected number of children born per woman in her fertile window, and $f(\cdot; \theta_2, \ldots, \theta_r)$ is a density function characterizing the PASFRS. Such a choice ensures that for any set of valid parameters $(\theta_2, \ldots, \theta_r)$ the PASFRS are positive and integrate to one without further constraints on the $r-1$ parameters and in the observed data (Bergeron-Boucher et al. 2017), thus facilitating estimation and inference. In this contribution, our main goal is to provide flexible, yet interpretable, models and inference procedures for $f(\cdot; \theta_2, \ldots, \theta_r)$ rather than $g(\cdot; R, \theta_2, \ldots, \theta_r)$. We shall, however, emphasize that when the interest is on learning the total fertility curve in equation (5.1), our approach can be easily combined with a Bayesian updating for the posterior distribution of R, thereby inducing a full posterior on $g(\cdot; R, \theta_2, \ldots, \theta_r)$.

Several specifications of $f(\cdot; \theta_2, \ldots, \theta_r)$ are illustrated in Hoem et al. (1981) leveraging the Hadwiger (inverse–Gaussian), Gamma, Beta, Coale–Trussell, Brass and Gompertz densities. Other formulations have been suggested by Peristera and Kostaki (2007), Bermúdez et al. (2012), Schmertmann (2003), and Chandola et al. (1999). More recently, Mazzuco and Scarpa (2015) proposed to use a generalization of the normal distribution, known as skew–normal, to fit age–specific fertility rates. Such a distribution is denoted as $y \sim \text{SN}(\xi, \omega, \alpha)$ and has density function equal to

$$f(y; \xi, \omega, \alpha) = 2\omega^{-1}\phi[\omega^{-1}(y-\xi)]\Phi[\alpha\omega^{-1}(y-\xi)], \tag{5.2}$$

where $\phi(\cdot)$ and $\Phi(\cdot)$ denote the density function and cumulative distribution function of the standard normal distribution, respectively, while $\xi \in \mathbb{R}$, $\omega \in \mathbb{R}_+$ and $\alpha \in \mathbb{R}$ represent the location, scale and skewness parameters. While direct interpretation of these parameters might be difficult, the first two moments of the skew-normal distribution have simple analytical expressions. In particular, the expectation of the random variable y is

$$\mathrm{E}(y) = \xi + \omega\delta\sqrt{2/\pi}, \tag{5.3}$$

whereas its variance is

$$\mathrm{var}(y) = \omega^2(1 - 2\delta^2/\pi), \tag{5.4}$$

with $\delta = \alpha(1+\alpha^2)^{-1/2}$ (Azzalini and Capitanio 2013). The properties of the skew–normal in equation (5.2) have been studied by Azzalini (1985) and other authors. One interesting feature is that, when $\alpha = 0$, equation (5.2) reduces to the density of a normal, thus allowing inclusion of both asymmetric ($\alpha \neq 0$) and symmetric ($\alpha = 0$) shapes in modeling the PASFRS via (5.2).[1] Indeed, Mazzuco and Scarpa (2015) have shown that in Italy the fertility schedule function has moved from a skewed to a symmetric shape.

Motivated by these considerations, we model PASFRS via a time–varying version of (5.2) and, taking a Bayesian approach, we allow flexible changes in this curve via suitable priors for its dynamic parameters ξ_t, ω_t and α_t. In this way, we define a new Bayesian skewed process, which allows forecasting of future PASFRS. As already mentioned, there is an abundance of models for forecasting of TFRs, while a coherent approach for PASFRs is still lacking. The method proposed in this chapter takes a first step toward addressing this important goal.

5.2.1 *Model Specification*

For every year $t = 1, \ldots, T$ and mother $i = 1, \ldots, n_t$, our data consist in artificial random samples of n_t women at the age of childbirth, where y_{it} represents the age of the i-th mother in year t. These artificial data are obtained by sampling, for each year t, a total of n_t age values from a discrete random variable with the proportionate age–specific fertility rates as probabilities, thereby obtaining a synthetic cohort generated by the dynamic PASFRS. As clarified in Sect. 5.3, the choice to rely on synthetic data is due to the computational intractability that would arise under BSP if the focus were on the full population. In fact, Bayesian inference under BSP requires sampling methods for multivariate truncated normals of dimension

[1]Common specifications, such as Hadwiger, Gamma, Gompertz, cannot assume a symmetric shape.

$\sum_{t=1}^{T} n_t$. Nonetheless, we will consider a sufficiently large n_t to allow efficient learning of the model parameters.

To further motivate the above construction, suppose that interest is on estimating how a fixed number of births n_t is distributed across the different ages, while the total intensity of fertility is kept fixed. This problem can be tackled via a multinomial distribution with cell counts corresponding to the number of mothers with a specific age, and a probability of falling in the k-th class (age equal to y_k) being proportional to $f(y_k; \xi, \omega, \alpha)$—the PASFR. Sampling from this hypothetical multinomial model is statistically equivalent to sampling from the discrete distribution mentioned above. Hence, the observed rates are effectively treated as data by our approach, and the uncertainty in the estimated parameters regulating the shape of PASFR will be fully incorporated via the posterior distribution, under our Bayesian approach to inference.

The aforementioned procedure allows to define a genuine likelihood based on a skew-normal specification. In fact, recalling the discussion in Sect. 5.2, we assume that each y_{it} has a skew–normal distribution with location ξ_t, scale ω_t and skewness parameter α_t, thereby obtaining

$$(y_{it} \mid \xi_t, \omega_t, \alpha_t) \sim \text{SN}(\xi_t, \omega_t, \alpha_t), \tag{5.5}$$

independently for each $i = 1, \ldots, n_t$ and $t = 1, \ldots, T$. Following a Bayesian approach to inference, we specify prior distributions for the parameters $\boldsymbol{\xi} = (\xi_1, \ldots, \xi_T)^\intercal \in \mathbb{R}^T$, $\boldsymbol{\omega} = (\omega_1, \ldots, \omega_T)^\intercal \in \mathbb{R}_+^T$ and $\boldsymbol{\alpha} = (\alpha_1, \ldots, \alpha_T)^\intercal \in \mathbb{R}^T$ in (5.5) to incorporate temporal interdependence across the fertility rates observed in the different years. Such priors can be seen as distributions quantifying experts' uncertainty in the model parameters, and the goal of Bayesian learning is to update such quantities in the light of the observed data to obtain a posterior distribution which is used for inference.

To address the above goal, while maintaining computational tractability, we specify independent Gaussian process (GP) priors (Rasmussen and Williams 2006), with squared exponential covariance functions, for the location and skewness parameters, thus obtaining

$$\boldsymbol{\xi}=(\xi_1, \ldots, \xi_T)^\intercal \sim \text{N}_T(\boldsymbol{\mu}_\xi, \boldsymbol{\Sigma}_\xi) \text{ and } \boldsymbol{\alpha}=(\alpha_1, \ldots, \alpha_T)^\intercal \sim \text{N}_T(\boldsymbol{\mu}_\alpha, \boldsymbol{\Sigma}_\alpha), \tag{5.6}$$

for any time grid $t=1, \ldots, T$, where $[\boldsymbol{\mu}_\xi]_j = m_\xi(t_j)$, $[\boldsymbol{\Sigma}_\xi]_{jl} = \exp(-\kappa_\xi ||t_j - t_l||_2^2)$, $[\boldsymbol{\mu}_\alpha]_j = m_\alpha(t_j)$, and $[\boldsymbol{\Sigma}_\alpha]_{jl} = \exp(-\kappa_\alpha ||t_j - t_l||_2^2)$. Note also that $m_\xi(\cdot)$ and $m_\alpha(\cdot)$ denote pre–selected GP mean functions, whereas the covariances in $\boldsymbol{\Sigma}_\xi$ and $\boldsymbol{\Sigma}_\alpha$ are specified so as to decrease with the time lag. Refer to Rasmussen and Williams (2006) for additional details on Gaussian processes. The priors for the square of the scale parameters ω_t, $t = 1, \ldots, T$ are instead specified as independent Inverse–Gamma distributions

$$\omega_t^2 \sim \text{Inv–Gamma}(a_\omega, b_\omega), \quad t = 1, \ldots, T. \tag{5.7}$$

Although the prior in equation (5.7) does not allow for explicit temporal dependence across different values of the scale parameters, we stress that the skewness parameters α_t and the locations ξ_t have a central role in controlling the mean and the variance of the random variable y_{it}, as outlined in equations (5.3) and (5.4). Hence, the GP priors in (5.6) induce temporal dependence also in the expectation and in the variance of the variable y_{it}, and are arguably sufficient to characterize its main dynamic evolution.

5.2.2 *Joint Likelihood and Posterior Distribution for* $\boldsymbol{\alpha}$

Assume, for the moment, that the parameters ξ_t and ω_t are fixed at $\xi_t = 0$ and $\omega_t = 1$ for each $t = 1, \ldots, T$. The focus of this simplifying assumption is to illustrate the key steps to obtain the joint posterior distribution for the vector $\boldsymbol{\alpha}$ induced by a Gaussian prior and the model (5.5). Recently, Canale et al. (2016) showed that the posterior distribution from a Gaussian prior combined with a skew–normal likelihood is an unified skew–normal (SUN) distribution, which is a family of distributions that includes the skew–normal one (Arellano-Valle and Azzalini 2006). In the following paragraph, we illustrate the multivariate extension of such a result, focusing on the analytical form of the resulting posterior distribution and its associated parameters.

For simplicity of exposition suppose, without loss of generality, that $n_t = n$ for $t = 1, \ldots, T$ and let $\mathbf{y}_t = (y_{1t}, \ldots, y_{nt})^\intercal$. Then, incorporating the above assumptions, the likelihood for $\boldsymbol{\alpha}$ induced by model (5.5) is

$$L(\boldsymbol{\alpha}) = \prod_{t=1}^{T}\prod_{i=1}^{n} 2\phi(y_{it})\Phi(\alpha_t y_{it}) \propto \prod_{t=1}^{T} \Phi_n(\alpha_t \mathbf{y}_t; \mathbf{I}_n) = \Phi_{nT}(\mathbf{Y}\boldsymbol{\alpha}; \mathbf{I}_{nT}), \quad (5.8)$$

where $\Phi_{nT}(\mathbf{Y}\boldsymbol{\alpha}; \mathbf{I}_{nT})$ is the cumulative distribution function of a nT–variate Gaussian with identity covariance matrix evaluated at $\mathbf{Y}\boldsymbol{\alpha}$. In (5.8), $\mathbf{Y}$ corresponds to a data matrix of dimension $nT \times T$ such that $\mathbf{Y}\boldsymbol{\alpha} = (y_{11}\alpha_1, y_{21}\alpha_1, \ldots, y_{it}\alpha_t, \ldots, y_{nT}\alpha_T)^\intercal$. Such a representation is useful to express the argument of $\Phi_{nT}(\cdot)$ in equation (5.8) as a linear term in $\boldsymbol{\alpha}$. The posterior distribution for $\boldsymbol{\alpha}$ is obtained combining the skew–normal likelihood in equation (5.8) with the Gaussian process prior. Formally, by applying the Bayes rule, we obtain $f(\boldsymbol{\alpha} \mid \mathbf{y}_1, \ldots, \mathbf{y}_T) \propto \phi_T(\boldsymbol{\alpha} - \boldsymbol{\mu}_\alpha; \boldsymbol{\Sigma}_\alpha)\Phi_{nT}(\mathbf{Y}\boldsymbol{\alpha}; \mathbf{I}_{nT})$, with

$$\begin{aligned} &\phi_T(\boldsymbol{\alpha} - \boldsymbol{\mu}_\alpha; \boldsymbol{\Sigma}_\alpha)\Phi_{nT}(\mathbf{Y}\boldsymbol{\alpha}; \mathbf{I}_{nT}) \\ &= \phi_T(\boldsymbol{\alpha} - \boldsymbol{\mu}_\alpha; \boldsymbol{\Sigma}_\alpha)\Phi_{nT}(\mathbf{s}^{-1}\mathbf{Y}\boldsymbol{\mu}_\alpha + \mathbf{s}^{-1}\mathbf{Y}(\boldsymbol{\alpha} - \boldsymbol{\mu}_\alpha); \mathbf{s}^{-2}), \end{aligned} \quad (5.9)$$

where $\mathbf{s} = \text{diag}[(\mathbf{Y}_1^\intercal \boldsymbol{\Sigma}_\alpha \mathbf{Y}_1 + 1)^{1/2}, \ldots, (\mathbf{Y}_{nT}^\intercal \boldsymbol{\Sigma}_\alpha \mathbf{Y}_{nT} + 1)^{1/2}]$. Recalling recent results in Durante (2019), equation (5.9) corresponds to the kernel of a SUN distribution. Specifically,

$$(\boldsymbol{\alpha} \mid \mathbf{y}_1, \ldots, \mathbf{y}_T) \sim \mathrm{SUN}_{T,nT}(\boldsymbol{\mu}_\alpha, \boldsymbol{\Sigma}_\alpha, \bar{\boldsymbol{\Sigma}}_\alpha \boldsymbol{\sigma}_\alpha \mathbf{Y}^\intercal \mathbf{s}^{-1}, \mathbf{s}^{-1}\mathbf{Y}\boldsymbol{\mu}_\alpha, \mathbf{s}^{-1}(\mathbf{Y}\boldsymbol{\Sigma}_\alpha \mathbf{Y}^\intercal + \mathbf{I}_{nT})\mathbf{s}^{-1}), \tag{5.10}$$

with $\bar{\boldsymbol{\Sigma}}_\alpha$ a full-rank correlation matrix such that $\boldsymbol{\Sigma}_\alpha = \boldsymbol{\sigma}_\alpha \bar{\boldsymbol{\Sigma}}_\alpha \boldsymbol{\sigma}_\alpha$. Complete algebraic derivations to obtain the above result are extensively described in Durante (2019, Theorem 1).

5.3 Posterior Computation

In the general setting, where $\boldsymbol{\xi}$ and $\boldsymbol{\omega}$ are unknown, the joint posterior for $(\boldsymbol{\xi}, \boldsymbol{\omega}, \boldsymbol{\alpha})$ does not admit a closed–form expression, and, hence, it is necessary to rely on MCMC methods. Here, we propose a Metropolis–within–Gibbs algorithm which combines the results in the previous section and other SUN properties to iteratively sample values from the full–conditionals of $\boldsymbol{\xi}$, $\boldsymbol{\omega}$ and $\boldsymbol{\alpha}$. In doing so, MCMC builds on a Markov chain which produces realizations from the posterior distribution $f(\boldsymbol{\xi}, \boldsymbol{\omega}, \boldsymbol{\alpha} \mid \mathbf{y}_1, \ldots, \mathbf{y}_T)$ after convergence (Gelfand and Smith 1990). A sufficiently large sample of values simulated from the joint posterior distribution is then used to make inference on functionals of the parameters via standard Monte Carlo integration (Casella and George 1992).

Given the current values of $\boldsymbol{\xi}$ and $\boldsymbol{\omega}$, the full–conditional for $\boldsymbol{\alpha}$ can be obtained via minor modifications of the results in the previous section. Indeed, if ξ_t and ω_t are known, the contribution of the generic y_{it} to the likelihood for $\boldsymbol{\alpha}$ is proportional to $\Phi[\alpha_t(y_{it} - \xi_t)/\omega_t] = \Phi(\alpha_t \bar{y}_{it})$. Hence, replacing each y_{it} with $\bar{y}_{it} = (y_{it} - \xi_t)/\omega_t$ in (5.8)–(5.9), the SUN full-conditional for $(\boldsymbol{\alpha} \mid \mathbf{y}_1, \ldots, \mathbf{y}_T, \boldsymbol{\xi}, \boldsymbol{\omega}) = (\boldsymbol{\alpha} \mid \bar{\mathbf{y}}_1, \ldots, \bar{\mathbf{y}}_T)$ has the same form of (5.10), with $\mathbf{Y}$ replaced by $\bar{\mathbf{Y}}$. To effectively use this result in a Metropolis–within–Gibbs algorithm, it is necessary to simulate from the distribution defined in equation (5.10). The following Lemma describes a constructive procedure for simulating from a SUN. See Azzalini and Capitanio (2013) and Durante (2019) for a formal proof.

Lemma 1 *If the full-conditional distribution for the skewness parameters comprising* $\boldsymbol{\alpha}$ *is* $(\boldsymbol{\alpha} \mid -) \sim \mathrm{SUN}_{T,nT}(\boldsymbol{\mu}_\alpha, \boldsymbol{\Sigma}_\alpha, \bar{\boldsymbol{\Sigma}}_\alpha \boldsymbol{\sigma}_\alpha \bar{\mathbf{Y}}^\intercal \bar{\mathbf{s}}^{-1}, \bar{\mathbf{s}}^{-1}\bar{\mathbf{Y}}\boldsymbol{\mu}_\alpha, \bar{\mathbf{s}}^{-1}(\bar{\mathbf{Y}}\boldsymbol{\Sigma}_\alpha \bar{\mathbf{Y}}^\intercal + \mathbf{I}_{nT})\bar{\mathbf{s}}^{-1})$, *then*

$$(\boldsymbol{\alpha} \mid -) \stackrel{\mathrm{d}}{=} \boldsymbol{\mu}_\alpha + \boldsymbol{\Sigma}_\alpha[\mathbf{V}_0 + \bar{\mathbf{Y}}^\intercal(\bar{\mathbf{Y}}\boldsymbol{\Sigma}_\alpha \bar{\mathbf{Y}}^\intercal + \mathbf{I}_{nT})^{-1}\bar{\mathbf{s}}\mathbf{V}_1],$$

with $\mathbf{V}_0 \sim \mathrm{N}_T(\mathbf{0}, \boldsymbol{\Sigma}_\alpha^{-1} - \bar{\mathbf{Y}}^\intercal(\bar{\mathbf{Y}}\boldsymbol{\Sigma}_\alpha \bar{\mathbf{Y}}^\intercal + \mathbf{I}_{nT})^{-1}\bar{\mathbf{Y}})$ *denoting a multivariate Gaussian and* $\mathbf{V}_1 \sim \mathrm{TN}_{nT}[-\bar{\mathbf{s}}^{-1}\bar{\mathbf{Y}}\boldsymbol{\mu}_\alpha, \mathbf{0}, \bar{\mathbf{s}}^{-1}(\bar{\mathbf{Y}}\boldsymbol{\Sigma}_\alpha \bar{\mathbf{Y}}^\intercal + \mathbf{I}_{nT})\bar{\mathbf{s}}^{-1}]$ *corresponding to a* nT*–variate Gaussian distribution with zero mean, covariance matrix* $\bar{\mathbf{s}}^{-1}(\bar{\mathbf{Y}}\boldsymbol{\Sigma}_\alpha \bar{\mathbf{Y}}^\intercal + \mathbf{I}_{nT})\bar{\mathbf{s}}^{-1}$, *and truncation below* $-\bar{\mathbf{s}}^{-1}\bar{\mathbf{Y}}\boldsymbol{\mu}_\alpha$.

Simulation from the SUN full–conditional distribution defined in Lemma 1 requires to sample from a nT–variate truncated Gaussian, which is very demanding for large values of nT. Recent developments in this direction involve slice sampling

(Liechty and Lu 2010) or Hamiltonian Monte Carlo (Pakman and Paninski 2014), with minimax tilting being the most efficient routine in moderate dimensions (Botev 2017). Despite these improved approaches, independent sampling from multivariate truncated Gaussian vectors is still unpractical when the dimension is greater than a few hundreds (Botev 2017). In these situations, Gibbs–sampling from sub–blocks of $\mathbf{V_1}$ provides an appealing solution (Chopin 2011), since multivariate truncated Gaussians are closed under conditioning (Horrace 2005), and sampling of sub–blocks of moderate size—e.g., around 50—can be done efficiently via minimax tilting (Botev 2017).

To obtain conjugacy in the full–conditional for the locations $\boldsymbol{\xi}$, we rely instead on the additive representation of the skew–normal distribution. Indeed, as a particular case of Lemma 1, we recall that if $z \sim \mathrm{N}(0, 1)$ and $w \sim \mathrm{N}(0, 1)$ independently, then $y = \xi + \omega[\delta|z| + (1-\delta^2)^{1/2}w] \sim \mathrm{SN}(\xi, \omega, \alpha)$, with $\alpha = \delta(1-\delta^2)^{-1/2}$. Hence, it is possible to recast the skew–normal likelihood in terms of a conditional Gaussian likelihood, given a set of latent variables z_{it}. More specifically, if y_{it} is marginally distributed as a $\mathrm{SN}(\xi_t, \omega_t, \alpha_t)$, by introducing latent observations z_{it}, we obtain

$$z_{it} \sim \mathrm{TN}_1(0, 0, 1) \text{ and } (y_{it} \mid z_{it}) \sim \mathrm{N}[\xi_t + \omega_t\delta_t z_{it}, \omega_t^2(1-\delta_t^2)],$$

with $\delta_t = \alpha_t(1+\alpha_t^2)^{-1/2}$, thereby allowing conditionally conjugate updates for $\boldsymbol{\xi}$ and a simple Metropolis step for $\boldsymbol{\omega}$. The complete Metropolis–within–Gibbs sampler algorithm for posterior computation iterates among the steps outlined below. Refer to the Appendix for detailed derivations.

[1] Latent variables z: Update every latent variable z_{it} from the truncated Gaussian full–conditional distribution

$$(z_{it} \mid -) \sim \mathrm{TN}_1[0, \delta_t(y_{it} - \xi_t)/\omega_t, (1-\delta_t^2)], \quad i = 1, \ldots, n, \quad t = 1, \ldots, T.$$

[2] Location vector $\boldsymbol{\xi}$: Given the current value of the latent variables z_{it} and of the parameters α_t and ω_t, we can recast our formulation as a regression model for transformed Gaussian data $y_{it}^* = y_{it} - \omega_t\delta_t z_{it}$, $i = 1, \ldots, n$, $t = 1, \ldots, T$. Hence, letting $\bar{\mathbf{y}}^* = (n^{-1}\sum_{i=1}^n y_{i1}^*, \ldots, n^{-1}\sum_{i=1}^n y_{iT}^*)^\intercal$, the full–conditional for $\boldsymbol{\xi}$ can be derived via Gaussian–Gaussian conjugacy and coincides with

$$(\boldsymbol{\xi} \mid -) \sim \mathrm{N}_T[(\boldsymbol{\Sigma}_{\xi}^{-1} + n\boldsymbol{V}_{\xi})^{-1}(\boldsymbol{\Sigma}_{\xi}^{-1}\boldsymbol{\mu}_{\xi} + n\boldsymbol{V}_{\xi}\bar{\mathbf{y}}^*), (\boldsymbol{\Sigma}_{\xi}^{-1} + n\boldsymbol{V}_{\xi})^{-1}],$$

where $\boldsymbol{V}_{\xi} = \mathrm{diag}[1/\omega_1^2(1-\delta_1^2), \ldots, 1/\omega_T^2(1-\delta_T^2)]$.

[3] Scale vector $\boldsymbol{\omega}$: For every time $t = 1, \ldots, T$, update ω_t independently with a Metropolis–Hasting step.

[4] Skewness vector $\boldsymbol{\alpha}$: Update $\boldsymbol{\alpha}$ from the full–conditional SUN distribution, replacing y_{it} with the transformed value $(y_{it} - \xi_t)/\omega_t$ in (5.10) and using Lemma 1.

Coherently with a Bayesian specification, forecasts for years $T+1, \ldots, T+q$ are obtained by treating the future observations $\mathbf{y}_{T+1}, \ldots, \mathbf{y}_{T+q}$ as missing data in the MCMC (Gelman et al. 2013). At each iteration, the parameters $(\xi_{T+1}, \omega_{T+1}, \alpha_{T+1}), \ldots, (\xi_{T+q}, \omega_{T+q}, \alpha_{T+q})$ are updated jointly with $(\boldsymbol{\xi}, \boldsymbol{\omega}, \boldsymbol{\alpha})$, after imputing the missing data $\mathbf{y}_{T+1}, \ldots, \mathbf{y}_{T+q}$ with values sampled from the conditional skew–normals in equation (5.5).

5.4 Forecasting Italian Fertility Rates

We apply the model defined in Sects. 5.2–5.3 to the proportionate age–specific Italian fertility rates from 1991 to 2014, creating an artificial population of $n = 500$ women for each year based on data at https://www.humanfertility.org/cgi-bin/main.php.

In performing posterior inference and forecasting, the GP priors for $\boldsymbol{\alpha}$ and $\boldsymbol{\xi}$ have been centered around 0 and 30 respectively, setting $m_\alpha(t_j) = 0$ and $m_\xi(t_j) = 30$. These values define our prior guess on the shape of the curve and on the average age at childbirth. The prior GP covariance parameters κ_α and κ_ξ are instead fixed at 100 to induce modest dependence across years. Finally, we set $a_\omega = 10$ and $b_\omega = 300$ to obtain prior means and standard deviations for the scales around 30 and 10, respectively. These values were elicited by inspecting the variance of the historical data, and centering the priors around this value, while inducing sufficient variability to deviate from this assumption, if required. We also conducted sensitivity analyses obtaining similar results under many hyper–parameters' settings. Posterior inference relies on 5000 MCMC samples after a burn–in period of 2000. These choices were sufficient for convergence, whereas mixing was not perfect, but still satisfactory.

The focus of inference is on the time–varying mean $\xi_t + \omega_t \delta_t \sqrt{2/\pi}$, variance $\omega_t^2(1-2\delta_t^2/\pi)$ and skewness parameter α_t of the age at childbirth under (5.5)—with $\delta_t = \alpha_t(1+\alpha_t^2)^{-1/2}$. The posteriors for these quantities can be easily computed from the MCMC samples of $(\xi_t, \omega_t, \alpha_t)$ and some key summaries are reported in Fig. 5.1. According to the upper panel, our empirical findings suggest that the average age at childbirth has increased in the last decades—a result which was expected and well investigated in the literature. This average age has moved from a minimum close to 28 years in 1991 to a maximum close to 31 years in 2010 and following years. The middle panel summarizes, instead, the posterior distribution for α_t, suggesting that the fertility rates have actually become symmetric in recent years and demonstrating the ability of the model to capture both symmetric and asymmetric shapes. Finally, the posterior distributions for the variance, reported in the bottom panel of Fig. 5.1, suggest a stable variability across the temporal window considered. Also these results are in line with the findings of Mazzuco and Scarpa (2015).

To validate the above results, Fig. 5.2 compares the histograms of the proportionate age–specific fertility rates, computed from the synthetic data, with the posterior distribution of $f(y_k; \xi_t, \omega_t, \alpha_t)$ in equation (5.2), for each age y_k, summarized via a pointwise posterior mean and the 95% credible intervals. Since the value of $f(y_k; \xi_t, \omega_t, \alpha_t)$ is a functional of model parameters, the posterior distribution for

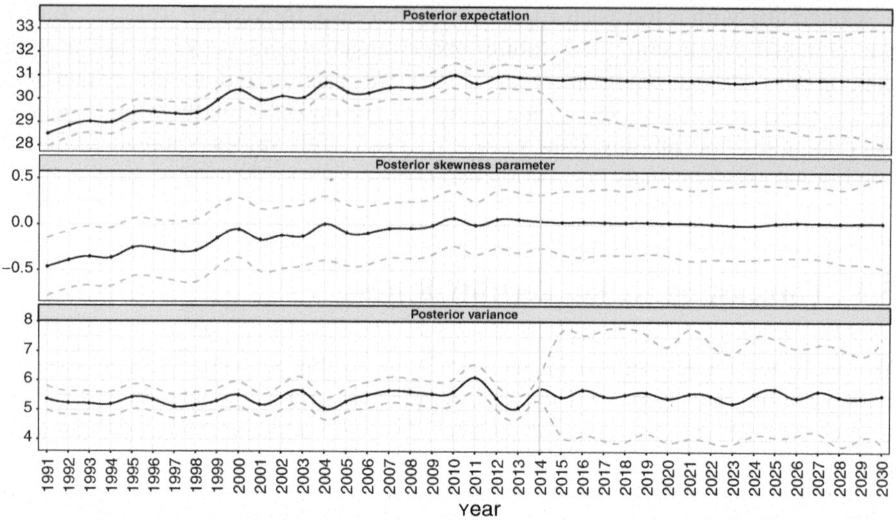

Fig. 5.1 Summaries of the posterior distribution for the mean, skewness parameter and variance of the skewed process for y_{it}. Dashed lines denote 95% credible intervals. Yellow vertical lines denote the last observed year

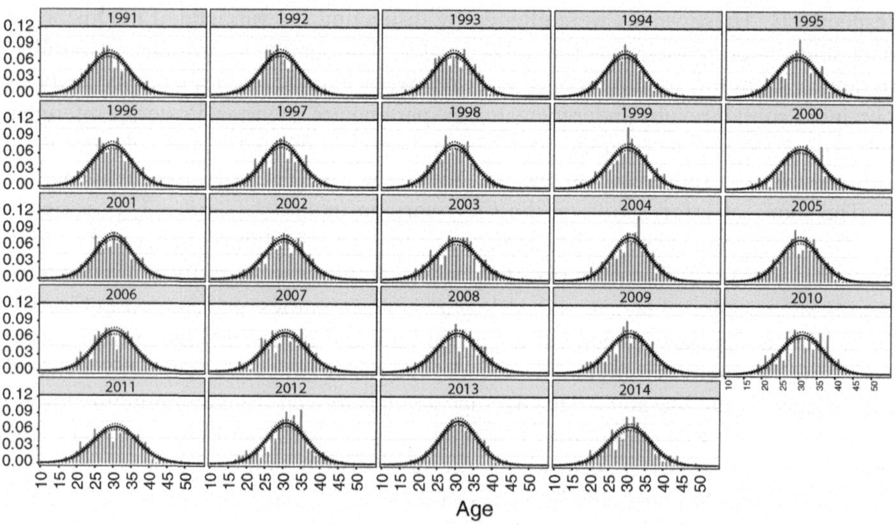

Fig. 5.2 For each year from 1991 to 2014, histograms of the proportionate age–specific fertility rates computed from the synthetic data, and summaries of the posterior distribution for $f(y_k; \xi_t, \omega_t, \alpha_t)$ in (5.2), for each age y_k. Black continuous line indicates pointwise posterior mean, while 95% credible intervals are denoted as dotted lines

$(\xi_t, \omega_t, \alpha_t)$ induces a posterior also for $f(y_k; \xi_t, \omega_t, \alpha_t)$, for each age y_k. Results suggest a satisfactory fit, with the rates arising from the artificial samples being close to the pointwise estimates. To summarize, posterior inference suggests that PASFRS have experienced a change in the last decade, which has impacted the location and shape of the curve while leaving variability stable. The goodness of fit of the proposed approach, in terms of adequacy with the empirical distribution of the artificial data, is satisfactory.

The results in terms of goodness of fit illustrated above motivate forecasts for the Italian PASFRS, producing these predictions for the 16 years after the last observed time. According to Fig. 5.1, forecasts for the posterior mean of the age at childbirth under the BSP model show a stable trend, which is coherent with the Italian fertility rates observed in the recent years. Also the forecasts for the variance and the skewness parameter of the age at childbirth are substantially stable.

We also compare our forecasting accuracy with the results from a default implementation of the approach proposed by Ševčíková et al. (2016) and available via the R library bayesPop (Ševčíková and Raftery 2016). The main routines of this library compute predictions for the TFR and life expectancies, and then obtain the cohort–specific fertility rates via post–processing of the MCMC output. We also highlight that the method available in bayesPop does not provide fertility rates for all the ages, but only for 5 years age groups. To compare these predictions with the results obtained from BSP, we represent the former as a step function with constant values within each age interval.

Results are reported in Fig. 5.3, with yellow curves referred to predictions from the BSP model and black step functions from bayesPop. The 90% credible intervals are illustrated as dotted lines. Direct comparison among the two approaches

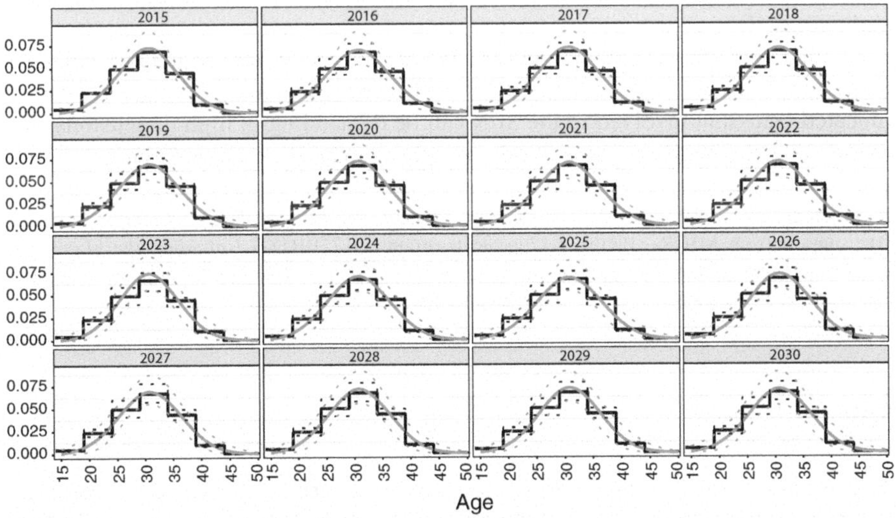

Fig. 5.3 Forecasted distribution for the BSP model (yellow) against those obtained under the package bayesPop. Dotted lines denote 90% credible intervals

suggests very similar results in terms of predicted probabilities, with both strategies assigning the highest probability of childbirth in the interval $(30-34]$. The credible intervals from BSP are wider than the competitor, likely due to the uncertainty in the dynamic components. This is not surprising, due to the assumptions made by Ševčíková et al. (2016) which may lead to under–coverage of the credible intervals when they are not met in practice.

5.5 Discussion

In this work we have proposed to model PASFRS via a Bayesian skewed process. Our specification incorporates symmetric and asymmetric shapes, while characterizing temporal dependence through the skew–normal parameters.

This approach takes a first step towards direct forecasting of PASFRS using Bayesian models. In facts, also Ševčíková et al. (2016) use a Bayesian framework to forecast PASFRS over time, but this is done within a hierarchical model applied to all countries which are further assumed to converge to a global pattern. The method proposed in this article provides, instead, single–country forecasts, borrowing information only from past PASFRS and not from other countries' patterns, nor from hypothetical global schedules. Results are comparable with Ševčíková et al. (2016), with a reasonably higher uncertainty of the forecasts.

Future extensions include methodological developments to allow joint modeling of multiple countries via a mixture of BSPs. This could also facilitate clustering of countries with respect to similarities in fertility patterns, thereby providing insights on important social aspects of developed countries. Also the inclusion of more complex dependence patterns among PASFRS and TFR could further improve predictions.

Another key improvement includes the reduction of the computational cost associated with posterior inference for BSP. The simulation of the nT–variate truncated Gaussian involved in the SUN can be demanding in high dimensions. An option to overcome this issue is to rely on approximate Bayesian inference.

Acknowledgements We thank the guest Editors for the suggestions on the first draft and acknowledge support from MIUR—PRIN 2017 project—grant 20177BRJXS *Unfolding the SEcrets of LongEvity: Current Trends and future prospects (SELECT). A path through morbidity, disability and mortality in Italy and Europe*—in the preparation of the final article.

Appendix

Here, we derive the key quantities involved in the algorithm described in Sect. 5.3.

Full conditional for z_{it}. Recall that $z_{it} \sim \text{TN}_1(0, 0, 1)$, and $(y_{it} \mid z_{it}) \sim \text{N}[\xi_t + \omega_t \delta_t z_{it}, \omega_t^2(1-\delta_t^2)]$. Hence, the full conditional for z_{it} is proportional to

$$f(z_{it})f(y_{it}\,|\,z_{it}) \propto \mathbf{1}(z_{it} > 0)\exp(-0.5z_{it}^2)\exp[-(y_{it}-\xi_t-\omega_t\delta_t z_{it})^2/2\omega_t^2(1-\delta_t^2)].$$

Focusing on the two terms in the exponents and applying classical Gaussian results, we obtain the kernel of a normal distribution with mean $\delta_t(y_{it} - \xi_t)/\omega_t$ and variance $(1 - \delta_t^2)$. Including the indicator function within such a kernel, we obtain

$$f(z_{it} \mid -) \propto \exp\left[-\frac{1}{2(1-\delta_t^2)}\left(z_{it} - \frac{\delta_t(y_{it} - \xi_t)}{\omega_t}\right)^2\right]\mathbf{1}(z_{it} > 0).$$

Hence $(z_{it} \mid -) \sim \mathrm{TN}_1[0, \delta_t(y_{it} - \xi_t)/\omega_t, (1-\delta_t^2)]$, for $i = 1, \ldots, n, t = 1, \ldots, T$.

Full conditional for $\boldsymbol{\xi}$. Recall that $y_{it}^* = y_{it} - \omega_t\delta_t z_{it}$ and let $\mathbf{y}_i^* = (y_{i1}^*, \ldots, y_{iT}^*)^\intercal$ denote the T-dimensional vector of scaled observations. Since $(\mathbf{y}_i^* \mid -) \sim \mathrm{N}(\boldsymbol{\xi}, \boldsymbol{V}_{\xi}^{-1})$, with $\boldsymbol{V}_{\xi} = \mathrm{diag}[1/\omega_1^2(1 - \delta_1^2), \ldots, 1/\omega_T^2(1 - \delta_T^2)]$, and $\boldsymbol{\xi} \sim \mathrm{N}_T(\boldsymbol{\mu}_{\xi}, \boldsymbol{\Sigma}_{\xi})$, by Gaussian–Gaussian conjugacy we obtain

$$(\boldsymbol{\xi} \mid -) \sim \mathrm{N}_T(\mathbf{S}_{\xi}^{-1}\mathbf{m}_{\xi}, \mathbf{S}_{\xi}^{-1}), \qquad \mathbf{S}_{\xi} = \boldsymbol{\Sigma}_{\xi}^{-1} + n\boldsymbol{V}_{\xi}, \quad \mathbf{m}_{\xi} = \boldsymbol{\Sigma}_{\xi}^{-1}\boldsymbol{\mu}_{\xi} + n\boldsymbol{V}_{\xi}\bar{\mathbf{y}}^*,$$

with $\bar{\mathbf{y}}^* = (n^{-1}\sum_{i=1}^n y_{i1}^*, \ldots, n^{-1}\sum_{i=1}^n y_{iT}^*)^\intercal$.

References

Alkema, L., Raftery, A. E., Gerland, P., Clark, S. J., Pelletier, F., Buettner, T., & Heilig, G.K. (2011). Probabilistic projections of the total fertility rate for all countries. *Demography, 48*(3), 815–839.

Arellano-Valle, R. B., & Azzalini, A. (2006). On the unification of families of skew-normal distributions. *Scandinavian Journal of Statistics, 33*(3), 561–574.

Azzalini, A. (1985). A class of distributions which includes the normal ones. *Scandinavian Journal of Statistics, 12*, 171–178.

Azzalini, A., & Capitanio, A. (2013). *The skew-normal and related families.* Cambridge: Cambridge University Press.

Bergeron-Boucher, M.-P., Canudas-Romo, V., Oeppen, J., & Vaupel, J. W. (2017). Coherent forecasts of mortality with compositional data analysis. *Demographic Research, 37*, 527–566.

Bermúdez, S., Blanquero, R., Hernández, J. A., & Planelles, J. (2012). A new parametric model for fitting fertility curves. *Population Studies, 66*(3), 297–310.

Billari, F., & Kohler, H. (2004). Patterns of low and lowest-low fertility in Europe. *Population Studies, 58*(2), 161–176.

Botev, Z. I. (2017). The normal law under linear restrictions: simulation and estimation via minimax tilting. *Journal of the Royal Statistical Society: Series B (Statistical Methodology), 79*(1), 125–148.

Canale, A., & Scarpa, B. (2015). Age-specific probability of childbirth. Smoothing via Bayesian nonparametric mixture of rounded kernels. *Statistica, 75*(1), 101–110.

Canale, A., Kenne Pagui, C. E., & Scarpa, B. (2016). Bayesian modeling of university first-year students' grades after placement test. *Journal of Applied Statistics, 43*(16), 3015–3029.

Casella, G., & George, E. I. (1992). Explaining the Gibbs sampler. *The American Statistician, 46*(3), 167–174.

Chandola, T., Coleman, D. A., & Hiorns, R. W. (1999). Recent European fertility patterns: Fitting curves to distorted distributions. *Population Studies, 53*(3), 317–329.

Chopin, N. (2011). Fast simulation of truncated Gaussian distributions. *Statistics and Computing, 21*(2), 275–288.

Durante, D. (2019). Conjugate Bayes for probit regression via unified skew-normal distributions. *Biometrika, 106*(4), 765–779.

Ediev, D. M. (2013). Comparative importance of the fertility model, the total fertility, the mean age and the standard deviation of age at childbearing in population projections. In *Meeting of the International Union for the Scientific Study of Population, Busan. Presented at the Meeting of the International Union for the Scientific Study of Population, Busan.*

Gelfand, A. E., & Smith, A. (1990). Sampling-based approaches to calculating marginal densities. *Journal of the American Statistical Association, 85*(410), 398–409.

Gelman, A., Stern, H. S., Carlin, J. B., Dunson, D. B., Vehtari, A., & Rubin, D. B. (2013). *Bayesian data analysis*. Boca Raton: Chapman and Hall/CRC.

Hadwiger, H. (1940). Eine analytische reproduktionsfunktion für biologische gesamtheiten. *Scandinavian Actuarial Journal, 1940*(3–4), 101–113.

Hoem, J. M., Madsen, D., Nielsen, J. L., Ohlsen, E., Hansen, H. O., & Rennermalm, B. (1981). Experiments in modelling recent Danish fertility curves. *Demography, 18*(2), 231–244.

Horrace, W. C. (2005). Some results on the multivariate truncated normal distribution. *Journal of Multivariate Analysis, 94*(1), 209–221.

Keilman, N., & Pham, D. Q. (2000). Predictive intervals for age-specific fertility. *European Journal of Population/Revue Européenne de Démographie, 16*(1), 41–65.

Kostaki, A., Moguerza, J. M., Olivares, A., & Psarakis, S. (2009). Graduating the age-specific fertility pattern using support vector machines. *Demographic Research, 20*, 599–622.

Liechty, M. W., & Lu, J. (2010). Multivariate normal slice sampling. *Journal of Computational and Graphical Statistics, 19*(2), 281–294.

Lutz, W., & Samir, K. C. (2010). Dimensions of global population projections: What do we know about future population trends and structures? *Philosophical Transactions of the Royal Society B: Biological Sciences, 365*(1554), 2779–2791.

Mazzuco, S., & Scarpa, B. (2015). Fitting age-specific fertility rates by a flexible generalized skew normal probability density function. *Journal of the Royal Statistical Society: Series A (Statistics in Society), 178*(1), 187–203.

Murphy, E. M., & Nagnur, D. N. (1972). A Gompertz fit that fits: Applications to Canadian fertility patterns. *Demography, 9*(1), 35–50.

Pakman, A., & Paninski, L. (2014). Exact Hamiltonian Monte Carlo for truncated multivariate Gaussians. *Journal of Computational and Graphical Statistics, 23*(2), 518–542.

Peristera, P., & Kostaki, A. (2007). Modeling fertility in modern populations. *Demographic Research, 16*, 141–194.

Raftery, A. E., Chunn, J. L., Gerland, P., & Ševčíková, H. (2013). Bayesian probabilistic projections of life expectancy for all countries. *Demography, 50*(3), 777–801.

Raftery, A. E., Alkema, L., & Gerland, P. (2014). Bayesian population projections for the United Nations. *Statistical Science, 29*(1), 58.

Rasmussen, C. E., & Williams, C. K. (2006). *Gaussian Processes for Machine Learning*. Cambridge: MIT.

Rindfuss, R. R., Morgan, P. S., & Offutt, K. (1996). Education and the changing age pattern of American fertility: 1963–1989. *Demography, 33*(3), 277–290.

Scarpa, B. (2014). Probabilistic and statistical models for conception. *Wiley StatsRef: Statistics Reference Online*.

Schmertmann, C. (2003). A system of model fertility schedules with graphically intuitive parameters. *Demographic Research, 9*, 81–110.

Ševčíková, H., & Raftery, A. E. (2016). Bayespop: Probabilistic population projections. *Journal of Statistical Software, 75*, 1–29.

Ševčíková, H., Li, N., Kantorová, V., Gerland, P., & Raftery, A. E. (2016). Age-specific mortality and fertility rates for probabilistic population projections. In *Dynamic demographic analysis* (pp. 285–310). Cham: Springer.

Chapter 6
A Three-Component Approach to Model and Forecast Age-at-Death Distributions

Ugofilippo Basellini and Carlo Giovanni Camarda

6.1 Introduction

Population projections and mortality forecasts have been studied since the beginning of the twentieth century. The seminal works of Whelpton (1928, 1936) and Lotka (1939) on the cohort component method and the stable population contributed significantly to the development and application of population projections. Mortality forecasts go back at least to the beginning of the twentieth century, as actuaries were concerned about the financial effects of mortality improvements on life annuities and pensions (Pollard 1987). It is however in the last three decades that mortality forecasting flourished, owing to the introduction and development of stochastic methodologies to project mortality.

Three functions can be used to analyse human mortality and its developments over age and time: the hazard, the survival and the probability density function (Klein and Moeschberger 2003). These functions describe the same stochastic phenomenon and are uniquely related between each other: one can derive any two of them by knowing the third one, without the need of additional information.

Electronic Supplementary Material The online version of this chapter (https://doi.org/10.1007/978-3-030-42472-5_6) contains supplementary material, which is available to authorized users.

U. Basellini (✉)
Max Planck Institute for Demographic Research (MPIDR), Rostock, Germany

Institut national d'études démographiques (INED), Aubervilliers, France
e-mail: basellini@demogr.mpg.de

C. G. Camarda
Institut national d'études démographiques (INED), Aubervilliers, France

S. Mazzuco, N. Keilman (eds.), *Developments in Demographic Forecasting*, The Springer Series on Demographic Methods and Population Analysis 49, https://doi.org/10.1007/978-3-030-42472-5_6

Despite the complementarity of the mortality functions, the majority of forecasting techniques is based on age-specific mortality rates or death probabilities (for comprehensive reviews, see Booth and Tickle 2008; Cairns et al. 2009; Shang et al. 2011; Stoeldraijer et al. 2013). Most of these models take advantage of the regularities typically found in age- and time-patterns, such as the predominantly downward trend in age-specific mortality observed in many developed countries during the last 60 years, and they extrapolate the trends in the future using statistical methods (Haberman and Renshaw 2011).

Nevertheless, the inspection of the other two functions can provide additional insights on mortality developments that one might not directly discern from a rate-based analysis. It is well known that the remarkable mortality improvements observed in these countries during the twentieth century are generally divided into two stages of mortality changes: compression and shifting dynamics (see, for example, Fries 1980; Wilmoth and Horiuchi 1999; Kannisto 2000; Bongaarts 2005; Canudas-Romo 2008). Broadly speaking, the first stage took place in the first part of the century, as significant reductions in infant and childhood mortality resulted in greater equality in lengths of life. In the second part of the century, mortality improvements at older ages became more prominent, resulting in higher average lifespans with stagnating equality.

The age-at-death distribution is an excellent function to inspect these dynamics of mortality changes. Mortality compression can be detected from the reduction in the variability of the distribution, while shifting corresponds to a translation of the distribution to higher ages without relevant changes in its shape. In addition, the distribution provides immediate information on key questions in mortality studies, such as the longevity of the population, and the inequality in ages at death.

Figure 6.1 shows changes in the age-at-death distribution of Swiss males between 1950 and 2016. The graphical inspection of the death distribution readily provides information on the population's longevity, which is typically measured by life expectancy at birth or, in low mortality countries, by the modal age at death (Kannisto 2001; Horiuchi et al. 2013). Additionally, the variability of lifespans within the population can be directly assessed from the spread of the distribution or its interquartile range. The increase in longevity as well as the reduction of lifespan variability for Swiss males during this period clearly emerge from Fig. 6.1. Moreover, changes in the distribution over time highlight the two dynamics of mortality: for example, it is evident that the shifting dynamic of mortality started around the 1970–1980s, becoming more prominent in most recent decades, while the compression dynamic had been strongest in the decades 1950–1970 and 1990–2010.

Despite providing direct information on mortality patterns and trends over time, surprisingly few methods have been proposed to forecast mortality from age-at-death distributions. Among the firsts to abandon the conventional approach of using mortality rates, Oeppen (2008) and Oeppen and Camarda (2013) proposed to forecast the density of single and multiple-decrement life tables, using methodologies borrowed from compositional data analysis. Bergeron-Boucher et al. (2017) expanded on this work, suggesting a coherent model based on life-table deaths of fifteen Western European countries. Furthermore, Basellini and Camarda

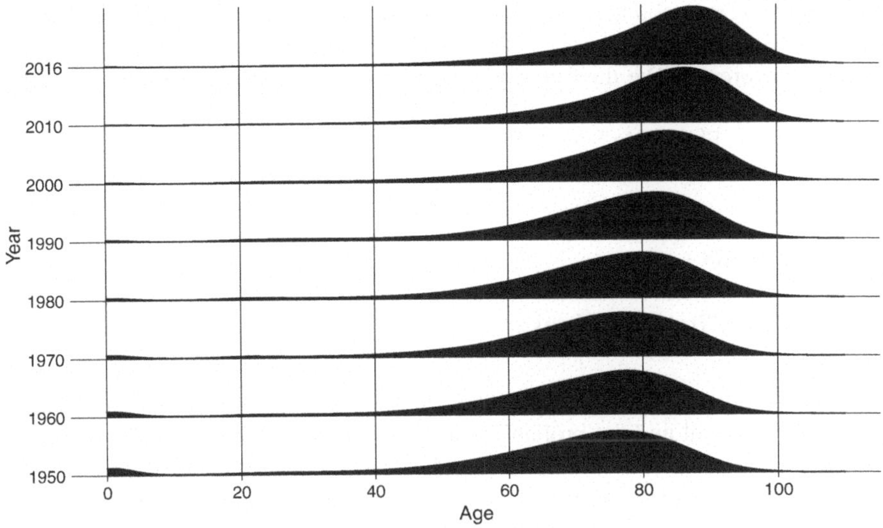

Fig. 6.1 Changes in the age-at-death distribution for Swiss males at selected years between 1950 and 2016. The orange area corresponds to the interquartile range of the distribution, whose value is reported in print. The dashed line depicts the modal age at death. Data have been smoothed for illustrative purposes. (Source: Authors' own elaborations on data retrieved from the Human Mortality Database 2019) (For the interpretation of the references to colors in this Figure, please refer to the electronic version of the chapter available online)

(2019) proposed a relational model to forecast adult mortality from age-at-death distributions. Finally, Pascariu et al. (2019) suggested a vector autoregressive model to forecast the statistical moments of the death distribution.

In this chapter, we contribute to the growing literature of forecasting the age-pattern of mortality from age-at-death distributions. Specifically, we extend the Segmented Transformation Age-at-death Distributions (STAD) model proposed by Basellini and Camarda (2019), which focuses on adult mortality only, to obtain mortality forecasts for the entire age range. While retaining the underlying methodology of the STAD model, here we introduce significant novelties to achieve our goal. In particular, our approach is based on two steps. First, we decompose the observed death counts into three additive mortality components, namely Childhood, Early-Adulthood and Senescent mortality. We perform this decomposition via the nonparametric approach proposed by Camarda et al. (2016). Secondly, we model and forecast each component-specific age-at-death distribution employing specialized versions of the STAD model. As such, the Three-Component STAD (3C-STAD) model allows us to capture mortality developments over the entire age range, and forecasts are obtained from the extrapolation of the model's parameters using standard time-series techniques.

This chapter is organized as follows. In Sect. 6.2, we overview the methods that we introduce as well as the data that we employ. In Sect. 6.3, we provide two illustrations of our methodology by forecasting female and male mortality in two high-longevity countries. In particular, we first assess the accuracy of point and interval forecasts of the 3C-STAD model by performing three out-of-sample validation exercises. We then present the 3C-STAD forecasts until the year 2050. In both cases, we compare the 3C-STAD with three other well-known forecasting methodologies. Finally, in Sect. 6.4 we summarize and discuss our results.

6.2 Methods

6.2.1 *Mortality Functions*

Human mortality can be analysed by any one of three complementary functions: the hazard, the survival and the probability density function (Klein and Moeschberger 2003). In demography, for a given calendar year t, these functions are generally known as the force of mortality $\mu(x,t)$ at age x, the probability of surviving from birth to age x, $\ell(x,t)$, and the age-at-death distribution $f(x,t)$.

The three mortality functions are uniquely related between each other, and knowing one of them allows one to determine the other two. In the following, without loss of generality, let $\ell(0,t)$, commonly labelled as the life-table radix, be equal to one, and let us drop the time index t to ease notation. The relationship that exists between the three functions at any age x is given by:

$$f(x) = \ell(x)\,\mu(x)\,. \tag{6.1}$$

The probability of surviving $\ell(x)$ can be derived from the other two mortality functions:

$$\ell(x) = \exp\left(-\int_0^x \mu(a)da\right), \quad \ell(x) = \int_x^\omega f(x)\,dx\,, \tag{6.2}$$

where ω is the highest age attained in the population. Thus, combining (6.1) and (6.2) demonstrates the complementarity of the three mortality functions.

Since Thiele (1871), demographers and actuaries described human mortality into three different components that operates principally, or almost exclusively, upon childhood, middle and old ages, respectively. The attempt to decompose those three components stimulated numerous approaches (cf. Sect. 6.4). In a general setting, the hypothesis can be expressed as follows:

$$\mu(x) = \mu_c(x) + \mu_e(x) + \mu_s(x)\,, \tag{6.3}$$

where the force of mortality $\mu(x)$ at age x is additively decomposed into three independent components, $\mu_c(x)$, $\mu_e(x)$, and $\mu_s(x)$. For ease of presentation, we labelled these mortality component with Childhood, Early-Adulthood and Senescence, respectively. However, they theoretically operate over all ages x.

Combining (6.1) and (6.3), the corresponding decomposition of the age-at-death distribution can be written as follows:

$$\begin{aligned} f(x) &= \ell(x)\,\mu_c(x) + \ell(x)\,\mu_e(x) + \ell(x)\,\mu_s(x) \\ &= f_c(x) + f_e(x) + f_s(x)\,. \end{aligned} \tag{6.4}$$

Note that the overall age-at-death distribution $f(x)$ is a proper density function, i.e. $\int_0^{\omega} f(x)\,dx = 1$. Conversely, component-specific age-at-death distributions do not individually sum to one when integrated over the entire age range (cf. Equation (6.11) for the corresponding probability mass constraint in a discrete setting).

6.2.2 *Data and Mortality Decomposition*

Whereas risk of death acts continuously, mortality functions and models can be displayed only at particular ages and years. For modelling and forecasting mortality and for a specific sex and population, available data are thus observed death counts, $d_{x,t}$, and central exposures to the risk of death, $e_{x,t}$, with ages $x = 0, \ldots, \omega$ and years t. In the following, we analyse the female and male populations of two high-longevity countries, Sweden and Switzerland, choosing a common time period (1950–2016) and with $\omega = 110+$. While Sweden was selected for the high standard in data quality, even at the oldest ages (Vaupel and Lundström 1994; Wilmoth and Lundström 1996), Switzerland was chosen for its atypical mortality development, especially for males, related to the strong HIV epidemic during the 1980s (Csete and Grob 2012). Data are taken from the Human Mortality Database (HMD 2019).

We assume that the number of deaths at age x and year t is a random variable $D_{x,t}$ that follows a Poisson process (Brillinger 1986):

$$D_{x,t} \sim \mathcal{P}(e_{x,t}\;\mu_{x,t}) \tag{6.5}$$

where the force of mortality $\mu_{x,t}$ is assumed to be constant over each year of age (i.e. from age x to $x+1$) and over each calendar year (i.e. from year t to $t+1$). This assumption implies that $\mu_{x,t}$ approximates the force of mortality at exact age $x + \frac{1}{2}$ and exact time $t + \frac{1}{2}$ (Cairns et al. 2009). Note that the notation $\mu_{x,t}$ is the discrete counterpart of the continuous notation $\mu(x,t)$ employed in Sect. 6.2.1. Moreover, death rates $m_{x,t} = d_{x,t}/e_{x,t}$ are the maximum likelihood estimators of the force of mortality $\mu_{x,t}$, if no structure is enforced over age and/or time.

The first step in the Three-Component Segmented Transformation Age-at-death Distributions (3C-STAD) model concerns the decomposition of the force of mortality into its three independent components $\mu_k(x)$, $k = c, e, s$. Instead of employing a parametric mortality model, we favour a non-parametric approach to avoid imposing a rigid structure and achieve a better fit to the observed data. For this purpose, we employ the Sum of Smooth Exponentials (SSE) model, which has been shown to provide insightful results for mortality analysis (Camarda et al. 2016; Remund et al. 2018). In the following, we provide a short overview of the SSE model; for a more detailed description of the model, we refer the interested reader to the original paper of Camarda et al. (2016).

The SSE belongs to the class of multiple-component models (also known as competing hazard models, Gage 1993), as it proposes an additive decomposition of the expected value of counts in multiple (smooth) components. In a given year t, let $\boldsymbol{\mu}$, $\boldsymbol{d}$ and $\boldsymbol{e}$ denote vectors over age of overall force of mortality, death counts and exposures, respectively. Within the SSE, we can model the force of mortality as the sum of three components $\boldsymbol{\gamma} = \text{vec}\left(\boldsymbol{\gamma}_c : \boldsymbol{\gamma}_e : \boldsymbol{\gamma}_s\right)$, where $\text{vec}\,(\cdot)$ arranges the elements of a matrix by column order into a vector. The expected value of the Poisson process $\boldsymbol{d} \sim \mathcal{P}(\boldsymbol{e} * \boldsymbol{\mu})$, where $*$ denotes the element-wise product, and $\boldsymbol{d}$ is expressed as a composition of exposures and mortality components, i.e. $\boldsymbol{e} * \boldsymbol{\mu} = \boldsymbol{C}\,\boldsymbol{\gamma}$, where the composition matrix $\boldsymbol{C} = [\boldsymbol{E} : \boldsymbol{E} : \boldsymbol{E}]$ is a block matrix that includes three times the diagonal matrix of population exposures $\boldsymbol{E} = \text{diag}(\boldsymbol{e})$ (one for each component of mortality). The composition matrix has the dual role of multiplying each component by the exposure times and of summing them to obtain the overall Poisson mean. The SSE model can be framed as a Composite Link Model (Thompson and Baker 1981), and estimation of the model's parameters can be obtained by a modified version of the iterative reweighted least squares (IWLS) algorithm (Eilers 2007).

The SSE model has several advantages over parametric decompositions of the force of mortality, which made it our favoured choice for the first step of the 3C-STAD. Although the SSE could accommodate parametric assumptions, it allows to model each component by assuming only smoothness over age (and eventually over time). We opted for this last more flexible setting. This can be achieved by expressing each component k as a linear combination of B-spline basis $\boldsymbol{B}_k$ and associated coefficients $\boldsymbol{\alpha}_k$:

$$\boldsymbol{\gamma}_k = \exp\left(\boldsymbol{B}_k\,\boldsymbol{\alpha}_k\right), \quad k = c, e, s. \tag{6.6}$$

Smoothness of $\boldsymbol{\gamma}_k$ is obtained by combining a large number of B-splines and a roughness penalty on the coefficients vector $\boldsymbol{\alpha}_k$ (Eilers and Marx 1996). Note that the exponential in (6.6) guarantees positive component-specific force of mortality, as one would expect. Furthermore, component-specific shape constraints can be easily specified and included in the estimation procedure by additional asymmetric penalties. Here, we enforce monotonic decreasing and increasing constraints on the Childhood and Senescent components, respectively, and a log-concave shape for the Early-Adulthood component. These constraints further aid the identifiability of the model by ensuring that the three components are not interchangeable.

Another advantage of the SSE methodology is that it adequately blends the transitions between components, without imposing sharp delimitations where one stops and another one continues. Moreover, we employ the two-dimensional extension of the SSE model. In this way we both account for the significant age-time interactions and avoid abrupt changes over time in the interaction of

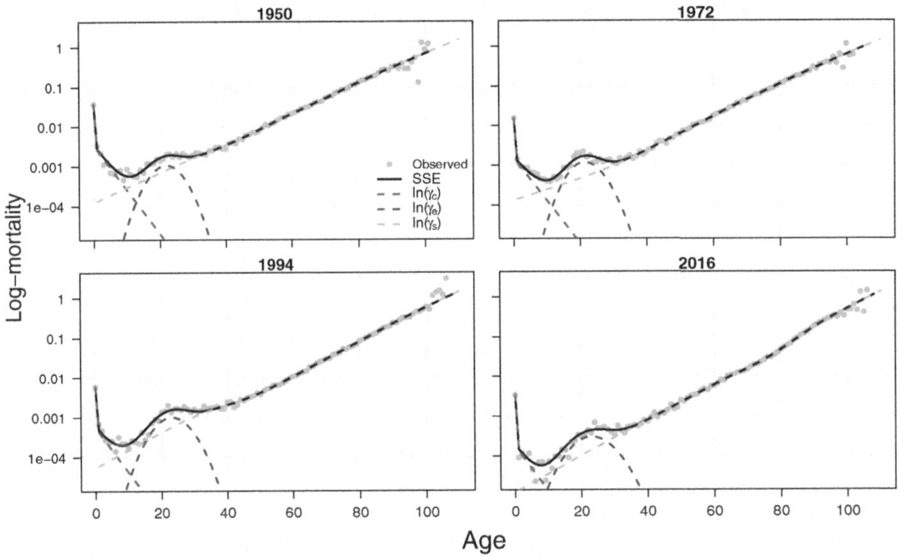

Fig. 6.2 Observed and fitted mortality rates (in log scale) for Swiss males at selected years between 1950 and 2016. The force of mortality is decomposed into Childhood (γ_c), Early-Adulthood (γ_e) and Senescent (γ_s) components via the two-dimensional SSE model. (Source: As for Fig. 6.1) (For the interpretation of the references to colors in this Figure, please refer to the electronic version of the chapter available online)

the components. A detailed description of year-to-year mortality fluctuations is relevant in a forecasting perspective. In the SSE model, at the cost of overfitting, this flexibility is achieved by a large number of B-splines with a low smoothing parameter in the time dimension.

Figure 6.2 shows an example of fitting the two-dimensional SSE model to Swiss males between 1950 and 2016: the three components of mortality clearly emerge, each one featuring the expected shape. Unlike the original SSE model, we start our analysis from age 0 which is treated in a specific manner. This particular age represents a clear discontinuity in the age-pattern of mortality, as mortality of newborns is sharply higher than death rates at later infant ages due to malformations, pre-term births and birth-related complications (Chiang 1984; Camarda et al. 2016). Hence, we incorporate the discontinuity in the first age of life by including, for the Childhood component, a specialized coefficient for this age, which is not penalized over age.

Outcomes from the SSE model allow us to obtain (i) the age-at-death distribution of each component over time (using standard life-table construction, Preston et al. 2001), and (ii) the expected number of deaths separated by component, $\hat{\boldsymbol{d}}_k = \boldsymbol{e} * \hat{\boldsymbol{\gamma}}_k$. This allows us to model and forecast age-at-death distributions independently for each component.

6.2.3 *Modelling Component-Specific Distributions*

The second step of the 3C-STAD consists in modelling the component-specific age-at-death distributions. Since different features characterize the three components, we deal differently with each one of them.

6.2.3.1 Senescent Mortality

We start by presenting the model employed for the Senescent component, originally proposed and described in greater details in Basellini and Camarda (2019). The Segmented Transformation Age-at-death Distributions (STAD) is a relational model that relates a fixed time-invariant reference distribution, denoted standard, to a series of observed distributions via a segmented transformation of the age axis. In general, consider two age-at-death distributions $f(x)$ and $g(x)$, where the former is the standard, and the latter any observed distribution. The STAD model can be expressed as $g(x) = f[t(x; \boldsymbol{\theta})]$, where the transformation function $t(x; \boldsymbol{\theta})$ is characterized by three parameters $\boldsymbol{\theta}$ that depend on: (i) the difference in modal ages at death between the two distributions, and (ii) the change in the variability of the two distributions *before* and *after* their modal ages.

Let $\nu_s = M_s^g - M_s^f$ denotes the difference between the mode of the Senescent distributions $g_s(x)$ and $f_s(x)$. The transformation function of the STAD model for the Senescent component, $t_s(\cdot)$, can then be written as:

$$t_s(x;\ \nu_s, b_s^\ell, b_s^u) = \begin{cases} M_s^f + b_s^\ell\, \tilde{x} & \text{if } x \leq M_s^g \\ M_s^f + b_s^u\, \tilde{x} & \text{if } x > M_s^g \end{cases} \tag{6.7}$$

where $\tilde{x} = x - \nu_s - M_s^f$, and b_s^ℓ and b_s^u denote the change in the variability of $g_s(x)$ with respect to $f_s(x)$ before and after the mode, respectively. Note that the superscript ℓ and u refer to the lower and upper segments of the age range (i.e. before and after the modal age at death).

The top panels in Fig. 6.3 explain graphically the mechanisms underlying the STAD model for the Senescence component. Given a standard distribution (black lines in the graphs), let us consider the simpler case in which we vary the parameter ν_s but keep the variability parameters equal to 1, that is, $b_s^\ell = b_s^u = 1$. The transformation function in Equation (6.7) then simplifies to $t_s(x) = x - \nu_s$, and the resulting distribution is shifted along the x-axis by an amount equal to ν_s. This case corresponds to a shifting mortality scenario (blue lines in the graphs): the new distribution has the same shape and variability of the standard, but it is translated by the shifting parameter.

A more general development of mortality can be described by different values of the variability parameters, which act jointly with ν_s to modify the age-pattern of the standard distribution. When the two parameters are greater (lower) than 1,

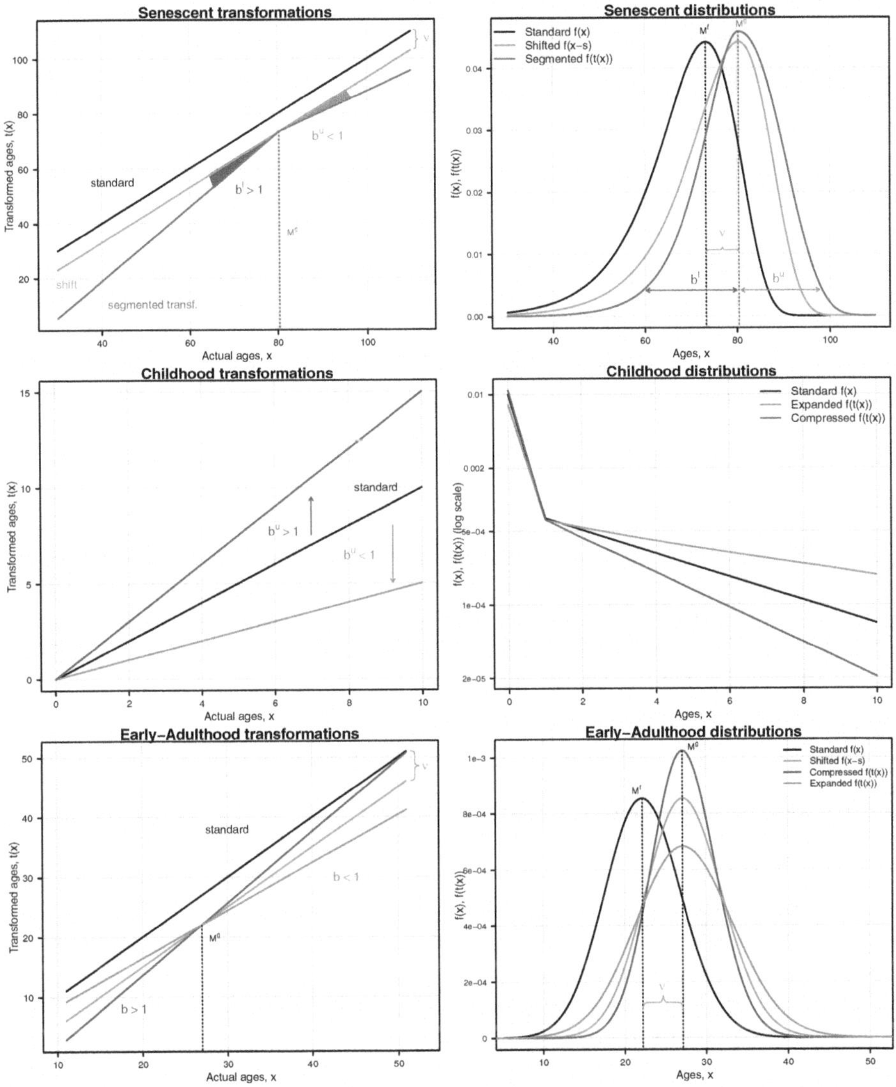

Fig. 6.3 A graphical representation of the transformation functions (left panels) for the three components of the 3C-STAD model, and their effects on the corresponding component-specific age-at-death distributions (right panels). (Source: Authors' own elaborations) (For the interpretation of the references to colors in this Figure, please refer to the electronic version of the chapter available online)

the variability of the segmented distribution is compressed (expanded) before and after the modal age at death with respect to the standard. In the top right panel of Fig. 6.3, the segmented distribution has a lower variability ($b_s^\ell > 1$) before the mode and a higher variability ($b_s^u < 1$) above the mode as compared to the standard distribution. As such, increases in the two parameters capture the compression dynamic of mortality, distinguishing between changes that occur before and after the modal age at death.

6.2.3.2 Childhood Mortality

The modal age at death for the Childhood component is invariably at age 0. The STAD is thus simplified and we drop from the transformation in (6.7) the part below the mode, i.e. we consider a left-truncated distribution with a constant mode at age 0. For the Childhood component, changes between the standard distribution, $f_c(x)$, and any observed distributions, $g_c(x)$, are modelled by varying the slope of the associated transformation of the age axis. In formulas, since $M_c^g = M_c^f = 0$, we can express the transformation of the age-axis as:

$$t_c(x;\ b_c^u) = b_c^u\, x\,. \tag{6.8}$$

The parameter b_c^u captures the change in the variability of the observed (left-truncated) distribution with respect to the standard distribution. The middle panels in Fig. 6.3 present this case. A parameter b_c^u larger than 1 will reduce the variability of the Childhood age-at-death distribution with respect to the standard one (purple lines). Vice versa, a slope smaller than 1 will lead to an increase of the variance of the associated distribution (orange lines).

6.2.3.3 Early-Adulthood Mortality

The Early-Adulthood component of mortality is a typical and distinguishable feature of the human mortality pattern, which has been observed and modelled since the very first approaches to mortality decomposition (e.g. Thiele 1871; Lexis 1878; Pearson 1897). Cause-of-death investigations of young excess mortality have often provided relevant policy recommendations (Heuveline 2002; Remund et al. 2018). As such, including this mortality component enhances the plausibility of fitted and forecast age-profiles, while improving the goodness-of-fit of the 3C-STAD model.

Transformations for the Early-Adulthood component account for changes in the component-specific modal age-at-death and for the variability of the observed distribution, $g_e(x)$, always with respect to the standard one, $f_e(x)$. Unlike the original STAD model, a linear transformation of the age axis without segmentation has been proven adequate for describing changes of the Early-Adulthood component over years. Therefore we do not differentiate between variability before and after the mode. This adaptation of the STAD can be thought as an Accelerated Failure Time model for age-at-death distributions, where the aging process is first shifted and then uniformly accelerated/decelerated with respect to the standard distribution.

Formally, we can write the transformation function for the Early-Adulthood component as:

$$t_e(x;\ \nu_e, b_e) = M_e^f + b_e\,\tilde{x} \tag{6.9}$$

where $\tilde{x} = x - \nu_e - M_e^f$, $\nu_e = M_e^g - M_e^f$ and the parameter b_e captures the change in the variability of the observed distribution $g_e(x)$ with respect to the standard $f_e(x)$. Bottom panels in Fig. 6.3 illustrates the effect of $t_e(\cdot)$ on a theoretical standard distribution. A shifting mortality scenario for Early-Adulthood could be achieved by different values of the parameter ν_e, keeping $b_e = 1$ (blue lines). Alternatively, a b_e smaller than 1 leads to an increase of the variability of the distribution, simultaneously before and after the observed mode (orange lines). A shrinkage of the age axis is achieved by a b_e larger than 1, and it prompts a $g(x)$ with lower variability with respect to the standard $f_e(x)$ (purple lines).

6.2.4 *Estimating and Forecasting the 3C-STAD Parameters*

Being equipped with the component-specific transformation functions, we can move from the theoretical description of the 3C-STAD model to its actual application for modelling and forecasting a series of age-at-death distributions over time. The first step needed to achieve this goal is the choice of the standard distribution $f_k(x)$ for each component. For the Senescent component, we start by aligning the observed distributions to a common modal age at death, using a landmark registration approach frequently employed in Functional Data Analysis (Ramsay and Silverman 2005). The alignment procedure corresponds to a plain shifting transformation of the observed densities, which preserve all their features except the modal value. The standard is then computed as the mean of the aligned distributions. This approach increases the representativeness of the standard, which does not conflate features of the distributions that occur at different distances with respect to the mode (for additional details and an explicative illustration, see Basellini and Camarda 2019, pp. 122–124). For the Childhood and Early-Adulthood components, we choose the standard as simple means of the observed distributions, as the alignment procedure is not required for the former, and it does not significantly improve the fit for the latter.

Table 6.1 summarizes all hypotheses made in the 3C-STAD model about each component, and the associated parameters that are needed to be estimated and

Table 6.1 Summary of the 3C-STAD model by component: type of transformation of the age axis, associated parameters and choice of the standard distribution

Component, k	Transformation, $t_k(\cdot)$	Parameters		Standard, $f_k(x)$
		Shift	Variability	
Senescence	Segmented at the mode	ν_s	b_s^ℓ, b_s^u	Mean of aligned distr.
Childhood	Left-Truncated, no shift	–	b_c^u	Mean of distr.
Early-Adulthood	Linear, shift at the mode	ν_e	b_e	Mean of distr.

forecast. Given the component-specific standard distributions, parameters of the transformation functions $t_k(\cdot)$ are estimated from the data by maximum likelihood. Here we make use of the outcomes of the SSE model (cf. Sect. 6.2.2), and expected number of deaths over age and time due to each component k, $d^k_{x,t}$ are modelled by the 3C-STAD. Given the actual exposures $e_{x,t}$ and assuming that component-specific expected deaths are Poisson distributed counts as in (6.5), we maximize the following log-likelihood function for each year t:

$$\ln \mathcal{L}\left(\boldsymbol{\theta}_{k,t} \mid d^k_{x,t}, e_{x,t}, v_{k,t}\right) \propto \sum_x \left[d^k_{x,t} \ln\left(\hat{\mu}^k_{x,t}\right) - e_{x,t}\,\hat{\mu}^k_{x,t}\right], \quad k = c, e, s \tag{6.10}$$

where $\hat{\mu}^k_{x,t}$ denotes the hazard of component k corresponding to the transformed distribution derived from $t_k(\cdot)$ applied in year t to the associated standard $f_k(x)$. In particular, the hazard $\hat{\mu}^k_{x,t}$ is derived from the age-at-death distribution $f_k(t_k(\cdot))$ using standard life-table formulas (Preston et al. 2001).[1] Note that the vector $\boldsymbol{\theta}_{k,t}$ contains only the variability parameter(s). For each year t, the shifting parameters v_s and v_e of the Senescent and Early-Adulthood components are computed as differences in the modal age at death between standard and observed distributions, as estimated by the SSE model.

Once the parameters have been estimated over all years t, we can model their trends using standard time-series methods. Mortality forecasts of the 3C-STAD model are then obtained by combining the extrapolated model's parameters with the time-fixed standard distributions. We combine univariate and multivariate approaches to achieve our goal. For the Senescent component, we employ the best fitting ARIMA(p,d,q) model for v_s, and a VAR(1) model for b^ℓ_s and b^u_s (as in Basellini and Camarda 2019). For the Childhood component, the parameter b^u_c is modelled with the best fitting ARIMA(p,d,q) model, while for the Early-Adulthood parameters v_e and b_e we employ a VAR(1) model.

The 3C-STAD acts directly on age-at-death distributions, therefore we must ensure that the sum over ages x of the three component-specific probability masses is equal to 1, that is:

$$\sum_x f_{x,t} = \sum_x \left(f^c_{x,t} + f^e_{x,t} + f^s_{x,t}\right) = 1 \tag{6.11}$$

for each year t. Consequently and in addition to the shifting/variability parameters, it is necessary to forecast the probability masses of the three components. In particular, we recognize the compositional nature of a set of component-specific age-at-death distributions: we are dealing with three non-negative components that always sum to a constant. We thus employ a Compositional Data methodology to model and forecast the time series of component-specific probability masses (Aitchison 1986; Pawlowsky-Glahn and Buccianti 2011). Specifically, we transform the probability masses for each component obtained by the SSE model using an

[1]One readily implemented approach to derive the hazard from age-at-death distribution in `R` is provided by the function `convertFx` in the `MortalityLaws` package (Pascariu 2018).

additive log-ratio transformation. This procedure produces two time-series that are unconstrained (i.e. they take values on the entire set of real numbers). The two transformed time-series are modelled and forecast with a VAR(1). We finally back-transform the results to obtain forecasts of the original time-series. For each forecast year, these back-transformed series sum up to 1 because they have been treated as compositional data. Note that this approach reduces the dimensionality of the forecasting problem for the probability masses by one dimension, i.e. from three to two time-series.

Finally, the complexity of our methodology requires a bootstrapping procedure to produce prediction intervals (PI, Efron and Tibshirani 1994). We take into account the uncertainty of the 3C-STAD parameters by simulating 1000 new time-series of all parameters from randomly resampled residual values. For each simulation, we then forecast mortality patterns and associated summary measures. From the obtained distribution of forecast simulations, we took the median as central forecast, and the lowest and highest deciles to construct 80% PI. Residual bootstrap of this type has already been employed to construct PI in mortality models (Bergeron-Boucher et al. 2017; Basellini and Camarda 2019).

Routines for estimating and forecasting the parameters of the 3C-STAD model were implemented in `R` (R Development Core Team 2018) and are available online.[2] Our routines take advantage of the `R` packages `forecast`, `demography`, `MortalitySmooth`, `MortalityLaws` and `vars` (Pfaff 2008a,b; Hyndman and Khandakar 2008; Camarda 2012; Hyndman et al. 2018a,b; Pascariu 2018).

6.3 Results

6.3.1 Out-of-Sample Validation

Here, we assess the predictive performance of the 3C-STAD model using out-of-sample validation. Specifically, we employ data of the Human Mortality Database (2019) for the female and male populations of Sweden and Switzerland for the period 1950–2016. For each population, we perform three exercises, corresponding to validation periods of 10 years (training period 1950–2006), 20 years (training period 1950–1996) and 30 years (training period 1950–1986). The common starting year of analysis, 1950, was chosen in order to have training periods longer than validation horizons for each exercise.

To assess the performance of our forecasts, we employ the standard life-table functions: life expectancy at birth (e_0) as measure of population's longevity, and age-specific mortality rates (in log scale, $\ln(m_{x,t})$), which measure the age-pattern and intensity of mortality. Additionally, we use the Gini coefficient (G_0), a measure

[2] `R` codes to replicate all results presented in this chapter are available at https://github.com/ubasellini/3C-STADmodel.

of lifespan inequality, whose importance for evaluating mortality forecasts has been recently highlighted (Bohk-Ewald et al. 2017).

We compare the performance accuracy of the 3C-STAD model with three other forecasting methodologies. First, given its prominence and wide application, we employ the original Lee-Carter (LC) model (Lee and Carter 1992). Second, since one limitation of the LC model is the lack of smoothness in the fitted and forecast mortality rates, we use the Hyndman-Ullah (HU) functional data model (Hyndman and Ullah 2007), which overcomes this limitation by smoothing the starting data as a first step. Third, we choose the CODA model proposed by Oeppen (2008): this model is indeed closer in spirit to the 3C-STAD, as it models and forecasts the age-at-death distribution. The LC and HU models were estimated and forecast with the R packages `forecast` and `demography` (Hyndman et al. 2018a,b; Hyndman and Khandakar 2008). The CODA model was fitted and forecast using the R codes provided in the Supplementary Material of Bergeron-Boucher et al. (2017).

Our evaluations of mortality forecasts are based on the accuracy of both point predictions and calibration of prediction intervals (PI), as both measures are relevant for the validation of probabilistic projections (Chatfield 2000). Greater accuracy in point forecasts occurs when point predictions are closer to the observed data. To evaluate point forecasts, we employ the mean absolute error (MAE), which is defined as:

$$\text{MAE} = \frac{1}{N} \sum_{t \in T} |\hat{y}_t - y_t|$$

where $\hat{y}_t$ is the point forecast at time t for either life expectancy at birth, mortality rates or Gini coefficient. Associated out-of-sample observed values are denoted by y_t. The set of validation years is T, and N is the total number of data used for validation. Note that for mortality rates, mean is computed over ages, too.

Greater calibration of PI is achieved when the proportion of out-of-sample data that falls within the calculated PI is closer to the given nominal level (for example, 80% or 95%). To evaluate interval forecasts, we compute the empirical coverage probability (ECP) of the 80% PI for each model (as in, for example, Shang et al. 2011; Raftery et al. 2013). For the sake of consistency and fairness, we computed the PI for all models by the same bootstrapping procedure, i.e. residual bootstrap of the time-series of the model's parameters (cf. Sect. 6.2.4).

In addition to the MAE and ECP, scoring rules can be used to assess calibration and sharpness of probabilistic forecasts simultaneously (for a review, see Gneiting and Katzfuss 2014). Scoring rules allow one to jointly assess point and interval predictions by providing a summary measure of the predictive performance that forecasters aim to minimize. Here, we employ the Dawid-Sebastiani score (DSS) (Dawid and Sebastiani 1999), which is given by:

$$\text{DSS}_t = \frac{\left(y_t - \mu_{F,t}\right)^2}{\sigma_{F,t}^2} + 2 \ln \sigma_{F,t} \,, \quad t \in T$$

where $\mu_{F,t}$ and $\sigma^2_{F,t}$ are the first two central moments of the probabilistic forecast at time t, y_t is the associated out-of-sample observed value, and T is the set of validation years. We then compute the mean value of the DSS for all the data used for validation.

Table 6.2 reports the point, interval and probabilistic forecast accuracy of the four models in the three out-of-sample scenarios as well as for all the four populations analysed here. Bold values correspond to better performances. In terms of point forecast, the 3C-STAD is the most accurate model, as its forecasts are more or as precise as those of the other models. Out of 36 indicators, the 3C-STAD outperforms 20 times. The LC is the second most precise model with 9 indicators, followed by the HU and CODA models, each with 8 and 3 indicators, respectively. Note that the sum does not add up to the total number of indicators due to the draw of some models for some specific measures (for example, both the 3C-STAD and LC models are equally best performers for the indicator G_0 for Swedish females in the 30y exercise). In terms of interval forecast, the CODA outperforms all other models, being more accurate for 15 indicators over 36. The 3C-STAD, LC and HU follow, each with 12, 11 and 7 indicators, respectively. Finally, if we consider point and prediction accuracy simultaneously using the DSS measure, we find that the 3C-STAD model is the best performer, outperforming the others for 12 indicators. The LC, CODA and HU models follow with 9, 8 and 7 indicators, respectively.

6.3.2 Forecast to 2050

Having assessed and compared the forecast accuracy of the 3C-STAD model, we now present its mortality forecasts for the four populations analysed until 2050. As in the previous Subsection, we compare projections based on the 3C-STAD model with those of LC, HU and CODA models.

Figure 6.4 shows the observed and forecast life expectancy at birth (e_0) and Gini coefficient (G_0) in the four populations for the years 1950–2050. In terms of e_0, the 3C-STAD forecasts are always more optimistic than those of the LC and HU model. With respect to CODA, the 3C-STAD is more optimistic for males and less optimistic for females. In terms of lifespan inequality, CODA forecasts are the most egalitarian in 2050 (lower values of G_0) for the female populations, while the 3C-STAD predicts more equality for males.

In Fig. 6.5, we compare the age-specific mortality rates forecasts in 2050 for all populations. Several differences emerge between the models from this age-pattern analysis. Mortality rates of the 3C-STAD are smooth, lacking the jagged features visible in the LC and CODA forecasts. This is a great advantage for long-term mortality projections (Li et al. 2013). Additionally, the Swedish projections of the 3C-STAD do not display an unexpected S-shape displayed by other models in the age range 60–100.

Table 6.2 Mean absolute error (MAE), empirical coverage probability (ECP) for the 80% PI, and mean Dawid-Sebastiani score (DSS) of the 3C-STAD, LC, CODA and HU forecasts of e_0, G_0 and $\ln(m_{x,t})$ for females and males in two countries and three out-of-sample exercises: validation periods of 10 years (training period 1950–2006), 20 years (1950–1996) and 30 years (1950–1986). Lower values of the MAE and of the DSS (in bold) correspond to greater forecast accuracy. Values of the ECP closer to the 80% nominal level (in bold) correspond to greater interval forecast accuracy. (Source: as for Fig. 6.1)

				Forecast Accuracy											
				Point forecast (MAE)				**Interval forecast** (ECP for 80% PI)				**Probabilistic forecast** (mean DSS)			
Country	Training period	Validation period	Measure	3C-STAD	LC	CODA	HU	3C-STAD	LC	CODA	HU	3C-STAD	LC	CODA	HU
Switzerland Females	1950–2006	10y	e_0	**0.11**	0.29	0.40	0.16	100%	100%	100%	**90%**	−1.44	−1.03	**−0.72**	−2.15
			G_0	0.08	0.11	0.09	**0.06**	100%	**80%**	90%	**80%**	−4.12	**−2.83**	−2.89	−3.98
			$\ln(m_{x,t})$	**0.19**	0.24	0.24	0.22	38%	35%	**47%**	37%	8.69	23.63	58.46	**−4.98**
	1950–1996	20y	e_0	0.13	**0.11**	0.39	0.12	100%	100%	100%	**95%**	−0.54	**−0.51**	−0.51	−2.13
			G_0	0.08	**0.06**	0.21	0.10	90%	100%	95%	**85%**	−3.49	−2.73	**−2.08**	−3.13
			$\ln(m_{x,t})$	**0.19**	0.24	0.23	0.23	51%	48%	**54%**	38%	**−0.59**	32.49	17.09	−6.02
	1950–1986	30y	e_0	0.74	0.43	0.45	**0.20**	**87%**	100%	97%	93%	0.22	**0.08**	−0.64	−0.96
			G_0	0.21	0.40	0.30	**0.13**	70%	63%	37%	**77%**	−0.76	**−0.03**	−1.10	−2.82
			$\ln(m_{x,t})$	0.22	0.28	0.23	**0.20**	54%	50%	**58%**	43%	**−2.78**	4.42	7.84	−7.59
Switzerland Males	1950–2006	10y	e_0	**0.19**	0.41	0.34	0.78	100%	**90%**	100%	0%	−1.44	−0.72	**−0.32**	−3.96
			G_0	0.13	0.21	**0.12**	0.26	**80%**	70%	100%	10%	−3.16	−2.02	−2.29	**−1.23**
			$\ln(m_{x,t})$	**0.17**	0.23	0.20	0.20	37%	32%	**53%**	31%	**−2.18**	22.42	38.49	−7.17
	1950–1996	20y	e_0	**1.39**	1.59	1.61	2.23	10%	20%	**25%**	0%	2.82	3.14	**2.65**	43.43
			G_0	**0.46**	0.74	0.65	1.01	15%	0%	**20%**	0%	**0.90**	6.38	1.52	51.82
			$\ln(m_{x,t})$	**0.25**	0.29	0.28	0.32	29%	29%	**43%**	17%	**5.49**	168121	56.82	6.37
	1950–1986	30y	e_0	**1.55**	1.63	2.27	1.94	37%	**47%**	30%	17%	3.90	**2.39**	4.04	31.51
			G_0	0.98	**0.64**	0.88	0.71	20%	**27%**	**27%**	17%	3.10	**1.84**	3.31	39.06
			$\ln(m_{x,t})$	0.31	**0.27**	0.31	**0.27**	25%	35%	**42%**	21%	**5.52**	90.05	9.40	8.64

Sweden Females	1950–2006	10y	e_0	0.12	**0.10**	0.38	0.15	**100%**	**100%**	**100%**	**100%**	−2.27	−1.56	**−0.59**	−2.27
			G_0	0.07	**0.05**	0.13	0.12	**80%**	90%	100%	50%	−4.16	−3.67	−2.75	**−2.33**
			$\ln(m_{x,t})$	**0.16**	0.18	0.22	**0.16**	37%	39%	**55%**	44%	8.02	**1.98**	77.68	−6.74
	1950–1996	20y	e_0	0.46	**0.17**	0.73	0.46	**90%**	100%	95%	20%	−0.82	−0.68	0.28	**−0.04**
			G_0	**0.06**	0.10	0.20	**0.06**	95%	90%	95%	**85%**	−3.92	−2.69	**−2.20**	−4.00
			$\ln(m_{x,t})$	**0.18**	0.19	0.22	0.19	43%	45%	**54%**	28%	8.52	−5.90	36.68	**−4.24**
	1950–1986	30y	e_0	0.69	0.53	1.43	**0.43**	23%	**97%**	7%	30%	0.92	−0.11	8.16	**0.02**
			G_0	**0.07**	**0.07**	0.34	0.09	**80%**	87%	20%	70%	−2.31	−2.72	**1.87**	−3.59
			$\ln(m_{x,t})$	**0.18**	0.21	0.27	0.19	**39%**	**39%**	34%	29%	**0.10**	17.38	71.52	0.16
Sweden Males	1950–2006	10y	e_0	**0.11**	0.38	0.41	0.81	**100%**	**100%**	**100%**	0%	−1.65	−0.95	**−0.90**	4.72
			G_0	0.10	0.09	**0.03**	0.04	**70%**	**90%**	100%	100%	−3.48	**−3.04**	−3.51	−4.13
			$\ln(m_{x,t})$	**0.17**	0.23	0.19	0.18	43%	26%	**49%**	27%	9.49	103.96	111.90	**−4.47**
	1950–1996	20y	e_0	**0.72**	1.35	1.34	1.69	**100%**	30%	15%	0%	**0.20**	2.27	5.28	16.06
			G_0	0.32	0.37	**0.26**	0.39	15%	10%	**40%**	0%	**−0.17**	−0.19	−0.90	1.50
			$\ln(m_{x,t})$	**0.20**	0.29	0.23	0.21	**51%**	21%	32%	27%	**1.05**	105.81	55.83	−3.14
	1950–1986	30y	e_0	2.65	**2.43**	2.59	3.14	7%	**13%**	7%	0%	18.49	**7.64**	72.16	149.89
			G_0	**0.40**	0.83	0.93	1.02	**23%**	17%	10%	10%	**0.01**	10.40	67.76	76.51
			$\ln(m_{x,t})$	**0.29**	0.38	0.31	0.31	18%	**28%**	25%	16%	**7.24**	83.55	42.46	35.03

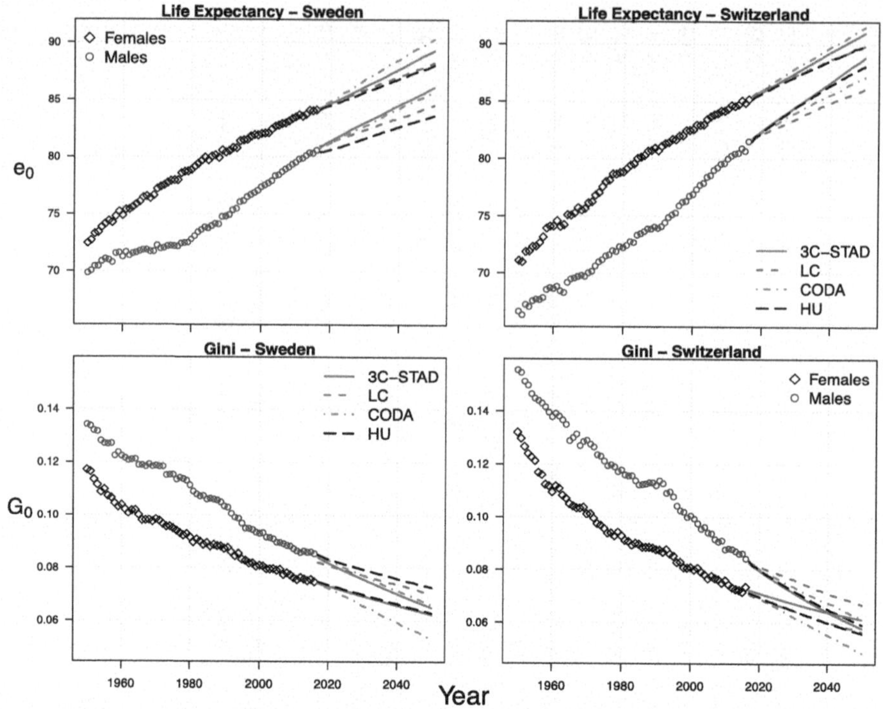

Fig. 6.4 Observed and forecast life expectancy at birth (e_0, top panels) and Gini coefficient (G_0, bottom panels) females and males in Sweden and Switzerland, 1950–2050. (Source: As for Fig. 6.1) (For the interpretation of the references to colors in this Figure, please refer to the electronic version of the chapter available online)

Finally, Fig. 6.6 shows the observed age-at-death distribution for the four populations in 2016, along with the 2050 forecasts of the four models. With respect to the other models, the 3C-STAD forecasts are characterized by greatest shift for all the populations. In addition to this, the 3C-STAD projections are also less compressed than those of other models, with the exception of Swedish males.

6.4 Discussion

Age-at-death distributions have generally been neglected for modelling and forecasting mortality, despite providing insightful information on mortality age-patterns and trends over time. In this chapter, we introduced a novel stochastic methodology to forecast mortality that is based on changes in age-at-death distributions. Our proposed Three-Component Segmented Transformation Age-at-death Distributions (3C-STAD) model captures and forecasts mortality developments over age and time by: (i) decomposing mortality into three independent components, namely

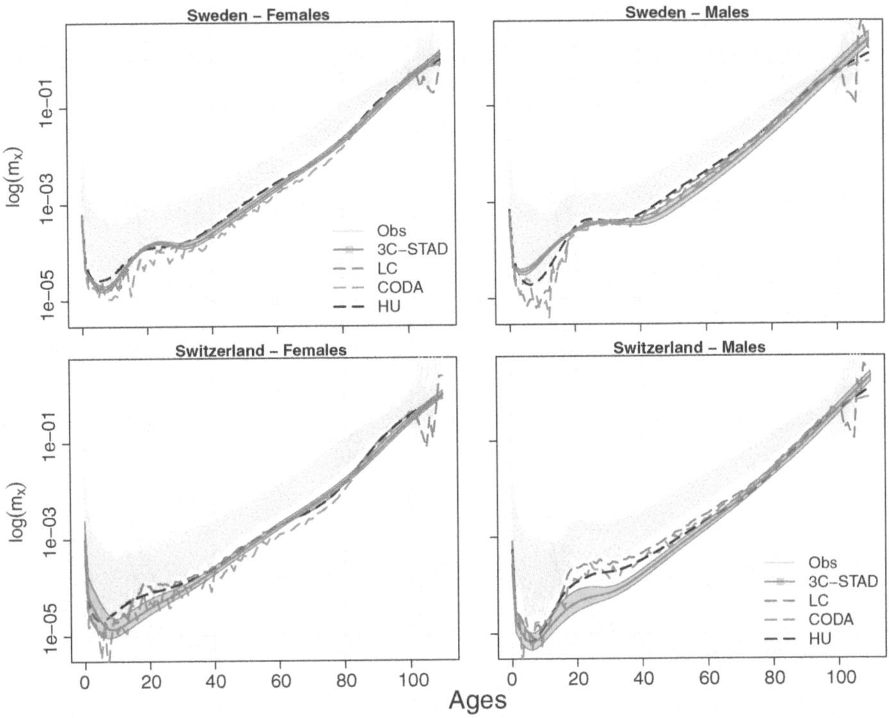

Fig. 6.5 Observed age-specific mortality rates in 1950–2016 (grey lines) and forecast rates of four models in 2050 for females and males in Sweden and Switzerland. Shaded areas correspond to 80% PI for the 3C-STAD model. (Source: As for Fig. 6.1) (For the interpretation of the references to colors in this Figure, please refer to the electronic version of the chapter available online)

Childhood, Early-Adulthood and Senescence, and (ii) modelling and forecasting changes in each component-specific age-at-death distributions.

The decomposition of the mortality age-pattern into multiple components has a long history in demographic analysis. In 1871, Thiele pioneered this decomposition by expressing the force of mortality as the sum of three independent components that operate principally, or almost exclusively, upon childhood, middle and old ages, respectively. Shortly afterwards, Lexis (1878) theorized a similar three-component decomposition, but he shifted the attention from the force of mortality to the age-at-death distribution. His ideas were followed upon and further elaborated by Pearson (1897), who divided the death density into five components, each one with its own distribution with different masses and degree of skewness. Finally, more recently, different parametric approaches have been proposed to decompose human mortality patterns (Siler 1979; Heligman and Pollard 1980; Kostaki 1992; de Beer and Janssen 2016; Mazzuco et al. 2018).

For our purposes, we performed a non-parametric decomposition using the Sum of Smooth Exponentials (SSE) model (Camarda et al. 2016). We favour this over other parametric approaches because it allows us to achieve a good fit to the

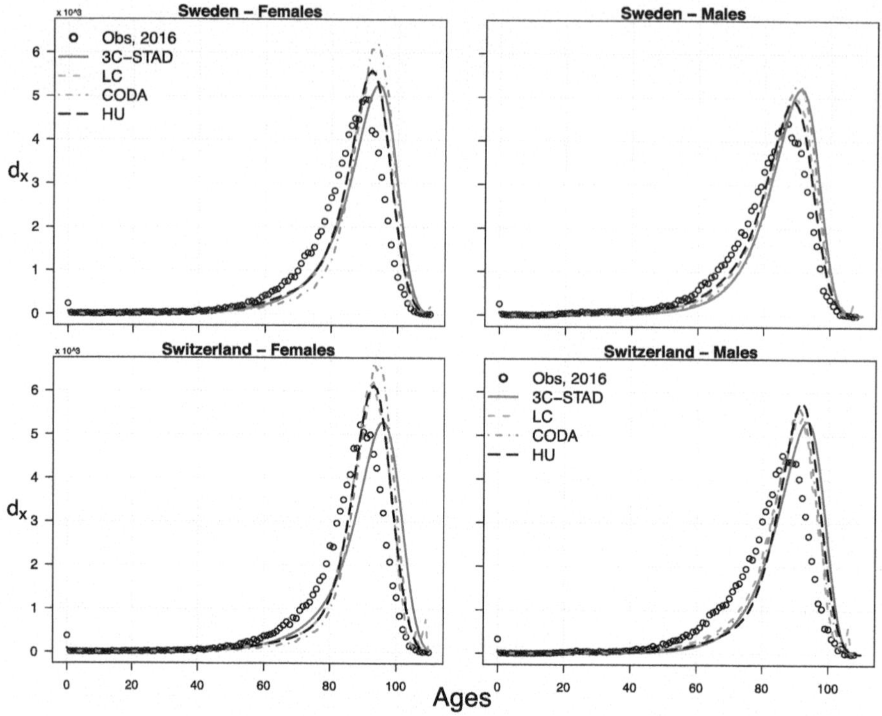

Fig. 6.6 Observed age-at-death distribution in 2016 (grey points) and forecasts of four models in 2050 for females and males in Sweden and Switzerland. (Source: As for Fig. 6.1) (For the interpretation of the references to colors in this Figure, please refer to the electronic version of the chapter available online)

observed data without imposing a rigid parametric structure, hence adapting the decomposition to a large and diverse range of mortality developments. Moreover, via the SSE model, we obtain smooth components with specific shape constraints, and a two-dimensional age-time perspective is incorporated into the mortality decomposition. Component-specific age-at-death distributions derived by the SSE model are then isolated to model and forecast their changes. To do so, we employ modified versions of the relational model proposed by Basellini and Camarda (2019), originally designed for forecasting only adult distributions of deaths.

We have applied the 3C-STAD model to the female and male populations of Sweden and Switzerland using data retrieved from the Human Mortality Database (2019). First, we assessed the point and interval forecast accuracy of the model by performing three out-of sample validation exercises. We have then forecast mortality for each population until 2050. In both cases, we compared the 3C-STAD projections with those of three well-known and employed methodologies: the Lee-Carter (LC, Lee and Carter 1992), the CODA (Oeppen 2008) and the Hyndman-Ullah (HU, Hyndman and Ullah 2007) models. We compare forecasts of summary measures, such as life expectancy as birth (e_0) and lifespan inequality (as measured by the Gini coefficient, G_0), as well as age-specific functions, such as death rates or age-at-death distributions.

The results of the out-of sample validation exercises show that the 3C-STAD produces accurate mortality forecasts, both in terms of point forecasts and prediction intervals (PI). In particular, the 3C-STAD was the most accurate model for point forecasts with respect to other models. Additionally, the 3C-STAD PI outperformed the other models for one indicator out of three (see Table 6.2).

Concerning interval forecasts, CODA was found relatively more accurate, a result that might be related to the fact that "the PI are wider with a CODA method than with an LC method" (Bergeron-Boucher et al. 2017, p. 546). However, when we considered point and interval forecasts simultaneously using a scoring rule, the wide PI of the CODA were penalized, and the 3C-STAD and LC models were preferred to the CODA. Within 3C-STAD framework, a possibility to improve estimation of PI would be to include the uncertainty related to the SSE decomposition. However, preliminary analyses showed that this approach raises computational burden without a significant widening of the forecast variability. It is likely that the reason is due to our usage of the SSE model. In the decomposition procedure, we aim to follow mortality data as close as possible, consequently the SSE model presents extremely small uncertainty. Nonetheless, we envisage alternative procedures to further improve estimation of the interval accuracy of the 3C-STAD model.

Mortality forecasts until 2050 for the four populations highlighted additional differences between models. The 3C-STAD and CODA forecasts of e_0 are generally more optimistic than those of the LC and HU models. Forecasting age-at-death distributions instead of mortality rates here translates into more optimistic forecast of life expectancy, a finding already observed elsewhere (Bergeron-Boucher et al. 2019). This could be an advantage, given that the LC forecasts have often under-predicted future gains in life expectancy (Lee and Miller 2001). Significant differences further emerge from an age-specific analysis of the different projections. On one side, the 3C-STAD forecast rates are inherently smooth, which is a desirable property especially for long-term projections (Li et al. 2013). On the other side, the 3C-STAD forecast age-at-death distributions are characterized by greater shifting and smaller compression than those of other models. These projections seem more plausible, given that the shifting mortality dynamic has replaced the compression one in high-longevity countries in the most recent decades (Canudas-Romo 2008; Bergeron-Boucher et al. 2015; Janssen and de Beer 2019).

In general, we regard three characteristics as desirable for any forecasting methodology. First, the model should be able to capture and forecast mortality trends that can move in different directions across ages. Second, the relevant dynamics of mortality changes observed during the last century, i.e. shift and compression, should be appropriately accounted for. Third, the forecast age-profile of mortality rates should be smooth, without implausible jaggedness where rates of adjacent age groups have very different and volatile values. Despite being one of the most employed forecasting methodology by public and private companies, the seminal LC model does not satisfy any of these properties. The single time index regulates the direction of change for mortality rates at all ages, i.e. mortality improvements occur in the same direction at all ages. Furthermore, the model cannot account for the two mortality dynamics, and forecasts age-pattern are very volatile and jagged (see Figs. 6.5 and 6.6).

Conversely, the 3C-STAD model meets all these three requirements. On one hand, the mortality decomposition allows us to capture and forecast mortality improvements across ages without rigid assumptions. Smoothness in the fitted and forecast age-profiles is a by-product of the non-parametric decomposition that we have employed. On the other hand, the 3C-STAD parameters capture and disentangle the shifting and compression mortality dynamics. The recently proposed model of Bardoutsos et al. (2018) is another example of projection methodology that satisfies these features.

Obviously, the 3C-STAD is not free of shortcomings, and neither we claim here that it outperforms all other forecasting methodologies. In addition to the width of the PI mentioned before, the computational time needed to produce mortality forecasts could be improved. The estimation of the two-dimensional SSE model in fact generally requires around thirty minutes, and speeding this step up will be required to shorten computational times. Future mortality values are obtained by forecasting eight time-series. Although this feature might pose issues in other situations, all of these series have clear demographic meanings and rather intelligible trends. Combination of univariate and multivariate time-series approaches has thus provided a reliable tool for overcoming this seemingly critical drawback of the 3C-STAD model. Different approaches in extrapolating the eight time-series will be pursuit, also for assessing consequences of specific future demographic scenarios. Moreover, in line with recent literature (Li and Lee 2005; Hyndman et al. 2013; Janssen et al. 2013; Bergeron-Boucher et al. 2017), future research will be directed towards the inclusion of coherence as an additional factor to improve forecasts for a group of (sub)populations.

To conclude, we have shown that the proposed 3C-STAD model offers great prospects for modelling and forecasting human mortality. In light of the generally pessimistic forecasts of the widely employed LC model (Li et al. 2013; Seligman et al. 2016), forecasting methodologies, such as the 3C-STAD, should be explored by pension and insurance providers to better assess their solvency needs, and by statistical bureaus to produce alternative population projections.

References

Aitchison, J. (1986). *The statistical analysis of compositional data*. London: Chapman and Hall.

Bardoutsos, A., de Beer, J., & Janssen, F. (2018). Projecting delay and compression of mortality. *Genus, 74*. Article number: 17.

Basellini, U., & Camarda, C. G. (2019). Modelling and forecasting adult age-at-death distributions. *Population Studies, 73*(1), 119–138.

Bergeron-Boucher, M.-P., Ebeling, M., & Canudas-Romo, V. (2015). Decomposing changes in life expectancy: Compression versus shifting mortality. *Demographic Research, 33*(14), 391–424.

Bergeron-Boucher, M.-P., Canudas-Romo, V., Oeppen, J., & Vaupel, J. W. (2017). Coherent forecasts of mortality with compositional data analysis. *Demographic Research, 37*(17), 527–566.

Bergeron-Boucher, M.-P., Kjærgaard, S., Oeppen, J., & Vaupel, J. W. (2019). The impact of the choice of life table statistics when forecasting mortality. *Demographic Research, 41*, 1235–1268.

Bohk-Ewald, C., Ebeling, M., & Rau, R. (2017). Lifespan disparity as an additional indicator for evaluating mortality forecasts. *Demography, 54*(4), 1559–1577.

Bongaarts, J. (2005). Long-range trends in adult mortality: Models and projection methods. *Demography, 42*(1), 23–49.

Booth, H., & Tickle, L. (2008). Mortality modelling and forecasting: A review of methods. *Annals of Actuarial Science, 3*(1–2), 3–43.

Brillinger, D. R. (1986). A biometrics invited paper with discussion: The natural variability of vital rates and associated statistics. *Biometrics, 42*(4), 693–734.

Cairns, A. J., Blake, D., Dowd, K., Coughlan, G. D., Epstein, D., Ong, A., & Balevich, I. (2009). A quantitative comparison of stochastic mortality models using data from England and Wales and the United States. *North American Actuarial Journal, 13*(1), 1–35.

Camarda, C. G. (2012). MortalitySmooth: An R package for smoothing poisson counts with *P*-splines. *Journal of Statistical Software, 50*, 1–24. Available on www.jstatsoft.org/v50/i01.

Camarda, C. G., Eilers, P. H., & Gampe, J. (2016). Sums of smooth exponentials to decompose complex series of counts. *Statistical Modelling, 16*(4), 279–296.

Canudas-Romo, V. (2008). The modal age at death and the shifting mortality hypothesis. *Demographic Research, 19*, 1179–1204.

Chatfield, C. (2000). *Time-series forecasting*. London: Chapman & Hall/CRC.

Chiang, C. L. (1984). *The life table and its applications*. Malabar: Krieger.

Csete, J., & Grob, P. J. (2012). Switzerland, HIV and the power of pragmatism: Lessons for drug policy development. *International Journal of Drug Policy, 23*(1), 82–86.

Dawid, A. P., & Sebastiani, P. (1999). Coherent dispersion criteria for optimal experimental design. *The Annals of Statistics, 27*(1), 65–81.

de Beer, J., & Janssen, F. (2016). A new parametric model to assess delay and compression of mortality. *Population Health Metrics, 14*. Article number: 46.

Efron, B., & Tibshirani, R. J. (1994). *An introduction to the bootstrap*. Boca Raton: CRC.

Eilers, P. H. (2007). Ill-posed problems with counts, the composite link model and penalized likelihood. *Statistical Modelling, 7*(3), 239–254.

Eilers, P. H. C., & Marx, B. D. (1996). Flexible smoothing with *B*-splines and penalties (with discussion). *Statistical Science, 11*(2), 89–102.

Fries, J. F. (1980). Aging, natural death, and the compression of morbidity. *New England Journal of Medicine, 303*(3), 130–135.

Gage, T. B. (1993). The decline of mortality in England and Wales 1861 to 1964: decomposition by cause of death and component of mortality. *Population Studies, 47*(1):47–66.

Gneiting, T., & Katzfuss, M. (2014). Probabilistic forecasting. *Annual Review of Statistics and Its Application, 1*(1), 125–151.

Haberman, S., & Renshaw, A. (2011). A comparative study of parametric mortality projection models. *Insurance: Mathematics and Economics, 48*(1), 35–55.

Heligman, L., & Pollard, J. H. (1980). The age pattern of mortality. *Journal of the Institute of Actuaries, 107*(1), 49–80.

Heuveline, P. (2002). An international comparison of adolescent and young adult mortality. *The ANNALS of the American Academy of Political and Social Science, 580*(1), 172–200.

Horiuchi, S., Ouellette, N., Cheung, S. L. K., & Robine, J.-M. (2013). Modal age at death: Lifespan indicator in the era of longevity extension. *Vienna Yearbook of Population Research, 11*, 37–69.

Human Mortality Database. (2019). University of California, Berkeley (USA) and Max Planck Institute for Demographic Research (Germany). Available at www.mortality.org or www.humanmortality.de (data downloaded on 15 February 2019).

Hyndman, R., & Khandakar, Y. (2008). Automatic time series forecasting: The forecast Package for R. *Journal of Statistical Software, 27*(3), 1–22.
Hyndman, R. J., & Ullah, M. S. (2007). Robust forecasting of mortality and fertility rates: A functional data approach. *Computational Statistics and Data Analysis, 51*(10), 4942–4956.
Hyndman, R. J., Booth, H., & Yasmeen, F. (2013). Coherent mortality forecasting: The product-ratio method with functional time series models. *Demography, 50*(1), 261–283.
Hyndman, R., Athanasopoulos, G., Bergmeir, C., Caceres, G., Chhay, L., O'Hara-Wild, M., Petropoulos, F., Razbash, S., Wang, E., & Yasmeen, F. (2018a). *Forecast: Forecasting functions for time series and linear models*. R package version 8.4.
Hyndman, R. J., Booth, H., Tickle, L., & Maindonald, J. (2018b). *Demography: Forecasting mortality, fertility, migration and population data*. R package version 1.21.
Janssen, F., & de Beer, J. (2019). The timing of the transition from mortality compression to mortality delay in Europe, Japan and the United States. *Genus, 75*. Article number: 10.
Janssen, F., van Wissen, L. J. G., Kunst, A. E. (2013). Including the smoking epidemic in internationally coherent mortality projections. *Demography, 50*(4), 1341–1362.
Kannisto, V. (2000). Measuring the compression of mortality. *Demographic Research, 3*(article 6). https://doi.org/10.4054/DemRes.2000.3.6.
Kannisto, V. (2001). Mode and dispersion of the length of life. *Population: An English Selection, 13*, 159–171.
Klein, J. P., & Moeschberger, M. L. (2003). *Survival analysis: Techniques for censored and truncated data* (2nd ed.). New York: Springer Science & Business Media.
Kostaki, A. (1992). A nine-parameter version of the Heligman-Pollard formula. *Mathematical Population Studies, 3*(4), 277–288.
Lee, R. D., & Carter, L. R. (1992). Modeling and forecasting US mortality. *Journal of the American Statistical Association, 87*(419), 659–671.
Lee, R., & Miller, T. (2001). Evaluating the performance of the Lee-Carter method for forecasting mortality. *Demography, 38*(4), 537–549.
Lexis, W. H. R. A. (1878). Sur la durée normale de la vie humaine et sur la théorie de la stabilité des rapports statistiques. *Annales de Démographie Internationale, 2*(5), 447–460.
Li, N., & Lee, R. (2005). Coherent mortality forecasts for a group of populations: An extension of the Lee-Carter method. *Demography, 42*(3), 575–594.
Li, N., Lee, R., & Gerland, P. (2013). Extending the Lee-Carter method to model the rotation of age patterns of mortality decline for long-term projections. *Demography, 50*(6), 2037–2051.
Lotka, A. J. (1939). Théorie analytique des associations biologiques. Part II. Analyse démographique avec application particuliere al'espece humaine. *Actualités Scientifiques et Industrielles* (780). Hermann et Cie, Paris, France.
Mazzuco, S., Scarpa, B., & Zanotto, L. (2018). A mortality model based on a mixture distribution function. *Population Studies, 72*(2), 191–200.
Oeppen, J. (2008). Coherent forecasting of multiple-decrement life tables: A test using Japanese cause of death data. In *Compositional data analysis conference*.
Oeppen, J., & Camarda, C. G. (2013). Coherent forecasting of multiple-decrement life tables: Compositional models for French cause of death data, 1925–2008. In *Joint Eurostat/UNECE work session on demographic projections*.
Pascariu, M. D. (2018). *MortalityLaws: Parametric mortality models, life tables and HMD*. R package version 1.7.0.
Pascariu, M. D., Lenart, A., & Canudas-Romo, V. (2019). The maximum entropy mortality model: Forecasting mortality using statistical moments. *Scandinavian Actuarial Journal, 8*, 661–685. https://www.tandfonline.com/doi/full/10.1080/03461238.2019.1596974.
Pawlowsky-Glahn, V., & Buccianti, A. (Eds.). (2011). *Compositional data analysis: Theory and applications*. London: Wiley.
Pearson, K. (1897). *The chances of death, and other studies in evolution* (Vol. 1). London: E. Arnold.
Pfaff, B. (2008a). *Analysis of integrated and cointegrated time series with R*. New York: Springer Science & Business Media.

Pfaff, B. (2008b). VAR, SVAR and SVEC models: Implementation within R package vars. *Journal of Statistical Software, 27*(4), 1–32.
Pollard, J. H. (1987). Projection of age-specific mortality rates. *Population Bulletin of the United Nations, 21–22*, 55–69.
Preston, S. H., Heuveline, P., & Guillot, M. (2001). *Demography. Measuring and modeling population processes*. Oxford: Blackwell.
R Development Core Team. (2018). *R: A language and environment for statistical computing*. Vienna: R Foundation for Statistical Computing.
Raftery, A. E., Chunn, J. L., Gerland, P., & Ševčíková, H. (2013). Bayesian probabilistic projections of life expectancy for all countries. *Demography, 50*(3), 777–801.
Ramsay, J. O., & Silverman, B. W. (2005). *Functional data analysis* (2nd ed.). New York: Springer.
Remund, A., Camarda, C. G., & Riffe, T. (2018). A cause-of-death decomposition of young adult excess mortality. *Demography, 55*(3), 957–978.
Seligman, B., Greenberg, G., & Tuljapurkar, S. (2016). Convergence in male and female life expectancy: Direction, age pattern, and causes. *Demographic Research, 34*, 1063–1074.
Shang, H. L., Booth, H., & Hyndman, R. (2011). Point and interval forecasts of mortality rates and life expectancy: A comparison of ten principal component methods. *Demographic Research, 25*(5), 173–214.
Siler, W. (1979). A competing-risk model for animal mortality. *Ecology, 60*(4), 750–757.
Stoeldraijer, L., van Duin, C., van Wissen, L., & Janssen, F. (2013). Impact of different mortality forecasting methods and explicit assumptions on projected future life expectancy: The case of the Netherlands. *Demographic Research, 29*, 323–354.
Thiele, T. N. (1871). On a mathematical formula to express the rate of mortality throughout the whole of life, tested by a series of observations made use of by the Danish Life Insurance Company of 1871. *Journal of the Institute of Actuaries and Assurance Magazine, 16*(5), 313–329.
Thompson, R., & Baker, R. (1981). Composite link functions in generalized linear models. *Applied Statistics, 30*(2), 125–131.
Vaupel, J., & Lundström, H. (1994). Longer life expectancy? Evidence from Sweden of reductions in mortality rates at advanced ages. In *Studies in the economics of aging* (pp. 79–102). Chicago: University of Chicago Press.
Whelpton, P. K. (1928). Population of the United States, 1925 to 1975. *American Journal of Sociology, 32*(2), 253–270.
Whelpton, P. K. (1936). An empirical method of calculating future population. *Journal of the American Statistical Association, 31*(195), 457–473.
Wilmoth, J. R., & Horiuchi, S. (1999). Rectangularization revisited: Variability of age at death within human populations. *Demography, 36*(4), 475–495.
Wilmoth, J. R., & Lundström, H. (1996). Extreme longevity in five countries. *European Journal of Population/Revue Européenne de Démographie, 12*(1), 63–93.

Chapter 7
Alternative Forecasts of Danish Life Expectancy

Marie-Pier Bergeron-Boucher, Søren Kjærgaard, Marius D. Pascariu, José Manuel Aburto, Jesús-Adrián Alvarez, Ugofilippo Basellini, Silvia Rizzi, and James W. Vaupel

7.1 Background

Forecasts of life expectancy have become essential in the estimation of future health care and pension costs and in planning social security policies. Demand for accurate mortality forecasts is high and new models are being introduced each year. One of the most commonly used is the Lee-Carter (LC) model (Lee and Carter 1992), which forecasts age-specific death rates in a log-linear way. Most high-income countries have recorded a log-linear decline of their age-specific death rates, as well as a linear increase of their life expectancy (White 2002). Given these regularities, linear extrapolation is a justifiable approach to predict future mortality and is at

Electronic Supplementary Material The online version of this chapter (https://doi.org/10.1007/978-3-030-42472-5_7) contains supplementary material, which is available to authorized users.

M.-P. Bergeron-Boucher (✉) · S. Kjærgaard · J.-A. Alvarez · S. Rizzi · J. W. Vaupel
Interdisciplinary center on population dynamics, University of Southern Denmark, Odense, Denmark
e-mail: mpbergeron@sdu.dk

M. D. Pascariu
Biometric Risk Modeling Chapter, SCOR Global Life, Paris, France

J. M. Aburto
Interdisciplinary center on population dynamics, University of Southern Denmark, Odense, Denmark

Department of Sociology & Leverhulme Centre for Demographic Science, University of Oxford, Oxford, UK

U. Basellini
Laboratory of Digital and Computational Demography, Max Planck Institute for Demographic Research (MPIDR), Rostock, Germany

S. Mazzuco, N. Keilman (eds.), *Developments in Demographic Forecasting*, The Springer Series on Demographic Methods and Population Analysis 49,
https://doi.org/10.1007/978-3-030-42472-5_7

the foundation of most forecasting models (Booth and Tickle 2008). However, when mortality development is not linear, reliance on such an assumption can be problematic.

Signs of stagnation in period life expectancy were observed in many low-mortality countries during the second half of the twentieth century. For example, life expectancy stagnated in Eastern European countries between the 1960s and 1980s, in the Netherlands between 1988 and the early 2000s (especially for females) and in Denmark in the 1980s. While each case of stagnation is unique, behaviors such as drinking and smoking play an important role in non-linear mortality development (Vallin and Meslé 2004; Stoeldraijer 2019). Effects from specific cohorts are also at play in some countries, i.e. stagnation or slower decline in mortality can result from childhood living conditions or harmful behavior such as smoking in adulthood, from certain birth cohorts (Lindahl-Jacobsen et al. 2016; Janssen and Kunst 2005). This chapter explores the difficulty in forecasting mortality when breaks in the trends are observed, using the example of Denmark.

In the 1950s, Denmark had one of the world's highest life expectancies for both sexes, but fell behind many other European countries in the following decades (Jarner et al. 2008). Especially, during the 1980s, female life expectancy stagnated and did not make significant gains until the mid-1990s (Christensen et al. 2010). This stagnation has been mainly attributed to high death rates for generations born between the two World Wars, due to high smoking prevalence and other risk factors (Lindahl-Jacobsen et al. 2016). Since the mid-1990s, life expectancy in Denmark has increased at a similar rate to that of other high-income countries, but continues to lag behind Sweden, a country similar to Denmark in many societal aspects (Christensen et al. 2010).

Such broken trends render forecasting more complex. Should the irregularities of the past be used in forecasting? The official forecasts of life expectancy in Denmark are based on data from 1990, to lower the effect of the stagnation period. However, Danish life expectancy is currently catching up with that of other high-income countries and the recent increase might not be representative of a long-term trend.

This chapter summarizes the conclusions of the *Forecasting Danish Life Expectancy and Age at Retirement Workshop*, held on December 10, 2018 in Odense, Denmark and can be divided into three main sections. First, methodological issues relating to forecasting mortality in Denmark are discussed. Second, the forecasting results and accuracy of different models are compared for Danish females and males and for both cohorts and periods. Third, implications of the different forecast models for Danish society are presented, both in terms of age at retirement and lifespan variability.

7.2 Methods

Danish official forecasts are based on the LC model (Lee and Carter 1992), with an adjustment of the initial parameters using the Lee and Miller (2001) variant and based on data since 1990 only (Hansen and Stephensen 2013). Whether the

Table 7.1 Summary of the forecast models compared

	Model	Reference	Indicator	Period forecast	Cohort forecast	Coherence
1	Random walk with drift (RWD)	Bell (1997)	m_{xt}	Yes	From period forecast	No
2	Lee-Carter (LC)	Lee and Carter (1992)	m_{xt}	Yes	From period forecast	No
3	Li-Lee (LL)	Li and Lee (2005)	m_{xt}	Yes	From period forecast	Yes
4	Compositional Data approach (CoDA)	Oeppen (2008)	d_{xt}	Yes	From period forecast	No
5	Coherent CoDA approach (CoDA-C)	Bergeron-Boucher et al. (2017)	d_{xt}	Yes	From period forecast	Yes
6	Constant increase (CI)	–	e_{0t}	Yes	No	No
7	Oeppen and Vaupel (OV) best practice increase	(Oeppen and Vaupel 2002, 2019)	e_{0t}	Yes	No	Yes
8	Double-gap (DG)	Pascariu et al. (2018)	e_{xt}	Yes	No	Yes
9	Maximum entropy model (MEM)	Pascariu et al. (2019)	Moments	Yes	No	No
10	Cohort Segmented Transformation Age at Death Distributions (C-STAD)	Basellini et al. (2020)	d_{xt}	No	Yes	No
11	Penalized composite link model (PCLM)	Rizzi et al. (2019)	d_{xt}	No	Yes	No

approach is optimal has not, however, been demonstrated. In this chapter, 11 models to forecast Danish life expectancy are compared (Table 7.1). The list of models is far from exhaustive, but provides an overview of a range of available forecast models.

7.2.1 Period Forecasts

The models here compared are extrapolative. The extrapolative approach is often preferred by statistical offices (Booth and Tickle 2008; Stoeldraijer et al. 2013). The models were selected based on their use of different indicators. Bergeron-Boucher et al. (2019) show that the use of different indicators for forecasting leads to significant differences in the results. Other forecasting models could have been used but we have limited the list to the models enumerated in Table 7.1, because they cover the variety of different life table indicators and also to limit the number of cross comparisons. For each indicator, at least one model is a coherent model (see Sect. 7.4.1 for further discussion on coherent models), with the exception of model nr. 9 based on statistical moments, as coherent models following such an approach have not been developed.

The first model involves applying a random walk with drift (RWD) to age-specific logged death rates. This approach is a simple log-linear extrapolation over time t of death rates (m_{xt}) at each age x independently (Bell 1997).

The second model is the Lee-Carter (LC) model. Lee and Carter (1992) popularized the use of the age-specific death rates and principal component analysis to forecast mortality. This method has been extensively used and many extensions have been suggested (Brouhns et al. 2002; Hyndman and Ullah 2007; Li et al. 2013; Li and Lee 2005; Booth et al. 2002, 2006; Lee and Miller 2001; Alho 1998). The model decomposes a centered matrix of log death rates indexed by time and age, using a singular value decomposition (SVD), into an overall level of mortality over time and the age-specific responses to this level. The time-level is extrapolated using time series models with a linear deterministic trend. The method has many advantages, including simplicity, easily interpretable parameters, and minimal subjective judgment (Booth and Tickle 2008). However, the age-specific responses, which can be interpreted as the age-specific rates of mortality improvement if multiplied by the time-level, are constant over time in this model, while evidence shows that they have been increasing, especially at older ages (Kannisto et al. 1994; Booth and Tickle 2008).

The third model is the Li-Lee (LL), which is an extension of the LC model to coherent forecasts for a group of populations (Li and Lee 2005). The LL model is based on the idea that closely related populations – e.g., provinces in a country or neighboring countries – are likely to have similar mortality trends. Forecasting such populations separately tends to increase their differences. Li and Lee (2005) thus suggest that the average of the populations be forecast using the LC model and then forecast the population-specific deviations from this average, using a stationary process. With this approach, the population-specific mortality trends are constrained so that they do not extensively diverge from the average.

Rather than using age-specific death rates, Oeppen (2008) suggests using the life table distribution of deaths (d_{xt}) to forecast mortality with Compositional Data Analysis (CoDA). CoDA is a framework to deal with compositional data, which are defined as positive values representing part of a whole and summing to a constant (e.g., percentages) (Pawlowsky-Glahn and Buccianti 2011). By treating life table deaths as compositional data and using a CoDA framework, the deaths are constrained to vary between 0 and the life table radix (e.g., 1 or 100,000), which conditions the relationship between components. Bergeron-Boucher et al. (2017) show that, by using Oeppen's CoDA approach, the rates of mortality improvement increase over time, providing more optimistic and less biased forecasts than the LC model. The fourth model is an adaptation of the LC model to CoDA using life table deaths distribution (Oeppen 2008) and the fifth model is an adaptation of the LL model to CoDA (Bergeron-Boucher et al. 2017). These models are respectively called CoDA and CoDA coherent (CoDA-C).

Models extrapolating life expectancy directly can also be used. Among them, we compare a simple approach extrapolating the life expectancy at birth e_{0t} using the mean rate of improvement in e_{0t} over past years. We call this approach constant increase (CI).

Alternatively, life expectancy can be assumed to increase by 2.2 years per decade. This increase is equal to the gains in the female best-practice in life expectancy, as defined by Oeppen and Vaupel (2002), since 1960. This approach is here called Oeppen and Vaupel (OV) best practice increase.

Another model based on life expectancy extrapolation is the double-gap (DG) model. The DG model is used to coherently forecast female and male life expectancy in a certain country or region with reference to a benchmark level, for example, the trend given by the long-term historical record life expectancy in the world. The sex-gap in life expectancy is assessed to forecast the male life expectancy in the analyzed population. The extrapolation process is based on classic time series methods (Pascariu et al. 2018).

The final period model is the maximum entropy method (MEM). The MEM makes use of the statistical properties of a probability density function in order to estimate the distribution of deaths of a population in the future (Pascariu et al. 2019). Time series methods for forecasting a limited number of central statistical moments are used and then a reconstruction of the future distribution of deaths using the predicted moments is performed. The estimation of the density function is made using the maximum entropy approach (Mead and Papanicolaou 1984).

7.2.2 Cohort Forecasts

All models selected in this chapter, so far, are designed to forecast period mortality. The first five models (RWD, LC, LL, CoDA and CoDA-C), based on age-specific data, can also be used to forecast cohort mortality by reading the period forecast matrices of death rates by time and age along a diagonal. With the CoDA and CoDA-C models, the forecast life table deaths distributions are transformed into death rates using life table calculations (Preston et al. 2001) and a similar reading is made. Additionally, we compared two models specifically designed to use cohort data to make forecasts: The Cohort Segmented Transformation Age-at-death Distributions

(C-STAD) model and a Penalized Composite Link Model (PCLM). True cohort forecasts, i.e. those based on cohort data only, have rarely been achieved (Booth and Tickle 2008), and the C-STAD and PCLM models are among the first to obtain such forecasts.

The C-STAD model is a method that has been recently proposed to model and forecast cohort mortality (Basellini et al. 2020). Specifically, the C-STAD is a relational model based on a warping transformation of the age axis of a reference distribution of deaths. The parameters of the transformation function capture mortality changes in terms of shifting and compression dynamics. Mortality forecasts are obtained from their extrapolation using standard time series models. The C-STAD is a generalization of the approach proposed by Basellini and Camarda (2019) to model and forecast adult period mortality from age-at-death distributions.

Another method recently proposed to forecast cohort age-at-death distributions is based on the PCLM (Penalized Composite Link Model) for ungrouping data (Eilers 2007; Rizzi et al. 2015). The counts of a cohort life table distribution of deaths are treated as realizations of a Poisson process. The age-at-death distribution is modeled by a penalized maximum likelihood, under the following assumptions: (i) the forecast age-at-death distribution is smooth; (ii) no deaths are observed after age 120; (iii) when the last observed age of deaths is far from the mode, the latter is a priori forecast with a simple ARIMA model. The PCLM smoothly redistributes the remaining deaths in the right-hand tail of the age-at-death distribution of a cohort not yet extinct (Rizzi et al. 2019).

7.3 Data

Observed death rates for Denmark were extracted from the Human Mortality Database (HMD 2019) by sex, and life tables were constructed using the standard procedure (Preston et al. 2001). When a death rate is equal to zero, the value was replaced by half of the minimum death rate observed in the dataset, as many of the models cannot be estimated with the presence of zeros. Zeros are, however, rare in the dataset. Overall, data from 1925 to 2016 for both females and males were extracted, but different fitting periods are used across the analyses.

For the LL, CoDA-C and DG models, a reference population is needed. For the LL and CoDA-C models, the reference population is the average mortality trend for Denmark, Sweden, the Netherlands and the United Kingdom. The average is the geometric mean of the death rates of these four countries for the LL model and the associated life table distribution of deaths for the CoDA-C. Data for these countries were also extracted from the HMD. The choice of the reference population is based on the analysis of Kjærgaard et al. (2016). The selected reference population provides the most accurate forecasts for Denmark and consists of countries with similar mortality trends that are geographically close to Denmark. For the DG model, the reference population is the best practice in life expectancy, as defined by Oeppen and Vaupel (2002) and based on countries within the HMD that have the highest life expectancy each year (Pascariu et al. 2018).

7.4 Methodological Challenges in Forecasting Life Expectancy in Denmark

7.4.1 Non-linear Trends

Figure 7.1 shows life expectancy at birth over time in Denmark and Sweden, for females and males. Segmented regressions (Muggeo 2003) have been applied to the trends. The slope of each segment and the year when a break occurs are marked in the figure. For both females and males, the increase in life expectancy was similar for Sweden and Denmark until the second half of the 1970s. After 1977, the Danish female life expectancy increase slowed down until 1995, thus lagging more and more behind Sweden. After 1995, female life expectancy in Denmark increased faster than in the previous period and faster than that of Sweden. The gap in life expectancy between these two countries has been closing in recent years. For males, the Swedish life expectancy increase accelerated in 1979, while in Denmark this break first occurred in 1992. However, the increase in life expectancy since the mid-1990s has been faster for Danish males than for Swedish males. As for females, the gap between the two countries has been closing since the mid-1990s.

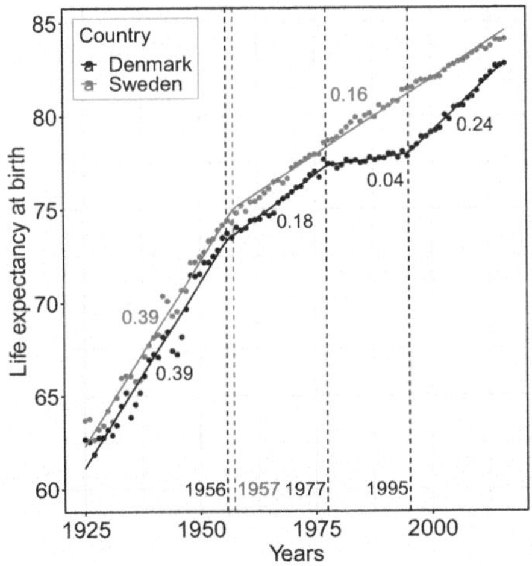

(a) Females

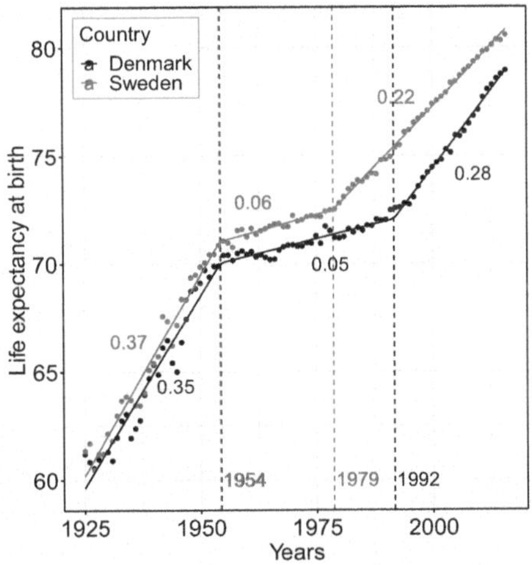

(b) Males

Fig. 7.1 Life expectancy at birth in Denmark (lower curve) and Sweden (upper curve) between 1925 and 2016, with segmented regressions, (**a**) Females and (**b**) Males

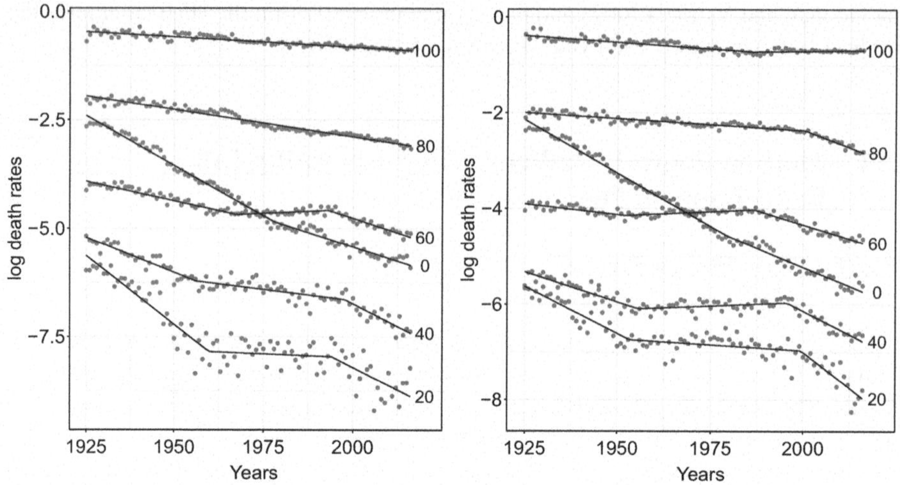

(a) Females (b) Males

Fig. 7.2 Log death rates in Denmark between 1925 and 2016 at specific ages, with segmented regressions, (**a**) Females and (**b**) Males

Breaks in trends are also observed in the age-specific death rates, especially between age 20 and 70 (Fig. 7.2). Imposing a linear development of past trends and extrapolating these trends in the future thus seems to be inadequate to forecast Danish mortality. Using non-linear or segmented trends could be an option. However, predicting when or if the next break would occur is arduous. When non-linearity in the trends is observed, Stoeldraijer (2019) suggests two approaches.

First, if the causes of the non-linear trends are known, information about these causes could be included in the forecasts. For example, the non-linearity of life expectancy in Denmark has been attributed to smoking (Christensen et al. 2010; Lindahl-Jacobsen et al. 2016). Adjusting for the distorting effect of smoking on mortality is thus likely to improve forecast accuracy (Janssen and Kunst 2007; Bongaarts 2014). Some authors have developed models to forecast mortality that account for smoking (Preston et al. 2014; Janssen et al. 2013; Wang and Preston 2009; Bongaarts 2006). Janssen et al. (2013) show that non-smoking mortality has more linear trends than all-cause mortality. However, risk factors (e.g., smoking) and other epidemiological information are often difficult to forecast as they often have non-linear trends; their relationship with mortality is often imperfectly understood; assumptions about future behaviors are often required; and data on, e.g., smoking or smoking-related mortality, are needed (Booth and Tickle 2008; Wilmoth 1995; Raftery et al. 2014). Given these constraints, epidemiological models are not compared here.

The second recommendation of Stoeldraijer (2019) is to use coherent forecast models (e.g., the LL model) for countries with less linear trends, especially if the causes of the non-linearity are unknown. White (2002) and Oeppen and Vaupel (2002) show that, among high-income countries, gains in life expectancy from countries lagging behind tend to be faster than those of leading countries. They also found that gains from leaders in life expectancy tend to slow down. White (2002) attributes these trends to a convergence in life expectancy towards a mean. Country-specific trends might deviate temporarily from the mean, but will eventually converge towards it. White (2002) also notices that the mean life expectancy among a group of high-income countries is more linear than country-specific trends. Oeppen and Vaupel (2002) find a nearly perfect linear trend in the increase in the record life expectancy over time. Both White (2002) and Oeppen and Vaupel (2002) conclude that these regularities (in the record or average) could be used to forecast mortality and highlight the need to consider mortality changes in an international perspective. Janssen and Kunst (2007) state "[...] we recommend using the experience of other countries not to set target values of life expectancy, but to create a broader empirical basis for the identification of the most likely long-term trend" (Janssen and Kunst 2007, p. 323).

7.4.2 *Length of Fitting Period*

Given the non-linear mortality trends in Denmark, a basic question is whether or not only recent trends should be used to forecast Danish life expectancy. Table 7.2 shows the difference in predicted life expectancy in 2066 with eight models, when different fitting periods are used: 1960–2016, 1975–2016 and 1990–2016. As the OV approach is not affected by a fitting period, this model is ignored in this section, as well as the models using cohort data. All the other models are sensitive to the fitting period, leading to differences of between 0.3 and 5.7 years for the same model in a 50-year forecast. The forecast results are as sensitive to the fitting period as they are to the model selected. The forecasts based on the most recent period are the most optimistic for both sexes and all models. The Danish population experienced fast improvements in mortality in the recent period and it is thus not surprising that forecasts based on data since the 1990s are more optimistic than those that take the period of stagnation into account.

Table 7.2 Forecasts of life expectancy at birth in 2066 using eight models and three fitting periods: 1960–2016, 1975–2016 and 1990–2016

	Females				Males			
	1960–2016	1975–2016	1990–2016	Range	1960–2016	1975–2016	1990–2016	Range
RWD	89.0	88.0	89.5	1.5	84.3	85.2	87.6	3.3
LC	87.2	87.4	89.0	1.8	83.9	85.6	87.5	3.6
LL	87.9	88.2	88.8	0.9	84.3	86.6	88.1	3.7
CoDA	89.2	88.4	89.8	1.4	85.5	87.2	89.7	4.2
CoDA-C	89.9	89.6	89.9	0.3	86.3	88.5	90.4	4.1
MEM	89.8	89.5	91.5	2.0	86.5	87.5	89.3	2.8
CI	90.6	89.8	92.5	2.7	86.5	88.3	92.2	5.7
DG	90.5	96.2	93.0	5.6	87.8	93.5	90.3	5.6
Range	3.4	8.8	4.2	–	3.9	8.3	4.7	–

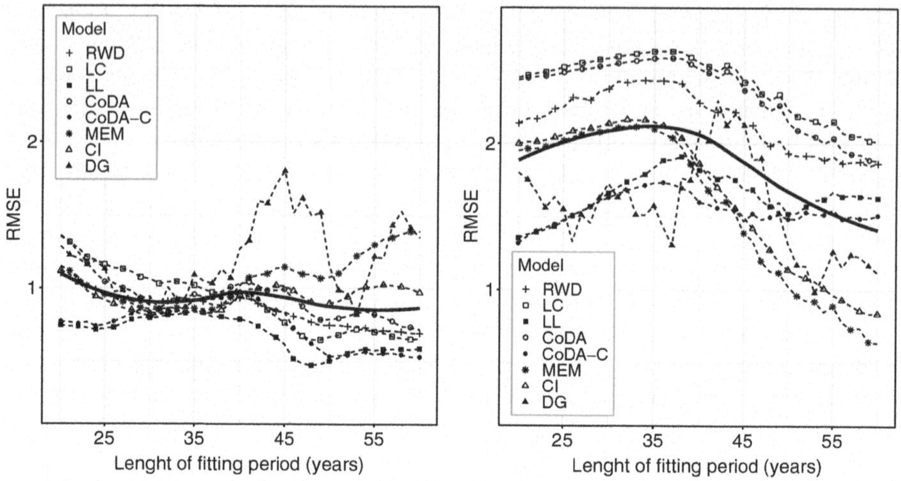

(a) Females (b) Males

Fig. 7.3 Average RMSE of life expectancy for a 20-year forecast with starting year from 1985 to 1997, by length of fitting period and model; and smoothed average across models (full line), (**a**) Females and (**b**) Males

To evaluate which length of fitting period would have produced the most accurate forecasts for Denmark, an out-of-sample analysis is performed. Data starting from the year 1985 to 1997 are forecast 20 years ahead based on different lengths of the fitting period. For example, life expectancy between 1985 and 2004 is forecast based on the previous 15 years (1970–1984) to the previous 60 years (1925–1984). This procedure is repeated for forecasts starting from 1985 to 1997. In total, 552 forecasts were made. The root mean square error (RMSE) of each forecast is calculated and averaged by length of the fitting period.

Figure 7.3 shows the RMSE for forecasts based on different lengths of fitting period. The results differ by model, but as a general conclusion, the longer the fitting period, the better. A general rule of thumb among forecasting experts is that the fitting period should be at least as long as the forecast horizon. Following this rule, a 20-year forecast should be based on, at least, 20 years of historical data. Our results suggest that longer fitting periods, rather than shorter ones, generally would have provided more accurate forecasts for recent mortality trends. A similar conclusion is drawn for a 50-year forecast (results not shown here). The results also suggest that the coherent models (LL and CoDA-C) are less sensitive to the length of the fitting period, especially for females. For males, a shorter fitting period for the LL and CoDA-C models would have been more accurate.

It is important to understand whether an observed period of stagnation or acceleration is the emergence of a new dynamic or a temporal effect. Janssen and Kunst (2007) argue that, because the stagnation in Denmark and also in Norway and the Netherlands is mainly attributable to smoking and was not observed in other countries, it should be regarded as a temporal effect and longer fitting periods should be preferred. Our results are in line with those of Janssen and Kunst (2007) and suggest that long fitting periods should be used to forecast Danish life expectancy. A new dynamic has been in place since the late 1950s (see Fig. 7.1), with gains in life expectancy being mainly attributable to mortality reductions at old ages and from cardiovascular diseases (Christensen et al. 2009; Vallin and Meslé 2010). Lee and Miller (2001) argue that using data since 1950, with the LC model, reduces the bias of the forecasts for the United States.

7.5 Forecasting with Different Models

7.5.1 Period Forecasts

Given the results of Sect. 7.4.2, a fitting period from 1960 is selected and we forecast life expectancy 50 years ahead with the models described in Sect. 7.2.1. As the official Danish forecasts are based on an LC model that uses data since 1990 only, we also use a similar approach which we call LC90.

In 2066, life expectancy at birth is forecast to be between 87.2 and 95.3 years for females and between 83.9 and 91.4 years for males (Fig. 7.4). The forecast results thus vary by the model selected. The most pessimistic model is LC and the most optimistic is the OV for both sexes, for the period selected.

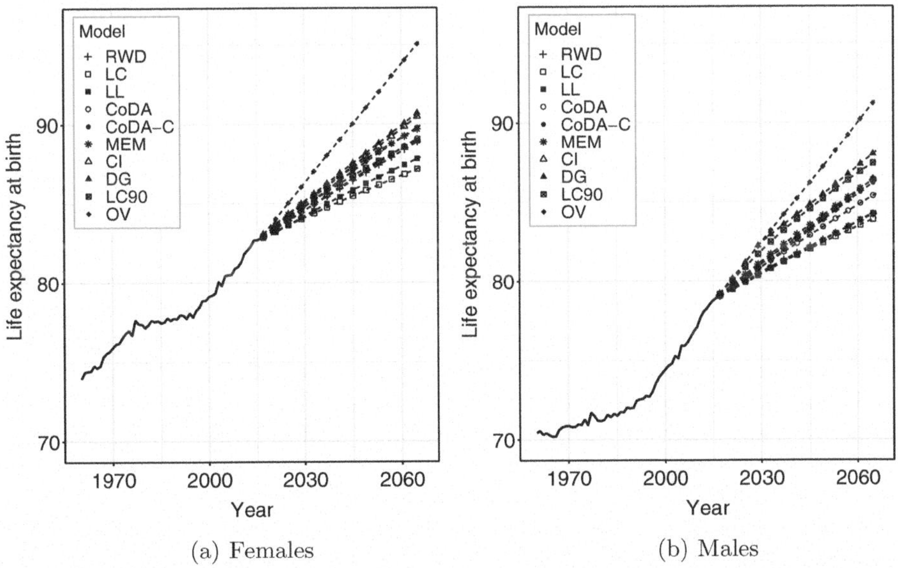

Fig. 7.4 Period life expectancy at birth forecast 50 years ahead using ten models, (**a**) Females and (**b**) Males

Table 7.3 Average RMSE of life expectancy at birth over forecast horizons of 6 to 26 years, with the two lowest values in bold and rankings displayed in parentheses, females and males

	RWD	LC	LL	CoDA	CoDA-C	MEM	CI	DG	OV
Females	1.15	1.40	0.98	1.08	**0.68**	0.99	0.99	1.11	**0.34**
	(8)	(9)	(3)	(6)	(2)	(5)	(4)	(7)	(1)
Males	2.16	2.34	1.78	2.29	1.66	1.89	1.95	**1.65**	**0.68**
	(7)	(9)	(4)	(8)	(3)	(5)	(6)	(2)	(1)

Given the variations across models, the forecast accuracy of the models is estimated by way of an out-of-sample analysis. Recent life expectancy trends are forecast for a horizon of 6 to 26 years using historical data, with 2016 being the final year of the forecast horizon, and the RMSE is calculated for each horizon and then averaged. For example, if the forecast horizon is 26 years, we use data from 1960 to 1990 as the fitting period and forecast life expectancy from 1991 to 2016. As the LC90 model is based on data from 1990, this approach is not evaluated but can be considered similar to the LC approach. The results are presented in Table 7.3. The OV approach would have been the most accurate to forecast recent life expectancy trends in Denmark. The increase in life expectancy of 0.22 years annually is close to the yearly gain in life expectancy observed in Denmark since the mid-1990s (Fig. 7.1). Aside from the OV approach, models using a reference population – i.e. LL, CoDA-C and DG – would have predicted recent life expectancy in Denmark more accurately than the other models. Danish life expectancy has been catching up with other countries in recent years and the results confirm that these models better capture this trend, as discussed in Sect. 7.4.1.

7.5.2 *Cohort Forecasts*

When looking at forecasts of cohort life expectancy (Table 7.4), the results among models described in Sect. 7.2.2 are similar for older cohorts. For example, females born in 1950 are predicted to live between 79.8 and 80.5 with all models, except the C-STAD model, which forecasts a life expectancy of 81.1. Differences across models are even smaller for males for this cohort, with a predicted life expectancy of between 74.4 and 74.9. As mortality was observed until age 66 in 2016 for this cohort, less variation is seen in the forecasts. As for the period forecasts, the difference across models increases with the forecast horizon. The models based on cohort experience – i.e. C-STAD and PCLM – tend to be more optimistic than the other models, which are based on period forecasts. These models are based on cohort data only. In order to fit the models and complete the mortality experience of a cohort, partial information on this specific cohort is needed. Reliable estimates are obtained for cohorts born up to 1970 and 1960, for C-STAD and PCLM, respectively. Thus, the C-STAD and PCLM models cannot be used to forecast mortality of more recent cohorts.

Table 7.4 Cohort life expectancy at birth for specific cohorts forecast with eight models, the range of the forecast values across the eight models and range across the six models based on period forecasts

	Females					Males				
	1950	1960	1970	1980	2018	1950	1960	1970	1980	2018
1. RWD	80.5	82.6	85.1	87.0	92.6	74.5	76.8	79.2	81.4	86.3
2. LC	80.0	81.8	83.9	85.3	89.1	74.4	76.6	79.0	81.0	85.3
3. LC90	80.2	82.3	84.8	86.7	91.5	74.9	77.8	80.9	83.7	89.8
4. LL	80.2	82.0	84.2	85.8	89.9	74.4	76.6	79.1	81.2	86.1
5. CoDA	80.3	82.3	84.8	86.7	92.0	74.5	76.9	79.5	81.9	87.5
6. CoDA-C	80.4	82.5	85.2	87.2	92.5	74.5	76.9	79.8	82.3	88.6
7. C-STAD	81.1	83.6	87.2	–	–	74.7	77.2	80.1	–	–
8. PCLM	79.8	82.8	–	–	–	74.6	77.3	–	–	–
Range 1–8	1.3	1.8	–	–	–	0.5	1.2	–	–	–
Range 1–6	0.5	0.8	1.3	1.9	3.5	0.5	1.2	1.9	2.7	4.5

7.6 Implications for Danish Society

Forecasts are key to planning economic, health, education and social policies, among others. Large variations in forecast results lead to greater uncertainty about costs, investments and policy planning. Two estimates derived from mortality forecasts are here compared across models: (1) Age at retirement and (2) Lifespan variability.

The forecasts presented in Sect. 7.5.1 are used to estimate the predicted age at retirement and lifespan variability, when possible. The DG, CI and OV models do not allow for an estimation of indicators based on life table statistics, other than e_0.

7.6.1 Age at Retirement

To ensure the sustainability of the Danish pension system, the Danish government implemented in 2007 a system where the pension age is increased if life expectancy is increasing. The legislation regulates the pension age 15 years ahead and it is based on life expectancy at age 60 and an expected increase of 0.6 years over a 15 years period. Based on this assumption, if the Danish population is expected to have a life expectancy at retirement age higher than 14.5 years, pension age is increased by a maximum of one year over a five year period. Changes to the pension age need to be approved by a majority in the Danish parliament. Regulations are voted on with 15 years notice every five years, with the next regulation coming up in 2020. Future pension ages have been decided until 2030 and pension ages until 2035 will be decided in 2020.

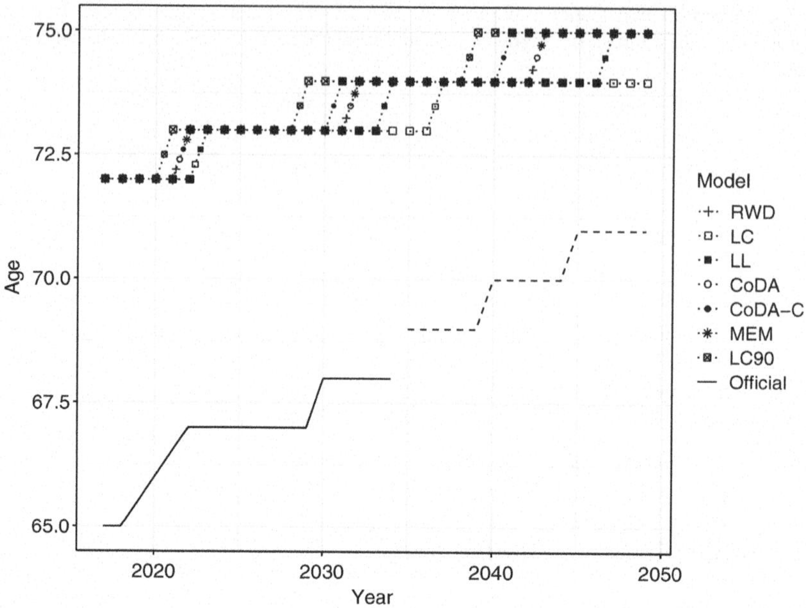

Fig. 7.5 Age with remaining life expectancy of 14.5 years, based on seven models, and official age at retirement, 2017–2049

As pension ages after 2030 are unknown, we focus on the desired number of years lived after retirement – i.e. 14.5 years – to evaluate the consequences of the different mortality forecasts. Figure 7.5 shows the age with a remaining life expectancy of 14.5 years ($x_{e(x)=14.5}$), for both sexes combined, forecast using different models. The Figure also shows the official pension age approved by the Danish parliament and the maximum increase in the pension age of one year every five years (dashed) after 2030. In 2016, the official pension age was 65 and $x_{e(x)=14.5}$ was 72. The gap between the official pension age and $x_{e(x)=14.5}$ persists in the forecasts, as the official pension age cannot increase faster than one year every five years. Nevertheless, the gap is expected to narrow for all models, if the pension age is increased by its maximum. A maximum increase in the pension age is likely if the policymakers want to bring the average number of years lived after retirement down to 14.5 years. A large gap between $x_{e(x)=14.5}$ and the pension age is forecast with all models, meaning that the expected number of years spent at retirement will be higher than 14.5.

Figure 7.6a shows the predicted number of years lived at retirement by sex, based on the Danish official pension age for the years where pension ages are determined. With all models, except the LC90 for males, the number of years lived after retirement is predicted to decline over time. The Danish population for most models is expected to be entitled to fewer years with a pension compared to older generations. Males are also expected to live fewer years after retirement than

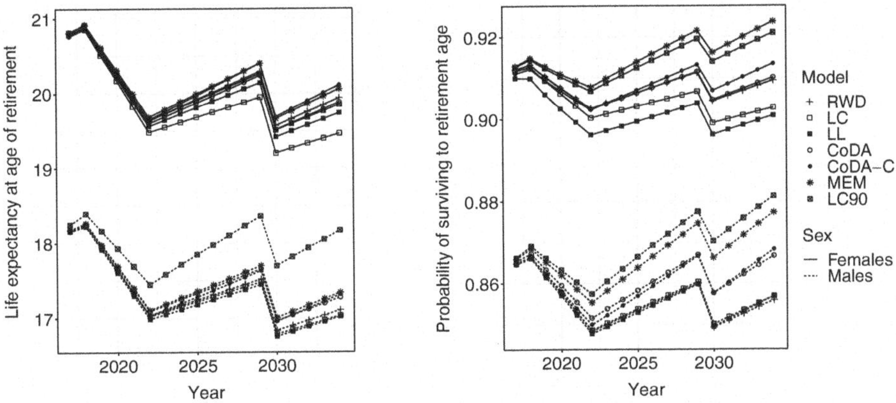

(a) Number of years lived at retirement

(b) Probability of surviving to retirement age

Fig. 7.6 Number of years lived at retirement and probability of surviving from birth to retirement age using seven forecasting models, Denmark, 2017–2034

are females. Similar trends are also observed for the cohort forecasts (results not shown here).

However, the models provide different trends when looking at the probability of surviving to the age at retirement (Fig. 7.6b). With the LC and LL models, the survival probability to age at retirement decreases until 2022 and then fluctuates at around 90.3% for females and 85.6% for males. For the MEM and LC90 models, an increase in the survival probabilities to retirement is expected, after an initial decline until 2022.

7.6.2 Lifespan Inequalities

Population health is often summarized by a single measure – life expectancy. However, standard measures of longevity, such as life expectancy, conceal variations in lifespan. Inequality in the length of life is an important indicator of the uncertainty in the timing of death and of heterogeneity in underlying population health at the macro level (van Raalte et al. 2018). Life expectancy and lifespan inequality are usually negatively correlated (Fig. 7.7) (Colchero et al. 2016; Vaupel et al. 2011). Here, we measure lifespan inequality with average life expectancy lost at death, denoted with $e^{\dagger}$ (Vaupel and Canudas-Romo 2003). For example, if an individual at time of death has 20 years of remaining life expectancy, then he/she contributes 20 years to lifespan inequality. Since 1960, Danish improvements in life expectancy and lifespan equality were halted by smoking-related mortality in those born between 1919 and 1939, while reductions in old-age cardiovascular mortality further held back lifespan equality (Aburto et al. 2018). It has been shown that, in Denmark, early

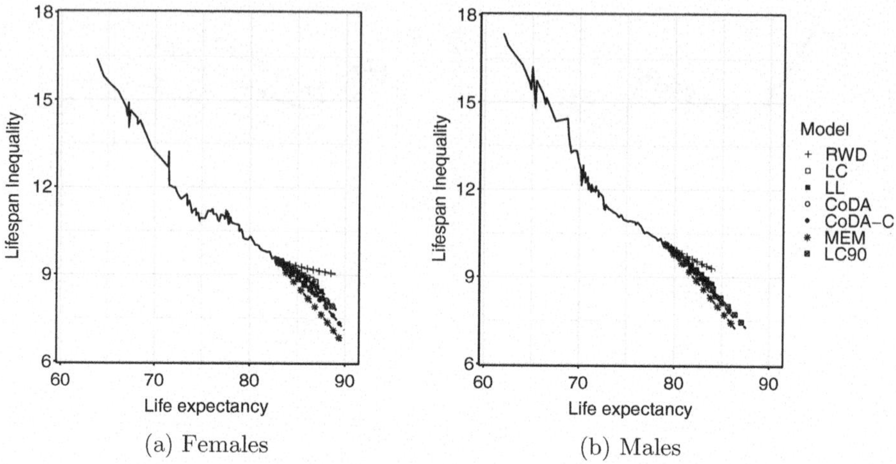

Fig. 7.7 Relation between life expectancy and lifespan inequality observed (lines) and forecast (shapes) between 1935 and 2066 in Denmark. **(a)** Females. **(b)** Males

deaths are more common in underprivileged groups, simultaneously reducing life expectancy and increasing lifespan inequality (Brønnum-Hansen 2017). Therefore, lifespan inequality, together with life expectancy, give a broader perspective on the effect of mortality changes on population health.

Moreover, evaluating the predictive ability of mortality forecasts is imperative, yet difficult. Accounting for lifespan inequality can help with this challenge (Bohk-Ewald et al. 2017). Therefore, we included lifespan inequality in our forecasting scenarios. As life expectancy at birth increases, lifespan inequality decreases (Fig. 7.7). However, at advanced ages, life expectancy increases can coincide with a rise in lifespan inequality (Engelman et al. 2010), as observed until the 1990s in Denmark when age at retirement was 65 (Fig. 7.8). Our mortality forecasts suggest a decrease in lifespan inequality from age at retirement in Denmark. This implies that ages at death after retirement could become more equal, which could help in the distribution of health resources by concentrating them in a narrow group of ages.

7.7 Discussion

The choice of model and fitting period leads to large variations in forecasts. Bergeron-Boucher et al. (2019) show that the choice of indicator to forecast mortality (e.g., death rates or life expectancy) also leads to significant differences in the forecasts, even when applying a similar extrapolative model on each indicator. Some scholars have proposed that assigning a higher weight to most recent observations would produce better forecasts (Hyndman and Shang 2009), a procedure that is not discussed in our analysis. Such an approach is equivalent to downplaying trends

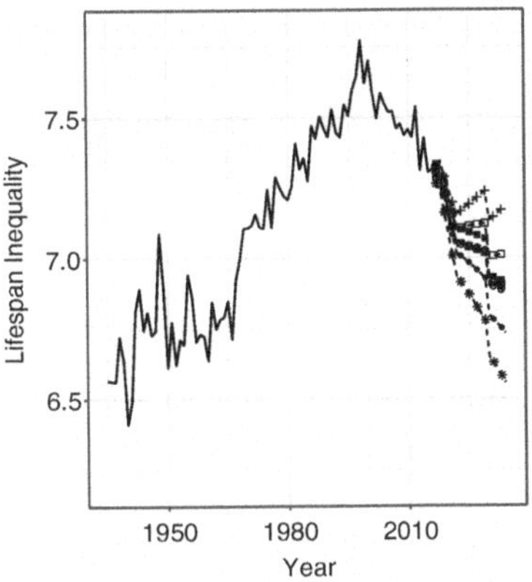

(a) Females

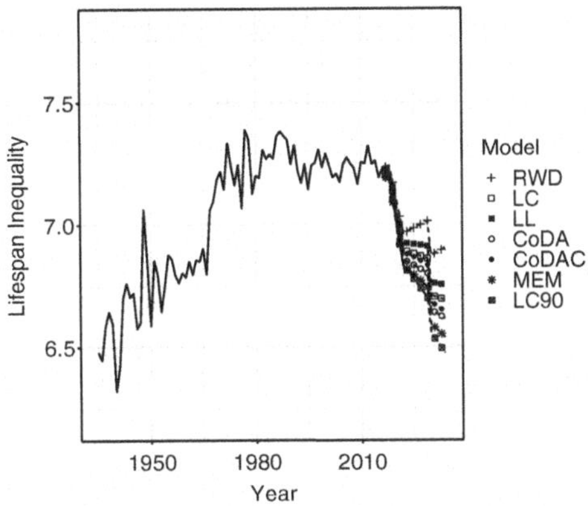

(b) Males

Fig. 7.8 Lifespan inequality observed (lines) and forecast (shapes) from the age at retirement between 1935 and 2034, Denmark. **(a)** Females. **(b)** Males

in the more distant past. Preliminary results suggest that this practice does not improve forecasts in all cases. For instance, when forecasting Danish mortality with commonly used models, such as the LC, the most accurate results were achieved without weighting schemes and by using long fitting periods. Despite our findings for Danish mortality, further research about how to weight historical data is necessary, in particular for countries exhibiting mortality deterioration and life expectancy reversals (e.g., former Soviet countries). Given the sensitivity of forecasts to these different factors, decisions have to be made by forecasters, which can often involve subjectivity, and choosing the optimal approach becomes a difficult task.

Nevertheless, our results show that the best extrapolative model to forecast recent period life expectancy in Denmark is based on a simple assumption of a 2.2 years' increase per decade, with the gap between Danish life expectancy and forecast best-practice life expectancy neither widening nor narrowing. The reason for this result is that, in our out-of-sample analysis, the increase during the validation period (1991–2016) was close to 2.2 years per decade. If other periods had been used for validation, this approach might not have shown similar performance. Aside from this OV approach, our results suggest that using coherent models, such as the LL, CoDA-C or the DG models would have provided more accurate forecasts of recent mortality trends in Denmark than other models. One could also argue that the OV approach is coherent, if life expectancy in all countries is assumed to increase at the same pace of that of a benchmark, which here is the best-practice. Additionally, the results show that a longer fitting period would have generally increased forecast accuracy. The stagnation in life expectancy in Denmark should thus be considered as a temporal effect and a model considering the catching up of Danish mortality trends towards other high-income countries should be preferred.

Stoeldraijer (2019) and Kjærgaard et al. (2016) found that forecasts with coherent models are sensitive to the choice of the reference population. Stoeldraijer (2019) found that the sensitivity of different coherent models differs between females and males, with the LL model being the most sensitive for females and the less sensitive for males, compared with two other coherent models. Kjærgaard et al. (2016) explore which reference population provides the most accurate forecasts and found that the optimal reference population differs across countries. The results of their analysis suggest that selecting a few countries with similar trends in life expectancy to the population of interest as the reference population increases forecast accuracy. This strategy was here used for the LL and CoDA-C models.

Accounting for smoking and cohort effects is also worth exploring when forecasting Danish mortality. However, as stated by Stoeldraijer (2019): "Because more assumptions are required in a method that incorporates smoking, a trade-off must be made between the advantage of being able to take the impact of smoking into account and the advantage of the objectivity of a pure extrapolation approach based on total mortality" (Stoeldraijer 2019, p. 21). As such, in this chapter we have limited our analyses to extrapolative models, often favored by statistical offices to produce official forecasts.

An important aspect of forecasting, which was not discussed in this chapter, is the prediction intervals. As the future is uncertain, it is important to estimate the uncertainty of a forecast. An indication of a likely range of values should thus be included when forecasting (Booth and Tickle 2008).

This chapter highlights the challenges in forecasting mortality in Denmark and the sensitivity of the forecasts to the different choices faced by the forecasters, e.g., which models, indicators and reference period should be used? Given that official forecasts are used to plan economic and social policies, these choices should be made carefully and analytically.

Replicability

The data and R codes used for the LC, LL, CoDA, CoDA-C and MEM models are publicly available at https://github.com/mpascariu/MortalityForecast. The DG model data and R codes are available in the *MortalityGaps* R package (Pascariu 2018) and at https://github.com/mpascariu/MortalityGaps.

Acknowledgements The authors wish to thank the participants to the *Workshop on Forecasting Danish Life Expectancy and Age at Retirement* held on December 10, 2018. A special thank you to Juha Alho, Henrik Bang, Marianne Frank Hansen, Søren Jarner, Christian Møller Dahl and Daria Kachakhidze for interesting and enlightening discussions.

References

Aburto, J. M., Wensink, M., van Raalte, A., & Lindahl-Jacobsen, R. (2018). Potential gains in life expectancy by reducing inequality of lifespans in Denmark: An international comparison and cause-of-death analysis. *BMC Public Health, 18*(1), 831.

Alho, J. M. (1998). A stochastic forecast of the population of Finland. *Statistics Finland Reviews, 4*(1), 32. Helsinki: Tilastokeskus.

Basellini, U., & Camarda, C. G. (2019). Modelling and forecasting adult age-at-death distributions. *Population Studies, 73*(1), 119–138. PMID: 30693848.

Basellini, U., Kjærgaard, S., & Camarda, C. G. (2020). An age-at-death distribution approach to forecast cohort mortality. *Insurance: Mathematics and Economics, 91*, 129–143.

Bell, W. R. (1997). Comparing and assessing time series methods for forecasting age-specific fertility and mortality rates. *Journal of Official Statistics, 13*(3), 279–303.

Bergeron-Boucher, M.-P., Canudas-Romo, V., Oeppen, J., & Vaupel, J. W. (2017). Coherent forecasts of mortality with compositional data analysis. *Demographic Research, 37*(17), 527–568.

Bergeron-Boucher, M.-P., Kjærgaard, S., Oeppen, J., & Vaupel, J. W. (2019). The impact of the choice of life table statistics when forecasting mortality. *Demographic Research, 41*(43), 1235–1268.

Bohk-Ewald, C., Ebeling, M., & Rau, R. (2017). Lifespan disparity as an additional indicator for evaluating mortality forecasts. *Demography, 54*(4), 1559–1577.

Bongaarts, J. (2006). How long will we live? *Population and Development Review, 32*(4), 605–628.

Bongaarts, J. (2014). Trends in causes of death in low-mortality countries: Implications for mortality projections. *Population and Development Review, 40*(2), 189–212.

Booth, H., & Tickle, L. (2008). Mortality modelling and forecasting: A review of methods. *Annals of Actuarial Science, 3*, 3–43.

Booth, H., Maindonald, J., & Smith, L. (2002). Applying Lee-Carter under conditions of variable mortality decline. *Population Studies, 56*(3), 325–336.

Booth, H., Hyndman, R., Tickle, L., & de Jong, P. (2006). Lee-Carter mortality forecasting: A multi-country comparison of variants and extensions. *Demographic Research, 15*(9), 289–310.

Brønnum-Hansen, H. (2017). Socially disparate trends in lifespan variation: A trend study on income and mortality based on nationwide Danish register data. *BMJ Open, 7*(5).

Brouhns, N., Denuit, M., & Vermunt, J. K. (2002). A poisson log-bilinear regression approach to the construction of projected lifetables. *Insurance: Mathematics and Economics, 31*(3), 373–393.

Christensen, K., Davidsen, M., Juel, K., Mortensen, L., Rau, R., & Vaupel, J. W. (2010). The divergent life-expectancy trends in Denmark and Sweden—And some potential explanations. In E. Crimmins, S. Preston, & B. Cohen (Eds.), *International differences in mortality at older ages: Dimensions and sources* (pp. 385–408). Washington, DC: National Academies Press.

Christensen, K., Doblhammer, G., Rau, R., & Vaupel, J. W. (2009). Ageing populations: The challenges ahead. *The Lancet, 374*(9696), 1196–1208.

Colchero, F., Rau, R., Jones, O. R., Barthold, J. A., Conde, D. A., Lenart, A., Nemeth, L., Scheuerlein, A., Schoeley, J., Torres, C., Zarulli, V., Altmann, J., Brockman, D. K., Bronikowski, A. M., Fedigan, L. M., Pusey, A. E., Stoinski, T. S., Strier, K. B., Baudisch, A., Alberts, S. C., & Vaupel, J. W. (2016). The emergence of longevous populations. *Proceedings of the National Academy of Sciences, 113*(48), E7681–E7690.

Eilers, P. H. (2007). Ill-posed problems with counts, the composite link model and penalized likelihood. *Statistical Modelling, 7*(3), 239–254.

Engelman, M., Canudas-Romo, V., & Agree, E. M. (2010). The implications of increased survivorship for mortality variation in aging populations. *Population and Development Review, 36*(3), 511–539.

Hansen, M. F., & Stephensen, P. (2013). Danmarks fremtidige befolkning. Technical report, Befolkningsfremskrivning 2013. DREAM rapport 2013. www.dreammodel.dk.

HMD. (2019). Human Mortality Database, University of California, Berkeley (USA), and Max Planck Institute for Demographic Research (Germany). http://www.mortality.org.
Hyndman, R. J., & Shang, H. L. (2009). Forecasting functional time series. *Journal of the Korean Statistical Society, 38*(3), 199–211.
Hyndman, R. J., & Ullah, S. (2007). Robust forecasting of mortality and fertility rates: A functional data approach. *Computational Statistics and Data Analysis, 51*(10), 4942–4956.
Janssen, F., & Kunst, A. E. (2005). Cohort patterns in mortality trends among the elderly in seven European countries, 1950–1999. *International Journal of Epidemiology, 34*(5), 1149–1159.
Janssen, F., & Kunst, A. (2007). The choice among past trends as a basis for the prediction of future trends in old-age mortality. *Population Studies, 61*(3), 315–326.
Janssen, F., van Wissen, L. J., & Kunst, A. E. (2013). Including the smoking epidemic in internationally coherent mortality projections. *Demography, 50*(4), 1341–1362.
Jarner, S. F., Kryger, E. M., & Dengsøe, C. (2008). The evolution of death rates and life expectancy in Denmark. *Scandinavian Actuarial Journal, 2008*(2–3), 147–173.
Kannisto, V., Lauritsen, J., Thatcher, A. R., & Vaupel, J. W. (1994). Reductions in mortality at advanced ages: Several decades of evidence from 27 countries. *Population and Development Review, 20*(4), 793–810.
Kjærgaard, S., Canudas-Romo, V., Bergeron-Boucher, M.-P., & Vaupel, J. (2016). The importance of the reference populations for coherent mortality forecasting models. In *European Population Conference*, Mainz
Lee, R. D., & Carter, L. R. (1992). Modeling and forecasting US mortality. *Journal of the American Statistical Association, 87*(419), 659–671.
Lee, R., & Miller, T. (2001). Evaluating the performance of the Lee-Carter method for forecasting mortality. *Demography, 38*(4), 537–549.
Li, N., & Lee, R. (2005). Coherent mortality forecasts for a group of populations: An extension of the Lee-Carter method. *Demography, 42*(3), 575–594.
Li, N., Lee, R., & Gerland, P. (2013). Extending the Lee-Carter method to model the rotation of age patterns of mortality decline for long-term projections. *Demography, 50*(6), 2037–2051.
Lindahl-Jacobsen, R., Rau, R., Jeune, B., Canudas-Romo, V., Lenart, A., Christensen, K., & Vaupel, J. W. (2016). Rise, stagnation, and rise of Danish women's life expectancy. *Proceedings of the National Academy of Sciences, 113*(15), 4015–4020.
Mead, L. R., & Papanicolaou, N. (1984). Maximum entropy in the problem of moments. *Journal of Mathematical Physics, 25*(8), 2404–2417.
Muggeo, V. M. R. (2003). Estimating regression models with unknown break-points. *Statistics in Medicine, 22*(19), 3055–3071.
Oeppen, J. (2008). Coherent forecasting of multiple-decrement life tables: A test using Japanese cause of death data. In *European Population Conference 2008*. European Association for Population Studies.
Oeppen, J., & Vaupel, J. W. (2002). Broken limits to life expectancy. *Science, 296*(5570), 1029–1031.
Oeppen, J., & Vaupel, J. W. (2019). The linear rise in the number of our days. In T. Bengtsson & N. Keilman (Eds.), Old and New Perspectives on Mortality Forecasting (pp. 159–166). Cham: Springer Open https://link.springer.com/content/pdf/10.1007%2F978-3-030-05075-7.pdf
Pascariu, M. (2018). *MortalityGaps: The double-gap life expectancy forecasting model*. R package version 3.1.2.
Pascariu, M., Canudas-Romo, V., & Vaupel, J. W. (2018). The double-gap life expectancy forecasting model. *Insurance: Mathematics and Economics, 78*, 339–350.
Pascariu, M. D., Lenart, A., & Canudas-Romo, V. (2019). The maximum entropy mortality model: Forecasting mortality using statistical moments. *Scandinavian Actuarial Journal, 8*, 661–685.
Pawlowsky-Glahn, V., & Buccianti, A. (2011). *Compositional data analysis: Theory and applications*. Chichester: Wiley.
Preston, S., Heuveline, P., & Guillot, M. (2001). *Demography: Measuring and modeling population processes*. Oxford: Blackwell Publishing.

Preston, S. H., Stokes, A., Mehta, N. K., & Cao, B. (2014). Projecting the effect of changes in smoking and obesity on future life expectancy in the United States. *Demography, 51*(1), 27–49.

Raftery, A. E., Lalic, N., & Gerland, P. (2014). Joint probabilistic projection of female and male life expectancy. *Demographic research, 30*, 795–822.

Rizzi, S., Gampe, J., & Eilers, P. H. C. (2015). Efficient estimation of smooth distributions from coarsely grouped data. *American Journal of Epidemiology, 182*(2), 138–147.

Rizzi, S., Kjærgaard, S., Bergeron-Boucher, M.-P., Lindahl-Jacobsen, R., & Vaupel, J. (2019). Forecasting mortality of not extinct cohorts. In *21st Nordic Demographic Symposium*, Reykjavik Iceland.

Stoeldraijer, L. (2019). *Mortality forecasting in the context of non-linear past mortality trends: An evaluation*. Ph.D. thesis, University of Groningen.

Stoeldraijer, L., van Duin, C., van Wissen, L., & Janssen, F. (2013). Impact of different mortality forecasting methods and explicit assumptions on projected future life expectancy: The case of the Netherlands. *Demographic Research, 29*(13), 323–354.

Vallin, J., & Meslé, F. (2004). Convergences and divergences in mortality: A new approach of health transition. *Demographic Research, S2*, 11–44.

Vallin, J., & Meslé, F. (2010). Will life expectancy increase indefinitely by three months every year? *Population and Societies* (473), 1. https://search.proquest.com/docview/823700331?pq-origsite=gscholar

van Raalte, A. A., Sasson, I., & Martikainen, P. (2018). The case for monitoring life-span inequality. *Science, 362*(6418), 1002–1004.

Vaupel, J. W., & Canudas-Romo, V. (2003). Decomposing change in life expectancy: A bouquet of formulas in honor of Nathan Keyfitz's 90th birthday. *Demography, 40*(2), 201–216.

Vaupel, J. W., Zhang, Z., & van Raalte, A. A. (2011). Life expectancy and disparity: An international comparison of life table data. *BMJ Open, 1*(1), e000128. https://bmjopen.bmj.com/content/bmjopen/1/1/e000128.full.pdf

Wang, H., & Preston, S. H. (2009). Forecasting United States mortality using cohort smoking histories. *Proceedings of the National Academy of Sciences, 106*(2), 393–398.

White, K. M. (2002). Longevity advances in high-income countries, 1955–1996. *Population and Development Review, 28*(1), 59–76.

Wilmoth, J. R. (1995). Are mortality projections always more pessimistic when disaggregated by cause of death? *Mathematical Population Studies, 5*(4), 293–319.

Chapter 8
Coherent Mortality Forecasting with Standards: Low Mortality Serves as a Guide

Heather Booth

8.1 Introduction

Mortality forecasts are an important component of population forecasting and are central to the estimation of longevity risk in actuarial practice. Planning by the state for health and aged care services and by individuals for retirement and later life depends on accurate mortality forecasts. The overall accuracy or performance of mortality forecasting has improved since Lee and Carter (1992) introduced stochastic forecasting of mortality to the demographic community, and further improvements can undoubtedly be made.

The series of new methods and method refinements contributing to improved performance include various extensions of the Lee-Carter method (e.g., Booth 2006; Booth et al. 2002, 2006; de Jong and Tickle 2006; Li and Li 2017; Li 2012; Li et al. 2013; Shang et al. 2011; Tickle and Booth 2014). The independently developed functional data approach of Hyndman and Ullah (2007) is a generalisation of Lee-Carter. Other approaches include general linear modelling (e.g., Ahmadi and Li 2014; Currie 2014; Renshaw and Haberman 2003, 2006), Bayesian methods (e.g., Cairns et al. 2011; Raftery et al. 2013), and compositional data modelling (Bergeron-Boucher et al. 2017), among others (Basellini and Camarda 2019; Booth and Tickle 2008; Camarda 2019; de Beer and Janssen 2016; Janssen 2018; Pascariu et al. 2018). However, the principal components approach, used in the Lee-Carter method, remains prominent.

A logical and fruitful development is coherent forecasting where the mortality experience of two or more populations are forecast jointly, with the expectation that forecast performance will be improved by borrowing strength from the complemen-

H. Booth (✉)
School of Demography, Australian National University, Canberra, Australia
e-mail: heather.booth@anu.edu.au

S. Mazzuco, N. Keilman (eds.), *Developments in Demographic Forecasting*, The Springer Series on Demographic Methods and Population Analysis 49, https://doi.org/10.1007/978-3-030-42472-5_8

tary, or 'other', population(s). Li and Lee (2005) introduced this idea by forecasting the mortality of a group of populations with similar mortality experience, identified as an integral part of model estimation. This common factor approach has been further developed by others (e.g., Li 2012).

The product-ratio method of coherent forecasting was proposed by Hyndman et al. (2013) following earlier unpublished work by Booth using ratios. The two examples used to illustrate the method forecast the mortality of two or more subpopulations within a country: the two sex-specific populations in sex-coherent mortality forecasting for Sweden and the populations of the several states of Australia in state-coherent mortality forecasting. It was noted that forecast accuracy and bias, averaged over the subpopulations, was improved by using the coherent method when compared with independent forecasts for each subpopulation. Further, forecast accuracy and bias were homogenised across the subpopulations, a feature of considerable benefit in actuarial and population projection applications. The generalisability of these findings to other countries has not previously been investigated. This study evaluates sex-coherent forecasting using a wide range of populations.

The use of an external standard or reference population in forecasting mortality has been variously proposed (Basellini and Camarda 2019; Fazle Rabbi 2019; Hyndman et al. 2013; Li and Lee 2005). The choice of external standard is often somewhat arbitrary; possible criteria include language, geographic proximity, political entity, and mortality level. However derived, a standard can be used in the product-ratio method to produce standard-coherent forecasts. By choosing an appropriate standard, the borrowed strength can be expected to result in a better forecast of the population of interest. This constitutes a novel application of the product-ratio method. This standard-coherent method is evaluated in this study.

8.2 Study Design

8.2.1 *Aim, Objectives and Hypothesis*

The overall aim of this study is to determine whether taking appropriate other mortality into account (by using the product-ratio method) improves the performance of mortality forecasting, as measured by accuracy, bias and robustness. This is addressed through three successive objectives.

The first objective is to evaluate the performance, compared with independent forecasts, of sex-coherent forecasting across a wide range of populations. It is expected, based on the example of Sweden in Hyndman et al. (2013) and preliminary research by the author that male mortality forecasts are improved when female mortality is taken into account, but not vice versa. Noting that female mortality is lower than male mortality, my hypothesis is that a low-mortality standard will serve as a better guide to future mortality, given the prevailing trend of decline, than a higher-mortality standard.

Based on this hypothesis, the second objective is to use a selection of low-mortality standards to evaluate the performance of standard-coherent forecasting across the range of populations. The third objective is to compare the forecast performance of independent, sex-coherent and standard-coherent forecasts in order to determine how these three methods rank for female and male mortality.

8.2.2 *Data*

Data are obtained from the Human Mortality Database ("Human Mortality Database," 2019) (HMD) for the period 1950–2014; this period was chosen to maximise as far as practicable the number of countries with available data. This resulted in a total of 21 countries (Table 8.1) being included in the analysis. The data comprise annual age-sex-specific central death rates, or mortality rates, and corresponding populations exposed to the risk of death.

The available data are for single years of age 0–109 and for the open-ended interval 110+. Initial evaluation of the mortality rates showed that, for all countries, observed rates at the oldest ages were lower in the earlier years of observation than in more recent years; it is assumed that this is the result of improved age at death

Table 8.1 Ranking of countries by sex-specific life expectancy in 2014

	Female		Male	
Country	e(0)	Rank	e(0)	Rank
Japan	86.81	1	80.51	5
Spain	85.60	2	80.08	7
France	85.43	3	79.27	11
Italy	85.15	4	80.55	4
Switzerland	85.11	5	80.93	2
Australia	84.56	6	80.59	3
Iceland	84.12	7	81.12	1
Portugal	84.12	7	77.92	18
Norway	84.10	9	80.03	8
Sweden	84.05	10	80.36	6
Canada	83.98	11	79.81	10
Finland	83.85	12	78.13	17
Austria	83.73	13	78.92	14
Belgium	83.51	14	78.57	15
Netherlands	83.29	15	79.88	9
Ireland	83.21	16	79.16	13
UK	82.99	17	79.25	12
Denmark	82.67	18	78.57	15
Czechia	81.73	19	75.72	20
USA	81.45	20	76.64	19
Hungary	79.24	21	72.26	21

reporting over time and selection effects rather than a real increase in mortality. In order to avoid erroneously modelling increasing mortality at the oldest ages, the data for ages 95 and older were combined into a revised open-ended interval. In other circumstances, it would be desirable to model mortality rates at the oldest ages (Buettner 2002). Here, however, there is little, if any, gain in doing so because the objective is to compare the performance of forecasting methods and because modelled rates would follow the same pattern in the standard as in the population of interest.

8.2.3 Choice of Standard

The evaluation of standard-coherent forecasting will obviously depend on the choice of standard. In line with the hypothesised role of a low-mortality standard, four leaders of the global mortality decline, measured in terms of life expectancy in 2014, were identified for use as standards. Table 8.1 shows 2014 life expectancy by sex for the 21 countries in the study. Countries with a total population size of less than one million were discounted in this process in order to avoid excessive fluctuation in the standard; this size criterion applies only to Iceland which, in fact, recorded the highest ranking male life expectancy in 2014 (Table 8.1). The sex-specific standards employed are Japan and Spain (1st and 2nd respectively for female life expectancy), and Switzerland and Australia (2nd and 3rd respectively for male life expectancy). These four countries were excluded from the analytical group of 17 countries on which the comparative analysis is based so as to maintain comparability of results.

8.2.4 Rolling Fitting Period

Any forecast is dependent on the particular fitting period used. Forecast error also depends on the particular year in the forecast period combined with forecast horizon. For evaluative purposes, it is important to take these influences into account as far as possible. This is done by appropriate averaging over forecasts. A rolling forecast origin is commonly used in the calculation of average error, so as to reduce the effect of fluctuations and abrupt changes in annual mortality rates in relation to the fitting period and the forecast period. In previous work, the rolling aspect has been restricted to the last year of the fitting period, or jump-off year, on the basis that time series methods give little weight to earlier data (Hyndman et al. 2013).

In this analysis, rather than fixing the first year of the fitting period, the length of the fitting period is fixed; the first and last years of the fitting period are simultaneously rolling. This is considered more robust, as a fixed first year of the fitting period could in some circumstances lead to systematic bias. Given 65 years of data and setting the maximum forecast horizon at 23 years (to obtain reliable results for up to 20 years), the fitting period length is fixed at 42 years. As the fitting period

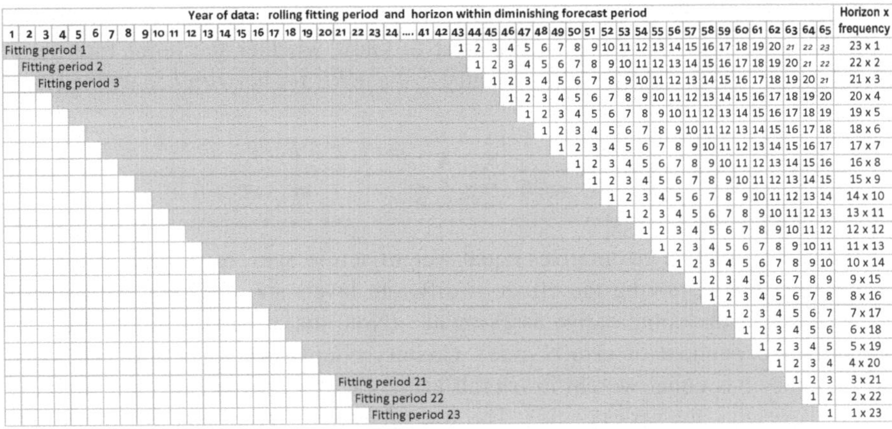

Note: Horizons 21 to 23 are not used because of low frequencies.

Fig. 8.1 Rolling fitting period of length 42 years, calendar years in forecast period (years 43–65) and forecast horizons (1–23 years)

is rolled forward in time, the forecast horizon is correspondingly reduced. Figure 8.1 illustrates how this procedure produces forecasts for horizons, h, of 1–23 years with diminishing frequency, there being 23 forecasts of $h=1$, 22 forecasts of $h=2$, ..., 2 forecasts of $h=22$ and 1 forecast of $h=23$. Forecasts based on three or fewer values are excluded from the evaluation; these are for horizons 21–23. Thus, the reported mean results cover horizons of 1–20 years, with greater confidence in means for shorter horizons deriving from larger numbers of observations.

8.2.5 Measures Used in Evaluation

The forecasts are evaluated using several measures, based on forecast error in the mortality rates at age x and time t for country c, $m(x, t, c)$. First, the accuracy of the point forecast is measured by the mean absolute relative error, *MARE*, in age-specific mortality rates, averaged over age and fitting period. For country c, the *MARE* for horizon h is defined as

$$MARE\,(h, c) = \frac{1}{(24-h)\times 96}\sum_{t=42}^{65-h}\sum_{x=0}^{95}\frac{\left|m\,(x, t+h, c)-\hat{m}\,(x, t+h, c)\right|}{m\,(x, t+h, c)}$$

where $\hat{m}\,(x, t+h, c)$ is the forecast rate for country c at age x and t is an index of year. For all horizons, the fitting period is 42 years of data starting in year $t=1$, 2,. . . ,23 and, correspondingly, the forecast period starts in year $t=43$, 44,. . . , 65 and ends in year $t=65$.

Second, the mean relative error, *MRE*, is used to assess bias. In demographic forecasting, it is often of primary interest to know whether the point forecast is biased and in which direction. For country *c*, the *MRE* for horizon *h* is defined as

$$MRE(h, c) = \frac{1}{(24 - h) \times 96} \sum_{t=42}^{65-h} \sum_{x=0}^{95} \frac{m(x, t + h, c) - \hat{m}(x, t + h, c)}{m(x, t + h, c)}$$

The use of relative errors gives equal weight across ages, regardless of the size of the rate, thus removing the effect of different levels and different age patterns of mortality in the comparative assessments. (Note that relative weights are conceptually independent of size of rate). Country comparisons are thus valid, and each country has equal weight in overall averages. Sex comparisons are similarly valid (all results are sex-specific). The use of relative errors also permits direct comparison of errors across horizons, and facilitates interpretation of averages and variability over horizons.

The units of analysis for evaluation and comparison are $MARE(h, c)$ and $MRE(h, c)$. Horizon-specific mean accuracy and bias, $MARE(h)$ and $MRE(h)$, are averages over countries; these describe the average 'horizon effect' in accuracy and bias, or degree to which forecast performance declines over time. Country-specific mean accuracy and bias, $MARE(c)$ and $MRE(c)$, are averages over horizons; these measure the degree of difficulty in forecasting mortality for each population. Overall mean accuracy and bias, *MARE* and *MRE*, are averages over countries and horizons:

$$MARE = \frac{1}{17} \sum_{c=1}^{17} MARE(c) = \frac{1}{20} \sum_{h=1}^{20} MARE(h) = \frac{1}{17 \times 20} \sum_{c=1}^{17} \sum_{h=1}^{20} MARE(h, c)$$

$$MRE = \frac{1}{17} \sum_{c=1}^{17} MRE(c) = \frac{1}{20} \sum_{h=1}^{20} MRE(h) = \frac{1}{17 \times 20} \sum_{c=1}^{17} \sum_{h=1}^{20} MRE(h, c)$$

It should be noted that *MRE* is a measure of net bias. The values of $MRE(h, c)$ are net across ages and across fitting periods. Additionally, $MRE(c)$ is net across horizons, $MRE(h)$ is net across countries, and the overall mean is net across horizons and countries. Absolute bias is used in some comparisons.

Third, the heterogeneity or standard deviations of accuracy and bias are used to assess method robustness. (Note these are not based on forecast variance as used in the estimation of the interval forecast; the interval forecast is not within the scope of the study.) Two measures of heterogeneity are used in parallel with the average measures. The first is the standard deviation across countries for each horizon:

$$SD_h(MARE) = \sqrt{\frac{1}{17} \sum_{c=1}^{17} (MARE(h, c) - MARE(h))^2}$$

and similarly for $SD_h(MRE)$. This measure shows the degree of country variation in the horizon effect. A low value is preferable as it indicates that the method is robust to different mortality conditions.

The second measure of heterogeneity is the standard deviation across horizons for each country:

$$SD_c(MARE) = \sqrt{\frac{1}{20}\sum_{h=1}^{20}(MARE\,(h,c) - MARE(c))^2}$$

and similarly for $SD_c(MRE)$. This shows the degree of variability over horizon in accuracy and bias for country *c*, due to the horizon effect, and a low value is preferable. The average of $SD_c(MARE)$ and $SD_c(MRE)$ over countries provides an overall measure of the degree of heterogeneity across horizons, which is used in comparing methods.

The study includes discussion of the sex-differences in accuracy and bias averaged over countries, $MARE_M(h) - MARE_F(h)$ and $MRE_M(h) - MRE_F(h)$, and of sex-differences in accuracy and bias averaged over horizons, $MARE_M(c) - MARE_F(c)$ and $MRE_M(c) - MRE_F(c)$. Note that these are not the accuracy and bias of the sex-difference in mortality.

8.3 Forecasting Methods

8.3.1 Functional Data Forecasting

The forecasting methods employed in this research draw on the functional forecasting approach of Hyndman and Ullah (2007). The Hyndman-Ullah functional data method (FDM) is a generalisation of the well-known Lee-Carter method (Lee and Carter 1992), and models and forecasts the natural logarithm of period age-specific mortality rates for a particular population or country (in this section, c is dropped from formulae). The functional data model is

$$\ln\,(m\,(x,t)) = a(x) + \sum_j b_j(x)k_j(t) + e\,(x,t) + \sigma\,(x,t)\;\;\varepsilon\,(x,t)$$

where $a(x)$ is the temporal average pattern of the logarithm of mortality by age and, for $j = 1,\ldots,J$ components, $b_j(x)$ is a 'basis function' and $k_j(t)$ is a time series coefficient. Broadly, the $k_j(t)$ represent annual rates of mortality decline averaged over age, while the $b_j(x)$ describe the age pattern of decline averaged over time. The parameters of the model are estimated after smoothing the data over age. Thus, the $a(x)$ and $b_j(x)$ are smooth functions of age. The pairs $(b_j(x), k_j(t))$ for $j = 1,\ldots,J$ are estimated using principal component decomposition. The error term $\sigma(x,t)\;\varepsilon(x,t)$

accounts for age-varying observational error; this is the difference between the observed rates and the smoothed rates. The error term $e(x, t)$ is modelling error, or the difference between the smoothed rates and the fitted rates from the model.

The FDM differs from the Lee-Carter method in several ways. First, as already noted, the $ln(m(x, t))$ are smoothed over age prior to modelling. This is done using nonparametric smoothing methods and assuming monotonic increase at ages 65 and older. Each year of data is smoothed by applying weighted penalized regression splines where the weights are equal to the approximate inverse variance of the rate, i.e., $m(x, t)\ E(x, t)$, where $E(x, t)$ is population exposed to risk, and deaths are assumed to follow a Poisson distribution (Booth et al. 2014).

Second, the FDM uses functional principal components and, unlike Lee-Carter, employs more than one component of the decomposition. Following previous research (Hyndman and Booth 2008; Hyndman et al. 2013), six components are used for all data sets in this study. The remaining J–6 components form the error term, $e(x, t)$. Third, there is no adjustment of the time coefficients (as was the case in the original Lee-Carter method). Fourth, rather than routinely employing the random walk with drift model for forecasting the time coefficients; the most appropriate autoregressive integrated moving average (ARIMA) models are selected based on statistical criteria (Shumway and Stoffer 2006).

8.3.2 Coherent Forecasting

Coherent forecasting takes the experience of two or more populations into account and ensures that the resulting forecasts for each population are 'non-divergent', which encompasses the conditions that they do not converge (and cross over) in the short term nor diverge in the long term (Li and Lee 2005). The product-ratio method for coherent forecasting (Hyndman et al. 2013) uses the FDM in jointly forecasting mortality for two or more populations.

For sex-coherent forecasting, the product function is the geometric mean of sex-specific rates, $p\left(x, t\right) = \sqrt{m_F\left(x, t\right) m_M\left(x, t\right)}$, where F denotes female and M denotes male. The ratio function is the square root of the ratio of sex-specific rates, $r\left(x, t\right) = \sqrt{m_M\left(x, t\right) / m_F\left(x, t\right)}$. Because of the symmetry in the two-population case, the inverse ratio is not needed. These two functions are independently forecast using the FDM. Coherence is achieved by restricting the forecast of the ratio to converge very slowly to its temporal average; in other words, the forecast of each time coefficient converges to stationarity. For further details, including the case of three or more populations, see Hyndman et al. (2013).

The forecasts of the product and ratio functions are combined to produce forecast mortality rates. Forecast male mortality at future t is:

$$\widehat{\sqrt{m_{\mathrm{F}}(\mathrm{x}, \mathrm{t})\ m_{\mathrm{M}}(\mathrm{x}, \mathrm{t})}} . \widehat{\sqrt{m_{\mathrm{M}}(\mathrm{x}, \mathrm{t}) / m_{\mathrm{F}}(\mathrm{x}, \mathrm{t})}} = \widehat{\sqrt{m_{\mathrm{M}}(\mathrm{x}, \mathrm{t})^2}} = \widehat{m}_{\mathrm{M}}(\mathrm{x}, \mathrm{t}) \qquad (8.1)$$

and forecast female mortality at future t is:

$$\sqrt{\widehat{m_F(x,t)\ m_M(x,t)}} \bigg/ \sqrt{\widehat{m_M(x,t)\ /m_M(x,t)}} = \sqrt{\widehat{m_F(x,t)^2}} = \widehat{m}_F(x,t) \qquad (8.2)$$

The product-ratio coherent method makes use of the fact that the product and ratio will behave roughly independently of each other, as long as the two populations have approximately equal mortality variances (Hyndman et al. 2013). The method is directly applicable to the mortality of any two populations for which the coherence of their future mortality is postulated. Thus, the method is appropriate for standard-coherent forecasting where standard mortality is taken into account in forecasting the mortality of the population of interest. In the above equations, this is achieved by replacing F by S to denote standard (for example Japan), and by replacing M by the country of interest (for example, France). The forecast for the country of interest is then obtained by Eq. 8.1. Note that Eq. 8.2 is not used as, under the hypothesis that a low-mortality standard will serve as a better guide to future mortality, the forecast for the standard should not be obtained by reference to a population with higher mortality. In applying the standard-coherent method, sex-specific mortality rates are used.

8.4 Evidence: A Comparison of Methods

In line with the objectives of this research, sex-coherent and standard-coherent forecasts are evaluated in terms of accuracy, bias and robustness, against independent forecasts and against each other. The basic units of analysis, sex-specific accuracy and bias measures by horizon and country, $MARE(h, c)$ and $MRE(h, c)$, are illustrated in Fig. 8.2 for independent forecasts of female mortality, each graph representing 340 data points. Typical of forecasts in general, accuracy declines ($MARE(h, c)$ increases) and absolute bias increases with forecast horizon. Given relative measures of accuracy and bias, the increases observed are entirely attributable to the horizon effect. While forecasts for most countries exhibit relatively modest increases in forecast error with horizon, a handful exhibit substantial increases. Similar patterns are found in the basic units of analysis for all three methods, for accuracy and bias, and for each sex (Fig. 8.8).

8.4.1 Sex-Coherent Forecasts

The comparison of sex-coherent forecasts with independent forecasts is summarised in Fig. 8.3 using ratios of sex-coherent to independent measures, or relative

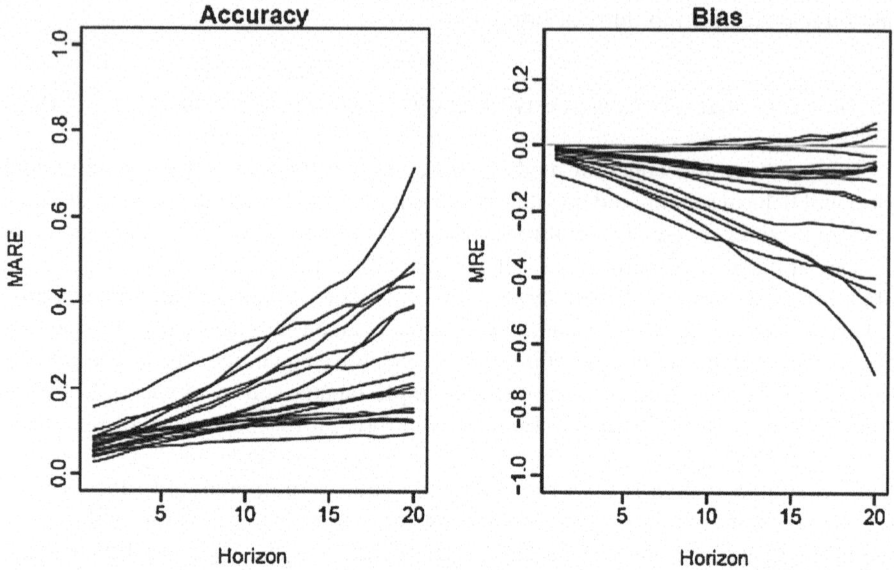

Fig. 8.2 Accuracy and bias by horizon and country, independent forecasts for female mortality

performance; see also Figs. 8.5 and 8.6, to be discussed later. The upper quadrants show country-specific relative accuracy and relative absolute bias, or ratios of averages over horizons, *MARE*(*c*) and $|MRE(c)|$, for female and male mortality forecasts. These results show that the sex-coherent method is advantageous for forecasting male mortality but disadvantageous for forecasting female mortality. For male mortality, taking account of female mortality improved forecast accuracy and bias for 13–14 of the 17 countries, with an overall improvement across countries of 11% in accuracy and 12% in bias. However, taking account of male mortality in forecasting female mortality improved accuracy and bias for only 3–4 of the 17 countries, resulting in an overall reduction of 11% in accuracy and an overall increase of 32% in bias.

Similar patterns occur in relative heterogeneity across horizons, seen in the lower quadrants of Fig. 8.3. For male mortality, sex-coherent forecasting reduced the standard deviations of accuracy and bias, $SD_c(MARE)$ and $SD_c(MRE)$, for 15 of the 17 countries, with an overall reduction of 21% for both measures compared with independent forecasts. For female mortality, however, sex-coherent forecasting produced increased standard deviations for all but 3–4 countries, with overall increases of 24% for accuracy and 43% for bias.

Together, these findings generally confirm that forecast performance is improved for male mortality but reduced for female mortality when comparing the sex-coherent forecasts with independent forecasts. The hypothesis that low mortality serves as a good guide to future mortality is therefore supported in the context of sex-coherent forecasting.

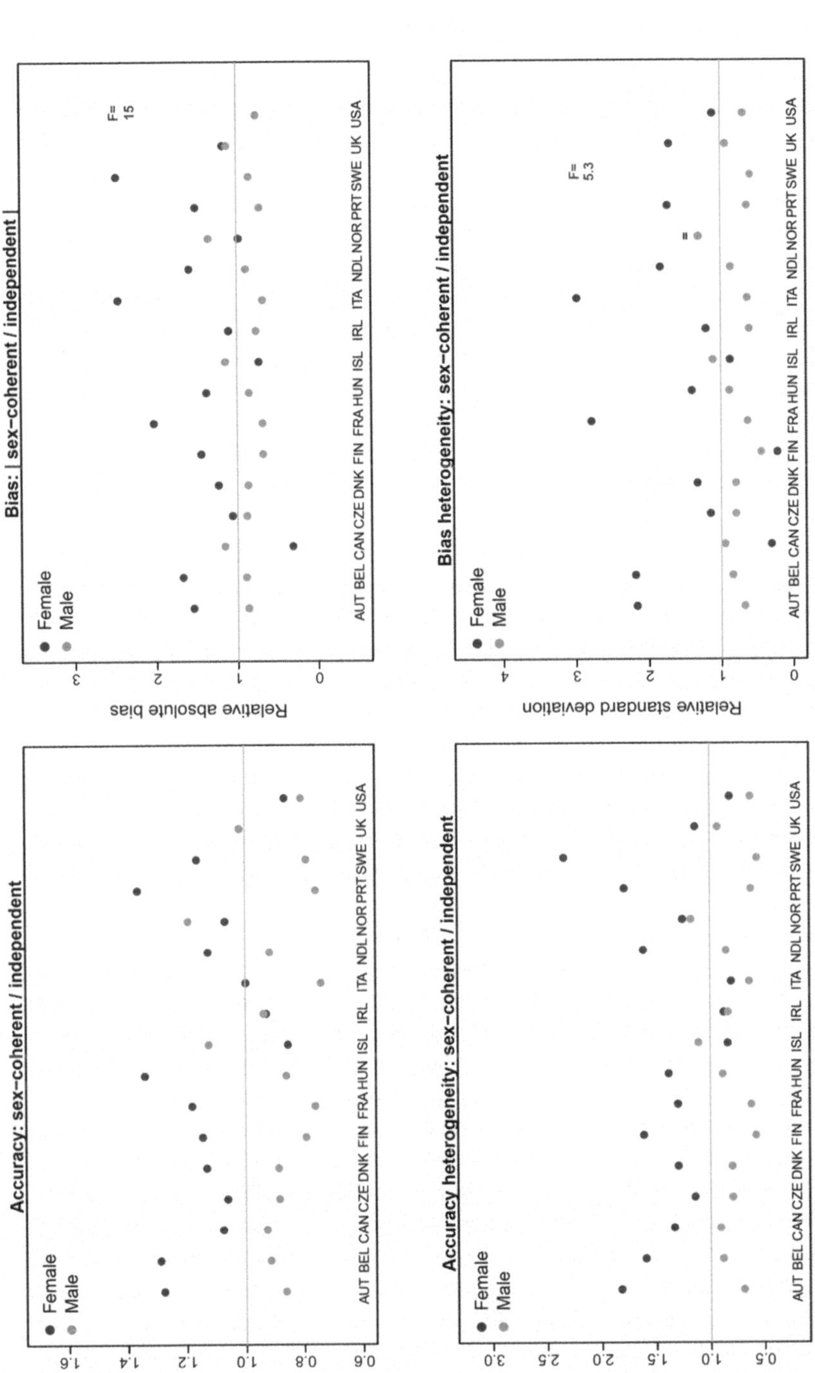

Fig. 8.3 Accuracy and bias of sex-coherent forecasts relative to independent forecasts by country and sex. Note: For bias, USA female is an outlier. For bias heterogeneity, Sweden female is an outlier and Norway female and male are equal (For the interpretation of the references to colors in this Figure, please refer to the electronic version of the chapter available online)

8.4.2 Standard-Coherent Forecasts

The second objective of the study involves evaluation of the efficacy of several low-mortality standards in improving the performance of mortality forecasts. The third objective is to rank forecasts produced by the three methods (independent, sex-coherent and standard-coherent). These objectives are addressed in this section. Results are presented for the standard-coherent method using the four low-mortality standards described earlier, with comparable results for independent and sex-coherent forecasts. The case of Japan as standard, chosen for its leadership in life expectancy, is considered in detail; the results presented in Figs. 8.4, 8.5 and 8.6 are accuracy and bias means and standard deviations. For the remaining three low-mortality standards, only summary results are shown.

8.4.2.1 Japan as Standard

The evaluation focusses first on the horizon effect. Forecast accuracy and bias are averaged across countries. The upper quadrants of Fig. 8.4 show horizon-specific average accuracy and bias, $MARE(h)$ and $MRE(h)$, for the three methods by sex. Comparing methods, the standard-coherent forecast is the most accurate at all horizons for both sexes. For male mortality, the sex-coherent forecast is more accurate than the independent forecast, but for female mortality the reverse is found, as previously noted. Similar patterns among methods occur for bias, revealing a systematic tendency in the forecasts (except standard-coherent forecasts for female mortality) to underestimate the extent of future mortality decline (see also Fig. 8.8). These findings also show that the horizon effect is stable on average: mean accuracy and bias worsen steadily over forecast horizon, with an increasing advantage of standard-coherent forecasting.

The corresponding standard deviations, $SD_h(MARE)$ and $SD_h(MRE)$, are compared in the lower quadrants of Fig. 8.4. Heterogeneity among countries is relatively low at shorter horizons, particularly for accuracy, but increases rapidly at longer horizons, a result of substantial increases for some countries but not others (Fig. 8.8). This heterogeneity is significantly reduced by standard-coherent forecasting, while being selectively modified by sex-coherent forecasting as previously noted.

Focussing now on countries, forecast accuracy and bias are averaged across horizons. Figures 8.5 and 8.6 (upper quadrants) show, for females and males respectively, country-specific average accuracy and bias, $MARE(c)$ and $MRE(c)$, by method. For many countries (17 for male mortality and 9–10 for female mortality), the standard-coherent forecast is the best among the three methods in terms of both accuracy and bias, and this is reflected in the overall means (shown top right) which are averages across countries. Again, the sex-coherent method performs less well than the independent method for female mortality (Fig. 8.5) but performs better for male mortality (Fig. 8.6). These rankings among methods are also found for the

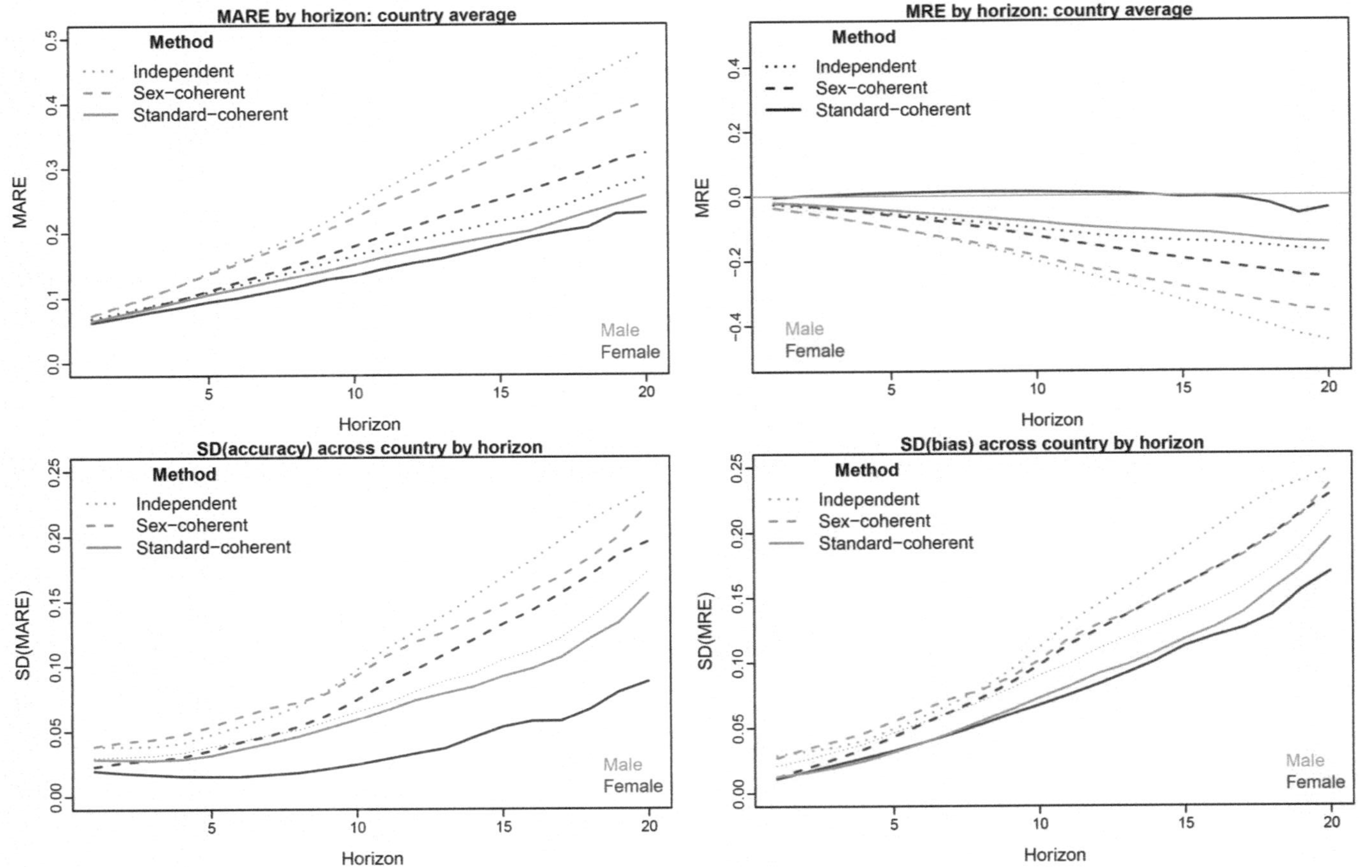

Fig. 8.4 Accuracy and bias by method (Japan as standard): country averages by horizon (For the interpretation of the references to colors in this Figure, please refer to the electronic version of the chapter available online)

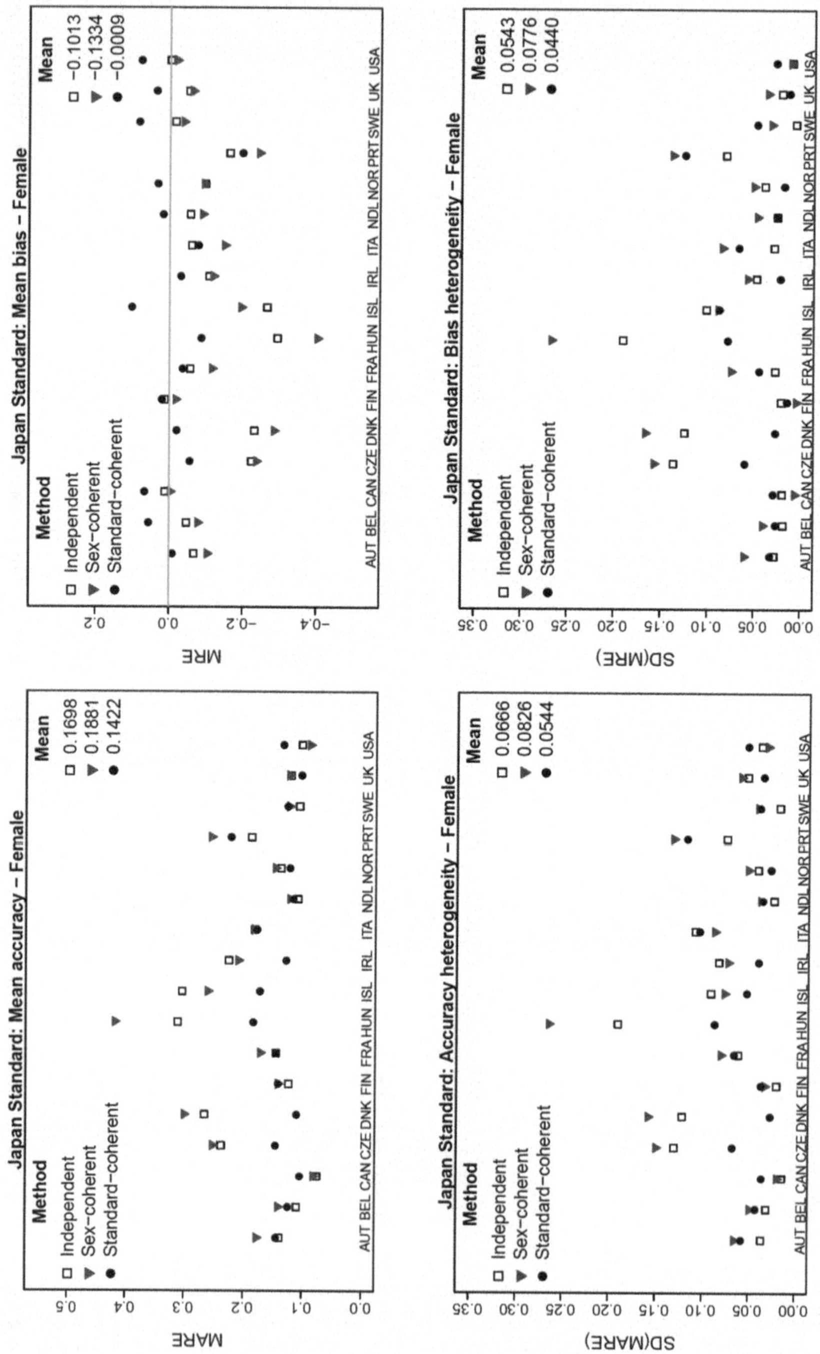

Fig. 8.5 Accuracy and bias by method (Japan as standard) by country, female mortality

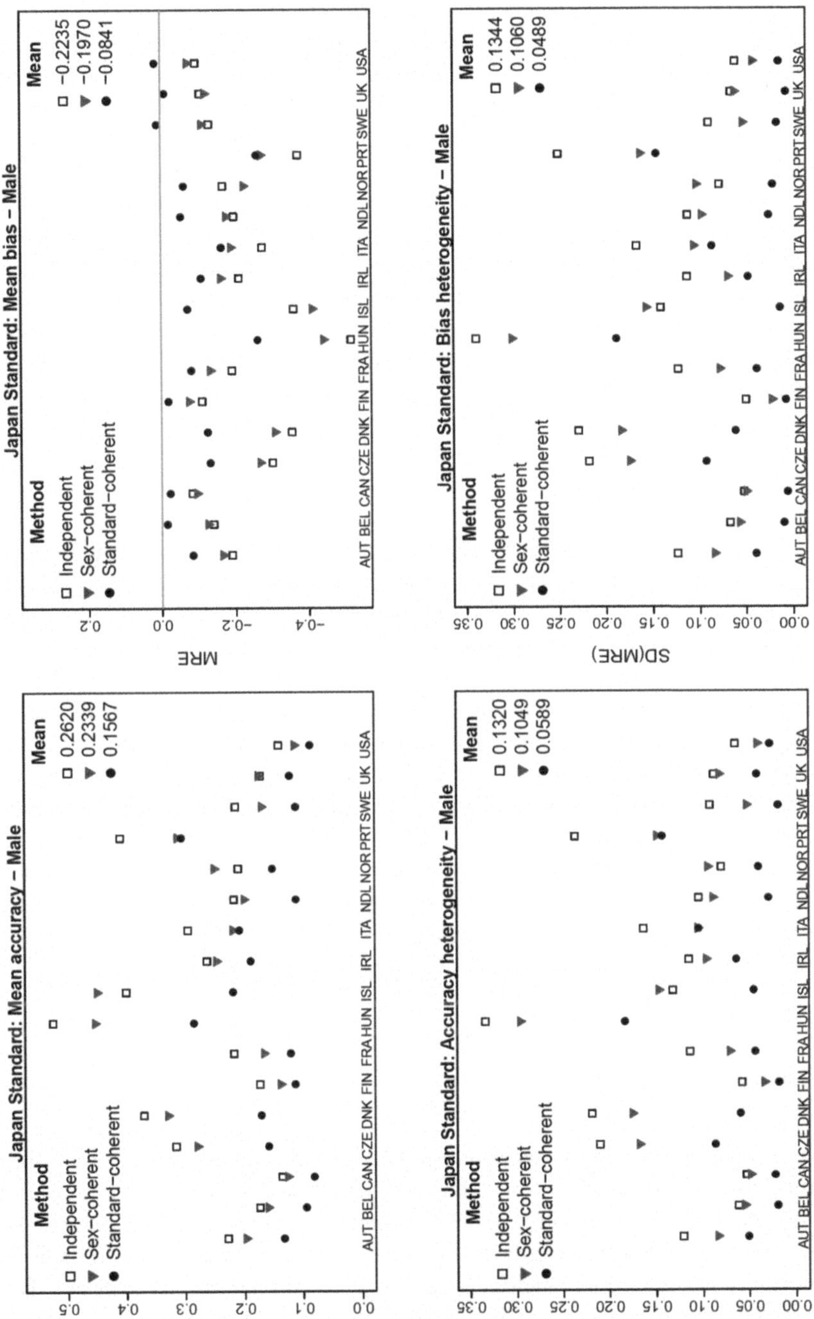

Fig. 8.6 Accuracy and bias by method (Japan as standard) by country, male mortality

standard deviations, $SD_c(MARE)$ and $SD_c(MRE)$, shown in the lower quadrants of Figs. 8.5 and 8.6.

This analysis identifies three countries, namely Czechia, Denmark and Hungary, for which forecasting errors are systematically largest when using the independent method, possibly due to their irregular patterns of mortality decline. Both female and male mortality in these countries gain substantially in performance from standard-coherent forecasting (Figs. 8.5 and 8.6). For Portugal, large gains also occur for male mortality, but losses in performance occur for female mortality. Small losses also occur for female mortality in populations for which forecast errors are low when using the independent method (Fig. 8.5). Overall, standard-coherent forecasting improves accuracy by 17% for female mortality and 41% for male mortality, while bias is reduced by 99% and 63% respectively. These results are generally consistent with the hypothesis that a low-mortality standard serves as a good guide to future mortality decline.

8.4.2.2 Other Standards

The efficacy of standard-coherent forecasting in improving forecast accuracy and bias clearly depends on the choice of standard. In this section, the three additional standards are considered; these are Spain, Switzerland and Australia. Summary results are shown in Table 8.2, comprising overall means and standard deviations, relative to independent forecasts, of accuracy and bias for the three methods and the four standards. (Note that as mean bias is a net measure, its size depends partly on the degree of counterbalancing of positive and negative biases; this explains the very low value for overall mean bias for female mortality when using Japan as standard, and also influences other values for bias.) For female mortality, the results obtained when using Spain, Switzerland and Australia as standard are similar to those for Japan as standard: the standard-coherent method improves accuracy and bias, and reduces across-country average heterogeneity across horizons. For male mortality, however, the effects are less consistent; when using Spain or Switzerland as standard, performance is reduced or only marginally improved.

8.5 Discussion

This analysis has evaluated the performance of two methods of coherent mortality forecasting in terms of the means and standard deviations of forecast accuracy and bias in female and male mortality in 17 low-mortality countries. The purpose of the evaluation was to test the hypothesis that low mortality serves as a good guide to future mortality when used in coherent forecasting, and high mortality does not. The findings support this hypothesis to a large extent but, for male mortality in particular, exceptions occur.

Table 8.2 Relative mean accuracy and bias by method and standard for female and male mortality, and relative sex-difference in accuracy and bias

	Independent	Sex-coherent	Japan-coherent	Spain-coherent	Switzerland-coherent	Australia-coherent
Female mortality						
Overall mean accuracy	1.000	1.108	0.834	0.861	0.894	0.791
Overall mean bias	1.000	1.318	0.005	0.453	0.791	0.576
Average SD(accuracy)	1.000	1.238	0.810	0.901	0.907	0.646
Average SD(bias)	1.000	1.430	0.803	0.812	0.919	0.649
Male mortality						
Overall mean accuracy	1.000	0.892	0.594	1.051	0.920	0.757
Overall mean bias	1.000	0.880	0.371	1.038	0.898	0.605
Average SD(accuracy)	1.000	0.793	0.439	1.080	0.970	0.685
Average SD(bias)	1.000	0.787	0.357	1.025	1.025	0.659
Sex-difference						
Overall mean accuracy	1.000	0.496	0.153	1.398	0.967	0.695
Overall mean bias	1.000	0.520	0.672	1.517	0.986	0.629
Average SD(accuracy)	1.000	0.339	0.061	1.263	1.034	0.725
Average SD(bias)	1.000	0.354	0.056	1.168	1.097	0.665

Note: Overall mean refers to mean accuracy and bias averaged over horizons and countries, *MARE* and *MRE* respectively. Average SD refers to the country-specific standard deviations across horizons, $SD_c(MARE)$ and $SD_c(MRE)$, averaged over countries. The sex-difference refers to the difference in accuracy and bias measures (and not to the difference in mortality)

8.5.1 Support for the Low-Mortality Hypothesis

The results show that sex-coherent forecasting improves forecast performance, relative to independent forecasting, for male mortality but not for female mortality. Average gains in performance for male mortality forecasting range from 11% to 21%, while average losses in performance for female mortality forecasting amount to 11–43% (Table 8.2). Given lower female mortality than male mortality in all countries in the study (Table 8.1), both results support the hypothesis.

At the same time, standard-coherent forecasting with each of the four low-mortality standards improves performance for female mortality, with gains of 8–99%. Again, these results support the hypothesis that low mortality serves as a good guide to future mortality, given that all four countries used as standards have low mortality relative to almost all other countries in the study (Table 8.1). For male mortality, however, standard-coherent forecasting with these low-mortality standards is not always advantageous. While using Japan or Australia as standard improves performance by 24–63%, using Switzerland or Spain as standard produces small gains or losses in performance. (The results for Spain as standard (not shown) indicate that poor performance cannot be attributable to high or similar male mortality in Spain compared with six of the populations considered (Table 8.1).) Thus, in the case of male mortality, the hypothesis is only partially supported by standard-coherent forecasting.

Further, for both female and male mortality, the lowest-mortality standard of the same sex does not produce the greatest gains in performance. The best performing standard for female mortality is Australia, chosen on the basis of male mortality, while the best performing standard for male mortality is Japan, chosen on the basis of female mortality. However, Japan and Australia serve as the two best guides for both female and male future mortality. These findings point to choice of low-mortality standard as an important consideration (Kjærgaard et al. 2016; Stoeldraijer 2019).

8.5.2 Ranking of Methods

Considering only Japan or Australia as standard, the ranking of methods by performance varies as a result of the differential effect of sex-coherent forecasting. For female mortality, the best method is standard-coherent forecasting, followed by independent forecasting, with sex-coherent forecasting in third place. For male mortality, standard-coherent forecasting is again best, followed by sex-coherent forecasting and then independent forecasting. These rankings hold for accuracy and bias, and for means and standard deviations. In most cases, these rankings also hold over forecast horizons.

8.5.3 Benefits of a Low-Mortality Standard

In the case of Japan as standard, the average trajectories of mean accuracy and bias change steadily over horizon (Fig. 8.4) and similar patterns are found for most individual countries. The horizon effects for accuracy and bias are considerably reduced by standard-coherent forecasting and heterogeneity across countries is also reduced. Thus confidence in standard-coherent forecasts is considerably greater than in independent forecasts which systematically overestimate future mortality rates and underestimate future life expectancy. Standard-coherent forecasting is also advantageous in reducing forecast error due to particular mortality conditions. The latter may be partially manifest in jump-off error indicated by error at $h = 1$. Jump-off error is greater on average for male mortality than for female mortality and, like the horizon effect, is reduced by standard-coherent forecasting (Fig. 8.4). Additionally, heterogeneity among countries with respect to forecast accuracy and bias is substantially reduced by standard-coherent forecasting; this is seen by horizon in the lower quadrants of Fig. 8.4, and is also evident in the upper quadrants of Figs. 8.5 and 8.6.

8.5.4 Homogenisation of Accuracy and Bias by Sex

One of the features of sex-coherent forecasting noted by Hyndman et al. (2013) is the homogenisation of forecast accuracy and bias for female and male mortality by horizon. Because forecast errors are generally smaller for female mortality than for male mortality, the opposing effects of sex-coherent forecasting result in smaller sex-differences in accuracy and bias. Figure 8.7 (upper quadrants) shows that sex-coherent forecasting substantially reduces the sex-difference in forecast accuracy and bias at longer horizons, compared with independent forecasting. This is the case for 14 of the 17 countries (Fig. 8.7 lower quadrants) and on average the sex-difference is reduced by 50% for accuracy and 48% for bias (Table 8.2).

Homogenisation by sex of forecast accuracy and bias is also an outcome of standard-coherent forecasting with Japan as standard, as also seen in Fig. 8.7. Compared with independent forecasting, Fig. 8.7 shows that standard-coherent forecasting substantially reduces the sex-difference in both forecast accuracy and bias, and in 16 of the 17 countries, resulting in overall reductions of 85% for accuracy and 33% for bias. Thus for accuracy, homogeneity by sex is greatest for the standard-coherent method (with Japan as standard) while for bias, homogeneity is greatest for the sex-coherent method. In both cases, independent forecasts are least homogeneous.

Greater homogeneity by sex of accuracy and bias is a significant advantage for forecasting practice, as it reduces the likelihood of unbalanced forecasts of female and male mortality. Increased confidence in the internal consistency of mortality forecasts is of direct benefit in actuarial applications and in forecasting the age-sex structure of populations.

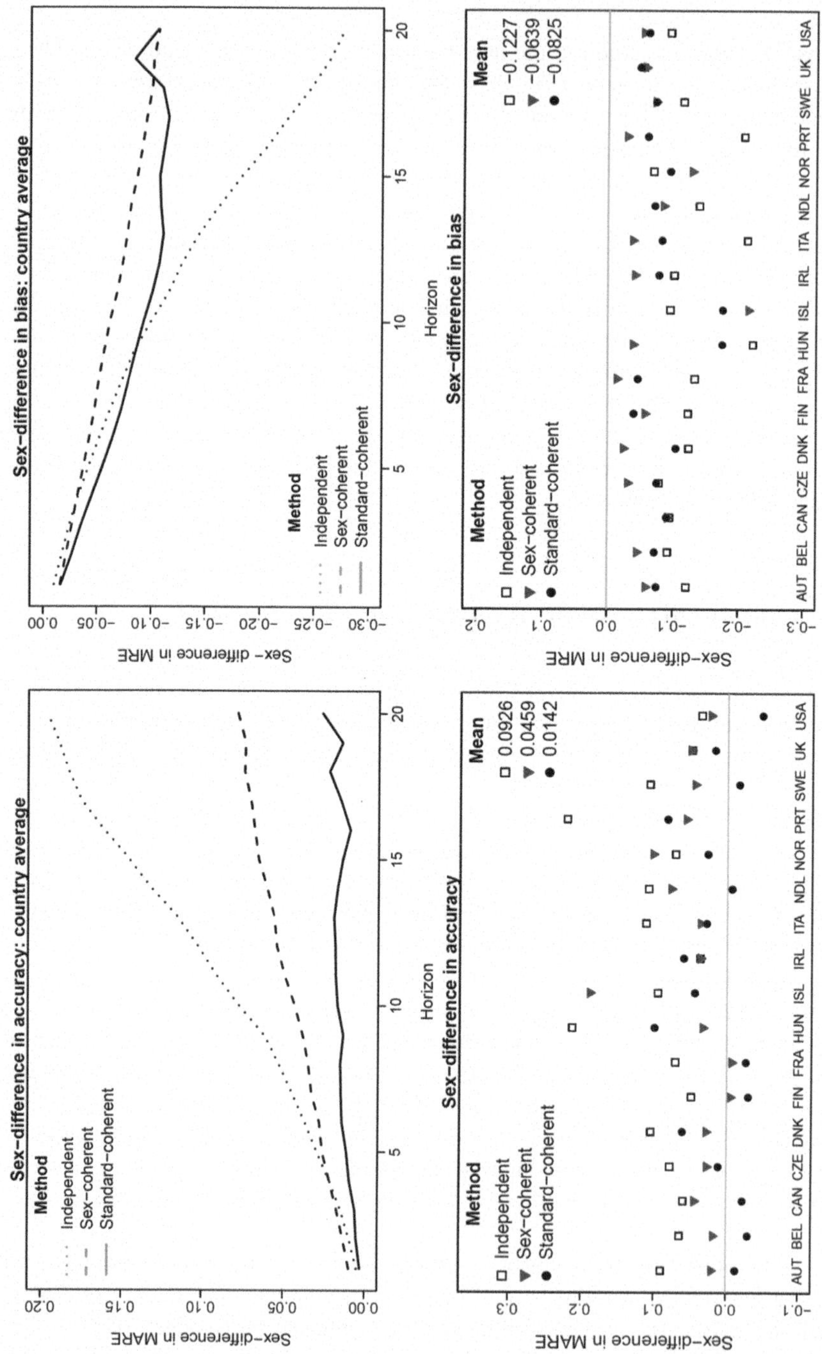

Fig. 8.7 Sex-difference (male – female) in accuracy and bias by method (Japan as standard)

Ratios of sex-differences in the overall means and standard deviations of accuracy and bias are shown for all methods and standards in Table 8.2. Sex-coherent forecasting reduces the sex-difference in the standard deviations of accuracy and bias by two-thirds. For standard-coherent forecasting, using Japan as standard very substantially reduces the sex-difference in performance while using Australia as standard reduces it by about one third. However, using Spain as standard is consistently disadvantageous for male mortality and hence for sex-differences, while using Switzerland as standard has little effect.

8.5.5 Strengths of the Study

An important and purposeful feature of this study is the use of relative measures of accuracy and bias: *MARE* and *MRE*. These measures aggregate and average the proportional forecast errors in age-specific mortality rates, with equal weight to each age, and are thus comparable across mortality levels and age pattern. This means that they are also comparable across horizons, countries and sex; differences and ratios are also comparable. This is a major strength of the study. Non-proportional errors, which are typically larger for higher rates, are influenced by decreasing mortality and portray a conservative horizon effect. In this study, increases in *MARE* and *MRE* with increasing horizon are not influenced by level of mortality.

A second strength is the use of a rolling fitting period, designed to avoid systematic effects in forecast errors arising from random temporal variation in the data in the fitting or forecast periods. By averaging over fitting periods, the effects of jump-off year (jump-off error), calendar year in the forecast period and horizon are averaged (Fig. 8.1). The fixed length of the rolling fitting period has little effect on forecast error, relative to a fixed first year. Indeed, the first year of the fitting period advances from 1950 to 1972, the latter completely omitting the period of mortality stagnation in the 1960s experienced in many low-mortality countries. By using a rolling start year of fixed length, the study takes into account as broad a range of mortality situations as possible.

The comparison of the three methods is further validated by their common use of FDM with identical parameters. Thus the comparison reveals the effects of taking other mortality into account through coherent forecasting. The two coherent methods are also directly comparable: the sex-coherent method is in fact a special case of the standard-coherent method where the standard is the other sex.

It is also of note that the study has a theoretical basis. Most studies introducing new methods have focussed on technical aspects and have been largely experimental.

8.5.6 Limitations

A common criticism of forecasting with the aid of a standard is that the standard itself is not forecast. In this study, the standard represents low mortality. As has been shown, it would be inappropriate to use coherent methods to forecast the standard because the other mortality would by definition be higher. In using standard-coherent forecasting, the forecast of the standard is not of interest. Rather, the standard should be forecast using the independent method, bearing in mind that such forecasts tend to overestimate future mortality (Fig. 8.8). The gains in accuracy for mortality forecasts for all other countries far outweigh this limitation. Further, it should be noted that the method does not require that the standard be forecast.

It should be borne in mind that the means and standard deviations of accuracy and bias are derived from the same forecasting errors in age-specific mortality rates. Given the nature of mortality data, large errors tend to be associated with less regular age and time patterns of change, which also produce large standard deviations across horizons and countries. Patterns across horizons and countries can therefore be expected to be similar. It should also be noted that the study uses heterogeneity in average error (the units of analysis) by horizon and country to assess robustness of methods. Given averaging over rolling fitting period, the study does not assess the accuracy of forecasts for individual calendar years in the forecast period.

The equal weight allocated to each age in the relative measures of accuracy and bias may be regarded as a limitation in situations where emphasis is required on ages where mortality rates are high. Weighting of *MARE* and *MRE* by age would address this requirement while still retaining the advantage of comparability across populations. In other circumstances, the mean absolute error and mean error may be used, but comparability across horizons, countries and sexes would be lost.

A further limitation of this study is that interval forecasts (Shang et al. 2011) are not considered. Conceptually, this follows from analysing accuracy and bias based on errors in the point forecast of age-sex-specific mortality rates, rather than on errors in the forecast distribution of these rates. Further, the rates used in calculation of these measures are net of random observational error by virtue of the smoothing procedure integral to functional data modelling, and the measures are further stabilised by averaging over age and fitting period. Thus, a significant component of the error contributing to the prediction interval of the forecast is excluded from consideration. Further research is needed to address the accuracy of prediction intervals in the framework of this analysis.

8.6 Conclusion

Coherent forecasting offers one approach to the reduction of error in mortality forecasts. Using the product-ratio method of coherent forecasting with functional data models, this study has shown that coherent forecasting with an empirical low-mortality standard can be highly advantageous in terms of forecast performance. Low-mortality-coherent forecasting has the ability to increase accuracy, reduce bias and limit the heterogeneity in these measures. Additionally, sex-differences in forecast performance are reduced, producing greater homogeneity by sex of accuracy and bias, thereby increasing confidence in forecasts by sex. These are important advantages in real world forecasting.

This study has provided clear guidance for female and male mortality forecasting. In both cases, a same-sex low-mortality-standard is optimal. For male mortality, sex-coherent forecasting is also advantageous, on average, but for female mortality sex-coherent forecasting is counterproductive. This study has identified Japan and Australia as the two standards producing the best forecast performance for both female and male mortality in the recent past, while Spain and Switzerland are much less useful as standards. Why this is so remains unclear. The hypothesis that low-mortality is a good guide to future mortality is largely supported, but the role of other features of the standard need further investigation.

Appendix

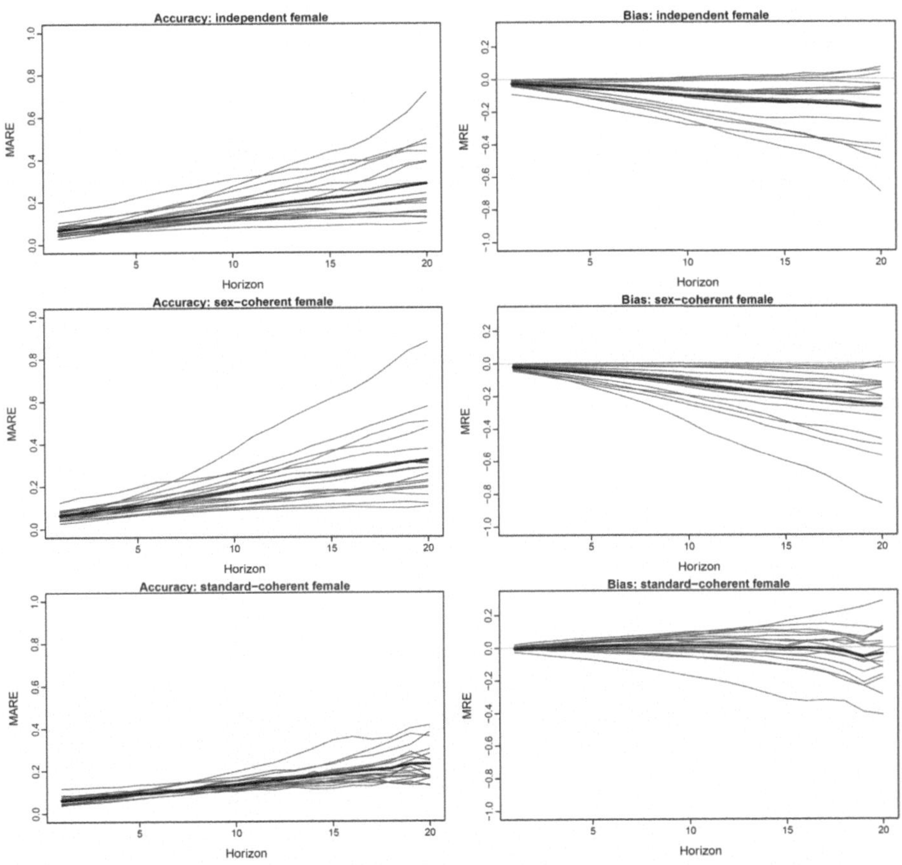

Fig. 8.8 Units of analysis: accuracy and bias by horizon and country for female and male mortality by method (Japan as standard). Note: Country average shown in black

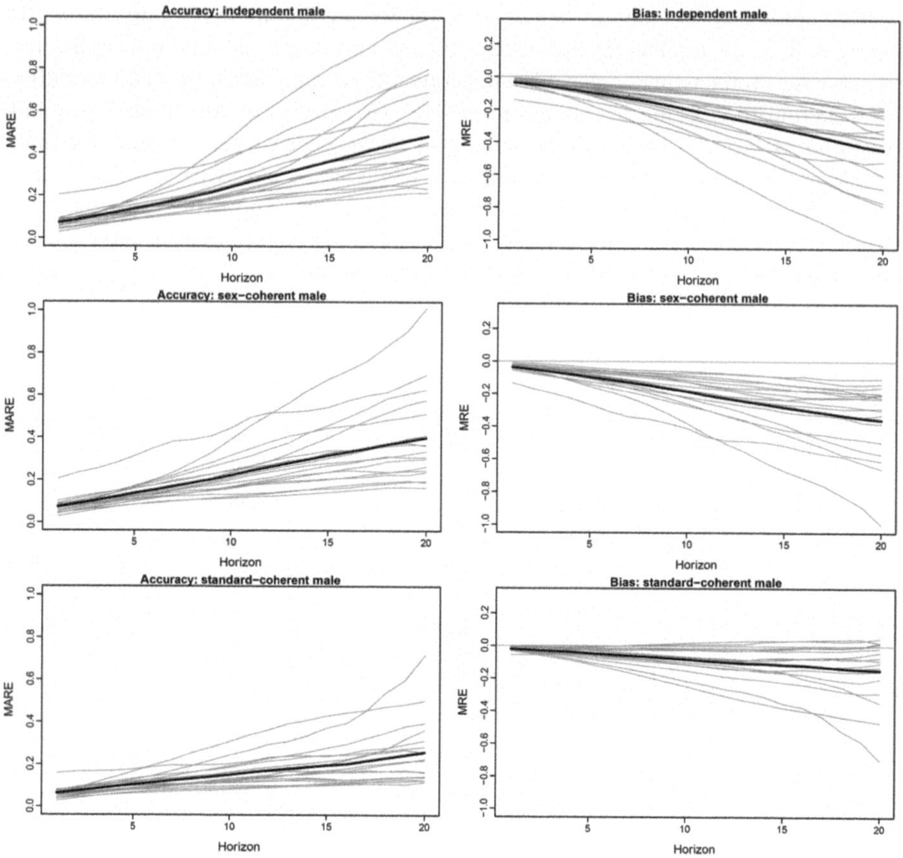

Fig. 8.8 (continued)

References

Ahmadi, S. S., & Li, J. S.-H. (2014). Coherent mortality forecasting with generalized linear models: A modified time-transformation approach. *Insurance: Mathematics & Economics, 59*, 194–221. https://doi.org/10.1016/j.insmatheco.2014.09.007.

Basellini, U., & Camarda, C. G. (2019). Modelling and forecasting adult age-at-death distributions. *Population Studies*, 1–20. https://doi.org/10.1080/00324728.2018.1545918.

Bergeron-Boucher, M.-P., Canudas-Romo, V., Oeppen, J., & Vaupel, J. W. (2017). Coherent forecasts of mortality with compositional data analysis. *Demographic Research, 37*, 527–566.

Booth, H. (2006). Demographic forecasting: 1980 to 2005 in review. *International Journal of Forecasting, 22*(3), 547–581. https://doi.org/10.1016/j.ijforecast.2006.04.001.

Booth, H., & Tickle, L. (2008). Mortality modelling and forecasting: A review of methods. *Annals of Actuarial Science, 3*(I/II), 3–43.

Booth, H., Maindonald, J., & Smith, L. (2002). Applying Lee-Carter under conditions of variable mortality decline. *Population Studies, 56*(3), 325–336. https://doi.org/10.1080/00324720215935.

Booth, H., Hyndman, R. J., Tickle, L., & De Jong, P. (2006). Lee-Carter mortality forecasting: A multi-country comparison of variants and extensions. *Demographic Research, 15*(9), 289–310.

Booth, H., Hyndman, R. J., & Tickle, L. (2014). Prospective life tables. In *Computational actuarial science, with R* (pp. 319–344). Boca Raton: CRC Press. https://doi.org/10.1201/b17230-11.

Buettner, T. (2002). Approaches and experiences in projecting mortality patterns for the oldest-old. *North American Actuarial Journal, 6*(3), 14–29. https://doi.org/10.1080/10920277.2002.10596053.

Cairns, A. J. G., Blake, D., Dowd, K., Coughlan, G. D., & Khalaf-Allah, M. (2011). Bayesian stochastic mortality modeling for two populations. *ASTIN Bulletin, 41*(1), 29–59. https://doi.org/10.2143/AST.41.1.2084385.

Camarda, C. G. (2019). Smooth constrained mortality forecasting. *Demographic Research, 41*(38), 1091–1130. https://doi.org/10.4054/DemRes.2019.41.38.

Currie, I. D. (2014). On fitting generalized linear and non-linear models of mortality. *Scandinavian Actuarial Journal*, (July), 1–28. https://doi.org/10.1080/03461238.2014.928230.

de Beer, J., & Janssen, F. (2016). A new parametric model to assess delay and compression of mortality. *Population Health Metrics, 14*(1), 1–21. https://doi.org/10.1186/s12963-016-0113-1.

de Jong, P., & Tickle, L. (2006). Extending Lee-Carter mortality forecasting. *Mathematical Population Studies, 13*, 1–18.

Fazle Rabbi, A. M. (2019). *Modified Lee-Carter methods with LASSO type smoothing and adjusting for lifespan disparity.* Ph.D. thesis. University of Padua.

Human Mortality Database. (2019). University of California, Berkeley (USA), and Max Planck Institute for Demographic Research (Germany). Retrieved from http://www.mortality.org on 30 June 2019.

Hyndman, R. J., & Booth, H. (2008). Stochastic population forecasts using functional data models for mortality, fertility and migration. *International Journal of Forecasting, 24*(3), 323–342. https://doi.org/10.1016/j.ijforecast.2008.02.009.

Hyndman, R. J., & Ullah, M. S. (2007). Robust forecasting of mortality and fertility rates: A functional data approach. *Computational Statistics and Data Analysis, 51*(10), 4942–4956. https://doi.org/10.1016/j.csda.2006.07.028.

Hyndman, R. J., Booth, H., & Yasmeen, F. (2013). Coherent mortality forecasting: The product-ratio method with functional time series models. *Demography, 50*(1), 261–283. https://doi.org/10.1007/s13524-012-0145-5.

Janssen, F. (2018, December 1). Advances in mortality forecasting: Introduction. *Genus*. Springer International Publishing. https://doi.org/10.1186/s41118-018-0045-7

Kjærgaard, S., Canudas-Romo, V., & Vaupel, J. W. (2016). The importance of the reference populations for coherent mortality forecasting models. In *European population conference*, Mainz, Germany.

Lee, R. D., & Carter, L. R. (1992). Modeling and forecasting U.S. mortality. *Journal of the American Statistical Association, 87*(419), 659–671.

Li, J. (2012). A Poisson common factor model for projecting mortality and life expectancy jointly for females and males. *Population Studies*, (November), 37–41. https://doi.org/10.1080/00324728.2012.689316.

Li, N., & Lee, R. (2005). Coherent mortality forecasts for a group of populations: An extension of the Lee-Carter method. *Demography, 42*(3), 575–594. https://doi.org/10.1353/dem.2005.0021.

Li, H., & Li, J. S.-H. (2017). Optimizing the Lee-Carter approach in the presence of structural changes in time and age patterns of mortality improvements. *Demography, 54*(3), 1073–1095. https://doi.org/10.1007/s13524-017-0579-x.

Li, N., Lee, R., & Gerland, P. (2013). Extending the Lee-Carter method to model the rotation of age patterns of mortality decline for long-term projections. *Demography, 50*(6), 2037–2051. https://doi.org/10.1007/s13524-013-0232-2.

Pascariu, M. D., Canudas-Romo, V., & Vaupel, J. W. (2018). The double-gap life expectancy forecasting model. *Insurance: Mathematics & Economics, 78*, 339–350. https://doi.org/10.1016/j.insmatheco.2017.09.011.

Raftery, A. E., Chunn, J. L., Gerland, P., & Sevčíková, H. (2013). Bayesian probabilistic projections of life expectancy for all countries – Springer. *Demography, 50*, 777–801. Retrieved from http://link.springer.com/article/10.1007/s13524-012-0193-x/fulltext.html?wt_mc=alerts.TOCjournals.13524.

Renshaw, A. E., & Haberman, S. (2003). Lee–Carter mortality forecasting with age-specific enhancement. *Insurance: Mathematics & Economics, 33*(2), 255–272. https://doi.org/10.1016/S0167-6687(03)00138-0.

Renshaw, A. E., & Haberman, S. (2006). A cohort-based extension to the Lee–Carter model for mortality reduction factors. *Insurance: Mathematics & Economics, 38*(3), 556–570. https://doi.org/10.1016/j.insmatheco.2005.12.001.

Shang, H. L., Booth, H., & Hyndman, R. (2011). Point and interval forecasts of mortality rates and life expectancy: A comparison of ten principal component methods. *Demographic Research, 25*(5), 173–214. https://doi.org/10.4054/DemRes.2011.25.5.

Shumway, R. H., & Stoffer, D. S. (2006). *Time series analysis and its applications: With R examples* (2nd ed.). New York: Springer.

Stoeldraijer, L. (2019). An evaluation of methods to coherently forecast mortality based on both quantitative and qualitative criteria. In *Mortality forecasting in the context of non-linear past mortality trends: An evaluation*. University of Groningen. Retrieved from https://www.rug.nl/research/portal/nl/publications/mortality-forecasting-in-the-context-of-nonlinear-past-mortality-trends-an-evaluation(70a8dbec-628a-42b9-afc6-cff076639040).html.

Tickle, L., & Booth, H. (2014). The longevity prospects of Australian seniors: An evaluation of forecast method and outcome. *Asia-Pacific Journal of Risk and Insurance, 8*(2), 1–34. https://doi.org/10.1515/apjri-2013-0004.

Chapter 9
European Mortality Forecasts: Are the Targets Still Moving?

Nico Keilman and Sigve Kristoffersen

9.1 Introduction and Problem Formulation

Many statistical agencies routinely produce population forecasts, and revise these forecasts when new data become available, or when current demographic trends indicate that an update is necessary. When the forecaster strongly revises, from one forecast round to the next one, a forecast for a certain target year (for instance the life expectancy in 2050), this indicates large uncertainty connected to mortality predictions. The aim of this chapter is to shed more light on the uncertainty in mortality forecasts, by analysing the extent to which life expectancy predictions for 2030 and 2050 were revised in subsequent rounds of population forecasts published by statistical agencies in selected countries. It updates and extends earlier work that focused on United Nations and Eurostat forecasts published between 1994 and 2004 (Keilman et al. 2008). There the conclusion was that life expectancy forecasts for 18 European countries for the year 2050 had been revised upwards systematically, by around 2 years on average during the 10-year publication period. A recent analysis based on official population forecasts for Norway published in the period 1999–2018 led to the same conclusion (Keilman 2018). Here we will show that the period of upward revisions seems to have ended for some European countries.

To predict the life expectancy for some future year appears to be similar to aiming at a moving target (Lee 1980). The forecaster tries to hit the value as well as she can, but we cannot expect that the first attempt will be successful. Next, there is a new attempt, but while the rifle was reloaded, the target appears to have moved upwards. This may go on for some forecast rounds. However, sometimes we notice hardly

N. Keilman (✉) · S. Kristoffersen
Department of Economics, University of Oslo, Oslo, Norway
e-mail: nico.keilman@econ.uio.no; sigvekr@student.ikos.uio.no

S. Mazzuco, N. Keilman (eds.), *Developments in Demographic Forecasting*, The Springer Series on Demographic Methods and Population Analysis 49,
https://doi.org/10.1007/978-3-030-42472-5_9

any revision from one forecast round to the next – in some cases, we even see a downward revision.

First, we illustrate this process with life expectancy assumptions for 2030 and 2050 included in official population forecasts of Austria, Denmark, the Netherlands, Norway, Sweden, and the United Kingdom. These countries were selected because the statistical agencies revise their population forecasts every 2 or 3 years. In addition, we show life expectancy assumptions for Japan, which is leading international trends in longevity. Next, we try to explain the systematic revisions by theories of anchoring (Tversky and Kahneman 1974; Kahneman 2011) and assumption drag (Ascher 1978).

9.2 Findings

Many methods have been used in the recent past to forecast mortality. Booth and Tickle (2008) give an extensive review. Most methods use some form of extrapolation: one assumes that the future trends in key parameters are a continuation of trends from the past. The key parameters could be age-specific mortality rates or the parameters in an underlying model. Some scholars have developed formal models for analysing *current* mortality trends in which risk factors and behavioural variables are linked to mortality at various ages, but such explanatory models are very rare in official demographic forecasts (the model employed by Statistics Netherlands is an exception; see below), for a number of reasons. These include the poor predictive performance of the models and the fact that future trends in explanatory variables (smoking, food habits, health care etc.) are as difficult to assess as future trends in mortality itself. See Bengtsson and Keilman (2019) for a recent overview.

Concerning the mortality forecasts presented here, the statistical agencies of Denmark, Japan, Netherlands, Norway, and Sweden use the Lee-Carter model (Lee and Carter 1992), or variations of it. The model variant used by Statistics Netherlands has two distinctive features: the role of smoking is explicitly modelled, and current trends in other countries than the Netherlands are included. The latter feature reduces the risk of extrapolating national idiosyncratic mortality trends. Mortality forecasts for Austria and the United Kingdom are based on assumed rates of decline in age-specific mortality rates in the future.

The Lee-Carter model assumes that a set of age-specific mortality rates observed for a number of years can be summarized in three sets of parameters. The first is a general age pattern of age-specific mortality, with one parameter value for each age. The second is a period index, with one parameter value for each year. The period index reflects falling mortality over time. However, the decrease is not the same for each age, and therefore the model contains an additional set of age-specific parameters, which modify the period index for each age. When used for projecting future mortality, one extrapolates the period index to future years, while keeping the two sets of age-specific parameters constant. Predicted age-specific mortality rates for a certain year can be summarized into a prediction for the life expectancy at birth

(LE) for that year. The model has been criticized for under-projecting long-term life expectancies (and even short-term life expectancies when using long time series with historical mortality rates); see Stoeldraijer et al. (2018), and the references therein. During some years, the LE increased faster than in other years. Therefore, it is difficult to select a certain period that can be thought to be representative for the future. Moreover, the non-linear nature of the model tends to slow down the increase in predicted LE. The result is a concave curve that eventually shows a tendency towards "flattening out" in the longer term.

Extrapolation of mortality based on constant rates of decline in age-specific mortality also leads to a concave curve for the LE as a function of time. A proportional improvement in mortality makes less and less difference in the expectation of life (Keyfitz and Caswell 2005, 81).

In what follows, we will focus on LE-values for men and women for 2030 and for 2050. We would like to stress that the LE is *not* the primary mortality indicator deliberately set to some value by the statistical agencies. Rather, it summarizes extrapolated age-specific mortality rates that were set either directly (Austria, the UK) or indirectly (through the Lee-Carter model and its parameters; see above). We acknowledge that many different age patterns of mortality can lead to the same value of the LE – yet we focus on the latter measure because it is a simple and straightforward indicator for checking the plausibility of assumptions on future mortality.

9.2.1 Descriptive Findings

Figure 9.1 plots assumed values for the LE in 2049/2050 for men and women in a series of forecasts for the populations in Denmark, Japan, and Norway. The assumptions refer to official forecasts made by statistical agencies in the three countries during the period 2000–2018. The data come from various sources, as listed in the Appendix.

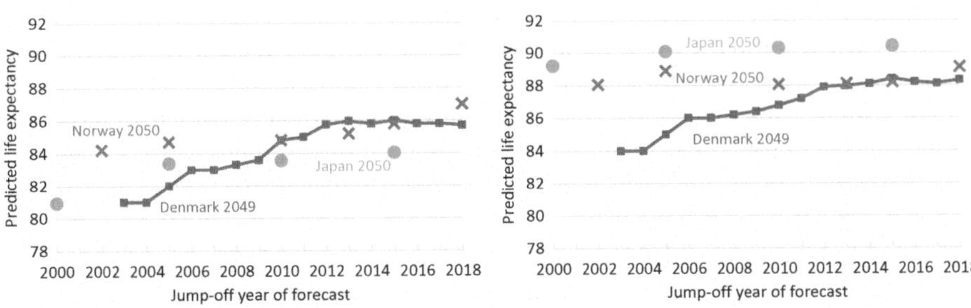

Fig. 9.1 Life expectancy predictions for Denmark, Norway, and Japan around 2050, forecasts prepared between 2000 and 2018. Left panel: men. Right panel: women. (Source: See Appendix)

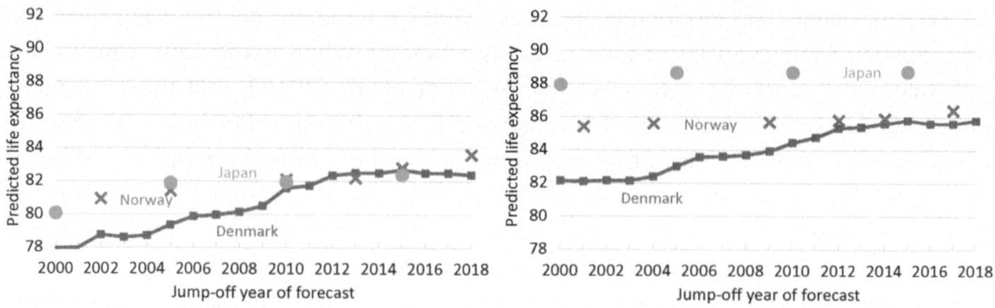

Fig. 9.2 Life expectancy predictions for Denmark, Norway, and Japan for the year 2030, forecasts prepared between 2000 and 2018. Left panel: men. Right panel: women. (Source: See Appendix)

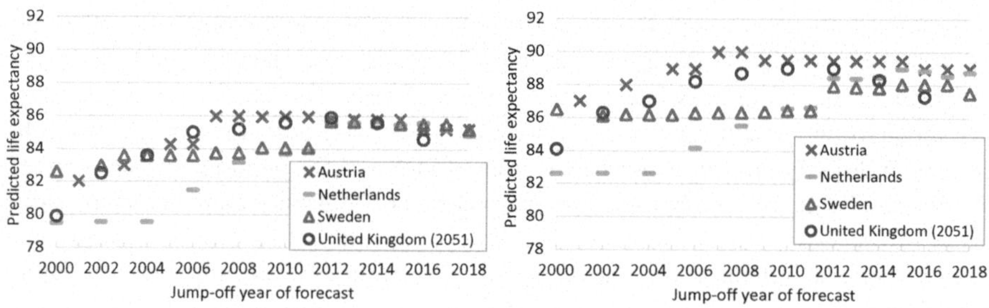

Fig. 9.3 Life expectancy predictions for Austria, the Netherlands, Sweden, and the United Kingdom around 2050, forecasts prepared between 2000 and 2018. Left panel: men. Right panel: women. (Source: See Appendix)

The graphs show a more or less systematic upward revision of LE-values from one forecast round to the next. For the case of Denmark, the upward trend appears to have ended around 2013. In the forecasts computed from 2013 onwards, there seems to be agreement about an LE for 2050 around 86 years for men and 88 years for women. For the other two countries, the forecasters show increased optimism in the sense that assumed LE-values were adjusted upwards in subsequent forecasts, although the revisions are not as strong as those for Denmark are during the period before 2013. One has to be a bit cautious concerning the LE of Japanese women, because we have only a few data points, and the upward revision from the 2010-forecast to the 2015-forecast is very modest.

The patterns that emerge for 2049/2050 in Fig. 9.1 are very similar to those for the year 2030 in the three countries; see Fig. 9.2. However, there is one exception: the 2030 predictions for Danish men computed between 2015 and 2018 show minor *downward* corrections. The "target" appears to move in opposite direction, compared to forecasts published before 2015.

Figures 9.3 and 9.4 show downward revisions in predicted LEs for 2030 and 2050 in four other countries: Austria, the Netherlands, Sweden, and the United Kingdom. The predictions for Austria appear to be the first ones for which upward revisions came to a halt: for both target years 2030 and 2050, this is visible starting

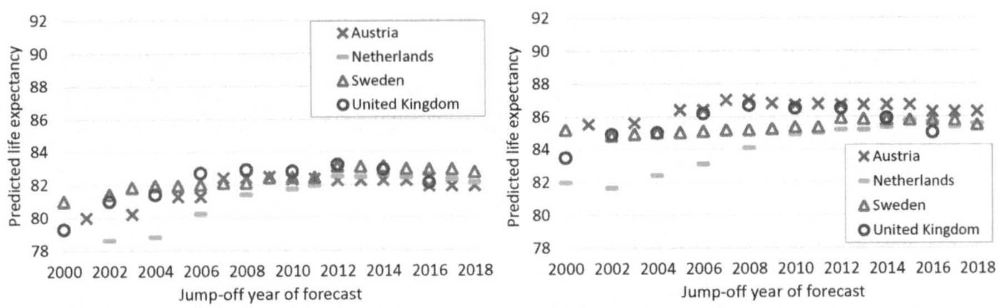

Fig. 9.4 Life expectancy predictions for Austria, the Netherlands, Sweden, and the United Kingdom for the year 2030, forecasts prepared between 2000 and 2018. Left panel: men. Right panel: women. (Source: See Appendix)

Fig. 9.5 Life expectancy at birth. (Source: See Appendix)

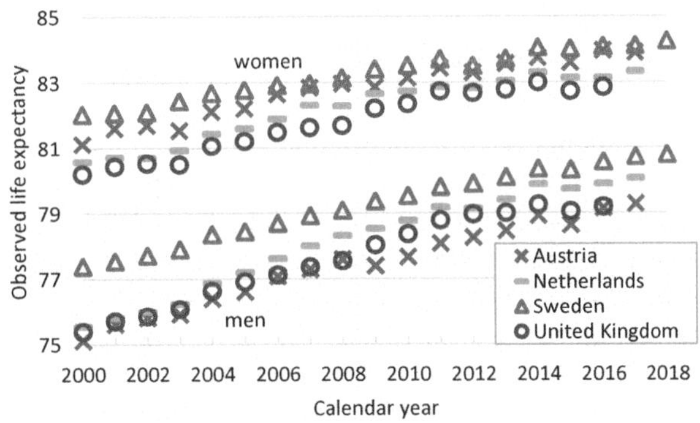

in 2007. Other countries followed a few years later. The cases of Sweden and the UK stand out with strong downward revisions in the last forecast, compared to the previous one. In the forecast of 2018, the 2050 LE-prediction for Swedish women was 0.55 years lower than the corresponding value in the forecast of 2017. For men and women in the UK, the 2050 predictions for LE fell by a whole year between 2014 and 2016, which makes a downward slope of half a year of life per calendar year. These revisions are of similar magnitude as those for Austria between 2015 and 2016 (−0.58 years). Also, note that LE-assumptions in Figs. 9.1, 9.2, 9.3 and 9.4 seem to converge over time, with much larger differences between countries for forecasts computed in the first decade of the century than in later forecasts.

An obvious question is whether the patterns shown in Figs. 9.3 and 9.4 are related to trends in actually observed LEs for recent years. Figure 9.5 may shed some led on this. We note that the upward trend in LE has weakened in all four countries in recent years, perhaps with the exception of men in Sweden. Thus, a possible explanation of the flat or even decreasing trends in predicted LE in Figs. 9.3 and 9.4 might be the fact that increases in actual LE tend to slow down, at least for Austria, Netherlands, and the United Kingdom. In other words, forecasters are possibly strongly guided by trends in the *current* value of the LE, when they predict the LE for future years. In Sect. 9.3, we will suggest psychological explanations for these findings.

Some evidence for an association between observed and predicted trends can be found in the justifications that statistical agencies give for the downward revisions. ONS (2017) writes, for the case of the United Kingdom, "... actual life expectancy has increased less than projected since mid-2014; this means that the life expectancy values for 2016 are lower, and also reduces the rate of increase in subsequent years." Statistics Netherlands justifies the downward revision by referring to the unfavourable mortality development in the last months of 2016 and the limited decrease in mortality in the first 8 months of 2017. At the same time, relatively low mortality in 2014 (and a rather high LE that year) led to high values for predicted LEs in 2030 and 2050 in the 2015-based forecast, in particular for women. This effect disappeared in later forecasts (Stoeldraijer et al. 2017).

9.2.2 A Simple Model

The process can be formalized as follows. For simplicity, we assume linearity both for observed and for extrapolated life expectancy trajectories, but with different slopes. Consider a time interval $[t_0,T]$, where t_0 is a certain year in the past, and T is some future year ("target year"). A forecaster has data on actual life expectancy values LE(t) for the time interval $[t_0, t_1]$ and is faced with the task of predicting the life expectancy LE(t) to year T, starting from the jump-off year t_1. Assume that actual life expectancy LE(t) follows a straight line with slope $b > 0$ on $[t_0, T]$. Assume further that the extrapolated trajectory is a straight line on $[t_1, T]$ with slope $b_e > 0$. Then the predicted life expectancy in year T, resulting from the prediction with jump-off year t_1, is $LE_1(T) = LE(t_1) + (T - t_1).b_e$. An updated forecast is made in year $t_2 > t_1$. The new extrapolation starts from $LE(t_2) = LE(t_1) + (t_2 - t_1).b$. The revised prediction for year T is now

$$LE_2(T) = LE(t_2) + (T - t_2).b_e = LE(t_1) + (t_2 - t_1).b + (T - t_2).b_e$$

The revised forecast $LE_2(T)$ differs from the previous forecast $LE_1(T)$ by an amount of

$$LE_2(T) - LE_1(T) = (t_2 - t_1).b + (T - t_2).b_e - (T - t_1).b_e = (t_2 - t_1).(b - b_e).$$

First, assume that $b_e < b$. The extrapolated life expectancy falls short compared to the actual life expectancy by an amount of $(b - b_e)$ annually. When the inter-forecast period is $(t_2 - t_1)$ years, the new life expectancy forecast for year T is higher than the previous one by $(t_2 - t_1).(b - b_e)$ years. This is the situation in Figs. 9.1 and 9.2.

Next, assume that life expectancy is extrapolated with the correct slope $(b_e = b)$. Then the new forecast for year T is the same as the previous one: $LE_2(T) - LE_1(T)$. Much of the data in Figs. 9.3 and 9.4 reflect this pattern.

Finally, assume that the increase in actual life expectance slows down, or even stagnates, whereas the extrapolations still follow a straight line with slope b_e. Then the difference $(b - b_e)$ may become negative, which implies a lower life expectancy forecast for year T compared to the previous forecast.

Note that the straight-line assumptions formulated above are not crucial for the qualitative results. As long as average annual increases over relevant time intervals are b and b_e for actual and extrapolated trends, respectively, we will see upward revisions for the predicted life expectancy in year T whenever the actual life expectancy improves faster than the extrapolated one $(b > b_e)$.

9.3 Possible Explanations: Assumption Drag and Anchoring

Why did population forecasters in the countries analysed here so often revise their views on people's length of life in an upwards direction? Or, to put it in terms of the simple model of Sect. 9.2.2: why did mortality forecasters under-predict so often the pace of annual LE-improvement? According to Pison (2018), French forecasters did not anticipate the sharp drop, after the Second World War, in adult mortality, old-age mortality in particular. There is no reason to assume that the situation was different in the seven countries analysed here until the beginning of this century. The decline in cardiovascular mortality explains much of the drop in adult mortality during the past 50 years. Falling numbers of cancer deaths contribute also. Forecasters did not foresee this decline, and relied heavily upon observed trends. Longevity improved only slowly during the 1950s and early 1960s, in particular for men. In some countries, there was even a stagnation or a decline. Examples are Denmark, the Netherlands, Norway, and Sweden. Therefore, forecasters assumed that the LE would increase very little in the immediate future, and that it would soon reach a maximum value ("ceiling", or "limit"; see Oeppen and Vaupel 2001). Indeed, statistical agencies in five of our countries used such a ceiling: Austria (until the 1990-based forecast, in which mortality was kept constant after 2015), Denmark (forecast of 1997, constant after 2012), Norway (forecast of 1990, constant after 2010), Netherlands (forecast of 1995, constant after 2010), and Sweden (forecast of 1994, constant after 2025). During the 1990s, however, the forecasters in these countries dropped the idea of a ceiling, and started to extrapolate a much longer increase in future LE, although the slope was not steep enough. French forecasters used an LE-ceiling up to the forecast published in 1986, but gave up this idea starting with the forecast published in 1995 (Pison 2018).

9.3.1 *Assumption Drag*

Forty years ago, Ascher (1978) analysed fertility forecasts in developed countries and noted that forecasters tend to rely strongly on recently observed data; they give less weight to the long-term trend. Figure 9.5 suggests that this "assumption drag" might hold for mortality, too: forecasters in Austria, the Netherlands, Sweden, and the UK revised assumed LE-values for 2030 and 2050 downwards, because they relied strongly on a weak upward trend of observed LEs in recent years. Here, "assumption drag" is to be understood as the maintenance of incorrect assumptions after their validity has been contradicted by the data. Why this practice? First, there might be a tendency among demographers to agree on incorrect assumptions because of socially validated beliefs, for example that there must be an upper limit to longevity, or a lower limit to fertility. Such a consensus makes it easier to reject conflicting evidence, such as new research results or data errors. Second, the complexity of advanced methods can mean that the results achieved are outdated, because all data are collected and processed and the high costs of advanced methods can mean that the forecasts simply tend to copy the underlying assumptions from a previous round.

Let us assume Ascher's assumption drag applies to mortality, too. The simple model of Sect. 9.2.2 states that it is primarily the *slope* in the LE between the jump-off year of the forecast and the year 2030/2050 that is under-predicted, not so much the *level*. Following this line of thought, Ascher's theory of assumption drag applies to improvements in the LE, rather than LE levels. The consequence may very well be that in future population forecasts, the downward revisions in Figs. 9.3 and 9.4 will come to a halt and that more or less stable patterns will emerge. This is more likely for 2030 than for 2050. After all, the closer we get to a certain target year, the easier it becomes to predict the LE for that year. Obviously, there is one additional important assumption underlying these speculations, namely that the long-term trend in LE expectancy is definitely upward, and that any periods of stagnation are only temporary.

9.3.2 Anchoring

The anchoring effect is one of the most solid tested phenomena in the world of experimental psychology. Tversky and Kahneman (1974; see also Kahneman 2011) discovered a cognitive bias, which takes place when we consider a particular value of an unknown quantity before estimating such quantity. The value we have considered or that has been shown to us before, strongly determines the estimate we are going to make, which will always be relatively close to that previous value, which is called the anchor. Once the anchor has been established, we evaluate whether it is high or low and then we adjust our estimate to that amount. This mental process finishes early, because we are not sure of the real amount. Therefore, our estimation is not usually far from the anchor. Thus, the idea of an adjust-and-anchor heuristic as a strategy for estimating uncertain quantities is as follows. Start from an anchoring number, assess whether it is too high or too low, and gradually adjust your estimate by mentally "moving" from the anchor. The adjustment typically ends prematurely, because people stop when they are no longer certain that they should move farther.

We can use the theory of anchoring to explain the patterns that we see in Figs. 9.1, 9.2, 9.3 and 9.4. To fix ideas, consider a forecast made every 3 years; let us say in 2012, 2015, and 2018. A forecaster confronted with the task of extrapolating LE between 2012 and 2030 uses recently observed values as an anchor. In spite of the fact that historical values have increased more or less linearly at a certain pace, a simple straight-line extrapolation with the same slope would move the prediction for 2030 too far away from the anchor value, and the forecaster decides to extrapolate with smaller annual improvements than historically. This may be a straight line, or, a decelerating (concave) curve. The next forecast round starts from the LE observed for 2015, and moves the complete extrapolated line or curve upwards. This is in essence the process described by the model in Sect. 9.2.2. Because the extrapolations do not increase fast enough, the new prediction for 2030 is higher than the old one for the same year. The whole procedure is repeated for 2018, and the result is an even higher LE-prediction for 2030. Figure 9.6 illustrates this process for the case of the United Kingdom.

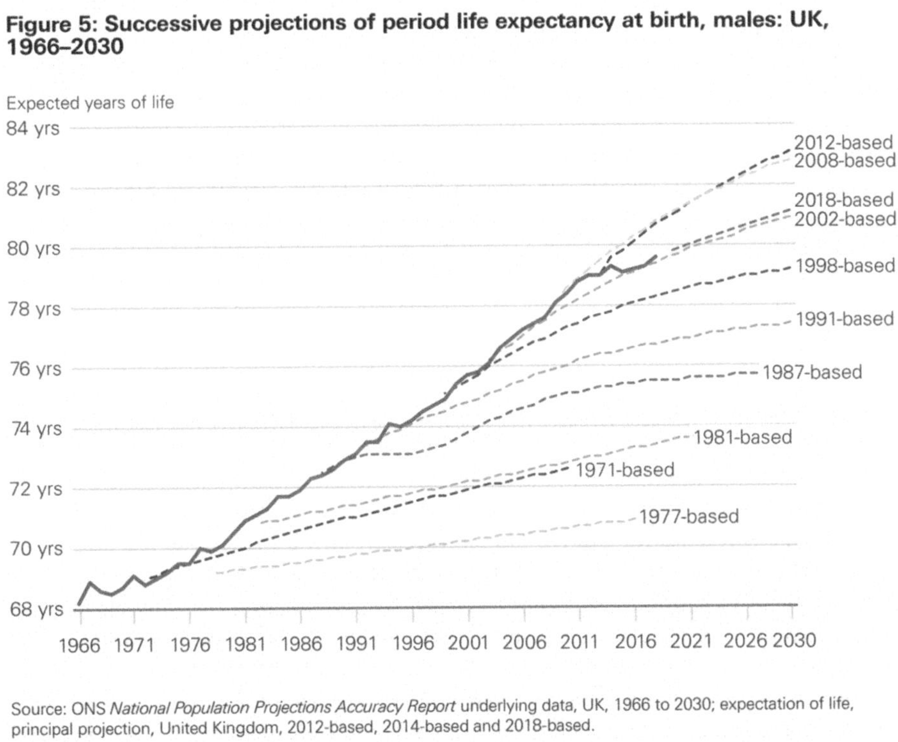

Fig. 9.6 Actual and projected period expectation of life at birth (EOLB), males, United Kingdom, 1966 to 2030, selected projections.

Between 1985 and 2012, the Office for National Statistics (ONS) did not extrapolate the LE according to a straight line, but used a concave curve. As argued in Sect. 9.2, not only extrapolations based on proportionate changes in age-specific mortality, but also those based on the Lee-Carter model will result in LE-improvements that diminish over time. In Sect. 9.2.2, we demonstrated that even with straight-line extrapolations, we would observe systematic upward revisions of predicted LEs for a certain target year if the slope of the extrapolation were less steep than that of actual values. This was the case for ONS-forecasts between 1971 and 1981 in Fig. 9.6.

The discussion so far attempts to explain the patterns in Figs. 9.1 and 9.2, where LE-predictions are systematically revised upwards. However, we can also use the theory of anchoring behaviour to explain downward revisions as in Figs. 9.3 and 9.4. When actual LE stagnates, the anchoring effect becomes stronger, and the extrapolations in the previous round of forecasts are considered too steep. As a result, the revised extrapolation curve is flatter than the original one, leading to a revised 2030-prediction that is close to the value in the previous round. This may explain the patterns we see for Danish men and women after 2011 in Figs. 9.1 and 9.2, and for Austrian men and women for forecasts with jump-off years between 2009 and 2015. *Very* strong anchoring may even lead to a downward revision; cf. the cases of Sweden and the UK in particular.

Kahneman (2011) notes that there are situations in which anchoring appears reasonable. People who are asked difficult questions clutch at straws, and the anchor is a plausible straw. To predict long-term trends in mortality is clearly difficult. Therefore, it is reasonable to use actual mortality trends as anchors. Yet one may wonder if forecasters, once being aware of the anchoring effect when formulating forecast assumptions, will learn from the errors they made in the past?

9.4 Conclusions

Life expectancy predictions for a certain target year (for instance, 2030, or 2050) computed by statistical agencies in some countries during the past decade have been revised upwards frequently. We noticed this in official LE-predictions for Denmark, Japan, and Norway. However, for a number of other countries (viz. Austria, the Netherlands, Sweden, the United Kingdom), such upward revisions are no longer visible. The LE-adjustments for 2030 and 2050 appear to be very small – they are even negative in the most recent forecasts for these countries. This means that in the current forecast, the forecaster is less optimistic about the LE in the target year than she was in the previous forecast. One possible explanation is that actual LE did not improve much, perhaps even stagnated, during the period between two forecasts. The patterns described here, illustrated by Figs. 9.1, 9.2, 9.3 and 9.4, are compatible with a situation in which the real (but unknown) LE until 2030 or 2050 improves faster than the predicted LE. We referred to two psychological factors that can be used to explain these patterns. The first one is an assumption drag, a term first coined by Ascher in 1978 in connection with fertility forecasts in developed countries in the 1960s, which tended to be far too high. The assumption drag involves a psychological mechanism according to which forecasters rely heavily on recently observed data, whereas they give less weight to long-term trends. The second psychological mechanism that one may use to explain upward and downward revisions of the LE in a series of population forecasts is an anchoring effect, discovered by Tversky and Kahneman. When a forecaster has to predict an unknown and uncertain quantity, he will start from a known value (the anchor), and predict a value that is close to that value.

The process with upward or downward revisions of predicted LE for a certain year in the future resembles the behaviour of a hunter, who aims at a moving target. Sometimes the target moves up (upward revision of the LE), sometimes down (downward revision). However, a simple model based on linear extrapolations of the LE suggests that upward revisions result simply from the fact that extrapolated LE does not improve as fast as actual LE. Downward revisions may be the result of a temporary stagnation of LE-improvement.

Acknowledgements We acknowledge gratefully the help of Alexander Hanika (Statistics Austria) and Annika Klintefelt (Statistics Denmark) in collecting data on historical forecasts for the two countries.

Appendix: Data Sources

Frank Hansen, M., Stephensen, P. (2013). Danmarks Fremtidige Befolkning: Befolkningsfremskrivning 2013.

Alexander Hanika (2019) Personal communication.

National Institute of Population and Social Security Research – IPSS (2012). http://www.ipss.go.jp/syoushika/tohkei/newest04/h4_2.html. Accessed: October 2018.

IPSS (2007). http://www.ipss.go.jp/syoushika/tohkei/suikei07/houkoku/katei/11-5.xls. Accessed: October 2018.

IPSS. http://www.ipss.go.jp/syoushika/tohkei/Mokuji/1_Japan/J_Detail_14.asp?fname=1_katei/1-2.htm&title1=%82P%81D%89%BC%92%E8%92l%95%5C&title2=%95%5C%82P%81%7C%82Q%81D%89%BC%92%E8%82%B3%82%EA%82%BD%95%BD%8B%CF%8E%F5%96%BD%81i%8Fo%90%B6%8E%9E%82%CC%95%BD%8B%CF%97%5D%96%BD%81j%82%CC%90%84%88%DA. Accessed: October 2018.

IPSS. http://www.ipss.go.jp/ppzenkoku/e/zenkoku_e2017/g_images_e/pp29gt0402e.files/sheet001.htm. Accessed: October 2018.

Office for National Statistics – ONS (2001). https://webarchive.nationalarchives.gov.uk/20160106011038/; http://www.ons.gov.uk/ons/rel/npp/national-population-projections-historic-series/2000-based-projections/index.html. Accessed: October 2018.

ONS (2003). https://webarchive.nationalarchives.gov.uk/20160106011038/; http://www.ons.gov.uk/ons/rel/npp/national-population-projections-historic-series/2002-based-projections/index.html. Accessed: October 2018.

ONS (2005). https://webarchive.nationalarchives.gov.uk/20160106011038/; http://www.ons.gov.uk/ons/rel/npp/national-population-projections-historic-series/2004-based-projections/index.html. Accessed: October 2018.

ONS (2007). https://webarchive.nationalarchives.gov.uk/20160105223341/; http://www.ons.gov.uk/ons/rel/npp/national-population-projections/2006-based-projections/index.html. Accessed: October 2018.

ONS (2009). https://webarchive.nationalarchives.gov.uk/20160105223341/; http://www.ons.gov.uk/ons/rel/npp/national-population-projections/2008-based-projections/index.html. Accessed: October 2018.

ONS (2011). https://webarchive.nationalarchives.gov.uk/20160105223341/; http://www.ons.gov.uk/ons/rel/npp/national-population-projections/2010-based-projections/index.html. Accessed: October 2018.

ONS (2013). https://webarchive.nationalarchives.gov.uk/20160105223341/; http://www.ons.gov.uk/ons/rel/npp/national-population-projections/2012-based-projections/index.html. Accessed: October 2018.

ONS (2015). https://webarchive.nationalarchives.gov.uk/20160105223341/; http://www.ons.gov.uk/ons/rel/npp/national-population-projections/2014-based-projections/index.html. Accessed: October 2018.

ONS (2017). National Population Projections: 2016-based statistical bulletin. https://www.ons.gov.uk/peoplepopulationandcommunity/populationandmigration/populationprojections/bulletins/nationalpopulationprojections/2016basedstatisticalbulletin. Accessed: October 2018.

ONS (2018). https://www.ons.gov.uk/peoplepopulationandcommunity/birthsdeathsandmarriages/lifeexpectancies/datasets/nationallifetablesunitedkingdomreferencetables. Accessed: October 2018.

Kaneko, R., Ishikawa, A., Ishii, F., Sasai, T., Iwasawa, M., Mita, F. and Moriizumi, R. (2006). Population projections for Japan: 2006–2055 outline of results, methods, and assumptions.

Statistics Denmark (2019). Population Projections for Denmark. https://www.dst.dk/en/Statistik/emner/befolkning-og-valg/befolkning-og-befolkningsfremskrivning/befolkningsfremskrivning. Accessed: January 2019.

Statistics Denmark. https://www.dst.dk/da/Statistik/Publikationer/StE/statistiske-efterretninger-emner?psi=486. Accessed: October 2018.

Statistics Netherlands (2019). https://opendata.cbs.nl/#/CBS/nl/navigatieScherm/zoeken?searchKeywords=*&page=1&year%5B%5D=Prognose. Accessed: June 2019.

Statistics Sweden (2002). https://www.scb.se/statistik/BE/BE0401/2003M00/BE18SM0201.pdf. Accessed: October 2018.

Statistics Sweden (2003). http://www.scb.se/statistik/BE/BE0401/2003I50/BE51ST0304.pdf. Accessed: October 2018.

Statistics Sweden (2004). http://www.scb.se/statistik/BE/BE0401/2003M00/BE0401_2004A01_SM_BE18SM0401.pdf. Accessed: October 2018.

Statistics Sweden (2005). https://www.scb.se/statistik/BE/BE0401/2005A01/BE0401_2005A01_SM_BE18SM050 1.pdf. Accessed: October 2018.

Statistics Sweden (2006). http://www.scb.se/statistik/_publikationer/BE0401_2006I50_BR_BE51ST0602.pdf. Accessed: October 2018.

Statistics Sweden (2018). Sveriges framtida befolkning 2018–2070. https://www.scb.se/hitta-statistik/statistik-efter-amne/befolkning/befolkningsframskrivningar/befolkningsframskrivningar/pong/publikationer/sveriges-framtida-befolkning-20182070/. Accessed: October 2018.

Statistics Sweden (2007). http://www.statistikdatabasen.scb.se/goto/en/ssd/PrognosLivslangd04. Accessed: October 2018.

Statistics Sweden (2008). http://www.statistikdatabasen.scb.se/goto/en/ssd/BefPrognosLivslangd. Accessed: October 2018.

Statistics Sweden (2009). http://www.statistikdatabasen.scb.se/goto/en/ssd/BefPrognosLivslang09. Accessed: October 2018.

Statistics Sweden (2010). http://www.statistikdatabasen.scb.se/goto/en/ssd/BefProgLivslangd2010. Accessed: October 2018.

Statistics Sweden (2011). http://www.statistikdatabasen.scb.se/goto/en/ssd/BefProgLivslangd2011. Accessed: October 2018.

Statistics Sweden (2012). http://www.statistikdatabasen.scb.se/goto/en/ssd/BefProgLivslangd2012. Accessed: October 2018.

Statistics Sweden (2013). http://www.statistikdatabasen.scb.se/goto/en/ssd/BefProgLivslangd2013. Accessed: October 2018.

Statistics Sweden (2014). http://www.statistikdatabasen.scb.se/goto/en/ssd/BefProgLivslangd2014. Accessed: October 2018.

Statistics Sweden (2015). http://www.statistikdatabasen.scb.se/goto/en/ssd/BefProgLivslangd2015. Accessed: October 2018.

Statistics Sweden (2016). http://www.statistikdatabasen.scb.se/goto/en/ssd/BefProgLivslangd2016. Accessed: October 2018.

Statistics Sweden (2017). http://www.statistikdatabasen.scb.se/goto/en/ssd/BefProgLivslangd2017. Accessed: October 2018.

References

Ascher, W. (1978). *Forecasting: An appraisal for policy makers and planners*. Baltimore: Johns Hopkins University Press.

Bengtsson, T., & Keilman, N. (Eds.). (2019). *Old and new perspectives on mortality forecasting*. Cham: Springer.

Booth, H., & Tickle, L. (2008). Mortality modelling and forecasting: A review of methods. *Annals of Actuarial Science, 3*(1 & 2), 3–43.

Kahneman, D. (2011). *Thinking, fast and slow*. London: Penguin Books.

Keilman, N. (2018). *Increasing (but Insufficient?) Optimism about future life expectancy*. NIUSSP 15 October 2018.

Keilman, N., Cruijsen, H., & Alho, J. (2008). Changing views of future demographic trends. In J. Alho, S. Hougaard Jensen, & J. Lassila (Eds.), *Uncertain demographics and fiscal sustainability* (pp. 11–33). Cambridge: Cambridge University Press.

Keyfitz, N., & Caswell, H. (2005). *Applied mathematical demography* (3rd ed.). New York: Springer.
Lee, R. (1980). Aiming at a moving target: Period fertility and changing reproductive goals. *Population Studies, 34*(2), 205–226.
Lee, R. D., & Carter, L. R. (1992). Modeling and forecasting US mortality. *Journal of the American Statistical Association, 87*(419), 659–671.
Oeppen, J., & Vaupel, J. (2001). Broken limits to life expectancy. *Science, 296*(5570), 1029–1031.
Pison, G. (2018). 1968-2018: Four demographic surprises in France over the last 50 years. *Population & Societies, 553*, 1–6.
Stoeldraijer, L., Van Duin, C., & Huisman, C. (2017). Bevolkingsprognose 2017–2060: 18,4 miljoen inwoners in 2060 (Population forecast 2017–2060: 18.4 million inhabitants in 2060). Statistische Trends, December 2017.
Stoeldraijer, L., Van Duin, C., Van Wissen, L., & Janssen, F. (2018). Comparing strategies for matching mortality forecasts to the most recently observed data: Exploring the trade-off between accuracy and robustness. *Genus, 74*(16), 1–20.
Tversky, A., & Kahneman, D. (1974). Judgment under uncertainty: Heuristics and biases. *Science, 185*(4147), 1124–1131.

Chapter 10
Bayesian Disaggregated Forecasts: Internal Migration in Iceland

Junni L. Zhang and John Bryant

10.1 Introduction

Ministries of Finance want national-level population forecasts. Almost all other users of population forecasts, from local councils, to market analysts, to planners of roads, supermarkets, and hospitals, want local-level forecasts.

Constructing local-level population forecasts is not easy. The most difficult part is estimating historical trends for demographic rates that can be extrapolated into the future. Fertility, mortality, and migration rates vary across subnational areas in ways that can be difficult to model. The age profiles of migrants coming to university towns, for instance, are dramatically different from the age profiles of migrants coming to rural areas (Wilson 2010). Moreover, the more finely a population is disaggregated, the smaller the number of observations that are available for each combination of classifying variables such as age, sex, and region. Random variation starts to dominate, and the underlying propensities become lost in the noise.

Traditional demographic techniques, which were designed for national-level datasets, are poorly suited to estimation and forecasting with sparse data. The most traditional demographic approach to estimating rates is to simply divide the number of observed events by the population at risk, and to do so separately for each

Electronic Supplementary Material The online version of this chapter (https://doi.org/10.1007/978-3-030-42472-5_10) contains supplementary material, which is available to authorized users.

J. L. Zhang (✉)
National School of Development, Peking University, Beijing, China
e-mail: junnizhang@163.com

J. Bryant
Bayesian Demography Ltd, Christchurch, New Zealand

S. Mazzuco, N. Keilman (eds.), *Developments in Demographic Forecasting*, The Springer Series on Demographic Methods and Population Analysis 49,
https://doi.org/10.1007/978-3-030-42472-5_10

combination of the classifying variables. When most cells have small numbers of events, however, estimates obtained by considering each cell separately are erratic and unreliable.

In response to these problems, demographers turn to some form of smoothing or modelling. Estimates for each cell are informed by data for neighbouring cells, and perhaps also by information about overall patterns. The classic method for smoothing migration rates, for instance, is model migration schedules (Rogers and Castro 1981). These allow demographers to construct typical age profiles for migration by specifying only a handful of parameters. More recent alternatives include splines, or other types of general-purpose statistical smoothing techniques. A second general approach is to use log-linear models, which provide parsimonious ways of representing the main patterns in the data (van Imhoff et al. 1997; Raymer and Rogers 2007; Rogers et al. 2010).

Demographic estimation and forecasting models based on model life tables, splines, or log-linear models have had many successes. But even these start to break down when cell counts become very small (Bernard and Bell 2015; Baffour and Raymer 2019). Standard log-linear models, for instance, cannot handle cell counts of zero.

As statisticians have long recognized, the ability to extract complex patterns from sparse datasets is a particular strength of Bayesian statistical methods (Gelman et al. 2014). Bayesian methods are, accordingly, becoming increasingly popular among demographers carrying out subnational estimates and forecasts (Lynch and Brown 2010; Schmertmann et al. 2013; Bijak and Bryant 2016; Alexander et al. 2017; Bryant and Zhang 2018). There are, of course, limits to how much can be inferred from any given dataset, even with the best available methods. However, Bayesian analyses also yield detailed measures of uncertainty, which can be used to inform users about these limits.

In this chapter, we present Bayesian forecasts for one particular component of local-level population change: internal migration, i.e., changes of residence within national boundaries. Getting internal migration right is essential to local-level forecasting, as internal migration is typically the biggest source of population change for small geographical units.

To illustrate the ability of Bayesian methods to cope with sparse data, we have chosen an extreme case: Iceland. The population of Iceland in 2018 was 348,450. Once the internal migration data for Iceland are disaggregated by sex, single-year-of-age, 8 regions of origin, 8 regions of destination, and calendar year, 66% of cells have values of zero. Using single years of age and calendar years, rather than, say, aggregating to 5-year units, increases sparsity. However, it reflects user needs. Consumers of population forecasts often want forecasts for particular years, or for age groups such as school ages that cannot be constructed from 5-year age-time blocks.

We begin the chapter with a review of the Icelandic data and migration trends. We then present a baseline model that tries to capture these trends in a parsimonious way. We subject the baseline model to some model checking, using 'replicate data' techniques. Based on these checks, we construct a revised, slightly more complicated model. We use held-back data to choose between the baseline and revised models. We then present forecasts from the best-performing of the two models.

Our recent book *Bayesian Demographic Estimation and Forecasting* (BDEF) (Bryant and Zhang 2018) also includes a chapter on internal migration in Iceland. However, the BDEF model uses confidentialised data, and has a component to account for the confidentialisation process, which is the main focus of that chapter. The BDEF component dealing with demographic rates is also simpler than the one presented here, and is not subjected to model testing or model comparison.

10.2 Data

Our first dataset is counts of internal migrations by region of origin, region of destination, single year of age (up to age 80+), sex, and calendar year. The data were obtained from the Statistics Iceland website.[1] The Statistics Iceland website states that the data come from the Register of Migration Data, and that a person is considered to have moved between regions if the person has stayed in the new region for at least one month. Altogether, the migration dataset has 181,440 cells.

These 181,440 cells do not include 'structural zeros', that is, cells where the count is zero by definition. In our case, since our definition of migration requires a change of region, a cell is a structural zero if the region of origin for the cell equals the region of destination. The figure of 66% of cells equalling zero cited above also does not include structural zeros. Among the non-zero cells, the median value is 2, and the maximum is 34.

To provide a feel for the sparsity of the data, Fig. 10.1 shows migration counts for three selected regions for a single year. The age profiles are jagged, and flows not involving the Capital Region are tiny, with most age groups having counts of zero.

In addition to migration counts, we also use a dataset giving resident population counts at 1 January of each year. These counts are disaggregated by region, age, sex, and year. The data were also obtained from the Statistics Iceland website.[2] The largest region in Iceland, Capital, had a population in 2018 of 222,484, and the smallest, Westfjords, had a population of 6,994.

We divide the data into a training set and a test set. The training set covers the years 1999–2008 and the test set covers the years 2009–2018. As we discuss below, we build our models using the training set, and choose the best model based on performance in the test set, before using the combined training and test sets to construct our final forecasts.

[1]Table *Internal migration between regions by sex and age 1986–2017—Division into municipalities as of 1 January 2018*, downloaded on 19 March 2019.

[2]Table *Population by municipality, age and sex 1998–2018—Division into municipalites as of 1 January 2018*, downloaded on 19 March 2019.

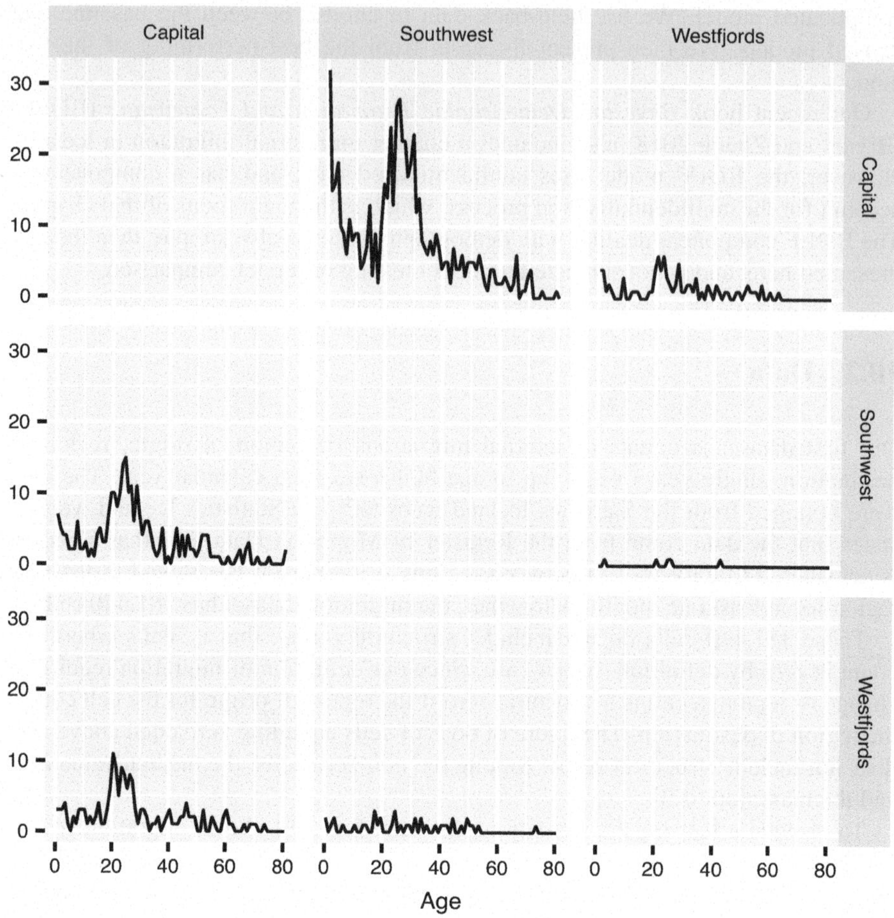

Fig. 10.1 Number of migrations of females in 2008, for three selected regions. Each row shows an origin region and each column shows a destination region: for example, row 2, column 1 shows migration from Southwest to Capital

10.3 Empirical Patterns

We begin by looking a little more closely at the data, starting with regional populations. Figure 10.2 shows regional population counts by age in 2008. Although the age profiles are broadly similar across regions, there are some important differences at the young adult ages. From about age 20, age profiles in most regions bend downwards. In Capital Region, however, the profile bends upwards. Even without seeing the migration data, we might suspect that young people are migrating from other regions into Capital Region.

Figure 10.3 shows direct estimates of migration rates by age, for each combination of origin and destination. We use the term 'direct estimate' to mean estimates

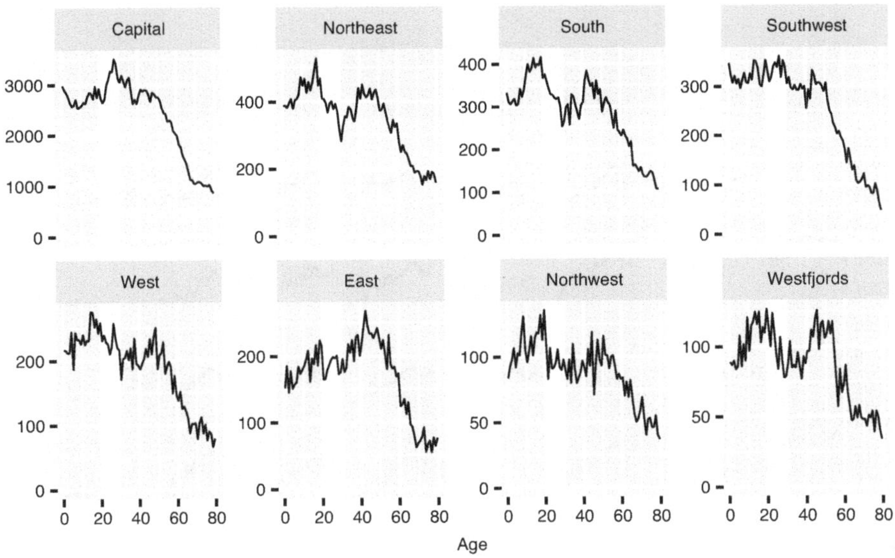

Fig. 10.2 Population aged 0–79, by single year of age and region in 2008. The regions are arranged by population size, from top left to bottom right. Each panel has a different vertical scale. The white vertical strips show ages 20–29

obtained by dividing the number of events in a given cell by the population at risk for that cell, as opposed estimates obtained from a statistical technique that pools information across cells. The estimated rates vary by two orders of magnitude across age and region, so, for clarity, we display them on a log scale. Comparing across columns, we can see that age-specific migration rates for migration into Capital Region have a more pronounced peak at the young adult ages than age-specific rates for migration into other regions. This is consistent with the observation that Capital region has proportionally more young people than other regions.

One sort of difference not readily apparent in Fig. 10.3, however, is sex differences. Females and males in Iceland seem to have very similar migration patterns.

Figure 10.4 displays a different aspect of the data, showing trends in migration between regions, for all age-sex groups combined. Once again, the rates are shown on a log scale. Migration rates into Capital Region, in the first column, are much higher than migration rates into any other region. There are hints of upward or downward trends, most notably for migration between Northwest and East regions, though in many cases it is difficult to be sure because of random variation in the rates.

Finally, Fig. 10.5 gives the age profiles for migration in 1999 and 2008. There appears to have been a slight shift in the age profile between these two years, particularly in the young adult ages.

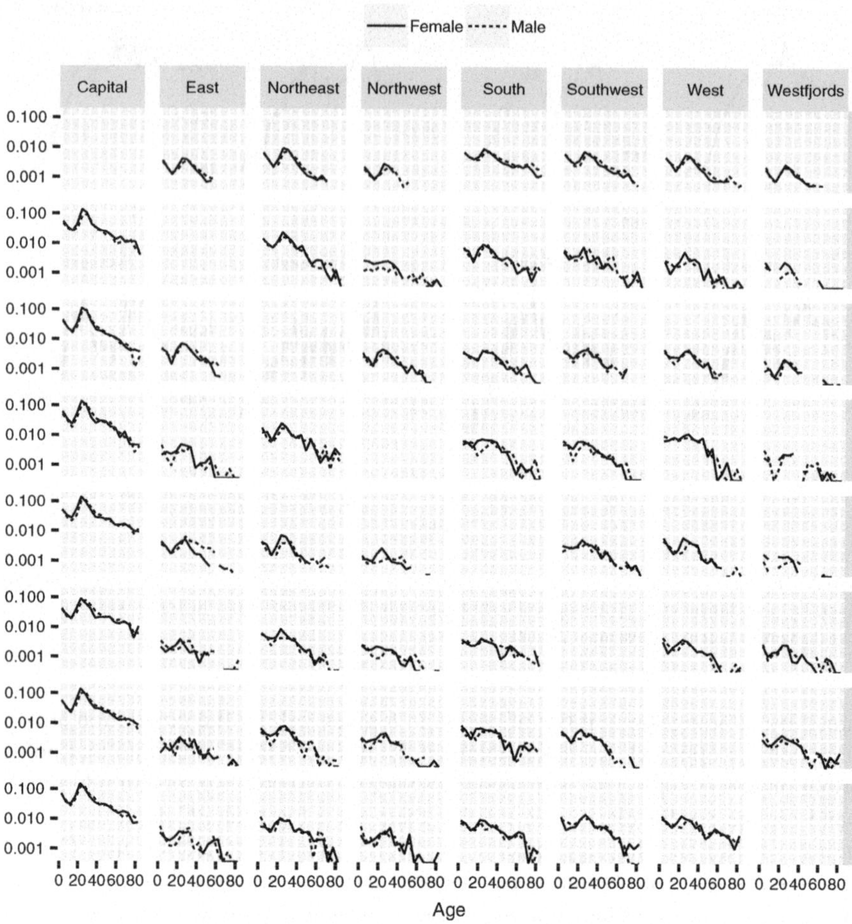

Fig. 10.3 Direct estimates of migration rates, by region of origin, region of destination, age, and sex, 1999–2008. Each row represents one origin region and each column represents one destination region. The rates are shown on a log scale. To reduce variability, the figure uses 5-year age groups, and uses average migration rates over the entire period 1999–2008

10.4 Baseline Model

10.4.1 Counts and Rates

Our baseline model tries to capture the main patterns in the migration data as simply as possible. Let y_{ijast} denote migrations between regions i and j by people in age group a and sex s during period t. As noted above, we define $y_{ijast} \equiv 0$ whenever $i = j$. Let p_{iast} denote the number of people at the start of period t in the population of region i, age group a and sex s. Let w_{iast} denote the number of person-years lived

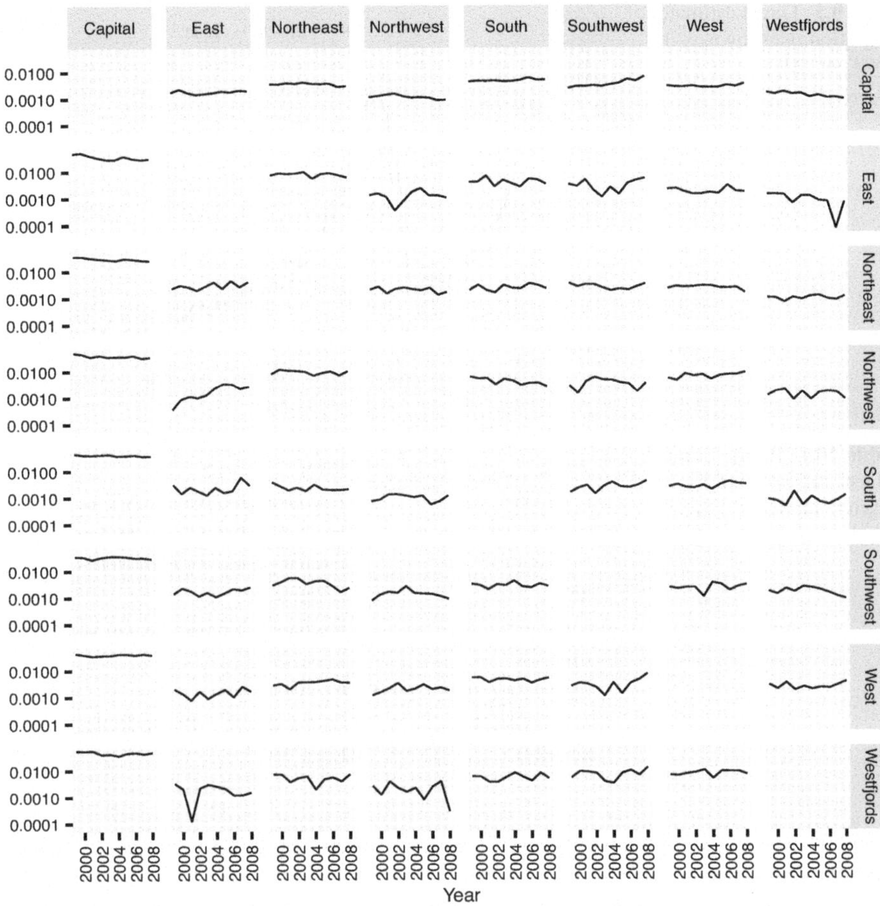

Fig. 10.4 Direct estimates of migration rates, by region of origin, region of destination, and time, 1999–2008. Each row represents one origin region and each column represents one destination region. The rates are shown on a log scale

during period t for the population of region i, age group a and sex s. Demographers commonly approximate the number of person-years lived using

$$\frac{\text{initial population} + \text{final population}}{2} \times \text{length of period},$$

which gives $w_{iast} = (p_{iast} + p_{i,a,s,t+1})/2$. We assume that, within each cell, migration counts follow a Poisson distribution,

$$y_{ijast} \sim \text{Poisson}(\gamma_{ijast} w_{iast}), \tag{10.1}$$

where γ_{ijast} is the underlying migration rate.

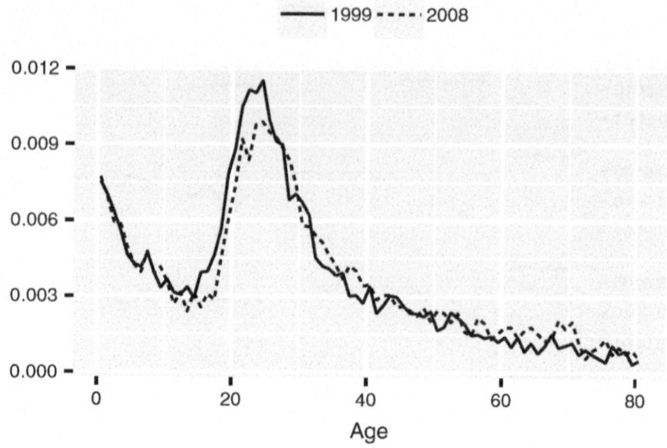

Fig. 10.5 Direct estimates of migration rates, by age, in 1999 and 2008

Table 10.1 Priors for main effects and interactions, baseline model

Term	Prior
(Intercept)	Exchangeable with known variance
region_orig	Exchangeable with covariates
region_dest	Exchangeable with covariates
age	Local trend
sex	Exchangeable with known variance
time	Local level
region_orig:region_dest	Exchangeable
region_dest:age	Exchangeable with covariates
age:time	Local level

Equation (10.1) allows for the fact that, for a given migration rate and exposure, the actual number of migrations is a random quantity. Standard log-linear models have no equivalent to Equation (10.1). This omission does not matter when cell counts are large, and variation due to the randomness of individual events is minor relative to variation due to differences in rates and exposures. However, ignoring random variation becomes problematic when cell counts are small. One consequence is the inability of such models to deal with cell counts of zero.

The migration rates γ_{ijast} are modelled using

$$\log \gamma_{ijast} \sim \mathrm{N}(x_{ijast}\beta, \sigma^2). \tag{10.2}$$

Vector β contains a combination of main effects and interactions, which are listed in Table 10.1. Vector x_{ijast}, which is composed of 0s and 1s, assigns the appropriate elements of β to each value for γ_{ijast}.

A main effect is a predicted difference for one variable that remains constant across values for all the remaining variables. In our model, for instance, a sex main effect is a female-male difference that remains constant across all possible combinations of region, age, and time. An interaction is a predicted difference that varies across values for one or more other variables. The age-destination interaction in our model, for instance, measures the way that migration age profiles vary across regions of destination.

An important feature of Equation (10.2) is that $x_{ijast}\beta$, the value for cell $ijast$ assembled from the various elements of β, is the *expected* value for log γ_{ijast}, not the *actual* value. The fact that Equation (10.2) uses a probability distribution implies that actual values differ in general from expected values. The typical size of the difference between actual and expected values is governed by the parameter σ. The smaller the value of σ, the tighter the fit. The parameter σ is estimated as part of the overall model-fitting process.

In models like that of Equations (10.1)–(10.2), the final estimate for each γ_{ijast} is a compromise between the predicted value calculated from $x_{ijast}\beta$ and the direct estimate calculated from y_{ijast} and w_{iast}. All else equal, the more observations there are for cell $ijast$, that is, the higher the values of y_{ijast} and w_{iast}, the closer the final value will be to the direct estimate. Models like that of Equations (10.1)–(10.2) perform a sort of local smoothing. Estimates are pulled towards the model predictions in cells where counts are small, but are left more-or-less unchanged in cells where counts are large. This is a sensible and effective way to smooth.

Effective smoothing is essential to demographic forecasting. A good forecast is one that carries forward into the future genuine, long-lasting features of the demographic series, and leaves out transient features or random noise.

10.4.2 Priors

Each main effect and interaction in β is given a prior distribution. In a Bayesian analysis, a prior distribution is a way of representing information about the system being modelled, beyond what is contained in the main datasets (Bryant and Zhang 2018, pp. 88–92). In our case, prior distributions allow us to encode some qualitative features of migration rates, beyond what is contained in the y_{ijast} and w_{iast}.

The prior for the sex effect β_s^{sex}, for instance, is

$$\beta_s^{\text{sex}} \sim \text{N}(0, 1). \tag{10.3}$$

This prior implies that, on a log scale, we expect female-male differences to be values like 0.1, −0.5, or 1.1, but not values like −18 or 400. This prior understates our actual knowledge. A differences of 0.1 on a log scale corresponds to a difference of about 10% on the original scale, which is about as large as we would expect to see for sex differences in Icelandic migration rates. In Bayesian terminology, our prior for the sex effect is 'weakly informative'. It places a constraint on the range of values that a parameter can take, but only a soft constraint. However, even a soft constraint can greatly speed up computations, and help the model distinguish between random noise and genuine differences.

The priors for the region-of-origin effect, region-of-destination effect, and origin-destination interaction all have the same basic form as the prior for sex. In the case of the region priors, however, the standard deviation parameter is estimated from the data rather than specified in advance. Values for two sexes do not provide enough information to estimate a standard deviation, but values for eight regions do. In addition, the priors for origin and destination include two covariates. The first covariate takes a value of 1 if the region is Capital, and 0 otherwise. The second covariate equals the log of population counts in 2008. By including these covariates, we are allowing for the fact that the Capital region is not like the other regions of Iceland, and that, as emphasised by gravity models of migration (Anderson 2011), migration rates tend to vary systematically with the population size of the origin and destination regions. In principle, we could refine the predictions by allowing the covariate to change over time, as regional population changed. However, this would greatly complicate the forecasting process, and regional population sizes are in any case relatively stable.

The time effect has a local level model (Prado and West 2010, ch. 4),

$$\beta_t^{\text{time}} \sim \text{N}(\alpha_t^{\text{time}}, \tau_{\text{time}}^2) \tag{10.4}$$

$$\alpha_t^{\text{time}} \sim \text{N}(\alpha_{t-1}^{\text{time}}, \omega_{\text{time}}^2). \tag{10.5}$$

A local level model is a generalisation of a random walk. Like a random walk, it allows for random shifts in the long-term mean of the series, but unlike a random walk, it also allows for one-off departures from this mean. The size of the long-term shifts is governed by ω_{time}, and the size of the one-off departures is governed by τ_{time}. The ω_{time} and τ_{time} parameters are both estimated from the data.

By using a local level model, we are ruling out the possibility of a long-term upward or downward trend in overall migration rates. This assumption is based on inspection of the Iceland data, as shown, for instance, in Fig. 10.4.

Age effects are modelled using a local trend model (Prado and West 2010, ch. 4),

$$\beta_a^{\text{age}} \sim \text{N}(\alpha_a^{\text{age}}, \tau_{\text{age}}^2) \tag{10.6}$$

$$\alpha_t^{\text{age}} \sim \text{N}(\alpha_{t-1}^{\text{age}} + \delta_{t-1}^{\text{age}}, \omega_{\text{age}}^2) \tag{10.7}$$

$$\delta_t^{\text{age}} \sim \text{N}(\delta_{t-1}^{\text{age}}, \varsigma_{\text{age}}^2). \tag{10.8}$$

A local trend model, through the parameter δ, allows for a persistent upward or downward trend. However, because the δ can vary, the size and direction of the trend can change. A local trend model thus allows for the fact that migration age profiles bend upwards through the teens and early twenties, and downwards after that.

Applying time-series models to age effects is an long-standing practice in statistical demography (e.g. Alho and Spencer (2005, pp. 281–282) or Congdon

(2008)). Time series models are based on the principle that neighbouring units are more highly correlated than distant units, an idea which is just as valid for age groups as it is for time periods.

The prior for the age-destination interaction has the same structure as the origin-destination interaction, in that it uses a normal distribution with a standard deviation that is estimated from the data. The prior also includes a covariate, the log of the 2008 population in each combination of age and destination. The prior for the age-time interaction uses a separate local level model for each age group, sharing the same $\tau_{\text{age:time}}$ and $\omega_{\text{age:time}}$ across age groups.

All standard deviation parameters that are not specified in advance are given priors constructed from half-t distributions. Half-t distributions are restricted to non-negative values, and favour values near 0. In all cases, we use distributions with 7 degrees of freedom. In our experience, results are generally insensitive to the exact choice of degrees of freedom, but a value of 7 provides a good tradeoff between robustness and speed of convergence. (See Sect. 10.4.4 for a discussion of model convergence.) We use scale parameters of 1 for σ and the main effects, and 0.5 for interactions. In doing so, we are implying that we expect interactions to be smaller than main effects (Gelman et al. 2008). All the priors for the standard deviations are, nevertheless, relatively weak. The *Prior Choice Recommendations* page[3] on the website for the Bayesian modelling language *Stan* discusses the advantages and disadvantages of the half-t prior and other priors.

10.4.3 Model Output

As with most Bayesian analyses, the output from the modelling is a sample from the posterior distribution for the unknown quantities. In our case, the unknown quantities are the γ_{ijast}, the standard deviation σ, the main effects and interactions, that is, β^{time}, $\beta^{\text{age:time}}$, and so on, and the parameters for each of the priors distributions.

We can use summaries of the posterior sample to describe the posterior distribution, in much the same way that a survey statistician uses summaries of a sample survey to describe the population. Thus if sample values for a particular rate are 0.0021, 0.0032, ..., 0.0019, and if the 50%, 2.5%, and 97.5% quantiles for these values are 0.0025, 0.0018, and 0.0030, then we can use 0.0025 as a point estimate for the rate and (0.0018, 0.0030) as a 95% 'credible interval'. Under the assumptions of the model, a 95% credible interval for a parameter has a 95% probability of containing the true value for that parameter.

[3]https://github.com/stan-dev/stan/wiki/Prior-Choice-Recommendations

10.4.4 Calculations

Estimates for the parameters in the model are obtained using computational methods known as Markov chain Monte Carlo (MCMC) (Gelman et al. 2014). Essentially, we start with an approximate answer, and then use a Gibbs sampler (Gelman et al. 2014, ch. 11) to cycle through the following steps:

- Draw values for the migration rates γ_{ijast}, conditional on y_{ijast}, w_{iast}, and the current values for all parameters other than the γ_{ijast}.
- Draw the main effects and interactions β, conditional on the γ_{ijast}, and all other parameters.
- Draw values for the remaining parameters, conditional on the γ_{ijast} and β.

The output from this process is a series of draws from the posterior distribution.

The techniques used to draw values for each set of parameters vary according to the conditional distribution of those parameters. Values for β, for instance, are drawn straight from normal distributions. Values for the γ_{ijast}, in contrast, are obtained through a Metropolis-Hastings step, in which new values are proposed and then accepted with probabilities that depend on the proposal distribution and on the posterior probabilities of the current and proposed values (Gelman et al. 2014, ch. 11). Values for standard deviation terms are drawn using a technique called slice sampling (Neal 2003).

We use multiple sets of starting values, and construct an independent chain starting from each set. Using multiple chains in this way can allow generation of more draws for the same amount of time, since the chains can be run in parallel on a multicore computer. It also provides a way of seeing whether the calculations are working as intended. If all is well, the chains should all converge to the same distribution of values. Depending on the quality of the initial approximate answers, it may take some time before this convergence occurs. Values generated during this initial burn-in period are discarded. Non-convergence across the chains can be detected using a statistic generally referred to as 'R-hat' (Gelman et al. 2014, p. 285). A value for an R-hat much above 1 indicates non-convergence.

In a model with as many parameters as ours, it is not feasible to calculate R-hats for all parameters. Instead, when a vector of parameters has more than 25 elements, we sample 25 elements and calculate R-hats only for those. We consider the model to have converged when the maximum of all observed R-hats is less than 1.1. By this point, R-hats for most of the cells we are monitoring are usually indistinguishable from 1.

For each model, we use 4 independent chains, each with a burnin of 15,000 iterations, and production of 15,000. We retain 1 out of every 60 iterations, yielding a sample of $4 \times 15{,}000 \div 60 = 1{,}000$ draws from the posterior distribution.

The calculations are all carried out using our own open source *R* packages **dembase** and **demest**. The *R* packages make use of *C* code for the most computationally-intensive part of the estimation. The packages can be downloaded from github.com/statisticsnz/R. All code for the Iceland migration example is available at: github.com/bayesiandemography/iceland_migration.

10.5 Model Checking Using Replicate Data

While building a model, we inevitably make many simplifications. Before we can trust the output from the model, we need to verify that, despite these simplifications, the model is still able to capture the substantively important features of the data. One effective way to check for important omissions in a model is to generate replicate data (Gelman et al. 2014, ch. 6). We illustrate with the example of regional time trends.

Our baseline model has a single, shared time trend. In other words, all region-to-region flows are assumed to shift upwards or downwards by the same percentage from year to year. If this assumption is too strong, it could materially affect forecasted values for future migration flows, which is an outcome of central importance to users of the migration forecasts.

Some region-to-region variation in time trends is indeed visible in Fig. 10.4. But, given the small numbers of observations, it is possible that these variations are random noise, and that the data are in fact compatible with the assumption of a single time trend.

To assess the compatibility of the data and the assumption of single time trend, we generate 19 synthetic or 'replicate' datasets, using our baseline model. We then compare the one actual dataset with the 19 replicate ones, to see if the actual dataset looks distinctive or out-of-place. If it does, we conclude that the single time trend assumption is too strong.

We generate a replicate dataset by randomly selecting a draw from the posterior sample, plugging the γ_{ijast} from that draw into Equation (10.1), and obtaining a set of simulated y_{ijast}. Repeating this process 19 times yields 19 replicate datasets. We could then, in principle, make 19 new versions of Fig. 10.4 and compare these with the original Fig. 10.4. Instead, we work with summary values. We fit a straight line to each of the $8 \times 7 = 56$ time series of origin-destination migration rates—in other words, to time series like those shown in each panel of Fig. 10.4. We then see whether the distribution of these slopes is similar across the actual and replicate datasets.

Figure 10.6 shows the results from these calculations. The actual dataset is clearly different from the replicate datasets. The baseline model fails to reproduce the observed variability in regional time trends.

10.6 Revised Model

In response to the results from the replicate data test, we construct a revised version of our model that, in addition to all the terms in the baseline model, includes an interaction between origin and time, and an interaction between destination and time. The priors for these interactions have the same structure as the age-time interaction in the baseline model. Each region has its own local level model, but standard deviation terms are shared across regions.

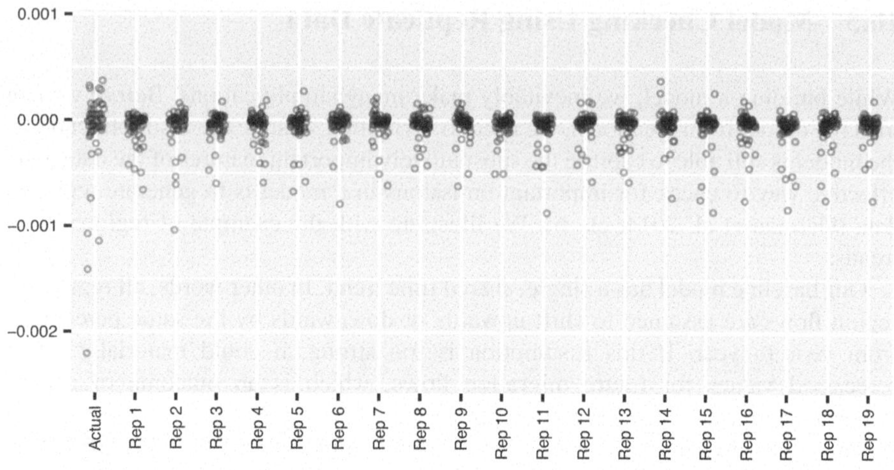

Fig. 10.6 Results of model checking for the baseline model. Using replicate data to test the ability of the baseline model to describe regional time series. Each point shows the slope from a straight line fitted to a time series for migration between a particular origin and destination. There are 56 points in each set. The first set of slopes are obtained from the actual dataset, and the remaining 19 are obtained from replicate datasets generated from the baseline model

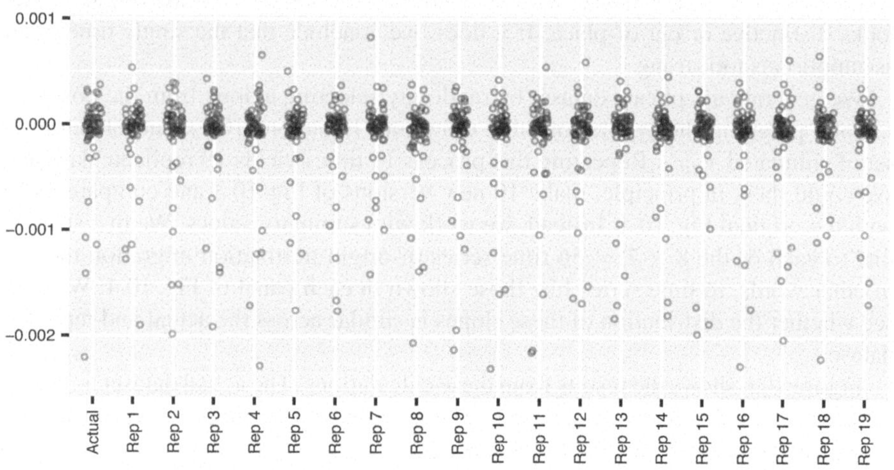

Fig. 10.7 Results of model checking for the revised model. An updated version of Fig. 10.6, using replicate data generated from the revised model rather than the baseline model

Figure 10.7 shows the results from applying the replicate data test to the revised model. The revised model performs much better than the baseline model. The distribution of slopes from the actual data is indistinguishable from the distributions generated under the replicate datasets.

In a full-scale analysis, we would repeat the test-and-revise process a few more times. For instance, we might use replicate data to test whether the data were consistent with the assumption of no overall trend upwards or downwards. If it turned out that the assumption was clearly violated, then we would extend the model accordingly.

10.7 Forecasts

Our forecasts use exactly the same set of assumptions as our estimates. Indeed, from a Bayesian point of view, there is no sharp distinction between forecasting and estimation. Forecasting is just estimation with missing data (Bryant and Zhang 2018).

We construct the forecasts by extending forward in time each draw from the posterior sample. With the baseline model, the process for extending the sth draw is as follows.

1. Plug values $\tau_{\text{time}}^{(s)}$ and $\omega_{\text{time}}^{(s)}$ into Equations (10.4) and (10.5), and then apply the equations iteratively to the end of the forecast period. This yields a forecasted set of time effects.
2. Plug values $\tau_{\text{age:time}}^{(s)}$ and $\omega_{\text{age:time}}^{(s)}$ into the prior model for age-time interactions, and iterate to obtain forecasted series of age-time interactions.
3. Plug the forecasted time effects, the forecasted age-time interactions, the non-time-varying elements of $\beta^{(s)}$, and $\sigma^{(s)}$ into Equation (10.2). Use Equation (10.2) to generate future values for the γ_{ijast}.

Carrying out these steps for $s = 1, \ldots, S$ yields a posterior distribution for migration rates for future years, which can be summarised and manipulated just like any other posterior distribution. Because the forecasts use the same sample of paramater values as the estimates, all the parameter uncertainty in the estimates propagates through into the forecasts.

10.8 Model Choice Using Held-Back Data

We have two models: a baseline model that does not include region-time interactions, and a revised model that does. At first sight, it might seem obvious that we should use our revised model for forecasting, since the replicate data checks imply that region-time interactions are needed to accurately reproduce the historical data. However, while replicate data checks can suggest directions for model improvement, they cannot provide definitive answers on which models will yield the best forecasts. Complex models that do a better job of explaining historical trends do not necessarily do a better job of predicting future values (Shmueli 2010). We use tests based on held-back data to make the final decision on which model to use.

Model choice using held-back data proceeds as follows:

1. Split the data into a training set and a test set.
2. Use the training set to make forecasts about values in the test set—one forecast for each model.
3. By comparing the forecasted values for the test set with the actual values, evaluate the performance of the models.
4. Based on the comparisons, choose a best model.

As noted above, our training data set consists of data for the years 1999–2008, and the test set consists of data for the years 2009–2018.

As well as providing a way of choosing a model, held-back data tests also give a sense of how the models will perform in practice. For instance, if, when measured against the test dataset, 80% credible intervals from a model only contain the true values only 50% of the time, then we would expect that the model to be overly optimistic in other settings as well.

The test data yields direct estimates of migration rates. We must be careful that the forecasted rates from our model are comparable to the direct estimates, in that they also reflect the randomness of the individual events. To do this, we take the forecasted γ_{ijast}, plug them into Equation (10.1), and use Poisson draws to obtain forecasted migration counts. Dividing the forecasted migration counts by exposures gives us the rates that we need.

Our first performance measure is median absolute error. This measure is constructed from the absolute differences between point forecasts and actual value from the test dataset. We obtain point forecasts by taking the medians of the posterior samples of the rates. The second measure is the proportion of values from the test dataset that lie within the credible intervals. We use 80% credible intervals for performance measurement, so ideally 80% or more of the test values should lie within our intervals. The third measure is the median width of the credible intervals: for the same coverage level, the narrower the intervals the better. We take medians of the absolute errors and of the intervals widths, rather than means, because both measures are highly skewed, with many small values and a few large values.

Ideally, we would like to make our comparisons at the lowest level of aggregation, that is, to compare forecasted rates classified by origin, destination, age, sex, and time with test-set rates classified in the same way. Unfortunately, with such sparse data, it is difficult to form credible intervals with the required degree of coverage, since a difference in migration counts of 1 or 2 can imply very large differences in coverage. We instead work with rates classified only by origin, destination, and time, which are considerably less lumpy.

When assessing the performance of the models, we do, however, distinguish between flows out of Capital Region and flows out of other regions. The population at risk of migration is so much larger for Capital Region than for other regions that the job of estimating and predicting migration is much easier. We would therefore expect model performance to differ between Capital Region and elsewhere.

Table 10.2 summarises the performance of the two models. The baseline and revised models have similar levels of accuracy, as measured by median absolute

Table 10.2 Comparison of performance of baseline and revised models, using 80 percent credible intervals

	Median abs. error	Median width	Coverage
Baseline: Capital	0.00044	0.00069	0.23
Baseline: Other	0.00075	0.00133	0.47
Revised: Capital	0.00056	0.00186	0.71
Revised: Other	0.00083	0.00238	0.73

error. Credible intervals from the baseline model are much narrower than credible intervals from the revised model. However, as can be seen in the third column of Table 10.2, the credible intervals from the baseline model are *too* narrow: they contain the true value far less than 80% of the time. The credible intervals from the revised model are much better calibrated, though not perfectly so.

Both models give more accurate predictions for flows from the Capital Region than for flows from other regions. This is not surprising: predictions for the Capital Region are based on more observations than the predictions for the other regions.

Forecasts from the revised model are less accurate than forecasts from the baseline model. However, the revised model is much better calibrated than the baseline model in that its actual coverage rate comes much closer to the nominal rate. We therefore base our forecasts on the revised model.

10.9 Estimates and Forecasts from the Revised Model

We look now at estimates and forecasts from the revised model. The estimates and forecasts are all based on data for the entire period 1999–2018. Figure 10.8 shows estimates of migration rates γ_{ijast} for females in 2018. As well as the modelled estimates, the figure also shows direct estimates, though, unlike the modelled estimates, the direct estimates are aggregated to 5-year age groups, to reduce variability.

Showing the direct estimates alongside the modelled estimates in Fig. 10.8 is a form of reality check on the modelled estimates. If the direct estimates departed in some systematic way from the modelled estimates, then we would suspect that the model had missed out an important feature of the data.

We should not, however, expect 95% of the direct estimates to lie within the 95% credible intervals for the γ_{ijast}. The direct estimates contain all of the original random variability in y_{ijast}. The model tries, as much as possible, to strip away this random variability.

Figure 10.8 illustrates the effects of the smoothing process discussed in Sect. 10.4.1, whereby the modelled estimates stay close to the direct estimates for flows involving Capital Region, where data are plentiful, and rely on predicted values from Equation 10.2 for other flows where data are scarce. This is typical behaviour for Bayesian hierarchical models. To obtain a sensible estimate of

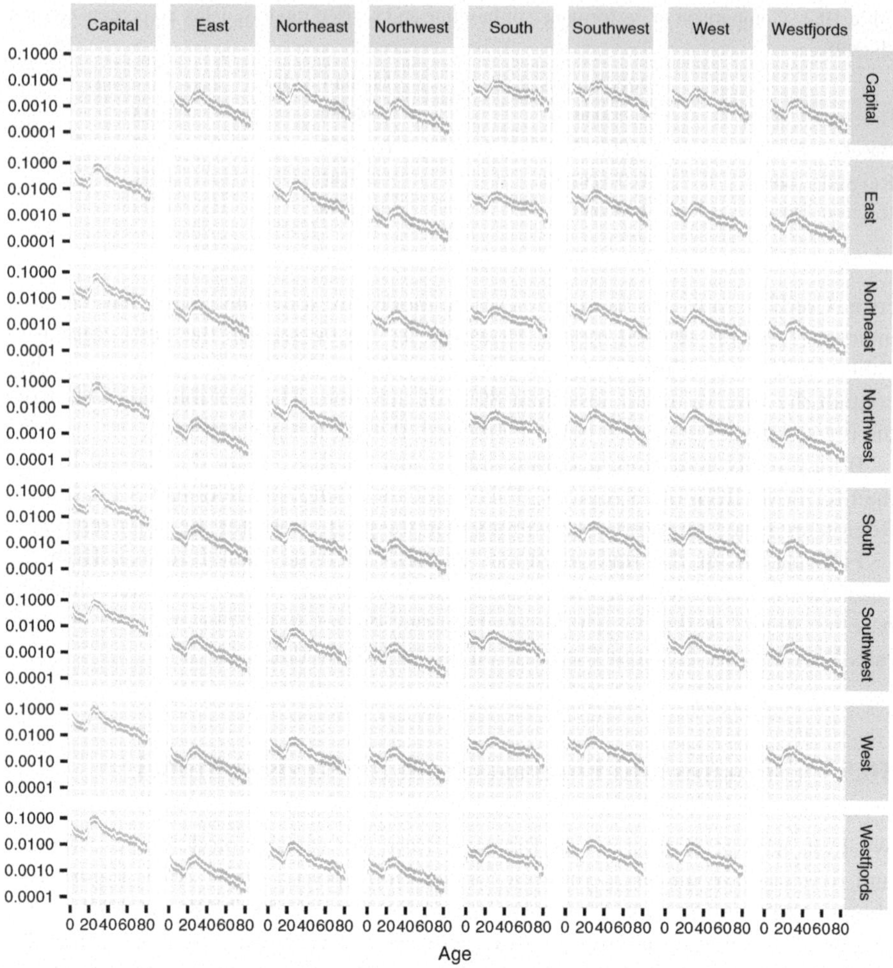

Fig. 10.8 Modelled and direct estimates of migration rates γ_{ijast}, by region of origin (rows), region of destination (columns), and age, for females in 2018. The modelled estimates come from the revised model, using data from the combined training and test datasets. The estimates are shown on a log scale. The grey bands represent 95% credible intervals and the white lines represent posterior medians, for single years of age. The dots represent direct estimates for 5-year age groups. The black dots represent estimates greater than 0, and the grey dots at the bottom of each panel represent estimates equal to 0, which are undefined on a log scale. As discussed in the text, we would not expect 95% of the direct estimates to lie within the 95% credible intervals for the γ_{ijast}

γ_{ijast} for each cell, the model not only uses information coming from the direct estimate for that cell, but also borrows information from all other cells. When data are plentiful such that the direct estimate is reliable, information from the direct estimate outweighs information from other cells. When data are scarce such that the direct estimate is unreliable, information from other cells receives a larger weight. For instance, in the panel for flows from East to Northwest, the direct estimate is nonzero for age group 25–29, and is zero for all other age groups. It is highly unlikely that the true underlying migration rates follow such an extreme age profile. The rates estimated by combining the East-Northwest data with information borrowed from other cells are much more plausible.

As can be seen by comparing across columns, the age profiles for modelled migration rates differ across destinations. The profile for Capital Region has a sharper peak at the young adult ages than the profile for East Region, for instance, which in turn has sharper peak than South Region. These differences would be difficult to see using direct estimates alone.

The overall level of migration also differs substantially from flow to flow, though this is partly obscured by the use of a log scale.

Figure 10.9 shows estimates and forecasts of migration rates into Capital region for females in selected single-year age groups. As is apparent in the figure, there is substantial uncertainty about underlying migration rates for young adults, even for years where data are available. Uncertainty does, nevertheless, grow further out into the forecast period.

Although, within each age group, migration rates are similar across regions, there are nevertheless differences. Migration rates appear to be higher for young adults from Westfjords, for instance, than they are for young adults from the Northeast.

With Fig. 10.10 we shift from the largest region of Iceland to the smallest. The vertical scale for Fig. 10.10 covers a much smaller range than the vertical scale for Fig. 10.9. People are much less likely to migrate to Westfjords Region than they are to Capital Region.

The data available for directly measuring migration into Westfjords are accordingly very limited. Between 1999 and 2018, for instance, there was not a single case of a 10-year-old migrating from Northwest Region to Westfjords. The model, nevertheless, yields estimates and forecasts that are intuitively reasonable. It implies, for instance, that underlying propensity for 10-year-olds in Northwest Region to migrate to Westfjords has been low, and will continue to be low, but is not zero. The model also virtually ignores the apparent spikes in migration rates suggested by the direct estimates. The model's behaviour in such cases is sensible, given the small counts that give rise to these spikes.

Switching from the training dataset for 1999–2008 to the full dataset for 1999–2018 produces only small differences in estimates for the same years. Figure 10.11 shows some representative examples. There do not appear to have been any major shifts in migration trends between the training period and the test period.

10.10 Discussion

It is still common in demography departments and statistics agencies to encounter rules of thumb stating that demographic rates cannot be calculated unless every cell in a table has, say, at least 5 observations, or at least 30 observations. In this

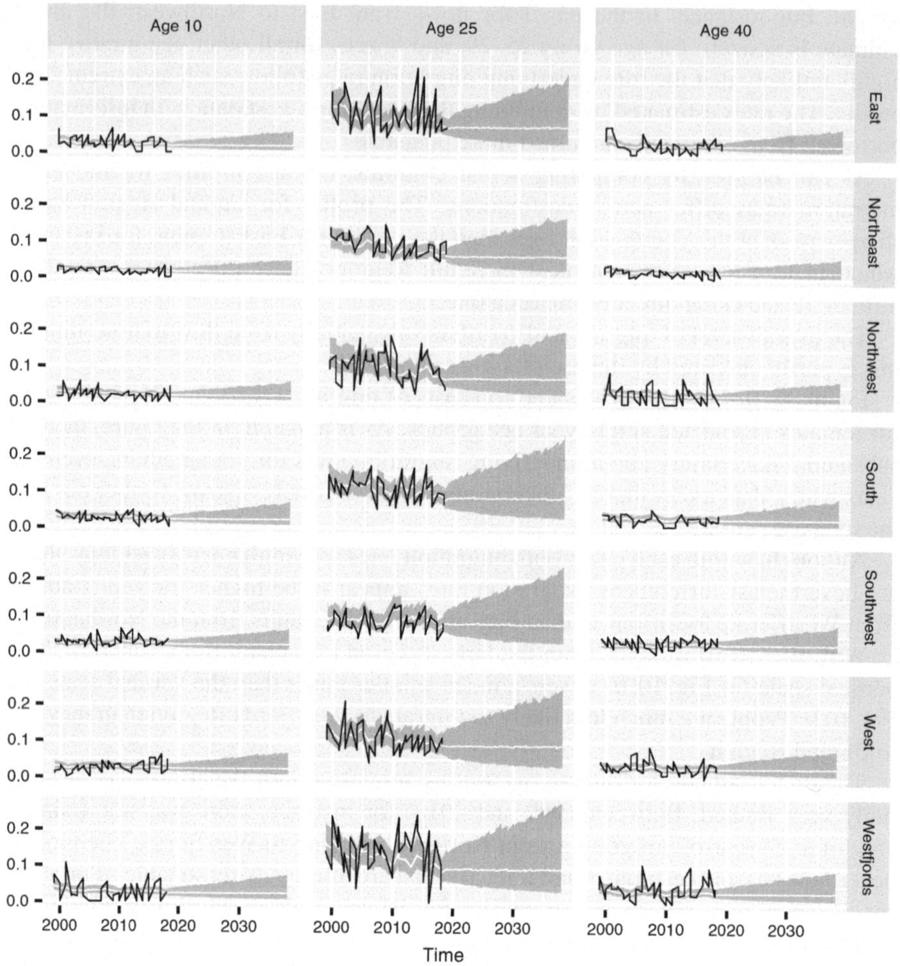

Fig. 10.9 Migration rates to Capital Region from other regions, for females in selected single-year age groups. The grey bands represent 95% credible intervals and the white lines represent posterior medians. The black lines represent direct estimates

chapter, we have broken all such rules. Of the 181,440 cells in our migration dataset, only 11,298 have 5 or more observations, and only 9 have 30 or more. And yet, while there is scope for further checking and refinement, the held-back data tests suggest that our revised model is already attaining respectable levels of accuracy and coverage. Moreover, using credible intervals or other uncertainty measures, consumers of the forecasts can be given guidance on how much trust to place in the rates, including rates calculated from small counts.

The availability of new methods for estimating and forecasting with sparse, complicated datasets, such as the methods we present in this paper, should prompt demographers and statisticians to rethink conventional rules of thumb about what

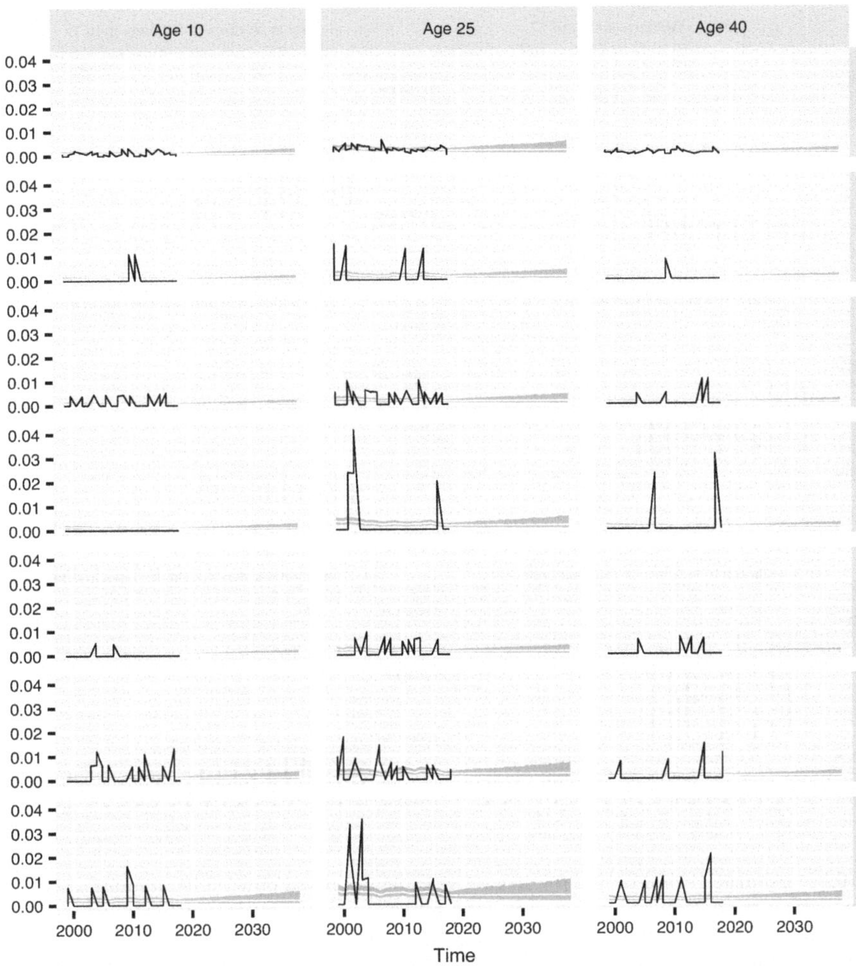

Fig. 10.10 Migration rates to Westfjords from other regions, for females in selected single-year age groups. The grey bands represent 95% credible intervals and the white lines represent posterior medians. The black lines represent direct estimates

is achievable in demographic forecasting. Users of demographer forecasts are demanding ever-more detail. Demographers and statisticians increasingly have the tools to meet these demands.

Of the remaining obstacles to the use of methods like the ones in this chapter, perhaps the most important is computation. Running all of the calculations in this chapter currently takes around 18 hours on a desktop computer. With these sorts of computation times, scaling up from 8 regions to 80 or 800 is difficult.

Speeding up computations is, however, a solvable problem. Our experience over several years is that improving algorithms and code yields steady improvements in speed, and we still have a long list of additional modifications to try. Moreover, the

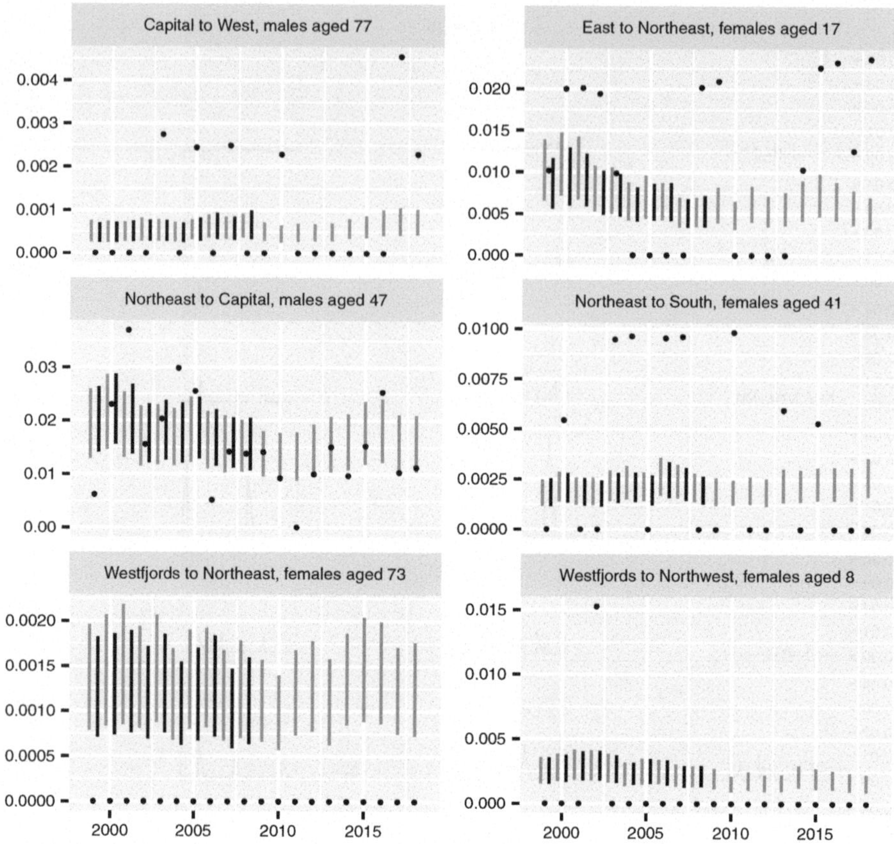

Fig. 10.11 Estimates based on the full dataset vs estimates based only on the training set. The dark grey lines show 95% credible intervals from fitting the revised model to the training set, and the light grey lines show 95% credible intervals from fitting the revised model to the full dataset. The black dots are direct estimates. Each panel shows a randomly-selected combination of origin, destination, age, and sex

rapid rise in distributing computing gives new options for attaining speed through brute force. We suspect that, before long, 80 or 800 regions will be well within reach.

References

Alexander, M., Zagheni, E., & Barbieri, M. (2017). A flexible Bayesian model for estimating subnational mortality. *Demography, 54*(6), 2025–2041.

Alho, J., & Spencer, B. (2005). *Statistical demography and forecasting*. Berlin-Heidelberg: Springer.

Anderson, J. E. (2011). The gravity model. *Annual Review of Economics, 3*(1), 133–160.

Baffour, B., & Raymer, J. (2019). Estimating multiregional survivorship probabilities for sparse data: An application to immigrant populations in Australia, 1981–2011. *Demographic Research, 40*, 463–502.

Bernard, A., & Bell, M. (2015). Smoothing internal migration age profiles for comparative research. *Demographic Research, 32*, 915–948.

Bijak, J., & Bryant, J. (2016). Bayesian demography 250 years after Bayes. *Population Studies, 70*(1), 1–19.

Bryant, J., & Zhang, J. L. (2018). *Bayesian demographic estimation and forecasting*. Boca Raton: CRC Press.

Congdon, P. (2008). Models for migration age schedules: A Bayesian perspective with an application to flows between Scotland and England. In J. Raymer & F. Willekens (Eds.), *International migration in Europe: Data, models and estimates*. Chichester: Wiley.

Gelman, A., Carlin, J., Stern, H., Dunson, D. B., Vehtari, A., & Rubin, D. (2014). *Bayesian data analysis* (3rd ed.). New York: Chapman and Hall.

Gelman, A., Jakulin, A., Pittau, M. G., & Su, Y.-S. (2008). A weakly informative default prior distribution for logistic and other regression models. *The Annals of Applied Statistics, 4*(2), 1360–1383.

Lynch, S. M. & Brown, J. S. (2010). Obtaining multistate life table distributions for highly refined subpopulations from cross-sectional data: A Bayesian extension of Sullivan's method. *Demography, 47*(4), 1053–1077.

Neal, R. M. (2003). Slice sampling. *The Annals of Statistics, 31*(3), 705–767.

Prado, R., & West, M. (2010). *Time Series: Modeling, Computation, and Inference*. Boca Raton: CRC Press.

Raymer, J., & Rogers, A. (2007). Using age and spatial flow structures in the indirect estimation of migration streams. *Demography, 44*(2), 199–223.

Rogers, A., & Castro, L. J. (1981). *Model migration schedules*. Laxenburg: International Institute for Applied Systems Analysis.

Rogers, A., Little, J., & Raymer, J. (2010). *The indirect estimation of migration: Methods for dealing with irregular, inadequate, and missing data*. Dordrecht: Springer Science & Business Media.

Schmertmann, C. P., Cavenaghi, S. M., Assunção, R. M., & Potter, J. E. (2013). Bayes plus Brass: Estimating total fertility for many small areas from sparse census data. *Population Studies, 67*(3), 255–273.

Shmueli, G. (2010). To explain or to predict? *Statistical Science, 25*(3), 289–310.

van Imhoff, E., van der Gaag, N., van Wissen, L., & Rees, P. (1997). The selection of internal migration models for European regions. *International Journal of Population Geography, 3*(2), 137–159.

Wilson, T. (2010). Model migration schedules incorporating student migration peaks. *Demographic Research, 23*, 191–222.

Chapter 11
Forecasting Origin-Destination-Age-Sex Migration Flow Tables with Multiplicative Components

James Raymer, Xujing Bai, and Peter W. F. Smith

11.1 Introduction

Estimates of future internal migration are required for making accurate population projections, and for policy development and planning. However, migration forecasting is complicated from a demographic modelling perspective in that it represents a transition from an origin population to a destination population. Andrei Rogers, Frans Willekens, Alan Wilson, and Phil Rees developed the multiregional population projection framework for including such transitions starting in the 1960s (Rogers 1966, 1968, 1975; Wilson and Rees, 1974a, b, 1975; Rogers and Willekens 1976; Willekens and Rogers 1978). However, methods for producing dynamic forecasts of interregional migration flows with measures of uncertainty are still relatively few.

In this chapter, we build from a range of earlier efforts that used multiplicative or log-linear models to forecast counts of migration flows by origin, destination, age and sex (Stillwell 1986; Willekens and Baydar 1986; Van Imhoff et al. 1997; Van der Gaag et al. 2000; Sweeney and Konty 2002; Van Wissen et al. 2008). In particular, this research extends the multiplicative component approach developed by Raymer et al. (2006) for projecting interregional migration in Italy and Raymer et al. (2017) for projecting Indigenous migration in Australia. We illustrate the forecast methodology by using origin-destination-age-sex tables representing

J. Raymer (✉) · X. Bai
School of Demography, Australian National University, Canberra, Australia
e-mail: james.raymer@anu.edu.au; xujing.bai@anu.edu.au

P. W. F. Smith
Department of Social Statistics and Demography and Southampton Statistical Sciences Research Institute, University of Southampton, Southampton, UK
e-mail: p.w.smith@soton.ac.uk

S. Mazzuco, N. Keilman (eds.), *Developments in Demographic Forecasting*, The Springer Series on Demographic Methods and Population Analysis 49,
https://doi.org/10.1007/978-3-030-42472-5_11

internal migration flows amongst Australia's state and territory populations. Our research extends the earlier efforts cited above by forecasting each multiplicative component separately and by integrating them together to provide forecasts of interregional migration by age and sex with measures of uncertainty. Modelling each component separately allows the forecaster more control by being able to specify different models for each component.

The forecasting model for internal migration advocated in this chapter is different from the current approach used by the Australian Bureau of Statistics (ABS), which projects gross flows of in-migration and out-migration to/from each state or territory separately from each other. While simpler to include in demographic accounting models, projections of in-migration and out-migration (or even worse, net migration) totals are not as reliable and are known to result in biased projections (Rogers 1990) and inaccurate uncertainty measures (Raymer et al. 2012). Here, biases refer primarily to projected measures that are systematically above (below) the observed values. Most often, biases in regional projections occur when net migration or in-migration rates are used. They are caused by the use of populations not 'at risk' of migration in the denominators. Thus, by focusing on the underlying structures of migration flows, we argue that more reliable projection models may be produced for both internal migration and the subsequent population totals and age-sex compositions. Moreover, when the internal migration projections inevitably fail to predict perfectly the future, we have more detailed information about the potential sources of error.

The structure of this chapter is as follows. We first explore how the internal migration patterns in Australia have changed since 1981. We then explore the stability in the underlying structures of migration flows over time, and identify the most important migration structures required for both estimation and projection. Finally, we illustrate the approach by predicting the observed flows with measures of uncertainty for the 2006–2011 and 2011–2016 periods based on historical migration flow data going back to the 1981–1986 period. We also produce and illustrate the results of forecasts for two time periods beyond the observed data, i.e., 2016–2021 and 2021–2026.

11.2 Multiplicative Component Calculations

Analysing and predicting the counts of migration flows may be considered from a categorical data analysis perspective. The basic categories are origin (*O*), destination (*D*), age (*A*) and sex (*S*). Migration flow tables typically include two or more of these categories. These tables can be decomposed into various hierarchical structures, not all of which are necessary for understanding or for producing accurate predictions. If certain (important) structures are unavailable, they can be imputed or 'borrowed' from auxiliary data sources. This general modelling framework comes from a sequence of papers on the age and spatial structures of internal migration (Willekens

Table 11.1 Notation for an origin-by-destination migration flow table

	Region of destination				
Region of origin	1	2	3	4	Total
1	0	n_{12}	n_{13}	n_{14}	n_{1+}
2	n_{21}	0	n_{23}	n_{24}	n_{2+}
3	n_{31}	n_{32}	0	n_{34}	n_{3+}
4	n_{41}	n_{42}	n_{43}	0	n_{4+}
Total	n_{+1}	n_{+2}	n_{+3}	n_{+4}	n_{++}

1983; Stillwell 1986; Van Imhoff et al. 1997; Rogers et al. 2002, 2003; Sweeney and Konty 2002; Raymer et al. 2006, 2017; Raymer and Rogers 2007; Van Wissen et al. 2008).

To begin, consider migration from origin i to destination j, denoted by n_{ij}. These counts may be organised in a two-way table, such as in Table 11.1 for migration between four hypothetical regions. Here, it is important to make a distinction between cell counts (n_{ij}) and marginal totals, i.e., the total number of out-migrants from each region (n_{i+}), the total number of in-migrants to each region (n_{+j}) and the overall level of migration (n_{++}). Note, within area movements ($i = j$) are excluded from the analyses.

For describing, analysing and projecting migration flow patterns over time, consider the following multiplicative decomposition of an origin-destination table:

$$n_{ij} = (T)(O_i)\left(D_j\right)\left(OD_{ij}\right), \tag{11.1}$$

where T is the total number of migrants (i.e., n_{++}), O_i is the proportion of all migrants leaving from area i (i.e., n_{i+}/n_{++}) and D_j is the proportion of all migrants moving to area j (i.e., n_{+j}/n_{++}). The interaction component OD_{ij} is defined as $n_{ij}/[(T)(O_i)(D_j)]$ or the ratio of observed migration to expected migration (for the case of no interaction). This general type of model is called a multiplicative component model and may be extended to include other categories, such as age or sex.

The data for this research were obtained from the Australian quinquennial censuses from 1981 to 2016 and include following characteristics:

- state or territory of current residence by state or territory of residence 5 years ago,
- five-year age groups (0–4, 5–9, ..., 80+ years), and
- sex.

We focus on the migration transitions between the eight states or territories of Australia: New South Wales (NSW), Victoria (VIC), Queensland (QLD), South Australia (SA), Western Australia (WA), Tasmania (TAS), Northern Territory (NT) and Australian Capital Territory (ACT). Note, in this study, we apply the forecast methodology described in the next section to a particular type of migration flows, namely, transitions between the place of residence 5-years ago and place of residence at the time of the census. However, the methodology may be applied to any type or category of migration flows so long as they are arranged in a categorical fashion. Other common types of migration flows include population or administrative register data on the number of moves (events) within a 1-year time interval and census or survey data on transitions based on current residence by place of birth, place of residence prior to last move, or place of residence 1 year ago (Bell et al. 2015).

For illustration of the multiplicative component calculations and their interpretations, the Australian interstate migration flow table and the corresponding multiplicative components for the 2011–2016 period are presented in Tables 11.2 and 11.3, respectively. For example, the number of persons who migrated from Australian Capital Territory (ACT) to New South Wales (NSW) ($n_{ACT,\,NSW}$) was 23,609 persons. The multiplicative components for this migration flow are equal to:

$$\begin{aligned} n_{ACT,NSW} &= (T)\,(O_{ACT})\,(D_{NSW})\left(OD_{ACT,NSW}\right) \\ &= (824{,}392)\,(0.054)(0.232)(2.281) \\ &= 23{,}609 \end{aligned}$$

Table 11.2 Interstate migration in Australia, 2011–2016

	Region of destination								
Region of origin	NSW	VIC	QLD	SA	WA	TAS	NT	ACT	Total
NSW	0	61,484	105,703	12,748	19,921	6590	6369	27,567	240,382
VIC	47,925	0	47,070	13,284	18,721	6932	5932	6725	146,589
QLD	77,163	46,585	0	10,611	21,071	7906	9710	7108	180,154
SA	12,904	19,813	15,507	0	7581	1800	3896	2250	63,751
WA	17,863	22,364	20,636	5741	0	4219	4733	2116	77,672
TAS	5356	9816	8944	1660	3645	0	725	794	30,940
NT	6629	6648	14,002	5610	5239	947	0	1253	40,328
ACT	23,609	8035	8295	1541	1818	600	678	0	44,576
Total	191,449	174,745	220,157	51,195	77,996	28,994	32,043	47,813	824,392

Table 11.3 Multiplicative components of interstate migration in Australia, 2011–2016

	O_i	D_j	$OD_{i,NSW}$	$OD_{i,VIC}$	$OD_{i,QLD}$	$OD_{i,SA}$	$OD_{i,WA}$	$OD_{i,TAS}$	$OD_{i,NT}$	$OD_{i,ACT}$
$T = 824{,}392$										
NSW	0.292	0.232	0.000	1.207	1.647	0.854	0.876	0.779	0.682	1.977
VIC	0.178	0.212	1.408	0.000	1.202	1.459	1.350	1.345	1.041	0.791
QLD	0.219	0.267	1.844	1.220	0.000	0.948	1.236	1.248	1.387	0.680
SA	0.077	0.062	0.872	1.466	0.911	0.000	1.257	0.803	1.572	0.609
WA	0.094	0.095	0.990	1.358	0.995	1.190	0.000	1.544	1.568	0.470
TAS	0.038	0.035	0.745	1.497	1.082	0.864	1.245	0.000	0.603	0.442
NT	0.049	0.039	0.708	0.778	1.300	2.240	1.373	0.668	0.000	0.536
ACT	0.054	0.058	2.281	0.850	0.697	0.557	0.431	0.383	0.391	0.000

From these calculations, we see that the overall level of interstate migration was 824,392 persons, the share of all migration from the ACT was 5.4% (i.e., 44,576 / 824,392 * 100), the share of all migration to NSW was 23.2% (i.e., 191,449 / 824,392 * 100), and that there was more than twice the expected value of migration between these two areas (i.e., 23,609 / (824,392 * 0.054071 * 0.232231) = 23,609 / 10,352). In Table 11.2, the largest flows are between the largest population states of NSW, Victoria (VIC) and Queensland (QLD). The smallest flows are between the smallest states or territories (Tasmania (TAS), Northern Territory (NT), and ACT). In Table 11.3, we see that the largest OD_{ij} ratios are between neighbouring states or territories, e.g., ACT and NSW, and the smallest are between states or territories that are far apart, e.g., TAS and NT.

Next, consider the multiplicative components for a four-way table of migration by origin, destination, age and sex. The multiplicative component model that fully explains this table is specified as:

$$n_{ijxy} =(T)(O_i)\left(D_j\right)(A_x)\left(S_y\right)\left(OD_{ij}\right)(OA_{ix})\left(OS_{iy}\right)\left(DA_{jx}\right)\left(DS_{jy}\right)\left(AS_{xy}\right)$$
$$\left(ODA_{ijx}\right)\left(ODS_{ijy}\right)\left(DAS_{jxy}\right)\left(ODAS_{ijxy}\right), \tag{11.2}$$

where A_x is the proportion of all migrants in age group x and S_y is the proportion of all migrants in sex group y. This model is a lot more complicated because there are now four main effects, six two-way interaction components, three three-way interaction components and one four-way interaction component between the origin, destination, age and sex variables. However, for the main effects and two-way interaction components, the interpretations of the parameters remain relatively simple. For example, the destination-age interaction (DA_{jx}) component is calculated as $n_{+jx+}/[(T)(D_j)(A_x)]$ and represents the ratio of observed age patterns of in-migration to each region divided by the expected age pattern of in-migration. Fortunately, the three-way and four-way interaction terms do not add much additional information and are rarely needed for estimation or projection (see, e.g., Van Imhoff et al. 1997; Smith et al. 2010). The same is true for the two-way interactions between origin and sex (OS_{iy}) and destination and sex (DS_{jy}). Thus, for most analyses, estimations and projections, the following reduced model may be used:

$$n_{ijxy} = (T)(O_i)\left(D_j\right)(A_x)\left(S_y\right)\left(OD_{ij}\right)(OA_{ix})\left(DA_{jx}\right)\left(AS_{xy}\right). \tag{11.3}$$

To illustrate the effectiveness of this model, consider the migration flows presented in Fig. 11.1. Here, we compare the observed and estimated age patterns of female internal migration between NSW and QLD for the 2006–2011 and 2011–2016 periods using the model specified in Eq. 11.3. Clearly, there are not much differences between the estimated and observed flows of migration in this case.

To assess the goodness-of-fit (g) between the observed and estimated migration flow tables, we focus on the following formula:

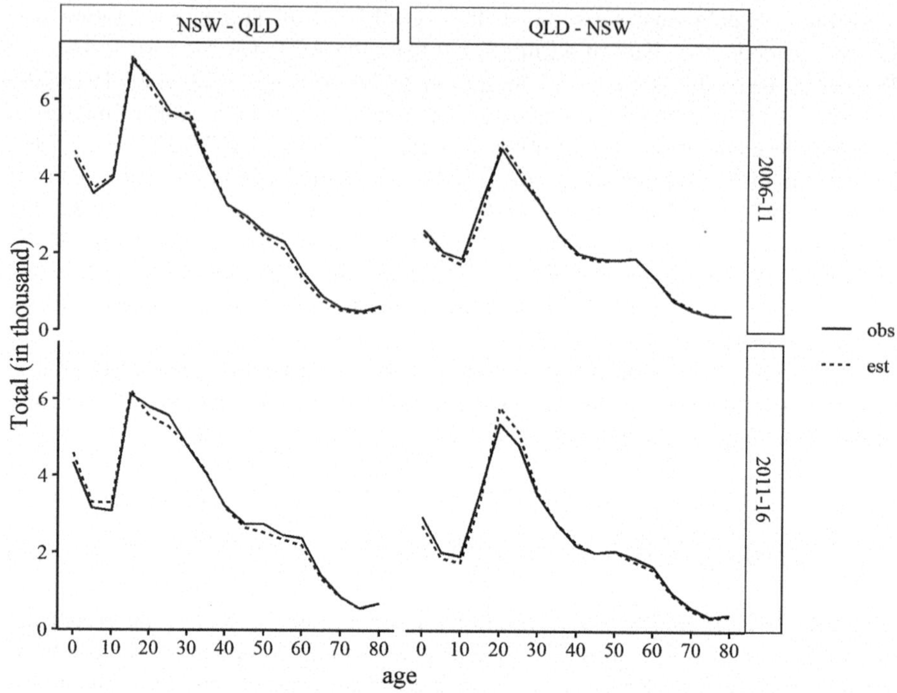

Fig. 11.1 Observed and estimated age patterns of female migration between New South Wales and Queensland, 2006–2011 and 2011–2016

$$g = \frac{100}{N} \sum_{i=1}^{N} \frac{\left| n_{ijxy} - \hat{n}_{ijxy} \right|}{\hat{n}_{ijxy}}$$

where N denotes the total number of cells in the origin-destination-sex-age table in a single period, which for our tables is equal to 1904, i.e., 8 origins $\times$ 8 destinations $\times$ 2 sexes $\times$ 17 age groups, not including the diagonal elements where $i = j$. The observed number of interstate migrants by age and sex is denoted by n_{ijxy} and the corresponding estimated flows is denoted by $\hat{n}_{ijxy}$. The test-statistics for the unsaturated model (Eq. 11.3) applied to the 2006–2011 and 2011–2016 data are 16.3% and 16.1%, respectively. For migration flows, we find this simple goodness-of-fit measure works well due to high likelihood of zeros in the observed data when broken down by origin, destination, age and sex. By placing the estimated values in the denominator, this allows us to provide measures for all predicted cell values.

In summary, multiplicative components are useful for analysing the key structures driving migration patterns. These can then be used for the purpose of estimating migration. Moreover, when particular interaction effects cannot be derived from available data, they may be obtained or calculated using other comparable data sets (e.g., interaction data from historical periods or from other populations). Since Snickars and Weibull (1977) found that historical migration tables provide much better estimates of current accessibility than any distance measure, historical data are often used to capture the spatial patterns of migration (see also Tobler 1995). For projection of internal migration patterns, this means we can effectively utilise trends exhibited by previous migration data sets.

11.3 Trends Over Time

In this section, we calculate and present each of the multiplicative components specified in Eq. 11.3 for the periods 1981–1986 to 2011–2016. The purpose of presenting these patterns is primarily to highlight the consistencies and/or any major deviations found in the trends over time, particularly since extrapolations of these components are combined and then used to predict future counts of migration by origin, destination, age, and sex.

The overall level components (T) and proportions of interstate migration in Australia are presented in Fig. 11.2 for the periods 1981–1986 to 2011–2016. During this time, total interstate migration increased from 717 thousand persons in 1981–1986 to 792 thousand persons in 1991–1996, followed by a decline to 774 thousand persons in 2006–2011 and then a sharp increase to 824 thousand persons in 2011–2016. While the total level of interstate migration demonstrated certain amount of fluctuation, its proportion in the total Australian population kept decreasing from around 5.5% in 1981–1986 to 4.4% in 2011–2016. The general decline in the propensity to migrate internally has been observed across Australia by

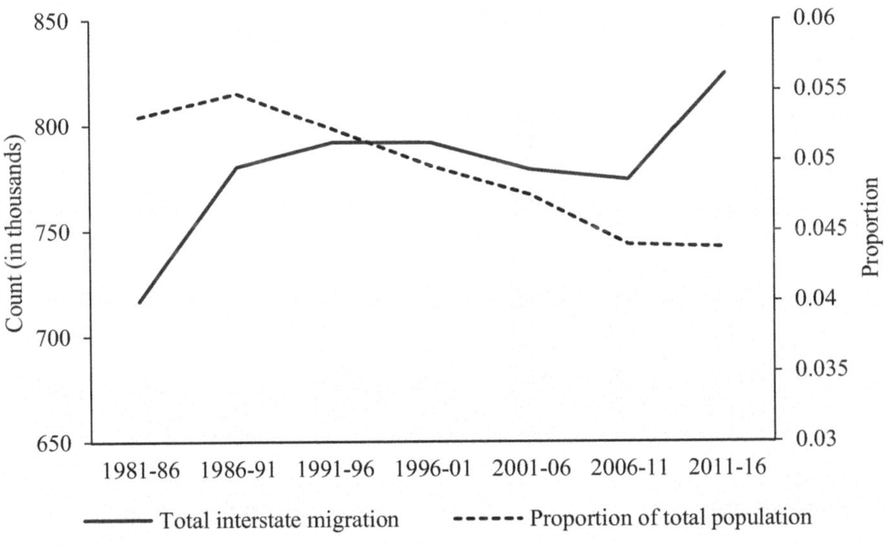

Fig. 11.2 Total level and proportion of interstate migration in Australian, 1981–1986 to 2011–2016

Bell et al. (2018), as well as in other developed countries (Cooke 2013; Champion et al. 2018). The underlying causes are thought to be population ageing and changing economic structures (i.e., manufacturing to service-based).

For the origin and destination main effect components (O_i and D_j, respectively) presented in Fig. 11.3, we see that the largest states of NSW, VIC and QLD contributed the largest shares of both out-migration and in-migration. While NSW

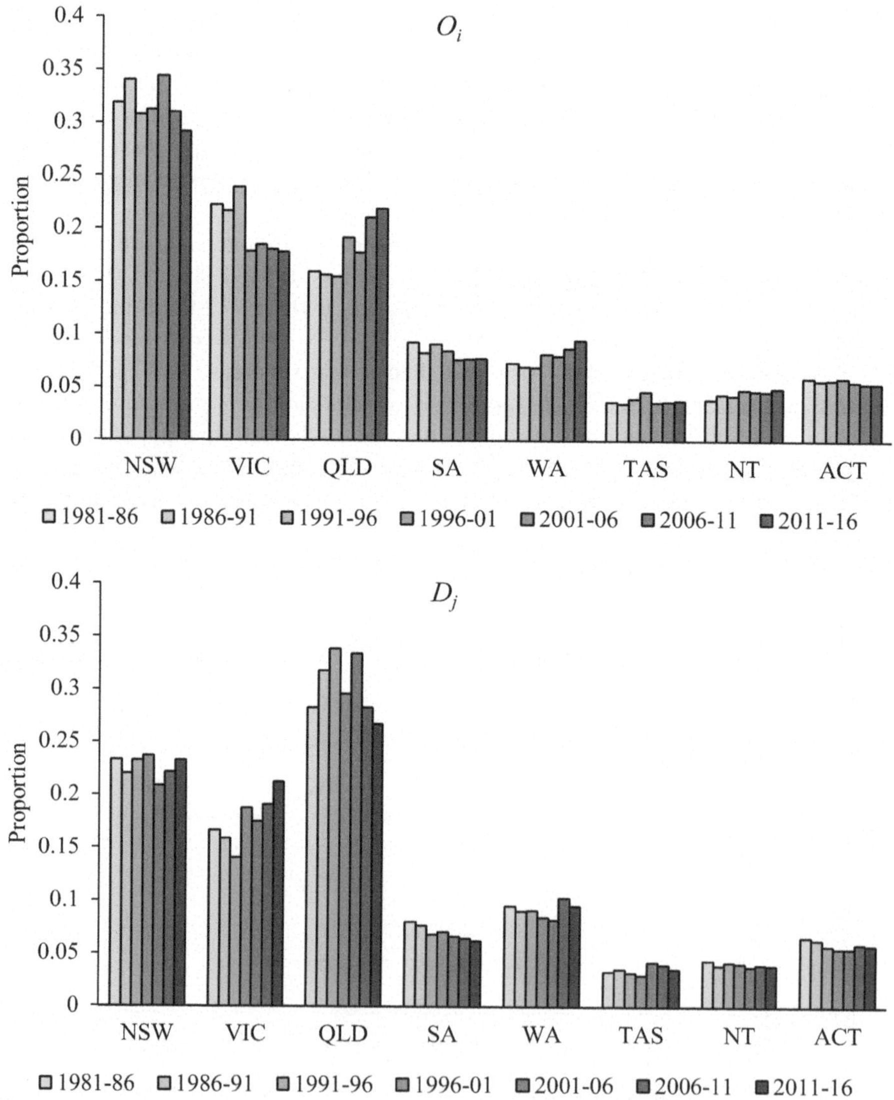

Fig. 11.3 Relative shares of out-migration (O_i) and in-migration (D_j) by state and territory in Australia, 1981–1986 to 2011–2016

consistently sent out the largest shares of interstate migrants from 1981–1986 to 2011–2016, it never received the largest share of in-migration – the largest share of in-migration was received by Queensland. Indeed, one of the distinctive features of internal migration in Australia over the past several decades is persistent net migration loss from New South Wales to other states in the country. Over 20 years ago, Burnley (1996) attributed this to high levels of immigration to and housing costs in Sydney.

The age and sex main effect components (A_x and S_y, respectively) of interstate migration are presented for the seven time periods in Fig. 11.4. For the age main effects, we find relative increases in shares of migration amongst 30–65 year olds and corresponding declines in the child age groups. These changes are likely caused by the ageing of the population. As for the main effect component for sex, there was a steady (albeit small) decrease in the share of male migrants from 52% in 1981–1986 to 49% in 2001–2006, which then held constant until the most recent period. This shift towards more female migration is likely caused by the increasing numbers of women seeking tertiary education and employment in Australia.

The values of the origin-destination (OD_{ij}), origin-age (OA_{ix}), destination-age (DA_{jx}) and age-sex (AS_{xy}) interaction components, presented in Figs. 11.5, 11.6, 11.7 and 11.8, respectively, represent ratios of observed to expected values. The expected values are calculated based on the multiplication of the overall level component (T) by the main effect components (O_i, D_j, A_x or S_y) corresponding to the two variables being interacted. Note, a value of 1.0 implies no difference from the expected value.

For the origin-destination components in Fig. 11.5, there are a couple of things to highlight. First, most of the values are above or below 1.0, which signifies the importance of this component in understanding the migration patterns. Second, there is relative stability in the ratios exhibited over time with all interactions, more or less, remaining the same in terms of being 'higher than expected' or 'lower than expected.' Third, the patterns exhibit clear trends over time, for example, the interaction between SA and NT has been steadily declining since the 1986–1991 period. Fourth, each origin has its own distinct destination patterns with, for example, ACT having more than twice the expected flows to NSW, and nearly half the expected flows to all other states and territories (except VIC which exhibits ratios of around 0.75). The interaction components for migration from VIC, on the other hand, are above 1.0 for state destinations but below 1.0 for territory destinations.

For the origin-age and destination-age components presented in Figs. 11.6 and 11.7, most of the ratios are near the value of 1.0 implying the state /territory age profiles of out-migration and in-migration resemble the overall age profile of migration (A_x). Notable differences in the out-migration age profiles (Fig. 11.5) include higher levels amongst retired age groups for VIC (before 2001) and QLD, relatively low levels of out-migration amongst older persons from WA, TAS (before 2001), NT, and ACT, and a sharp and consistent peak of 15–19 year olds leaving TAS. Notable differences in the in-migration age profiles (Fig. 11.6) include VIC receiving relatively more young adults (in recent periods) and fewer older migrants,

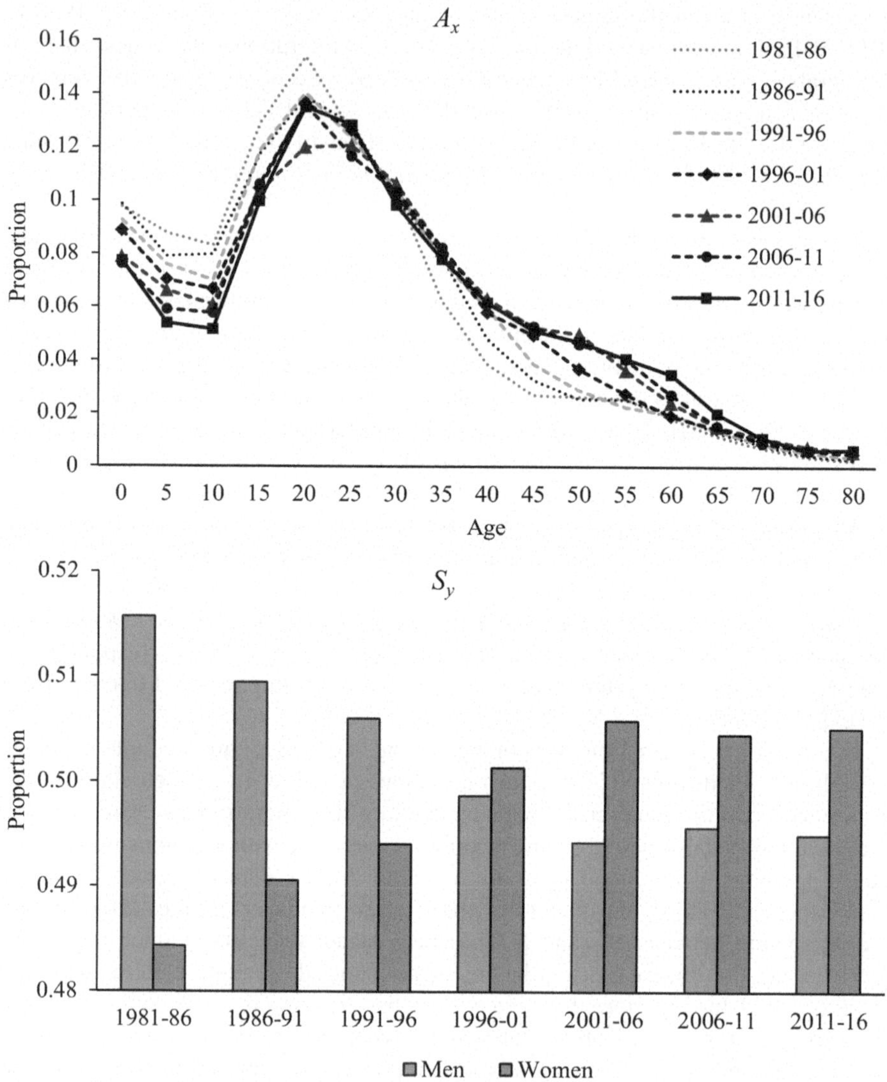

Fig. 11.4 Age (A_x) and sex (S_y) main effect components of interstate migration in Australia, 1981–1986 to 2011–2016

with the opposite occurring for QLD. WA, NT and ACT received considerably fewer older migrants, whereas it was the opposite for TAS. Finally, TAS appears to be growing as a retirement destination while at the same time becoming less attractive to young adults.

Finally, for the female age-sex interaction components (AS_{xy}) presented in Fig. 11.8, we find, for ages above 65 years, there has been a decreasing trend in the

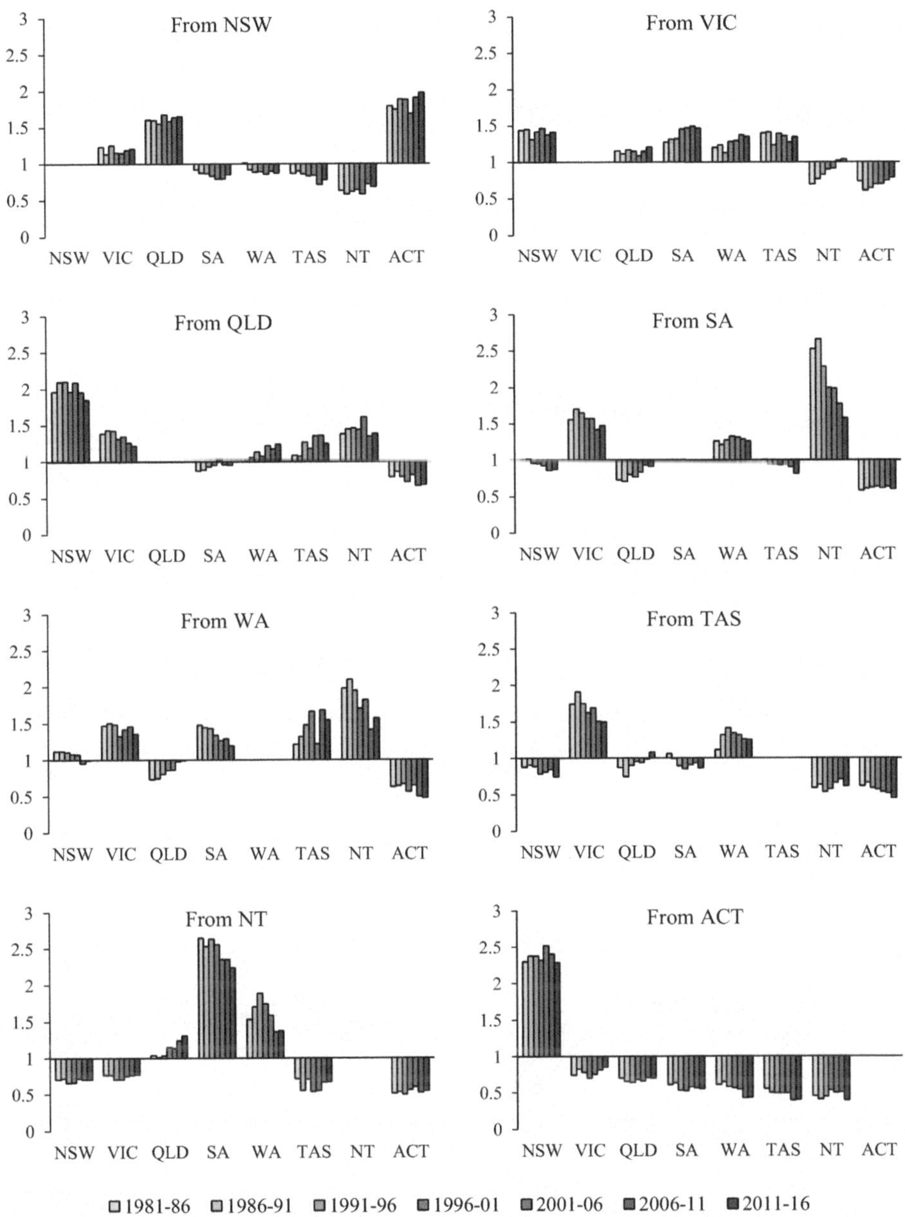

Fig. 11.5 Origin-destination (OD_{ij}) interaction components of interstate migration in Australia, 1981–1986 to 2011–2016

ratios towards 1.0. In general, it can be said that males and females have similar age profiles of migration, except in older age groups where there are more females in the population due to their lower mortality rates.

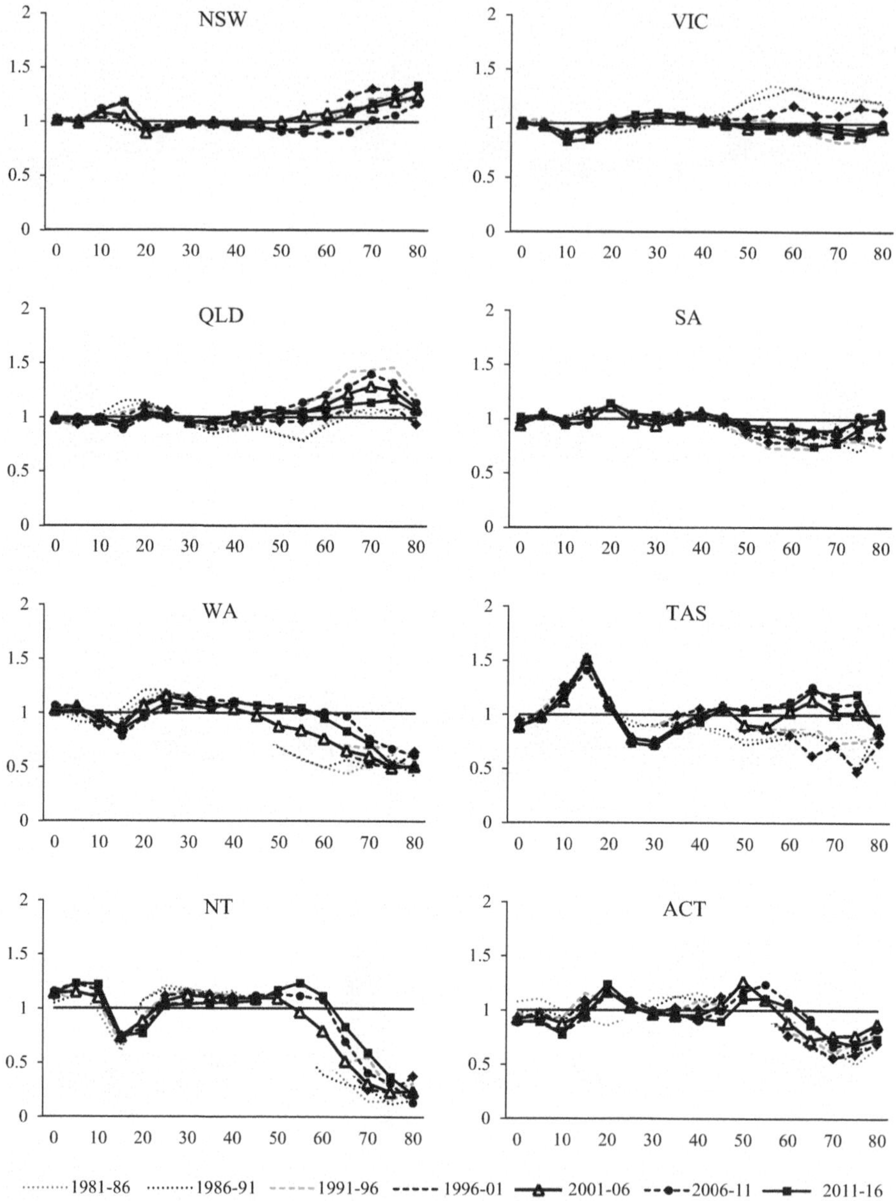

Fig. 11.6 Origin-age (OA_{ix}) interaction components of interstate migration in Australia, 1981–1986 to 2011–2016

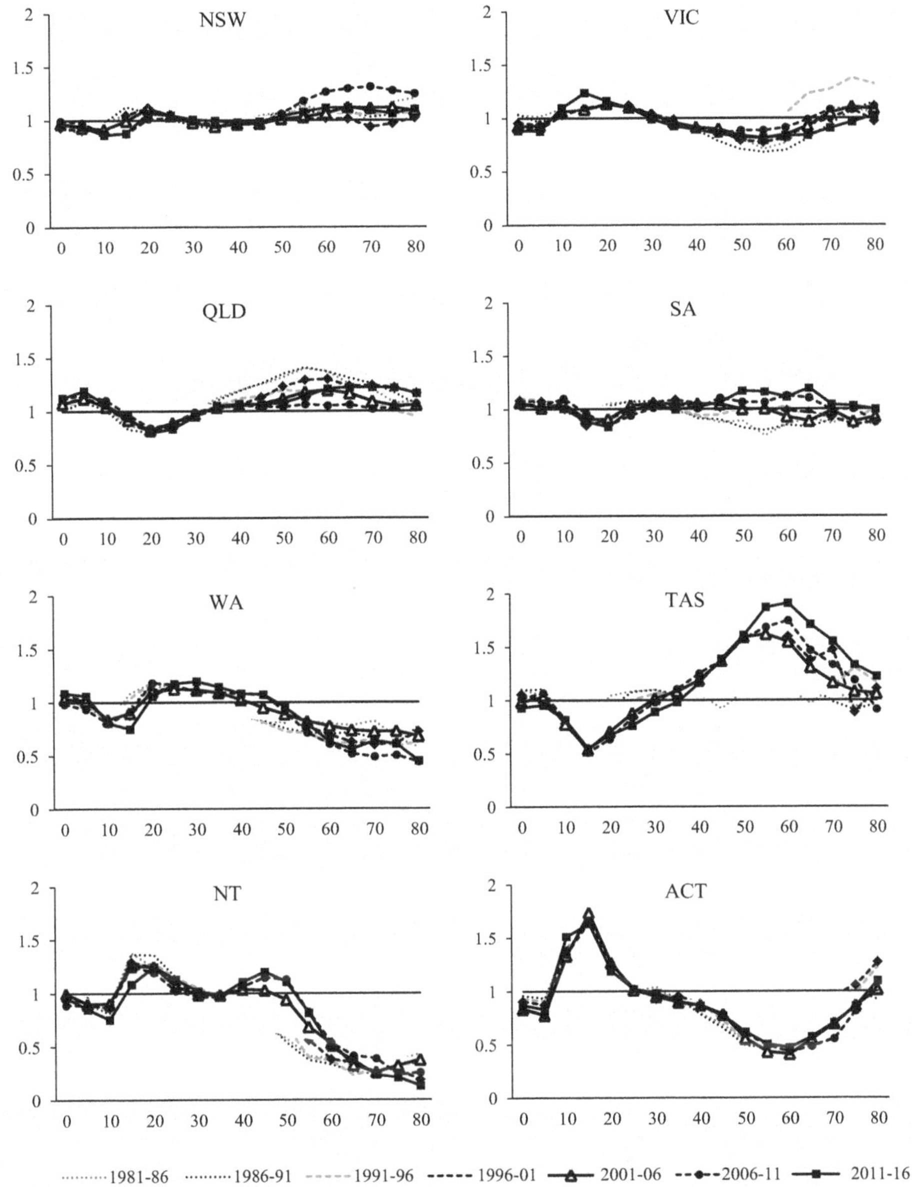

Fig. 11.7 Destination-age (DA_{jx}) interaction components of interstate migration in Australia, 1981–1986 to 2011–2016

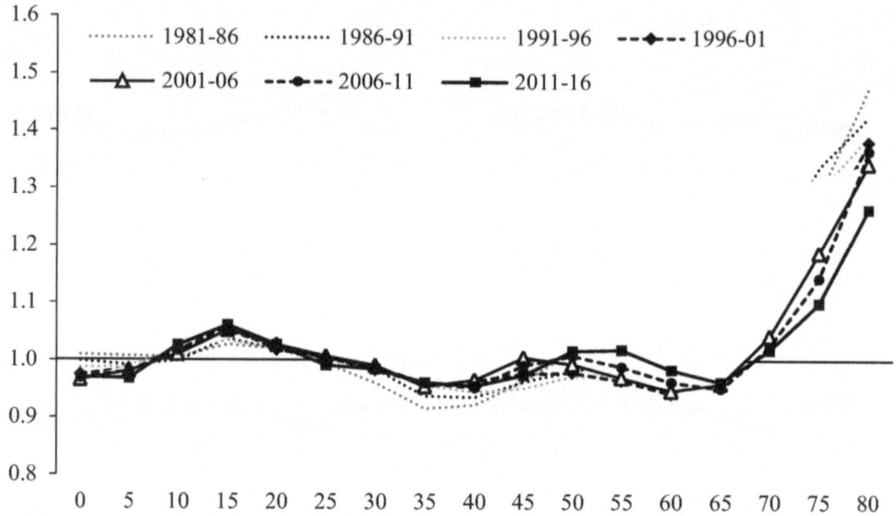

Fig. 11.8 Age-sex (AS_{xy}) interaction components for female interstate migration in Australia, 1981–1986 to 2011–2016

11.4 Forecasts

In this section, we show how the multiplicative component model can be used to produce predictions of internal migration by origin, destination, age and sex. The emphasis is on extrapolating each of the multiplicative components separately and then combining them to derive the forecasts of internal migration. For illustration, we first apply simple linear and log-linear trend extrapolations to each of the components specified in Eq. 11.3 to produce predictions of the 2006–2011 and 2011–2016 flows. For instance, the formulas of the linear and log-linear trend models for OD_{ij} components, respectively, are:

$$OD_{ij}(t) = \alpha + \beta\, Y(t) + \varepsilon(t) \text{ and} \tag{11.4}$$

$$\ln\left[OD_{ij}(t)\right] = \alpha + \beta Y(t)_t + \varepsilon(t) \tag{11.5}$$

where $OD_{ij}(t)$ denotes the OD_{ij} component at time t, $Y(t)$ denotes the corresponding year, and α and β denote the intercept and slope parameters estimated using ordinary least squares regression applied to the training sample data. The extrapolations are based on the 1981–1986 to 2001–2006 multiplicative components. Note, as part of the modelling process, the predicted main effect components are rescaled so that they sum to 1.0 and, when two-way interaction components are included, all predicted values are rescaled to match the estimated overall level (T) component.

In comparing the goodness-of-fit statistics for the linear and log-linear trend models, we find little difference between the two approaches. The linear model produced slightly lower g values of 24.1% and 30.7% for the 2006–2011 period and 2011–2016 period, respectively, compared to 24.4% and 31.2%, respectively for the log-linear model. Note, calculations of the mean squared error (MSE), mean absolute error (MAE) and symmetric mean absolute percentage error (SMAPE) goodness-of-fit measures also resulted in similar values for the linear and log-linear trend models, where:

$$MSE = \frac{1}{N}\sum_{i=1}^{N} \left(n_{ijxy} - \hat{n}_{ijxy}\right)^2,$$

$$MAE = \frac{1}{N}\sum_{i=1}^{N} \left|\hat{n}_{ijxy} - n_{ijxy}\right| \; and$$

$$SMAPE = \frac{100}{N}\sum_{i=1}^{N} \frac{\left|\hat{n}_{ijxy} - n_{ijxy}\right|}{\left(\left|n_{ijxy}\right| + \left|\hat{n}_{ijxy}\right|\right)/2},$$

where N denotes the total number of cells (i.e., 1904) in the origin [i] by destination [j] by sex [y] by age [x] table [$i \neq j$], n denotes the observed number of interstate migrants, and $\hat{n}$ denotes the corresponding estimated flows. In the end, because the difference was so small (see also Fig. 11.9), we decided to use the log-linear trend model because it ensured positive predicted values.

11.4.1 Model Selection

To identify the best multiplicative model for forecasting origin-destination-age-sex tables of migration, we predicted a range of unsaturated models starting with the model specified in Eq. 11.3 and used the g measure as a basis for comparison. All models used log-linear trend extrapolation to predict the component values for 2006–2011 and 2011–2016 based on the observed values from 1981–1986 to 2001–2006.

We tested and compared four models. Model 1 includes extrapolations of all components specified in Eq. 11.3. Model 2 replaces the extrapolations for the OA, DA and AS components with the most recent observed component values (i.e., 2001–2006) and held them constant for the holdout sample forecasts. Model 3 only includes extrapolations for the overall level and main effect components and held all two-way interaction components constant at the 2001–2006 values. Finally, Model 4 only extrapolated the overall level component. The remaining components represented the observed 2001–2006 values. These four models are specified as follows:

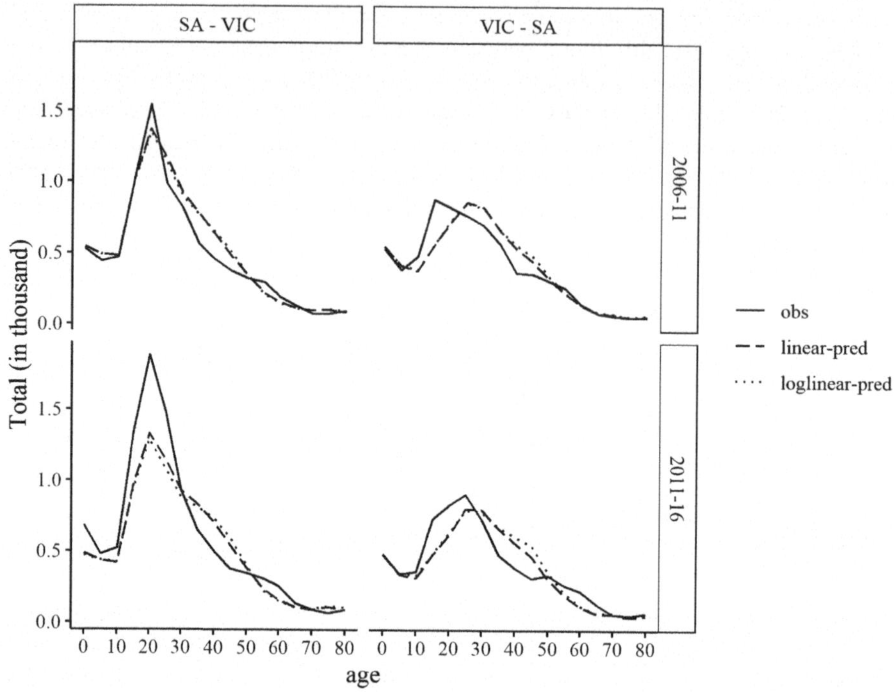

Fig. 11.9 Observed and predicted female flows of migration between Victoria and South Australia, 2006–2011 and 2011–2016

Model 1 $n_{ijxy}= (\hat{T})(\hat{O}_i)(\hat{D}_j)(\hat{A}_x)(\hat{S}_y)(\widehat{OD}_{ij})(\widehat{OA}_{ix})(\widehat{DA}_{jx})(\widehat{AS}_{xy}),$

Model 2 $n_{ijxy}= (\hat{T})(\hat{O}_i)(\hat{D}_j)(\hat{A}_x)(\hat{S}_y)(\widehat{OD}_{ij})(OA_{ix})(DA_{jx})(AS_{xy}),$

Model 3 $n_{ijxy}= (\hat{T})(\hat{O}_i)(\hat{D}_j)(\hat{A}_x)(\hat{S}_y)(OD_{ij})(OA_{ix})(DA_{jx})(AS_{xy}),$

Model 4 $n_{ijxy}= (\hat{T})(O_i)(D_j)(A_x)(S_y)(OD_{ij})(OA_{ix})(DA_{jx})(AS_{xy}),$

where the 'hat' symbol denotes log-linear extrapolation. The goodness-of-fit values, including g, MSE, MAE and SMAPE, for these four models are presented in Table 11.4. Surprisingly, there was very little difference between the overall goodness-of-fit tests. The 'best' performing model for both holdout sample prediction periods was the simplest model, Model 4, that only extrapolated the overall level component and held the remaining components fixed at the observed 2001–2006 values. We did not expect Model 4 to perform as well as the other models. Presumably, it did so because the historical trend data used to predict the multiplicative components forced the predicted values further away from the holdout sample than was observed in the most recent period used in the training sample.

Table 11.4 Goodness-of-fit statistics of different forecast models for internal migration

Measure	Model	2006–2011	2011–2016
g (%)	*(T)*	24.1	30.3
	(T)(O)(D)(A)(S)	24.9	31.1
	(T)(O)(D)(A)(S)(OD)	24.6	31.5
	(T)(O)(D)(A)(S)(OD)(OA)(DA)(AS)	24.4	31.2
MSE	*(T)*	39,300	66,981
	(T)(O)(D)(A)(S)	39,537	80,410
	(T)(O)(D)(A)(S)(OD)	43,050	87,791
	(T)(O)(D)(A)(S)(OD)(OA)(DA)(AS)	38,449	72,110
MAE	*(T)*	71	92
	(T)(O)(D)(A)(S)	73	104
	(T)(O)(D)(A)(S)(OD)	74	108
	(T)(O)(D)(A)(S)(OD)(OA)(DA)(AS)	75	108
SMAPE (%)	*(T)*	19.0	21.5
	(T)(O)(D)(A)(S)	20.1	23.3
	(T)(O)(D)(A)(S)(OD)	19.8	23.3
	(T)(O)(D)(A)(S)(OD)(OA)(DA)(AS)	20.1	24.3

11.4.2 Forecasting Internal Migration by Age and Sex with Measures of Uncertainty

In this section, we introduce uncertainty measures to Model 4, which turned out to be both the most effective and simplest model. As stated above, we predict the overall level component for the two most recent periods based on a simple log-linear extrapolation. The estimated total levels of interstate migration are 814,176 persons for the 2006–2011 period and 829,022 persons for the 2011–2016 period. The corresponding observed values were 774,013 persons and 824,392 persons, respectively.

In addition to the point predictions, we include 80% and 95% prediction intervals. These are calculated by simulating predictions of each of the components in the model specified in Eq. 11.3, assuming normal distributions for the logged components. For the components held constant over time, we use a random walk model where the variance of the errors is equal to the observed variance in each of the differenced logged components. For instance, for OD_{ij} components,

$$\ln\left[OD_{ij}\,(\,t)\right] = \ln\left[OD_{ij}\,(t-1)\right] + \varepsilon(t).$$

The overall level component is predicted using a linear regression model on the log scale, Eq. 11.5. Here, the variance is equal to the prediction error variance under the model. We used random walk models because they were relatively simple and resulted in good fits for our tests. Note, had the results been less satisfactory, we could have considered other time series models (e.g., AR(1)). Finally, the simulated

Table 11.5 Calibration (%) of holdout sample predictions of Australian internal migration by age and sex, 2006–2011 and 2011–2016

	2006–2011		2011–2016	
Model	80%	95%	80%	95%
Log-linear	85%	96%	88%	98%
Random walk	85%	95%	85%	97%

components were combined by multiplying them together to provide realisations for the predicted migration flows by origin, destination, age and sex and for each time period. The presented prediction intervals set out below are the empirical quantiles of 1000 simulated predicted flows.

We introduce two models to forecast the inter-state migration flows: (1) log-linear forecasting of the total levels and random walk of the other components around the observed values in the last period (2001–2006), and (2) random walk of both the overall level (T) and the other components around the last observed values. To evaluate the forecasting models, we calculate the coverage of the nominal 80% and 95% prediction intervals as the percentage of the observed origin-destination-sex-age flows that lie within the intervals. These calibration statistics are presented in Table 11.5 as the percentage of the total number of observations, excluding the diagonals, where $i = j$, in the origin-destination-age-sex tables. While they may not provide accurate estimates of the coverage of the nominal intervals, if there is correlation between the migration flows within and/or between years, they can indicate failures in the measures of uncertainty. However, in general, we find that the calibration statistics for both intervals for both models are reassuringly close to the nominal values.

The predicted and observed levels of out-migration, in-migration and net migration for the 2006–2011 and 2011–2016 periods are presented in Fig. 11.10 for the eight states and territories in Australia. The results were obtained from Model 4 that included log-linear forecasts for the total levels and random walk forecasts for the other components. In general, we find the predicted means are close to the observed values in both periods and that the prediction intervals cover the observed values. There were, however, two notable differences between observed and estimated totals. The first is the results for NSW, where the mean level of out-migration was much higher for both the 2006–2011 and 2011–2016 periods. The other is QLD, where the predicted means of in-migration were higher than the observed values. In both cases, however, the 95% prediction interval covered the observed values. These differences can largely be explained by the unanticipated changes to the O_i and D_j components in the model observed during the 2006–2011 and 2011–2016 periods (see Fig. 11.3).

The observed and estimated female age-specific patterns of in-migration and out-migration are presented in Figs. 11.11 and 11.12, respectively, for the 2011–2016 period. During this time period, the mean number of female migrants were overestimated by around 0.7%, while the corresponding number of male migrants were overestimated by around 0.4%. We also find that the interstate migration of younger age groups, especially the 20–24 year old age group, are underestimated,

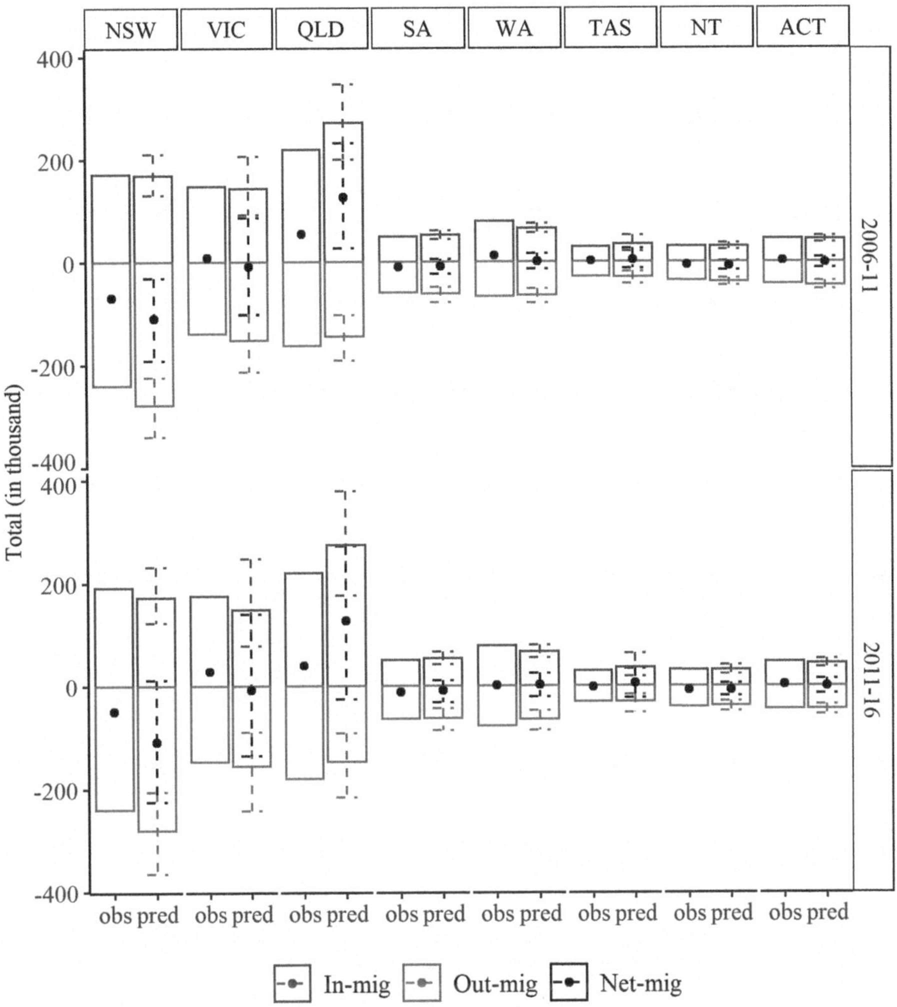

Fig. 11.10 Observed and forecasted in-migration, out-migration and net migration by state and territory in Australia, 2006–2011 and 2011–2016
Note: Values shown on the y-axis represent the counts of interstate migration measured in thousands. Error bars represent the 95% prediction intervals for the forecasted flows.

while the middle age groups are overestimated. These differences can be partially attributed to unanticipated increases in the proportions of migrants aged 20–25 years in 2006–2011 and 2011–2016 (see Fig. 11.4).

In summary, we found the multiplicative component model did well in predicting the observed patterns of migration by origin, destination, age and sex, particularly when the uncertainty in the predictions is taken into account. If this model were to be put into practice, more attention could be placed on the extrapolation of the age-specific components, especially if the aim was to reduce uncertainty in the forecasts.

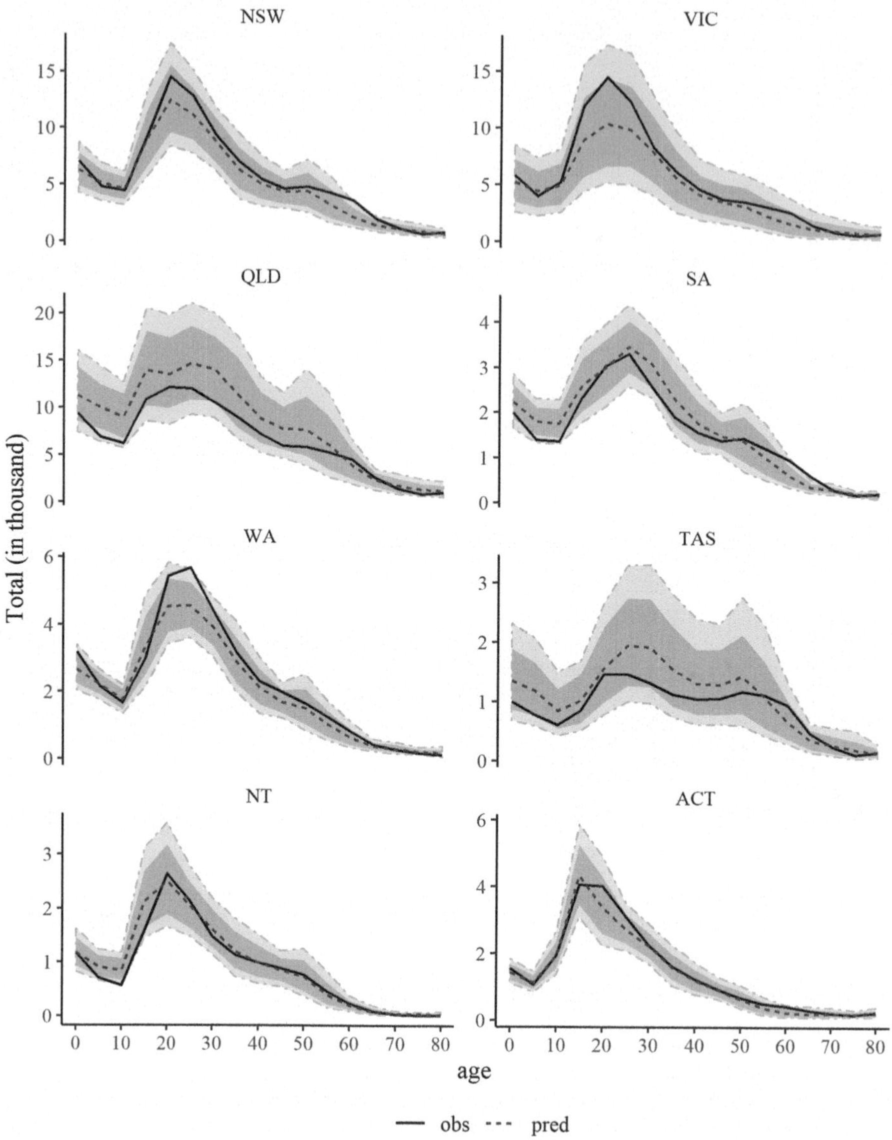

Fig. 11.11 Observed and estimated age-specific female in-migration with 80% and 95% prediction intervals (in thousands) by state and territory in Australia, 2011–2016

In our illustration, we found some of the predicted age patterns differed considerably from the observed values.

In addition to the holdout sample forecasts, we applied the method described above to the whole time series of data from 1981–1986 to 2011–2016 and forecasted the internal migration tables forward for the periods 2016–2021 and 2021–2026.

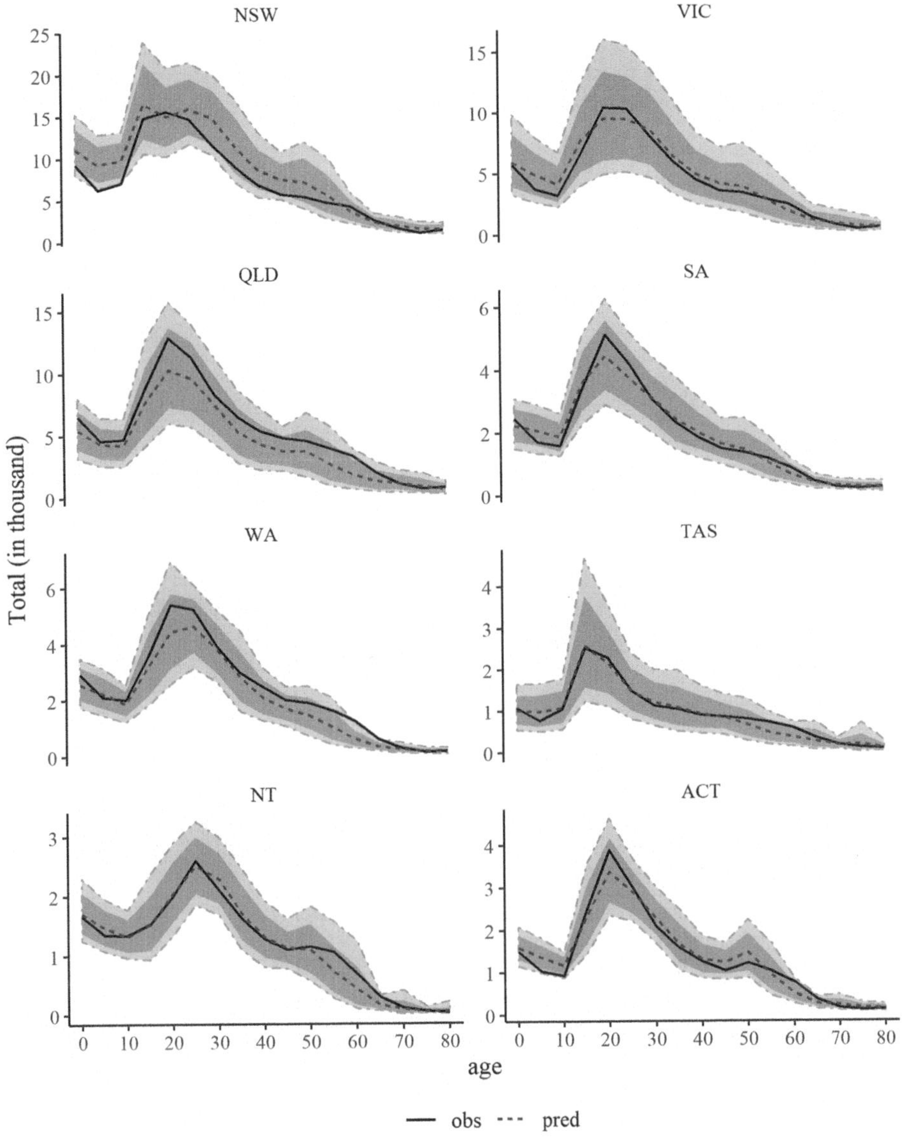

Fig. 11.12 Observed and predicted age-specific female out-migration with 80% and 95% prediction intervals (in thousands) by state and territory in Australia, 2011–2016

The forecasted total number of interstate migrants is 825,915 persons in 2016–2021 with 95% prediction interval ranging between 757,295 and 894,984 persons. For the 2021–2026 period, the forecasted total number of interstate migrants increased to 835,248 persons with the 95% prediction interval ranging between 762,748 and 916,675 persons. In Fig. 11.13, we present the forecasted in-migration, out-

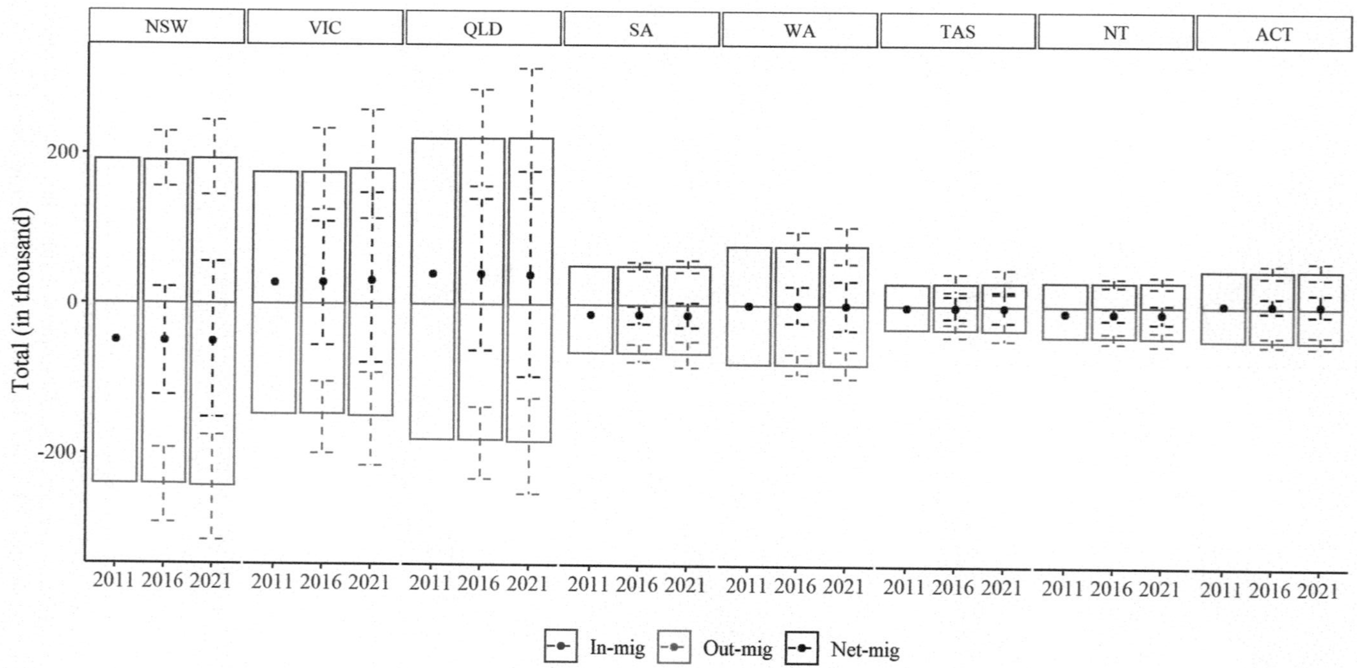

Fig. 11.13 In-migration, out-migration and net migration by state and territory in Australia for observed 2011–2016 flows and forecasted 2016–2021 and 2021–2026 flows

Note: Years at the horizontal axis denotes the starting years of each 5-year periods from 2011–2016 to 2021–2026. Values shown on the vertical axis represent the counts of interstate migration measured in thousands. Error bars represent the 95%prediction intervals for the forecasted flows.

migration and net internal migration for each state and territory for the two periods with comparisons to the observed levels in 2011–2016. In general, we find the levels of internal migration very stable over time. NSW and QLD are forecasted to keep contributing the largest amounts of out-migration and in-migration. Finally, to illustrate the performance of the model on forecasting age-sex-specific migration flows between pairs of origins and destinations, we present the age profiles for female migrants moving between NSW and QLD, representing a major internal migration flow in the system, and SA and TAS, representing a relatively small flow, in Fig. 11.14.

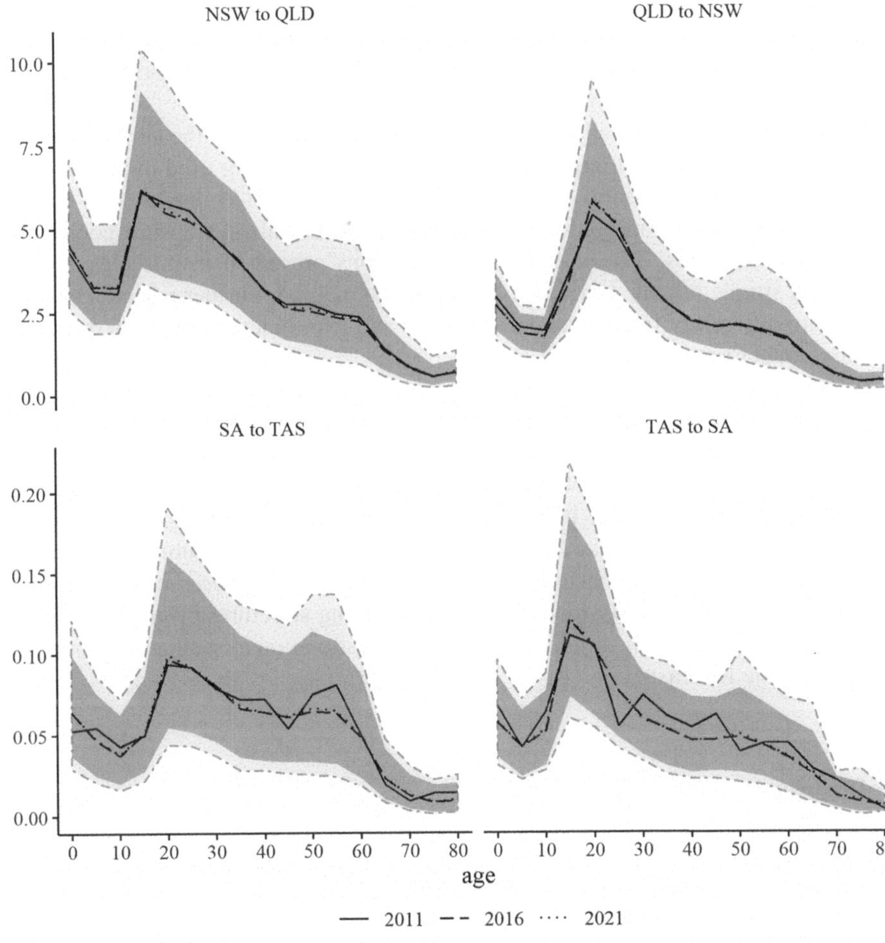

Fig. 11.14 Age-specific female migration flows (in thousands) between selected states in Australia for the observed 2011–2016 flows and forecasted 2016–2021 and 2021–2026 flows
Note: The areas with dark and light grey colours represent the 95% prediction intervals for the forecasted flows in 2016–2021 and 2021–2026 respectively.

11.5 Conclusion

In this chapter, we have shown how the multiplicative component projection model may be used to provide future estimates of internal migration by origin, destination, age and sex with measures of uncertainty. It extends earlier research using multiplicative or log-linear models to forecast internal migration (Stillwell 1986; Willekens and Baydar 1986; Van Imhoff et al. 1997; Van der Gaag et al. 2000; Sweeney and Konty 2002; Raymer et al. 2006; Van Wissen et al. 2008; Raymer et al. 2017) by modelling each component separately and integrating uncertainty. The methodology is relatively simple and robust. It directly provides the forecasted sizes of migration flows that can be used to construct transition probabilities for use in multiregional cohort component projection models, assuming one could also infer the probability of staying or not migrating, or aggregate them for use in standard 'single region' cohort component projection models.

Further research is needed to examine the appropriateness of the simple extrapolation method for each multiplicative component before being used in practice. In particular, it would be useful to assess the forward forecasted results with future measured values as good holdout sample results do not always ensure good out-of-sample predictions. The underlying assumptions presented in this chapter are admittedly simple but our aim was to illustrate the method. Further research should investigate differently forecasting assumptions and experimentations with different data and longer time series.

In conclusion, we hope that the methodology presented in this chapter will inspire improving methods for forecasting internal migration. Internal migration has become increasingly important as a component of population change, in both developing and developed societies (White 2016). Also, many countries have internal migration flow data by origin, destination, age and sex – our research has shown how onc can make better use of these data to make future predictions of internal migration. The basic argument is that migration processes evolve over time in predictable ways. By modelling the underlying structures of migration flow tables, we are able to both simplify the process of estimation as well as improve the accuracy of the forecasts.

References

Bell, M., Charles-Edwards, E., Ueffing, P., Stillwell, J., Kupiszewski, M., & Kupiszewska, D. (2015). Internal migration and development: Comparing migration intensities around the world. *Population and Development Review, 41*(1), 33–58.

Bell, M., Wilson, T., Charles-Edwards, E., & Ueffing, P. (2018). Australia: The long-run decline in internal migration intensities. In T. Champion, T. Cooke, & I. Shuttleworth (Eds.), *Internal migration in the developed world: Are we becoming less mobile?* (pp. 147–172). Abingdon: Routledge.

Burnley, I. H. (1996). Associations between overseas, intra-urban and internal migration dynamics in Sydney, 1976-91. *Journal of the Australian Population Association, 13*(1), 47–65.

Champion, T., Cooke, T., & Shuttleworth, I. (Eds.). (2018). *Internal migration in the developed world: Are we becoming less mobile?* Abingdon: Routledge.

Cooke, T. (2013). Internal migration in decline. *The Professional Geographer, 65*, 664–675.

Raymer, J., & Rogers, A. (2007). Using age and spatial flow structures in the indirect estimation of migration streams. *Demography, 44*(2), 199–223.

Raymer, J., Bonaguidi, A., & Valentini, A. (2006). Describing and projecting the age and spatial structures of interregional migration in Italy. *Population Space and Place, 12*(5), 371–388.

Raymer, J., Abel, G. J., & Rogers, A. (2012). Does specification matter? Experiments with simple multiregional probabilistic population projections. *Environment and Planning A, 44*(11), 2664–2686.

Raymer, J., Biddle, N., & Campbell, P. (2017). Analysing and projecting Indigenous migration in Australia. *Applied Spatial Analysis and Policy, 10*(2), 211–232.

Rogers, A. (1966). Matrix methods of population analysis. *Journal of the American Institute of Planners, 32*(1), 40–44.

Rogers, A. (1968). *Matrix analysis of interregional population growth and distribution*. Berkeley: University of California Press.

Rogers, A. (1975). *Introduction to multiregional mathematical demography*. New York: Wiley.

Rogers, A. (1990). Requiem for the net migrant. *Geographical Analysis, 22*(4), 283–300.

Rogers, A., & Willekens, F. (1976). Spatial population dynamics. *Papers of the Regional Science Association, 36*(1), 3–34.

Rogers, A., Willekens, F., Little, J. S., & Raymer, J. (2002). Describing migration spatial structure. *Papers in Regional Science, 81*, 29–48.

Rogers, A., Willekens, F., & Raymer, J. (2003). Imposing age and spatial structures on inadequate migration-flow datasets. *The Professional Geographer, 55*(1), 56–69.

Smith, P. W. F., Raymer, J., & Giulietti, C. (2010). Combining available migration data in England to study economic activity flows over time. *Journal of the Royal Statistical Society: Series A (Statistics in Society), 173*(4), 733–753.

Snickars, F., & Weibull, J. W. (1977). A minimum information principle: Theory and practice. *Regional Science and Urban Economics, 7*(1–2), 137–168.

Stillwell, J. (1986). The analysis and projection of interregional migration in the United Kingdom. In R. Woods & P. Rees (Eds.), *Population structures and models: Developments in spatial demography* (pp. 160–202). London: Allen & Unwin.

Sweeney, S. H., & Konty, K. J. (2002). Population forecasting with nonstationary multiregional growth matrices. *Geographical Analysis, 34*(4), 289–312.

Tobler, W. (1995). Migration: Ravenstein, Thornthwaite, and beyond. *Urban Geography, 16*(4), 327–343.

Van der Gaag, N., Van Imhoff, E., & Van Wissen, L. (2000). Internal migration scenarios and regional population projections for the European Union. *International Journal of Population Geography, 6*, 1–19.

Van Imhoff, E., Van der Gaag, N., Van Wissen, L., & Rees, P. (1997). The selection of internal migration models for European regions. *International Journal of Population Geography, 3*, 137–159.

Van Wissen, L., Van der Gaag, N., Rees, P., & Stillwell, J. (2008). In search of a modelling strategy for projecting internal migration in European countries. In J. Poot, B. Waldorf, & L. Van Wissen (Eds.), *Migration and human capital* (pp. 49–74). Cheltenham: Edward Elgar.

White, M. J. (Ed.). (2016). *International handbook of migration and population distribution*. Dordrecht: Springer.

Willekens, F. (1983). Log-linear modelling of spatial interaction. *Papers of the Regional Science Association, 52*, 187–205.

Willekens, F., & Baydar, N. (1986). Forecasting place-to-place migration with generalized linear models. In R. Woods & P. Rees (Eds.), *Population structures and models: Developments in spatial demography* (pp. 203–244). London: Allen & Unwin.

Willekens, F., & Rogers, A. (1978). *Spatial population analysis: Methods and computer programs* (Research Report 78-18). Laxenburg: International Institute for Applied Systems Analysis.

Wilson, A. G., & Rees, P. H. (1974a). Accounts and models for spatial demographic analysis 2: Age-sex disaggregated populations. *Environment and Planning A, 6*(1), 101–116.
Wilson, A. G., & Rees, P. H. (1974b). Population statistics and spatial demographic accounts. *Journal of the Royal Statistical Society, Series D (The Statistician), 23*(3–4), 229–257.
Wilson, A. G., & Rees, P. H. (1975). Accounts and models for spatial demographic analysis 3: Rates and life tables. *Environment and Planning A, 7*(2), 199–231.

Chapter 12
New Approaches to the Conceptualization and Measurement of Age and Ageing

Sergei Scherbov and Warren C. Sanderson

12.1 Introduction

People's views on population ageing are influenced by the statistics that they read about it. The statistical measures in common use today were first developed around a century ago, in a very different demographic environment. For around two decades, we have been studying population ageing and have been arguing that its conventional portrayal is misleading. In this chapter, we summarize some of that research, which provides an alternative picture of population ageing, one that is more appropriate for twenty-first century. More details about our new view of population ageing can be found in. (Sanderson and Scherbov 2019). Population ageing can be measured in different ways. An example of this can found in the UN's *Profiles in Ageing, 2017*. One way is to report on the forecasted increase in the number of people 60+ years old in the world.

> According to data from World Population Prospects: the 2017 Revision, the number of older persons—those aged 60 years or over—is expected to more than double by 2050 and to more than triple by 2100, rising from 962 million globally in 2017 to 2.1 billion in 2050 and 3.1 billion in 2100. Globally, population aged 60 or over is growing faster than all younger age groups. (United Nations n.d.)

A second way, also discussed in that report, is based on our research.

In this chapter we discuss the two ways of measuring population ageing. Conventional measures of population ageing consider people old at a fixed chronological age without regarding how healthy they are and how they function. Our measures of population ageing (Sanderson and Scherbov 2005, 2007, 2008, 2010, 2013,

S. Scherbov (✉)
International Institute for Applied Systems Analysis (IIASA), Laxenburg, Austria
e-mail: scherbov@iiasa.ac.at

S. Mazzuco, N. Keilman (eds.), *Developments in Demographic Forecasting*, The Springer Series on Demographic Methods and Population Analysis 49,
https://doi.org/10.1007/978-3-030-42472-5_12

2014) consider people old based on their characteristics, which can differ over time, space, and across subgroups. We will show that the choice of measures to assess population ageing makes a substantial difference, one that could potentially affect the assessment of policies with respect to population ageing.

Before we begin a discussion of population ageing, we must first define what population ageing is. There are several definitions of ageing at the population level. In the *UN report on World Population Ageing: 1950–2050* (United Nations 2002) population ageing is defined as "the process by which older individuals become a proportionally larger share of the total population". The Encyclopedia of Population (Demeny and McNicoll 2003) defines ageing of population as "a summary term for shifts in the age distribution (i.e., age structure) of a population toward older ages". Population ageing is often measured "by increases in the percentage of elderly people of retirement ages" and "The median age – the age at which exactly half the population is older and another half is younger – is perhaps the most widely used indicator" (Demeny and McNicoll 2003). Since the study of population ageing is often driven by a concern over the sustainability of pension systems, the old age dependency ratio (the number of individuals of retirement ages compared to the number of those of working ages) is also frequently used as a measure of population ageing.

Our view of population ageing is broader than this. It is based not only the chronological ages of people, but on their characteristics as well. So the first step in specifying our new measures of population ageing is to define who is elderly based on population-level characteristics.

Conventionally, the elderly are defined as those above age 60- or 65-years-old. This boundary or *old-age threshold* is, then, kept fixed. In 1916 an American sociologist Isaac Rubinow (1913, 14) defined age 65 as an old age threshold

> Age 65 is generally set as the threshold of old age since it is at this period of life that the rates for sickness and death begin to show a marked increase over those of the earlier years.

More than 100 years have passed since this definition of old-age threshold was introduced. People live much longer now and in many developed countries life expectancy at age 65 increased by around 10 years since Rubinow suggested his old-age threshold. Not only people live longer, but they are also healthier, stronger physically and cognitively perform better. However, in the conventional statistics of population ageing, people as old as age 65 and sometimes even 60 are classified as being old.

12.2 Characteristic Approach to the Measurement of Population Ageing

Conventional measures of ageing consider people being old at a fixed chronological age, usually at age 65. They do not distinguish where or when people lived. When conventional measures of ageing are applied, the old age threshold for a person living in a region with low life expectancy, say Burkina Faso, is the same as for a person living in Japan or other places with high life expectancy. Moreover, a 65-year-old person living today will be considered as old as a person of the same age who was living 100 years ago or who will be living 100 years from now. Conventional measures of ageing recognize only one characteristic of people – chronological age. But ageing is a multidimensional phenomenon and chronological age is only one of its relevant dimensions. Other characteristics of people such as physical and mental health are ignored in conventional measures of ageing.

Sanderson and Scherbov (2013) developed what they called the *characteristics approach* to the measurement of population ageing. This approach considers people old depending not only on their chronological age, but on other characteristics, such as health, physical strength, and cognitive abilities. When those characteristics change in time and space, the threshold of old-age becomes dynamic.

Using the terminology in Sanderson and Scherbov (2014), we call the ages that correspond to different characteristics of people "α-ages." To define α-ages, we begin with $C_t(\alpha)$, a schedule of some characteristic relevant to the study of population ageing (such as mortality hazard or remaining life expectancy), that defines the values of the characteristic at each chronological age α at a time or place denoted by t. We call these relationships "characteristic schedules". Generally, characteristic schedules change over time and are different from place to place. If $C_t(\alpha)$ is continuous and monotonic in α, it can be inverted to obtain the schedule of chronological ages associated with each value of the characteristic at time or place t.

α-ages can be calculated from the inverse of the characteristic schedules. For example, $\alpha_{\kappa,\,t} = C_t^{-1}(\kappa_t)$ is the α-age associated with the characteristic level κ_t in situation t.

In the simplest case the level of the characteristic does not change over time, so that κ has no t subscript. For example, if the time-invariant characteristic was a remaining life expectancy of 15 years, the α-age, the age at which that remaining life expectancy was attained for Germans (average of both sexes) in 2017 was 71 years. We call the α-ages based on invariant characteristics *constant characteristic ages*.

Different characteristics may be used to define thresholds reflecting different features of population ageing. To our knowledge, (Ryder 1975) was the first to do this. Ryder's old-age threshold was based on remaining life expectancy. A health-based characteristic could be also used to mark the entrance to old age. Health is a complex quality, but a rough and readily accessible measure of it is the corresponding age-specific mortality rate. In this case, α-ages based on the life-table mortality rate mx would provide ages of comparable population health across space and time (Cutler et al. 2007; Vaupel 2010; Fuchs 1984) and could also be used to define an old-age threshold.

When the characteristic under consideration is remaining life expectancy, we have a special term for α-ages. We call them *prospective ages* and measures derived from prospective ages are called prospective measures of ageing. For example, if we derive the old age threshold based on a constant remaining life expectancy, we call this the prospective old age threshold (POAT). Based on the prospective old age threshold, we have produced several prospective measures of population ageing.

Usually we define the prospective old age threshold as age that corresponds to a remaining life expectancy of 15 years (Sanderson and Scherbov 2010, 2013). In the 1970–1980s that was the level of the remaining life expectancy at age 65 in many countries with high life expectancies. Once the prospective old age threshold is defined, the prospective old age dependency ratio (POADR) and prospective proportion old (PPO) could be derived as well:

$$\text{POADR} = \frac{\text{Number of people older than the POAT}}{\text{Number of people ages 20 to the POAT}}$$

$$\text{PPO} = \frac{\text{Number of people older than the POAT}}{\text{Total number of people}}$$

The POADR appears on the UN website, *Profiles in Ageing, 2017,* for all UN countries and for the years 1980, 2015, 2030, and 2050. (https://population.un.org/ProfilesOfAgeing2017/index.html). The comparison between the conventional old-age dependency ratio and the prospective one on that website provides a simple way to assess the quantitative implications of the different approaches to the measurement of population ageing.

The prospective measure analogous to the median age is the prospective median age. In this case the population characteristic – remaining life expectancy – is not constant. To calculate prospective median age, we select a standard year. The prospective median age is the age in the standard year when the level of characteristic – remaining life expectancy at the median age– is the same as it is in the year of interest. Put differently, the prospective median age can be derived as $pma_{t,\,s} = C_s^{-1}(\kappa_t)$, where $pma_{t,s}$ is the prospective median age in year t, using the characteristic schedule of year s as a standard and κ_t is the median age of the population in year t.

We illustrate the notions introduced above with a country specific example. Figure 12.1 illustrates the concept of prospective age with data for Spanish females. Each line in this graph corresponds to constant remaining life expectancy and, therefore, a constant prospective age. For example, the line marked as 70, shows the age (y axis) when remaining life expectancy was the same as for a 70-year-old female in the year 2010. We read from this chart, that a 70-year-old person in 2010 had the same remaining life expectancy and prospective age as a 63-year-old woman in 1970. Or if we take a line that corresponds to the prospective age 40 in 2010, we can see that a woman at age 40 in 2010 had the same prospective age as a 30-year-old woman had around 1960. This provides a justification for the famous saying that 40 is the new 30.

Three features of Fig. 12.1 stand out. First, in 2010, the vertical distance between the lines is constant. This occurs because of the way in which the Figure is constructed. In 2010, the value along each line is assumed to be at the age indicated for that line. The second noteworthy feature is that the lines are roughly parallel. If no one died at ages below 80, then the lines would be perfectly parallel. The lines are roughly parallel because after age 30 most deaths do occur at advanced

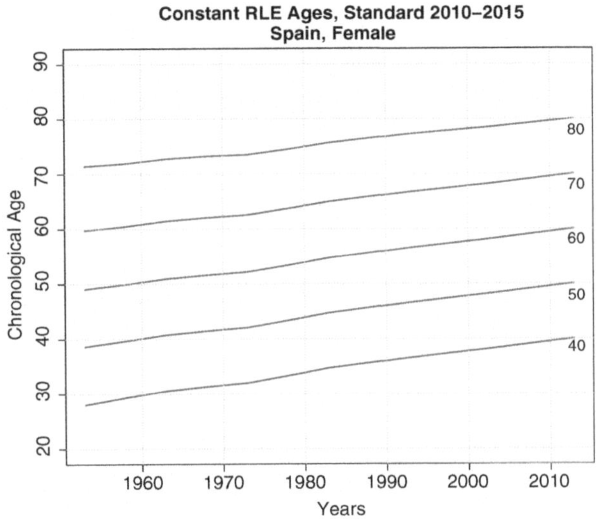

Fig. 12.1 Prospective ages for Spanish females. Each line indicates prospective age that corresponds to remaining life expectancy in 2000 for a particular age. Remaining life expectancy is constant along each line. (Source: United Nations 2017)

ages. Finally, the lines are also roughly linear. This arises because improvements in mortality conditions in Spain were quite regular. Had there been a morality crisis in the period covered by the Figure, the lines would not have been so linear.

Prospective ages have an analog in economics. They are like the use of constant dollars to compare values from one period to another by taking inflation into account, Prospective age serves an analogous purpose by comparing ages taking the increase in life expectancy into account. Any kind of financial data that can be represented in dollar terms can be converted into constant dollars by using an appropriate price index. Similarly, chronological ages can be converted into prospective ages using appropriate life tables.

Figure 12.2 illustrates the dynamics of the prospective old age threshold for several selected Western European countries. The same selection of countries is applied for Figs. 12.3, 12.4, 12.5, 12.6, 12.7, 12.8 and 12.9. The countries that we have chosen are the Western European countries with the largest population, plus Sweden, which represents the Scandinavian countries. Later in the chapter (see Fig. 12.10), we present data for Western Europe as a whole.

As we can observe from this figure, the prospective old age threshold has increased by about 6–8 years. In 1955 it was around age 63–64 while in 2015 it reached the level of 71–73 years. The increase in the prospective old age threshold is about 0.13 years per calendar year. This is similar to increases in remaining life expectancy around the same ages. This is a relatively recent phenomenon that occurs because most of the increase in life expectancy in low mortality countries comes at the older ages.

In the left panels of Figs. 12.3 and 12.4, we present conventional measures of ageing applying the old age threshold fixed at age 65 for the same countries. In the right pane we present prospective measures that use the prospective old age

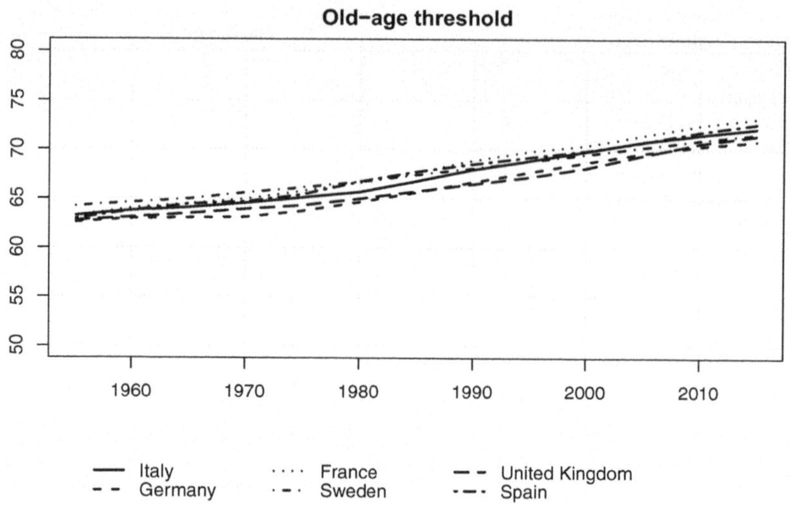

Fig. 12.2 Prospective old-age threshold (age when remaining life expectancy = 15 years) for several selected countries of Western Europe for both genders combined, 1955–2015. (Source: authors' calculations based on United Nations 2017)

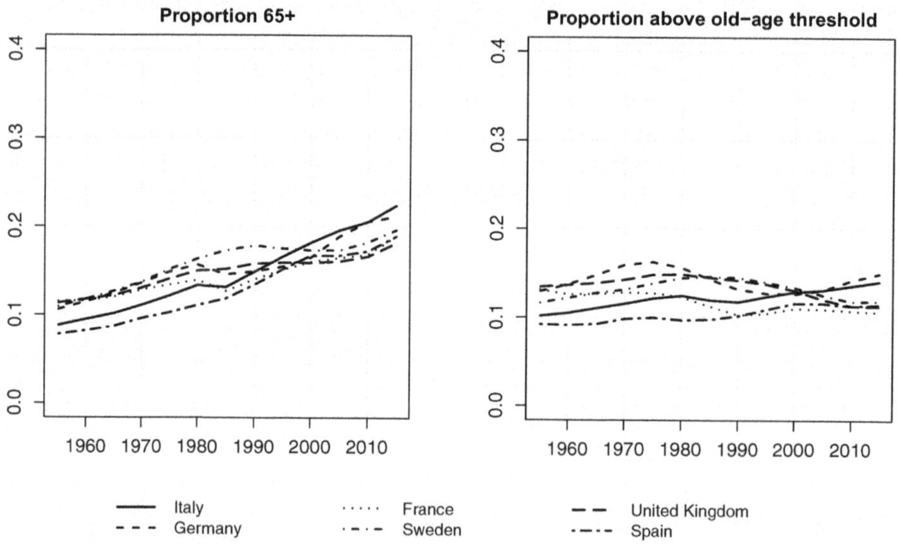

Fig. 12.3 Proportion of people 65+ and proportion of people with the remaining life expectancy 15 years or less (selected European countries), 1955–2015. (Source: authors' calculations based on United Nations 2017)

threshold presented in Fig. 12.2. While conventional measures indicate that there was a considerable population ageing in the past 60 years, prospective measures, in contrast, show that there was little or none.

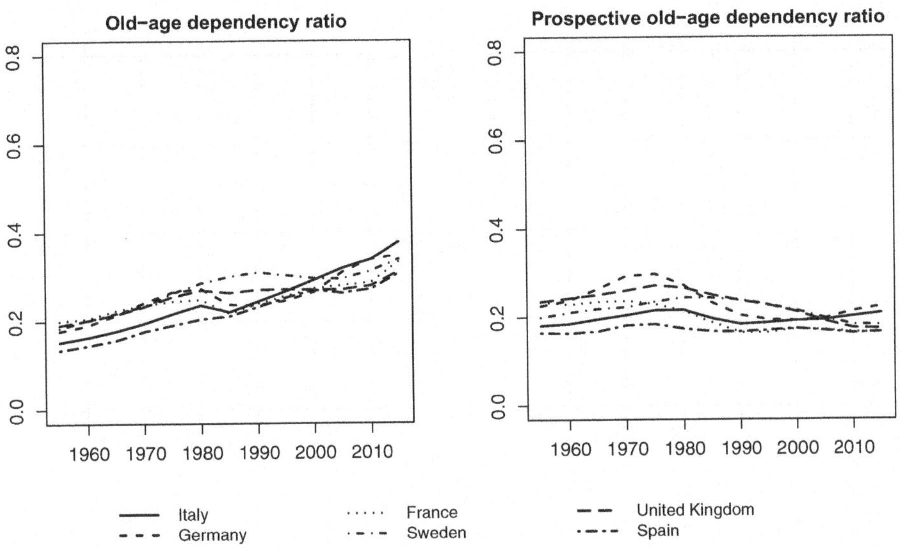

Fig. 12.4 Old-age dependency ratio and prospective old-age dependency ratio (selected European countries), 1955–2015. (Source: authors' calculations based on United Nations 2017)

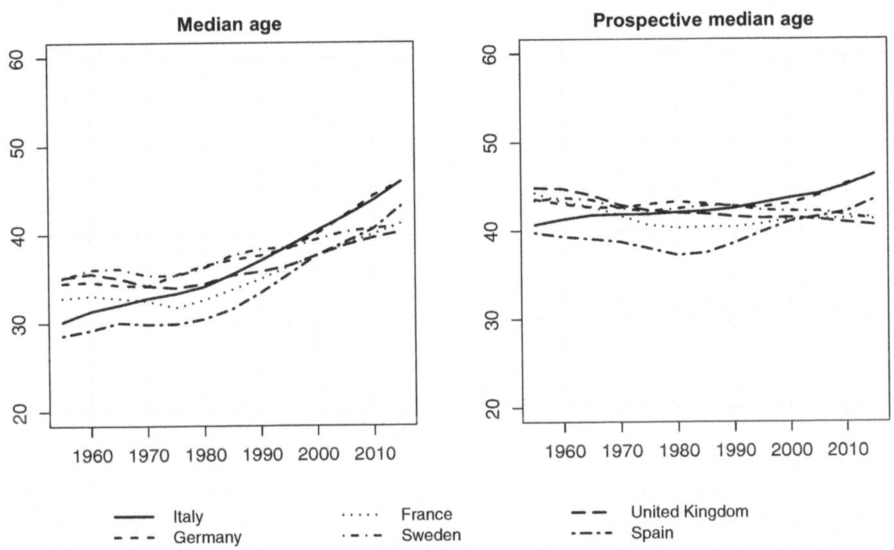

Fig. 12.5 Median age and prospective median age (selected European countries), 1955–2015. (Source: authors' calculations based on United Nations 2017)

In Fig. 12.5 we observe that while traditional median age increased by about 10 years in the recent 60 years in our group of Western European countries, its prospective analog virtually stayed constant.

As we have shown above it makes a substantial difference what type of measure we use to assess past population ageing. If we use conventional measures of ageing where only fixed chronological age defines the old age threshold then we observe that in the recent 60 years considerable population ageing occurred. Using examples of several Western European countries we showed that the proportion of old people and old age dependency ratios almost doubled during that time. Also, during the same period the median ages increased by almost 10 years. However, using measures of ageing that incorporate characteristics of people a very different picture of ageing is observed. According to all three prospective measures there was virtually no population ageing in our selected Western European countries. Moreover, in some cases we can even observe that populations as a whole became somewhat younger.

12.3 Future Ageing

Using forecasts in the 2017 Revision of World Population Prospects (UN 2017) it is possible to study how population ageing may develop in the future. Here we again consider two types of ageing measures – conventional and prospective ones. As was described above, to calculate prospective measures of ageing we need first to compute the POAT, the age at which forecasted remaining life expectancy is 15 years.

Figure 12.6 shows the dynamic of the POAT for the 6 selected Western European countries. By the end of the century the POAT in the 6 Western European approaches age 80.

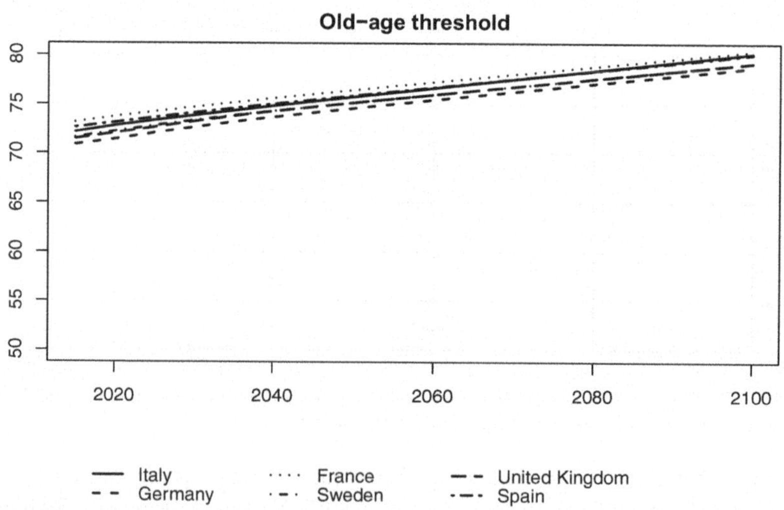

Fig. 12.6 Prospective old age threshold (age when remaining life expectancy = 15 years) for several selected countries of Western Europe for both genders combined, 2015–2100. (Source: authors' calculations based on United Nations 2017)

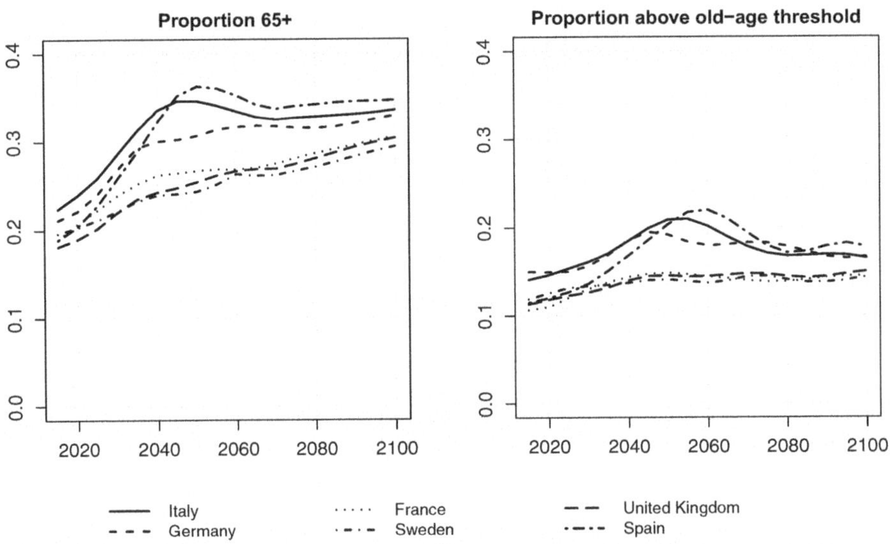

Fig. 12.7 Proportion of people 65+ and proportion of people with the remaining life expectancy 15 years or less (selected European countries), projections, 2015–2100. (Source: authors' calculations based on United Nations 2017)

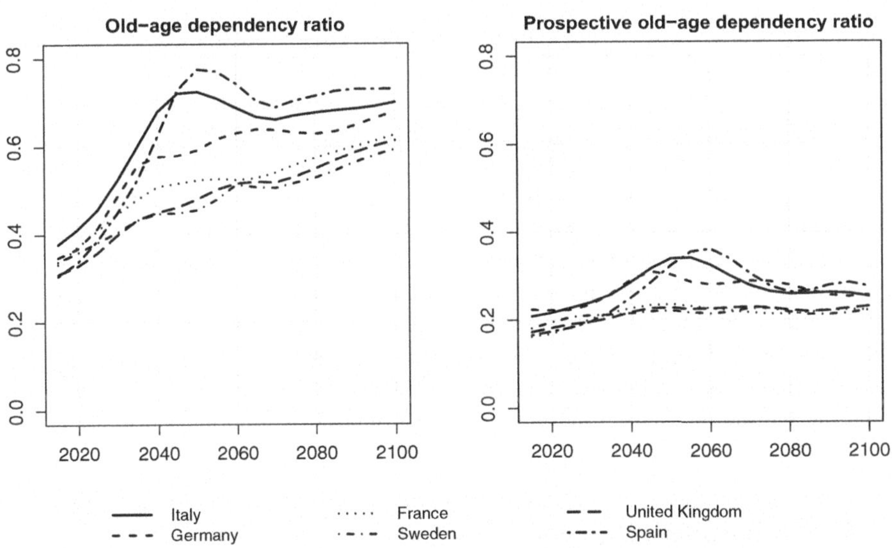

Fig. 12.8 Old-age dependency ratio and prospective old-age dependency ratio (selected European countries), projections, 2015–2100. (Source: authors' calculations based on United Nations 2017)

In Figs. 12.7 and 12.8 we present conventional and prospective measures of ageing projected up to 2100. We see there that both conventional and prospective measures are forecast to increase through the remainder of the century with a bump

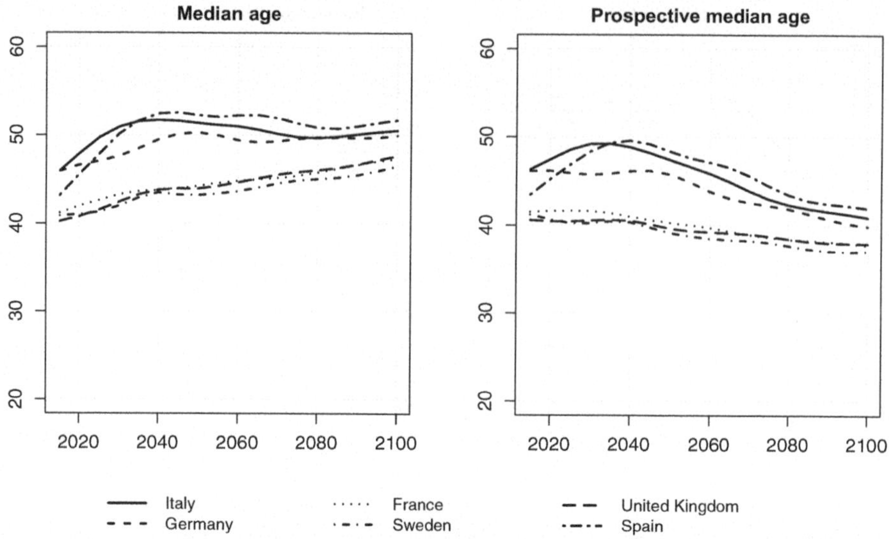

Fig. 12.9 Median age and prospective median age ratio (selected European countries), projections, 2015–2100. (Source: authors' calculations based on United Nations 2017)

around the middle of the century for Italy and Spain that reflects specifics of the age composition caused by a rapid fertility decline in the 1980s. However, the share of people above age 65 by the end of the century is forecasted to be about 30%. The prospective proportion old, though reaches only around half that.

The dynamics of the old age dependency ratio is very similar to the dynamics of the proportion old except that by the end of the century the prospective old- age dependency ratios are only around a third of the conventional ones.

Forecasts of conventional and prospective median ages shown in Fig. 12.10. The two measures of population ageing exhibit opposite trends. While the median age increases by the end of the century by about 5–7 years its prospective analog decreases by 3–5 years. These observations indicate that although median-aged people in the 6 populations will be older in 2100 than today, they will also have longer remaining life expectancies than today's median-age people.

12.4 Probabilistic Ageing

In this section we employ probabilistic population projections, that were developed by the UN using Bayesian hierarchical models (Raftery et al. 2012; Sevcikova et al. 2015). There are several different approaches to probabilistic population projections that were developed in recent decades. However, we will not discuss this issue here since there is a substantial literature on the subject (Alho 1990; Lee 1998; Lutz et al. 1999, 2001; Keilman et al. 2002; Booth 2006).

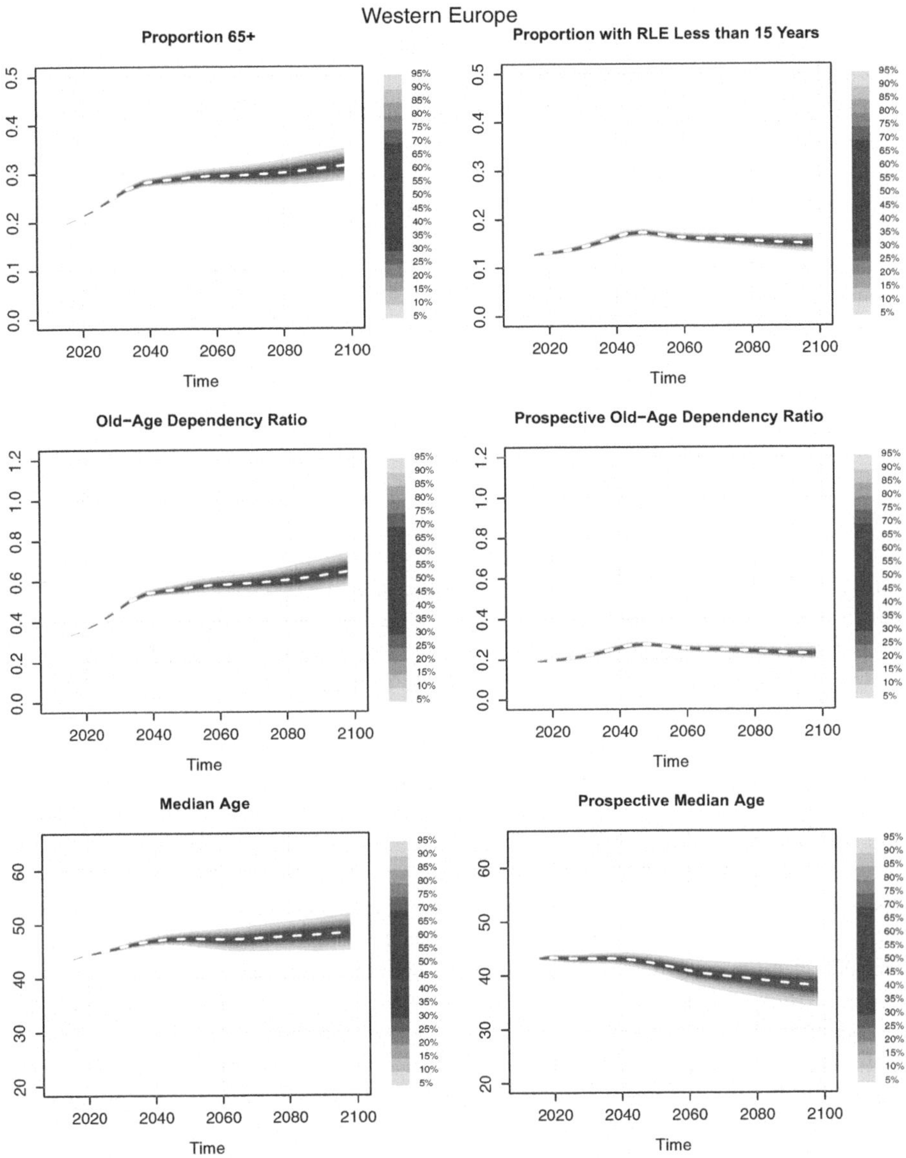

Fig. 12.10 Probabilistic forecasts for three measures of population ageing based on chronological ages and three based on prospective ages, Western Europe 2015–2100. (Source: authors' calculations based on United Nations 2015)

In this section we follow Sanderson et al. (2017, 2019) and merge two methodologies, prospective measures of population ageing and probabilistic population forecasts. Using this we compare the speed of change and variability in forecasts of the conventional proportion old and prospective proportion old, the old age dependency ratio and the prospective old age dependency ratio, and the median age and the prospective median age.

Future distributions of conventional and prospective measures of ageing were computed from 1000 stochastic trajectories of population age structures and associated life tables over the 2015–2100 period for Western Europe. These trajectories were provided by the UN's Population Division (UN 2015).

Results of this analysis are presented in Fig. 12.10 which has 3 panels, upper, middle and bottom. The left side of each panel presents conventional measure and the right side prospective measures.

The upper panel of Fig. 12.10 shows the change over time of the probability distributions of the proportion of the population who are 65+ years old and its prospective analog.

In 2015, the proportion of the population 65+ years-old in Western European countries was 19.7%. The median forecast of this proportion rises to 29.0% in 2050, with a 90% prediction interval of 27.8–30.4%. The forecasts indicate that the increase in the conventional proportion of old people in the population will slow down between 2040 and 2080 and will then speed up again. By 2100, the median forecast of the proportion of the population categorized 65+ years-old is 31.7%, with a 90% prediction interval of 28.5–35.4. The median forecast of the prospective proportion of the population counted as old (those with remaining life expectancy of 15 years or less) is around 12.7% in 2015. This proportion increases to around 17.2% in 2045 where it reaches the maximum, with a 90% prediction interval of 16.5–18.0, and gradually decreases in the following decades. The median forecast of this proportion is 14.1 in 2100, with a 90% prediction interval of 12.9–16.8%.

The middle panel, which compares the forecasted distributions of conventional and prospective old-age dependency ratios looks similar to the upper panel except for the levels of the measures. In the bottom pane we show the probability distributions of the conventional and the prospective median ages. We compute the prospective median ages as the ages in the life table of 2015, in which people have the same remaining life expectancy as at the median age in specific years. Since the UN publishes life tables for 5 year age intervals, the 2015 life table was interpolated on the basis of the UN life tables for 2010–15 and 2015–20.

In Western Europe in 2015, the conventional and the prospective median ages were both 43.5 years. The median forecast of the conventional median age is 47.3 for 2050, with a 90% prediction interval of 45.9–48.7, and is 48.6 in 2100, with a 90% prediction interval of 45.1–52.0. The median probabilistic forecast of the conventional median age increases rapidly from 2015 to 2040, and there is virtually no chance that it will be ever lower than its 2015 value at any time during this century. The median forecast of the prospective median age is also expected to increase between 2015 and 2040. In 2040, the median forecast of the prospective median age is 42.0, and the 90% prediction interval between 40.5 and 43.7. By 2100, the median forecast of the prospective median age is 37.9, and the 90% prediction interval is between 33.8 and 41.4. Based on the UN's probabilistic forecasts, it is highly unlikely that the prospective median age of the population in Western Europe region will be higher in 2100 than it was in 2015.

As we see the use of prospective measures not only produces different levels of ageing compared to their conventional analogs, but it may also produce different trends.

It is also important to note that the standard deviations of the forecasts of the prospective proportion of the population who are old and the prospective old age dependency ratios are less than their counterparts that do not use prospective ages. As was discussed in detail in Sanderson and Scherbov (2015b), the major reason for that is that in conventional measures the trajectories with higher life expectancy will have more people above age 65. In case of prospective measures, higher life expectancy leads to a higher old age threshold. Higher old age thresholds decrease both the prospective proportion old and the prospective old age dependency ratio. Thus, higher life expectancies produce two offsetting effects on the prospective measures. However, in case of median age and its prospective analog the situation is different because prospective median age uses the median age as an input, while the prospective old age dependency ratio does not use the conventional old age dependency ratio as an input. Thus, the distribution of median ages affects the distribution of prospective median ages.

12.5 Discussion

Population ageing is a multidimensional phenomenon, but chronological age is the only dimension that is traditionally used in its measurement. Assuming the people are old at a fixed chronological age, say 65, means that we consider people's characteristics invariant at this age. But this is very far from reality. Consider Italian men. In 1910, their life expectancy at birth was 46.32 year and 100 years later in 2010 it was 79.56 or more than 30 years higher. Of course, a very strong impact on the changes to life expectancy at birth occurred due to a drop in mortality at younger ages. Still, their life expectancy at age 65 in 1910 was 11.16 years and 100 years later it was18.35 years, or more than 7 years higher. The age when the remaining life expectancy reached 15 years or less in 1910 was about 59. In 2010 it was above 69. If we select another characteristic that might serve as a proxy for morbidity, which is mortality rate, then the mortality rate of Italian males at age, 65 in 2010 was the same as the mortality rate of a male at age 49 in 1910. On the other hand, the mortality rate at age 65 in 1910 corresponds to the mortality rate at age 76 in 2010.

People's characteristics are very different, but conventional methods ignore them and do not distinguish people living today and 100 years ago. But this is not the end of the story. Country or regional differences in longevity are also enormous. Russian men in 2010 at age 65 had the same mortality rates as Italian men had at age 77 in the same year. In measuring ageing conventional methods ignore regional differences in characteristics of people of the same age as well.

As we learned in this chapter accounting for characteristics of people makes a very big difference regarding conclusions that are made with respect to the past and the future of ageing. Prospective measures paint a much less gloomy picture. In this chapter, we touched only prospective measures, which uses remaining life expectancy as a characteristic of choice. If instead of life expectancy we would have selected mortality rates as a characteristic of interest, the picture of future ageing would be painted even more optimistic.

The use of the characteristic approach has an additional advantage; it converts characteristics of people to the metric of age. This is very useful because it allows us to construct aggregate indicators of ageing based simultaneously on different characteristics of people.

Population ageing will certainly be the source of many challenges in twenty-first century. But there is no reason to exaggerate those challenges through mismeasurement. The approach presented in this chapter reconceptualizes age based on the characteristics of people and allows the construction of new multidimensional measures of ageing.

The discussion of our approach to the study of population ageing has been based on period life table measures. This was necessary to present our core concepts simply, but it is far to limiting. First, cohort life table could also be used, but much more importantly, many characteristics of people can be used to study population ageing using the methods described above. More detailed descriptions of how our methods can be applied can be found in (Sanderson and Scherbov 2017, 2019). An analytic discussion of the differences between results based on period and cohort life tables can be found in (Sanderson and Scherbov 2007).

We have not discussed the connections between health and ageing in this chapter. This is a complex and controversial topic (Christensen et al. 2008; Angel et al. 2015). We address it in (Sanderson and Scherbov 2019) where we investigate years of healthy life expectancy following the prospective old-age threshold using data from the SHARE survey (Munich Center for the Economics of Aging 2013). We show there that in the European countries for which data were available, years of healthy life expectancy from the prospective old-age threshold onward have been roughly constant from 2004 to 2012. In other words, we did not find evidence to suggest that health during the period of old-age was either improving or deteriorating.

We have used the methodology described in this chapter in a number of related contexts. In (Sanderson and Scherbov 2015b; Ediev et al. 2019), we showed that faster increases in life expectancy lead to slower population ageing when prospective measures are used. In (Sanderson and Scherbov 2015a, 2019), we showed how our methodology can be used to compute an intergenerationally equitable public pension age.

Acknowledgements This project has received funding from the European Union's Horizon 2020 research and innovation program under grant agreement No 635316 (Project Name: Ageing Trajectories of Health: Longitudinal Opportunities and Synergies, ATHLOS).

References

Alho, J. M. (1990). Stochastic methods in population forecasting. *International Journal of Forecasting, 6*(4), 521–530.

Angel, R. J., Angel, J. L., & Hill, T. D. (2015). Longer lives, sicker lives? Increased longevity and extended disability among Mexican-origin elders. *The Journals of Gerontology: Series B, 70*(4), 639–649. https://doi.org/10.1093/geronb/gbu158.

Booth, H. (2006). Demographic forecasting: 1980 to 2005 in review. *International Journal of Forecasting, 22*(3), 547–581.

Christensen, K., McGue, M., Petersen, I., Jeune, B., & Vaupel, J. W. (2008). Exceptional longevity does not result in excessive levels of disability. *Proceedings of the National Academy of Sciences, 105*(36), 13274–13279. https://doi.org/10.1073/pnas.0804931105.

Cutler, D. M., Liebman, J. B., Shepard, M., & Smyth, S. (2007). *An expanded model of health and retirement* (Retirement research center paper NB07-15). Cambridge, MA: National Bureau of Economic Research. http://www.nber.org/programs/ag/rrc/NB07-15%20Cutler,%20Liebman%20Summary.pdf.

Demeny, P. G., & McNicoll, G. (2003). *Encyclopedia of population*. New York: Macmillan Reference USA.

Ediev, D. M., Sanderson, W. C., & Scherbov, S. (2019). The inverse relationship between life expectancy-induced changes in the old-age dependency ratio and the prospective old-age dependency ratio. *Theoretical Population Biology, 125*(February), 1–10. https://doi.org/10.1016/j.tpb.2018.10.001.

Fuchs, V. R. (1984). "Though much is taken": Reflections on aging, health, and medical care. *The Milbank Memorial Fund Quarterly-Health and Society, 62*(2), 143–166.

Keilman, N., Pham, D. Q., & Hetland, A. (2002). Why population forecasts should be probabilistic – Illustrated by the case of Norway. *Demographic Research, 6*(May), 409–454. https://doi.org/10.4054/DemRes.2002.6.15.

Lee, R. D. (1998). Probabilistic approaches to population forecasting. In W. Lutz, J. W. Vaupel, & D. A. Ahlburg (Eds.), *Frontiers of population forecasting. A supplement to Vol. 24, 1998, population and development review* (Vol. 24, pp. 156–190). New York: The Population Council. http://www.jstor.org/discover/10.2307/2808055?uid=3737528&uid=2129&uid=2&uid=70&uid=4&sid=21104606072223.

Lutz, W., Sanderson, W. C., & Scherbov, S. (1999). Expert-based probabilistic population projections. In W. Lutz, J. W. Vaupel, & D. A. Ahlburg (Eds.), *Frontiers of population forecasting. A supplement to Vol. 24, 1998, population and development review* (pp. 139–155). New York: The Population Council. www.jstor.org/discover/10.2307/2808054?uid=3737528&uid=2129&uid=2&uid=70&uid=4&sid=21104606072223.

Lutz, W., Sanderson, W. C., & Scherbov, S. (2001). The end of world population growth. *Nature, 412*(6846), 543–545. https://doi.org/10.1038/35087589.

Munich Center for the Economics of Aging. (2013). *The Survey of Health, Ageing and Retirement in Europe (SHARE)*. Munich: Munich Center for the Economics of Aging. http://www.share-project.org/.

Raftery, A. E., Li, N., Ševčíková, H., Gerland, P., & Heilig, G. K. (2012). Bayesian probabilistic population projections for all countries. *Proceedings of the National Academy of Sciences, 109*(35), 13915–13921. https://doi.org/10.1073/pnas.1211452109.

Rubinow, I. (1913). *Social insurance: With special reference to American conditions*. New York: H. Holt and company.

Ryder, N. B. (1975). Notes on stationary populations. *Population Index, 41*(1), 3–28. https://doi.org/10.2307/2734140.

Sanderson, W. C., & Scherbov, S. (2005). Average remaining lifetimes can increase as human populations age. *Nature, 435*(7043), 811–813. https://doi.org/10.1038/nature03593.

Sanderson, W. C., & Scherbov, S. (2007). A new perspective on population aging. *Demographic Research, 16*(January), 27–58. https://doi.org/10.4054/DemRes.2007.16.2.

Sanderson, W. C., & Scherbov, S. (2008). *Rethinking age and aging* (Population bulletin vol. 63 no. 4). Washington, DC: Population Reference Bureau. http://www.prb.org/pdf08/63.4aging.pdf.
Sanderson, W. C., & Scherbov, S. (2010). Remeasuring aging. *Science, 329*(5997), 1287–1288. https://doi.org/10.1126/science.1193647.
Sanderson, W. C., & Scherbov, S. (2013). The characteristics approach to the measurement of population aging. *Population and Development Review, 39*(4), 673–685. https://doi.org/10.1111/j.1728-4457.2013.00633.x.
Sanderson, W. C., & Scherbov, S. (2014). Measuring the speed of aging across population subgroups. *PLoS One, 9*(5), e96289. https://doi.org/10.1371/journal.pone.0096289.
Sanderson, W. C., & Scherbov, S. (2015a). An Easily Understood and Intergenerationally Equitable Normal Pension Age. In The Future of Welfare in a Global Europe, edited by Bernd Marin, 193–220. Farnham, UK: Ashgate.
Sanderson, W. C., & Scherbov, S. (2015b). Faster increases in human life expectancy could lead to slower population aging. *PLoS One, 10*(4), e0121922. https://doi.org/10.1371/journal.pone.0121922.
Sanderson, W. C., & Scherbov, S. (2017). A unifying framework for the study of population aging. *Vienna Yearbook of Population Research, 2016*(14), 7–39. https://doi.org/10.1553/populationyearbook2016s007.
Sanderson, W. C., & Scherbov, S. (2019). *Prospective longevity: A new vision of population aging*. Cambridge: Harvard University Press.
Sanderson, W. C., Scherbov, S., & Gerland, P. (2017). Probabilistic population aging. *PLoS One, 12*(6), e0179171. https://doi.org/10.1371/journal.pone.0179171.
Sanderson, W. C., Scherbov, S., & Gerland, P. (2019). The end of population aging in high-income countries. *Vienna Yearbook of Population Research, 16*(2018), 1–13. https://doi.org/10.1553/populationyearbookXXXX.
Sevcikova, H., Li, N., Kantorová, V., Gerland, P., & Raftery, A. E. (2015). *Age-specific mortality and fertility rates for probabilistic population projections* (Working Paper arXiv:1503.05215 [stat.AP]). Seattle: Center for Statistics and the Social Sciences University of Washington. http://arxiv.org/abs/1503.05215.
UN. (2015). *World population prospects: The 2015 revision*. New York: Department of Economic and Social Affairs, Population Division. http://esa.un.org/unpd/wpp/.
UN. (2017). *World population prospects: The 2017 revision*. New York: Department of Economic and Social Affairs, Population Division. http://esa.un.org/unpd/wpp/.
United Nations. (2002). *World population ageing: 1950–2050* (ST/ESA/SER.A/207). New York: Department of Economic and Social Affairs, Population Division, United Nations.
United Nations. (n.d.) *Global issues: Ageing*. https://www.un.org/en/sections/issues-depth/ageing/. Accessed 9 May 2019.
Vaupel, J. W. (2010). Biodemography of human ageing. *Nature, 464*(7288), 536–542. https://doi.org/10.1038/nature08984.

The manufacturer's authorised representative in the EU is Springer Nature Customer Service Centre GmbH, Europaplatz 3, 69115 Heidelberg, Germany. If you have any concerns regarding our products, please contact ProductSafety@springernature.com

Printed and bound by CPI Group (UK) Ltd, Croydon, CR0 4YY
22/09/2026
02221061-0008